MW00649984

EVOLUTIONARY CRIMINOLOGY

EVOLUTIONARY CRIMINOLOGY

TOWARDS A COMPREHENSIVE
EXPLANATION OF CRIME

RUSSIL DURRANT
School of Social and Cultural Studies
Victoria University of Wellington
Wellington, New Zealand

TONY WARD
School of Psychology
Victoria University of Wellington
Wellington, New Zealand

AMSTERDAM • BOSTON • HEIDELBERG • LONDON
NEW YORK • OXFORD • PARIS • SAN DIEGO
SAN FRANCISCO • SINGAPORE • SYDNEY • TOKYO

ELSEVIER
Academic Press is an imprint of Elsevier

Academic Press is an imprint of Elsevier
125 London Wall, London EC2Y 5AS, UK
525 B Street, Suite 1800, San Diego, CA 92101-4495, USA
225 Wyman Street, Waltham, MA 02451, USA
The Boulevard, Langford Lane, Kidlington, Oxford OX5 1GB, UK

Copyright © 2015 Elsevier Inc. All rights reserved.

This book and the individual contributions contained in it are protected under copyright by
the Publisher (other than as may be noted herein).

No part of this publication may be reproduced or transmitted in any form or by any means,
electronic or mechanical, including photocopying, recording, or any information storage
and retrieval system, without permission in writing from the publisher. Details on how to
seek permission, further information about the Publisher's permissions policies and our
arrangements with organizations such as the Copyright Clearance Center and the Copyright
Licensing Agency, can be found at our website: www.elsevier.com/permissions.

Notices
Knowledge and best practice in this field are constantly changing. As new research and
experience broaden our understanding, changes in research methods, professional
practices, or medical treatment may become necessary.

Practitioners and researchers must always rely on their own experience and knowledge
in evaluating and using any information, methods, compounds, or experiments described
herein. In using such information or methods they should be mindful of their own safety
and the safety of others, including parties for whom they have a professional responsibility.

To the fullest extent of the law, neither the Publisher nor the authors, contributors, or
editors, assume any liability for any injury and/or damage to persons or property as a
matter of products liability, negligence or otherwise, or from any use or operation of any
methods, products, instructions, or ideas contained in the material herein.

Library of Congress Cataloging-in-Publication Data
A catalog record for this book is available from the Library of Congress

British Library Cataloguing-in-Publication Data
A catalogue record for this book is available from the British Library

ISBN: 978-0-12-397937-7

For information on all Academic Press publications
visit our website at http://store.elsevier.com/

Working together
to grow libraries in
developing countries

www.elsevier.com • www.bookaid.org

Publisher: Nikki Levy
Acquisition Editor: Nikki Levy
Editorial Project Manager: Barbara Makinster
Production Project Manager: Caroline Johnson
Designer: Matthew Limbert

Typeset by TNQ Books and Journals
www.tnq.co.in

Printed and bound in the United States of America

Contents

I

THE EVOLUTIONARY FRAMEWORK

2. Evolutionary Theory and Human Evolution

3. Evolutionary Behavioral Science

9. Social-Structural and Cultural Explanations

III

RESPONDING TO CRIME

10. Punishment, Public Policy, and Prevention

11. The Rehabilitation and Reintegration of Offenders

12. Looking Forward from the Perspective of the Past

Preface

Our overall argument in this book is straightforward: we aim to make the case that we can significantly advance our understanding of criminal behavior and the way we respond to crime by drawing on the explanatory resources of evolutionary theory. Evolutionary explanations have become increasingly prominent in many academic fields in the social and behavioral sciences, but they have been largely ignored by criminologists. We think that this neglect is unwarranted. Although an evolutionary approach will not replace existing criminological theories—indeed, we argue that it can be fruitfully *integrated* with extant approaches—it can substantially enrich our understanding of criminological phenomena, open up new lines of inquiry, and offer guidance on the most effective ways of responding to crime. In short, we think that the arguments and materials presented in this book will be of significant interest to criminologists, forensic psychologists, practitioners, and anyone interested in understanding and managing criminal behavior.

Our overall aim may be straightforward, but providing satisfactory explanations for any human behavior—including the subject matter of this book, criminal behavior—entails rather more complexity. Humans are the product of evolutionary processes and understanding those processes and how they have shaped our psychological and behavioral characteristics over millions of years is an essential part of the explanatory story. In this respect we are much like any other species. However, we—unlike other animals—also have a cultural history that has led to substantial changes in the way that we live and the nature of our interactions with others, and understanding this history and how it shapes our behavior is also crucial. Humans also have a developmental history: our behavior, including our propensity to commit crime, is influenced by the complex interplay of genetic, epigenetic, and environmental processes that we experience across the life course. Finally, we are embodied organisms with thoughts, emotions, awareness, and a capacity for agency that allows us to make choices that both shape and are shaped by the ecological, social, and cultural environment in which we are embedded. Understanding the interplay of these various types of explanation, we argue, is a crucial task for all social and behavioral scientists, and is essential for the development of criminological theories.

In order to make sense of this complexity, we need to be armed with a clear understanding of evolutionary theory, and how evolutionary explanations relate to other types of explanations in criminology. This is the primary task we tackle in the first part of this book. Inevitably some of this material will be familiar to readers well versed in evolutionary biology and evolutionary psychology, but we think it is important to provide a clear overview of the key ideas and concepts. Moreover, there is a growing recognition of the importance of nongenetic inheritance in evolutionary processes and, more specifically, the role of culture and gene–culture coevolutionary processes in human evolution. These ideas are central to the arguments that are developed in this book, but may be less familiar to many readers. In Chapter 4, we provide a framework, drawing in part from Tinbergen's (1963) idea that there are four types of explanations (those that focus on evolutionary history, evolutionary function, development, and proximate processes) that play complementary roles in explaining behavior, that can help us to understand how evolutionary explanations "fit in" with other types of explanations in criminology. With this evolutionary framework in place, in Part II of the book we turn our attention to explanations of crime. In the five chapters that form the second part of the book, we begin with an overview of evolutionary altruism and cooperation, and then focus on each level of explanation in turn. In Part III of the book we discuss how the approach that we have developed can provide guidance in our efforts to manage crime by looking at punishment, prevention, and rehabilitation.

Understanding why individuals commit crime and how the propensity to engage in crime varies across time and space is an important task, for criminal behavior is responsible for a significant amount of harm in society. Our responses to crime can also be the source of significant harm and the overarching pragmatic goal of criminology and criminal justice is to manage crime in ways that reduce the adverse effects associated with it. In order to do this, we must be armed with the best explanatory accounts that are available because attempts to intervene based on an incorrect or incomplete understanding of the phenomena of interest are likely to be ineffective. In recent years, biosocial criminologists have made a persuasive case that criminology has neglected biological explanations to its detriment and that the future of criminological theorizing will need to recognize the complex interplay of biological and social processes in the etiology of crime. The arguments that we advance in this book are very much in the spirit of this claim. Although evolutionary explanations barely feature in the education of criminologists, and this book, to the best of our knowledge, is only the second authored monograph dedicated to the topic of evolution and crime in the last decade, we believe that "evolutionary criminology" holds much promise for advancing our explanations of crime and how best to manage it.

Russil Durrant
Tony Ward
October, 2014

Acknowledgments

We would first like to thank the editors at Academic Press for their (patient) help and support with this book.

Russil Durrant would like to give special thanks to Carolina and Zoe for their support and encouragement (with extra thanks to Zoe for all your help on the references); Tony Ward for his unflagging enthusiasm for this project and his stimulating academic support over the years. Thanks also to my colleagues at the Institute of Criminology, and to Leo, Bea, and Mavis for being there.

Tony Ward would like to thank Carolyn Wilshire and Alex Ward for many stimulating conversations on theoretical issues and human behavior. Thanks so much to Roxy Heffernan for helping me develop the Agency Model of Risk. I would like to acknowledge the intellectual input from Tony Beech and Richard Siegert over the years on evolutionary ideas. Russil Durrant has been amazing to work with, a true scholar. Finally, thanks to Leo (the very fluffy dog) for helping me unwind when I most needed it!

List of Figures

List of Tables

CHAPTER

1

Criminology and Evolutionary Theory

INTRODUCTION

Depending on exactly when one wants to let off the starting gun, criminology as an organized field of scholarly inquiry is no more than about 140 years old (Godfrey, Lawrence, & Williams, 2008). The phenomenon of crime is, of course, much older. How much older? The first codified laws of which we have any detailed knowledge come from Babylonia around 1760 BCE, so the origin of crime as "lawbreaking" dates from this period. All human groups, however, set norms that prescribe acceptable behavior and mete out punishment to those individuals who violate these norms (Boehm, 2012), and the phenomena that are the primary foci of criminologists—violence, rape, punishment, and the appropriation of resources from others—are part of the "deep history" (Shryock & Smail, 2011) of humankind. In their efforts to provide explanations for criminal behavior, criminologists, forensic psychologists, and others largely focus on proximate factors such as the psychological characteristics of offenders, their developmental history, and the social structure in which they are embedded. These types of explanations are clearly important. They have proven valuable in the development of theories and models of offending that have had some success in both accounting for crime and guiding approaches to effectively managing criminal behavior. We suggest, however, that our understanding of crime and the way that we respond to it can be significantly enriched through a consideration of the more distal causes of criminal behavior—those that reside in the evolutionary history of our species. Moreover, a more comprehensive approach to understanding crime and responding to criminal behavior, we claim, can be achieved through the integration of evolutionary approaches with those that focus on more proximal causal factors.

In this book we make one—longish—argument for this approach. Our aim in this opening chapter is more modest. We first clarify what we take

© 2015 Elsevier Inc. All rights reserved.

as the core subject matter of criminology. Then we make the empirical case that—despite the interdisciplinary aspirations of many criminologists—mainstream criminology has almost completely neglected evolutionary explanations in its attempts to understand the nature of crime and our responses to it. We consider several possible reasons for this neglect and suggest that the time is ripe for a careful consideration of how evolutionary approaches can be integrated within criminology. In the remainder of the book we elaborate on and illustrate how this can be accomplished.

THE SUBJECT MATTER OF CRIMINOLOGY

Not all criminologists are in complete agreement about exactly what discipline they are part of, and some argue that criminology should not be considered an academic discipline at all (Garland, 2011). We suggest, however, that criminology can reasonably be described as an applied social and behavioral science. As such, criminology is organized around a particular set of phenomena—very roughly, crime and our responses to crime—rather than a specific level of analysis like sociology or psychology (Agnew, 2011a). In this respect, criminology is somewhat like medicine—an applied area of study undergirded by a number of basic sciences or academic disciplines. For criminology, the key areas of inquiry include—but are not limited to—sociology, psychology, anthropology, political science, history, and law. As we note below, some of these disciplines—notably sociology—feature more prominently than others, and one of the main aims of this book is to argue for a more thoroughgoing inclusion of evolutionary biology into the field of criminology.

Even if we accept that criminology can be reasonably considered a discipline in its own right, there remains some disagreement regarding the scope of its domain, and criminologists have devoted a considerable amount of energy to the task of defining just what constitutes "crime." The most straightforward approach, paraded in every introductory textbook, is to define crime in legal terms: criminal acts are those that violate the criminal law and are therefore subject to sanction by the state. The major objection to this definition is that by defining crime in purely legal terms, the subject matter of criminology becomes a moving target, as what constitutes a criminal act varies both historically and cross-culturally. Many also argue that this definition of crime is both too narrow *and* too broad: it excludes many harmful acts while including many that result in relatively little or no harm (Agnew, 2011a). In response to these objections (and others), many criminologists prefer a definition of crime that is not yoked exclusively to what is currently proscribed by the law, while others have suggested that the focus on crime sensu stricto is a mistake and urge the acceptance of a "crime-free criminology" (Gottfredson, 2011). Agnew (2011a, p. 187) argues for a more inclusive definition of crime that can be defined as "acts that cause blameworthy harm, are condemned by the public, and/or are sanctioned by the state." We think that there is much merit in Agnew's analysis. A much simpler solution, however, is to accept that *crime* should be defined in purely legal terms, but the *subject matter* of criminology includes more than just crime. How much more? We suggest, largely consistent with Agnew's (2011a) approach, that criminologists should be concerned with three overlapping kinds of phenomena:

1. Intentionally harmful acts;
2. Acts that violate consensually held social norms and are subject to sanctions by group members; and
3. Acts that violate codified laws and are subject to punishment by the state.

Most criminologists accept that harmful acts form a central component of the subject matter of their discipline. Agnew suggests that the focus should be on *blameworthy harms*, with harm defined as acts that violate fundamental human rights. We think there is much value in this more inclusive perspective on harm, but—consistent with our overall evolutionary approach—suggest that *intentionally harmful acts are those carried out voluntarily that negatively affect the biological fitness of others*. Murder is the ultimate in intentionally harmful acts, because it entails the elimination of any further opportunities to promote reproductive success by the victim. Many other acts also negatively affect biological fitness in lesser ways. Bullying, verbal derogation, and sexual harassment, for instance, may all reduce or limit the survival or reproductive opportunities of others (e.g., through a reduction in status or reputation). This broad definition also encompasses the many harmful acts that have been the focus of critical criminologists such as state-sponsored collective violence, discrimination, corporate maleficence, and the failure to provide health care to those in need. Acts that harm the environment or other species can also be included here, as they have an impact on the biological fitness of other species. Of course, some of these acts are going to be of more enduring interest to criminologists than others (state-sponsored genocide understandably attracts more attention than the use of pesticides to eradicate insect populations), and defining intentional harm in this way does not necessarily imply that these acts are either morally wrong or that they should be subject to sanctions by the state.

The second set of overlapping phenomena that we suggest should form the subject matter of criminology concerns those acts that violate consensually held social norms. These acts are largely those that Agnew refers to in his definition as "condemned by the public." There are two key aspects to these acts. First, they violate consensually held social norms. The importance of social norms for group cohesion and collective action is a recurring theme in this book and features prominently in evolutionary approaches to understanding the nature of human cooperation (e.g., Bowles & Gintis, 2011; Richerson & Boyd, 2005; see Chapter 5). All human groups have norms that are typically explicitly articulated and that prescribe the domain of appropriate behavior. Many of these norms clearly relate to intentionally harmful acts, but norms also regulate a wide class of behaviors such as what food can be eaten and when, who is an appropriate marriage partner, and how individuals of different standing should address one another. Second, these acts are subject to some form of sanction by group members—from verbal admonishments to social exclusion and physical punishment.

The final set of acts that we suggest should form the subject matter of criminology are those that violate the criminal law and are subject to punishment by the state—in short, criminal acts.

Much of the subject matter of criminology concerns behaviors that are intentionally harmful, violate consensually held norms, *and* break the law. There are, however, important acts that fall into only one or two of these classes of behavior and that, arguably, should also be of interest to criminologists. The three sets of phenomena, when viewed through the lens of evolutionary theory, also have a relatively clear history. Intentionally harmful acts are clearly the oldest class of behaviors in evolutionary terms and reflect the relentless logic of natural and sexual selection (see Chapter 2), as organisms that manage to advance their own survival and reproductive success at the expense of others are more likely to be represented in subsequent generations. As such, intentionally harmful acts predate the origin of our species and—given suitable license to the term "intentional"—must have been present in the earliest organisms. The second set of behaviors that form the subject matter of criminology are, however, much more recent. Although some have argued that chimpanzees have something like a sense of "social justice," and a number of species may "police" in-group behavior that threatens group functioning (see Brosnan & de Waal, 2012; Clutton-Brock & Parker, 1995), the existence of consciously articulated social norms is unique to our lineage, probably emerging sometime around two million years ago (see Chapter 2). The final set of acts is more recent still, because it relies on the emergence of both writing (criminal acts are codified) and the state.

In sum, we suggest that the subject matter of criminology is largely concerned with: (1) acts that are intentionally harmful, that violate consensually held social norms, and/or violate codified laws and are subject to sanction by the state; (2) the consequences of these acts for others ("victims"); and (3) responses to these acts in terms of punishment, prevention, and rehabilitation. We appreciate that there are many criminologists who would not be entirely satisfied with how we construe the field of criminology. Brisman (2012), for instance, contends that criminology is more than the study of crime (even broadly construed) and responses to crime, and suggests that we should also study—among other topics—"what crime *means* to people" (p. 60) and what crime (and responses to crime) can tell us about cultural values and social structures. Similarly, many criminologists are interested in how crime and responses to crime are represented, with a particular focus on the presentation and consumption of crime in the media and what that can tell us about the nature of society. Inevitably, like most academic disciplines, there will be no sharp lines that perfectly describe the domain of criminology; inevitably there will also be topics of central and more peripheral interest. Criminology may be more than the study of crime (and harms and violations of norms) and our responses to crime (and how that information can be deployed in real world contexts), but few would deny—we think—that this is its central mission.

EVOLUTIONARY EXPLANATIONS IN CRIMINOLOGY

Many—perhaps most—criminologists are willing to accept that criminology is, in principle, an interdisciplinary subject. McLaughlin and Newburn (2010a, p. 2), for instance, assert that criminology is "a field of inquiry where people from a variety of intellectual and scholarly backgrounds come together to engage in research and deliberation." Not all would agree that this is the case in practice, despite the fairly widespread existence of "integrative" approaches. Many criminologists, for instance, note that criminological theory tends to be dominated by sociological approaches (e.g., DeKeseredy, 2012). Some have noted the relative neglect and misrepresentation of psychological theories and approaches in criminology (e.g., McGuire, 2004; Webber, 2010), and we think it is fair to say that criminology has not made as thorough use of contemporary psychological science in its theorizing as it might have. Others draw attention to the failure of criminology to fully incorporate biological approaches and argue that the adoption of "biosocial criminology" will lead to a paradigm shift in criminology with revolutionary consequences (Wright & Cullen, 2012). Although we think that a paradigm shift in the strict Kuhnian sense is unlikely in the near future, we are certainly in agreement that (1) criminology as a discipline has neglected biological approaches, and (2) that the inclusion of these approaches would significantly enrich our study of crime.

It is not uncommon for academics with a particular research interest or theoretical orientation to lament the lack of interest in their favored area of research, and there is always a temptation to overstate this neglect. We think, however, that a fairly sound case can be made for the near invisibility of evolutionary theory in mainstream criminology. We make this case using three main sources of data: surveys of members of the American Society of Criminology, textbook coverage of evolutionary approaches, and coverage of evolutionary approaches in leading criminology journals. Evolutionary approaches have not been completely neglected, however, and we follow the foregoing analysis with a brief historical overview of evolutionary ideas in criminology.

In the following section we discuss reasons why evolutionary approaches are relatively neglected and make the case that the time is ripe for this oversight to be corrected.

The Neglect of Evolutionary Explanations in Criminology

In a study by Walsh & Ellis (2004), attendees at the 1997 American Society of Criminology conference were sent a questionnaire that tapped into their views concerning their favored criminological theory and the most important causes of crime, along with a number of other questions. The 147 respondents generated a list of 23 different theories with "social-control," "self-control," and "differential association" the three most favored approaches. Only one respondent selected an evolutionary approach ("neo-Darwinism"). Respondents were also asked to rate a list of 24 possible causes of "serious and persistent criminal behavior" in terms of their importance on a scale ranging from 0 (of no importance) to 9 (extremely important). Topping the list of causes were "unfair economic system" ($M = 6.29$), "lack of empathy" ($M = 6.14$), and "lack of educational opportunities" ($M = 6.08$). "Evolutionary factors" were rated the least important of the 23 causes ($M = 1.37$). In a replication of this study, Cooper, Walsh, and Ellis (2010) sent questionnaires asking similar questions to all members of the American Society of Criminology having an e-mail address in 2007. The 1218 respondents provided a roughly similar pattern of results as in the first study—at least with respect to their views on evolutionary theory. No participant chose evolutionary theory as the favored criminological theory (although it is notable that 21 did select "biosocial theory"), and "evolutionary factors (natural selection)" were again viewed as the least important in explaining criminal behavior ($M = 1.64$). In sum, the results of these two studies suggest that American criminologists place almost no value on evolutionary approaches to understanding criminal behavior, a result that is largely consistent with the perceived importance of evolutionary approaches in the social sciences more generally (e.g., Perry & Mace, 2010).

Another way of exploring the importance accorded evolutionary approaches in criminology is to sample coverage of evolution and evolutionary theory in criminology textbooks. Although textbooks necessarily offer condensed and sometimes superficial coverage of topic areas, their attention to particular theories and approaches is a useful indication of what criminologists view as most important. Criminology is also blessed with a relatively large number of textbooks, readers, and the like devoted to criminological theory, and in principle these may provide the clearest indication of the importance accorded by criminologists to different theoretical perspectives. In order to examine the coverage of evolutionary theory in criminological textbooks, we took all introductory criminology textbooks and textbooks, readers, and encyclopedias on criminological theory published between 2000 and 2012 and held in the Victoria University of Wellington library as our sample. We then tabulated the number of indexed pages that referred to "evolution," "evolutionary theory," "evolutionary psychology," and related subjects—e.g., "evolutionary neuroandrogenic theory" and "sociobiology"—along with the actual amount of text (in pages) devoted to these approaches. The final sample comprised 21 introductory criminology textbooks and 14 books devoted to criminological theory (including the *Encyclopedia of Criminological Theory*).

The results revealed that a total of 21 books had some indexed reference to evolutionary approaches. In other words, 37 percent of all introductory criminology textbooks and criminological theory books published since 2000 and held in the Victoria University of Wellington library had no indexed reference to evolutionary approaches at all. Overall, an average of just under two pages a book were devoted to evolutionary approaches, representing 0.39 percent of the total pages in all of the books analyzed. If we restrict our analysis to those books that did mention evolutionary approaches, we find that on average just over three pages were devoted to evolutionary approaches, representing 0.6 percent of the total pages in those books. Only two books in the total sampled— Walsh & Ellis (2006) and Marsh (2011)—devoted 10 or more pages to evolutionary approaches.

The results of this study are fairly clear: introductory textbooks on criminology and criminological theory largely ignore evolutionary approaches. Coverage of evolutionary theory does, however, vary quite a bit among the textbooks sampled. However, the fact that 37 percent of the books had no indexed reference to evolutionary approaches suggests that many criminologists believe that evolution simply has no place in criminology. To put these results in perspective, it would be a major oversight if an introductory criminology or criminological theory textbook had no coverage of, say, strain or social-control theory. Two recent books on criminological theory provide good examples of the relative neglect of evolutionary approaches. Akers & Sellers (2009) provide a 401-word overview of criminological theories. The book includes the usual range of theoretical approaches, including individual chapters devoted to "conflict theory" "Marxism and critical theory," and "feminist theory"; one chapter is provided on biological approaches, with just under two pages allocated to evolutionary theory. McLaughlin & Newburn (2010b) also provide a detailed overview of major criminological theories (featuring chapters by some of the key architects of criminological theory), and despite including

13 chapters devoted to "new approaches," there is no indexed reference to evolutionary approaches at all. The main point of this exercise—we hasten to add—is not to chastise the writers of criminological textbooks, as their task is to reflect the state of play, not necessarily to set the agenda. However, it is clear that evolutionary theory does not feature prominently in the kind of information that criminologists believe is important for students to learn. Given that our sample is one of convenience, we also need to note that the results of our analysis may not be representative of criminology textbooks in general.

A third way of exploring the coverage of evolutionary approaches in criminology is to look at the representation of evolutionary ideas in leading criminology journals. To this end we examined all references to "evolutionary theory" and "evolutionary psychology" (exact phrases) anywhere in the text of articles published between 2000 and 2014 in three leading criminology journals—*Criminology, British Journal of Criminology*, and *Theoretical Criminology*. For comparison purposes, we also examined references to other theoretical approaches in criminology, including "strain theory," "control theory," "rational choice theory," "cultural criminology," and "critical criminology" (exact phrases). As can been seen in Table 1.1, the results of this analysis are fairly clear and largely support the idea that evolutionary approaches have had a relatively limited role to play in criminology as a discipline. Indeed, when the results of the three journals are combined, we see that criminologists are 12 times more likely to refer to either "control theory" or "critical criminology" than they are to evolutionary theory.

To summarize, criminology as an academic discipline has neglected the role of evolution in the development of explanations for criminal behavior. We have perhaps belabored this point a little, and in our focus

TABLE 1.1   The Representation of Evolutionary Theory and Other Theoretical Approaches in Criminology Journals from 2000 to 2014 (Number of Articles)

	Criminology	*British Journal of Criminology*	*Theoretical Criminology*	Total
Evolutionary theory	37	5	2	44
Evolutionary psychology	32	6	4	42
Strain theory	175	23	28	226
Control theory	497	31	21	549
Rational choice theory	144	37	17	198
Cultural criminology	251	55	73	379
Critical criminology	290	130	108	528

on mainstream criminology we have neglected a rich vein of theoretical and empirical work that has employed evolutionary theory to understand crime and our responses to it. This book provides a detailed exploration of this research, but it is worth pausing at this point to highlight some of this work.

Evolutionary Explanations in Criminology

Many introductory criminology textbooks begin and end their coverage of "evolutionary approaches" with the work of Cesare Lombroso. Evolutionary theories of crime were prominent in the latter half of the nineteenth century, and Lombroso's work is certainly the best known of these perspectives. Although Lombroso recognized that a number of factors played a role in the etiology of criminal behavior, he is chiefly remembered for his view that criminals were "evolutionary throwbacks" to an earlier, more primitive stage in human evolution (Rafter, 2008). Other scholars that drew on the concept of evolution in their theories of crime include Henry Maudsley, Richard Dugdale, Richard von Krafft-Ebing, and Francis Galton (Rafter, 2008), and their work exemplified a strong interest in the biological origins of criminal behavior in nineteenth-century criminology.

Although biological approaches to crime still featured in the first half of the twentieth century, they made very little explicit use of evolutionary theory, instead focusing on various genetic, bodily, and constitutional factors as epitomized in the work of William Sheldon (Rafter, 2008). Moreover, the rise of sociological approaches to understanding crime in the first half of the twentieth century significantly shifted attention to the social and ecological context in which criminal behavior occurs. Indeed, from the first couple of decades of the twentieth century, biological approaches in general, and evolutionary approaches in particular, declined across the various social and behavioral sciences, as behaviorism became the dominant paradigm in (North American) psychology, and anthropologists largely shifted their attention to the role of culture in explaining human behavior (Degler, 1991; Plotkin, 2004). The revival of evolutionary theory in the social sciences began in the 1960s and 1970s, and was felt most prominently in anthropology and psychology, although evolutionary approaches in psychology did not really gain anything like mainstream acceptance until the early part of the twenty-first century. As Barkow (2005) notes, some social sciences let this Darwinian revival almost completely pass them by—sociology is the most notable example, but, as we argued above, criminology has also failed to incorporate evolutionary approaches in any meaningful way.

There are a few exceptions, however. One example is the evolutionary ecological theory of criminal behavior developed by Cohen and

Machalek (1988) and extended by Vila and colleagues (Savage & Vila, 2002; Vila, 1994, 1997). This approach draws strongly from both behavioral ecology and the idea of cultural evolution (see Chapter 3) in advancing the idea that criminality is the outcome of developmental processes shaped by both biological and sociocultural factors. In short, due to their specific biological characteristics and sociocultural environment, some individuals are more likely to acquire "strategic styles" that lead to criminal behavior, given relevant opportunities. Another example is provided by Ellis's (2005) evolutionary neuroandrogenic theory of criminal behavior. Ellis draws on the theory of sexual selection (see Chapter 2) to argue that "aggressive and acquisitive criminal behaviour evolved as an aspect of human reproduction, especially among males" (Ellis, 2005, p. 288). At a proximate level, Ellis maintains, the sex hormone testosterone (which is present at much higher levels in men compared with those in women) plays an important role in competitive and victimizing behavior, particularly when coupled with low intelligence and impaired cognitive functioning. Ideas drawn specifically from evolutionary psychology (see Chapter 3) have also had some—relatively limited—coverage in mainstream criminological and sociological journals (e.g., Armit, 2011; Brannigan, 1997; Kanazawa & Still, 2000; Savage & Kanazawa, 2002; Wood, 2011), and evolutionary ideas form one component of the newly emerging paradigm of "biosocial criminology" that has been showcased in several recent books (Walsh, 2009; Walsh & Beaver, 2009; Walsh & Bolen, 2012) and special issues of criminology journals (Delisi, 2009; Walsh, 2012). To date, as far as we are aware, there has also been one recent book written by criminologists devoted to using evolutionary theory to understand criminal behavior and our responses to crime (Roach & Pease, 2013).

If we cast our gaze beyond criminology as an academic discipline, and its more mainstream publication outlets, and consider evolutionary approaches to topics that fall within the purview of criminology, then it is clear that there is now an extensive evolutionarily informed literature on crime and our responses to crime. We will engage with this material in depth throughout this book, but it is worth pointing out that evolutionary theory has been employed to explain a diverse range of criminological phenomena including aggression, violence, and homicide (Archer, 2009a, 2009b; Daly & Wilson, 1988; Duntley & Buss, 2011), psychopathy (Glenn, Kurzban, & Raine, 2011; Mealey, 1995), sexual offending (McKibbin, Shackelford, Goetz, & Starrat, 2008), theft (Kanazawa, 2008), drug use (Durrant, Adamson, Todd, & Sellman, 2009), collective violence (Durrant, 2011; van Vugt, 2009; Wrangham, 1999), punishment (Peterson, Sell, Tooby, & Cosmides, 2010), and rehabilitation (Ward & Durrant, 2011), and some scholars have argued for a subdiscipline devoted to these topics, dubbed "evolutionary forensic psychology" (Duntley & Shackelford, 2008a, 2008b).

WHY DO CRIMINOLOGISTS LARGELY IGNORE EVOLUTIONARY THEORY AND WHY SHOULD THIS CHANGE?

Despite the existence of work that has employed evolutionary theory to understand criminal behavior, it is clear that this research is largely absent from mainstream criminology—surveyed criminologists think it is unimportant, criminology textbooks largely ignore it, and it does not feature strongly in leading criminology journals. Why is this the case? Perhaps criminologists ignore evolutionary approaches because they simply have no need for them: all is well in the house of criminology; existing theoretical approaches more than satisfactorily account for the phenomena of interest; and these theoretical approaches guide practice in ways that serve best to reduce the harms caused by crime and the responses to crime. Criminologists as a group do not necessarily agree on a great deal but we think that few—if any—criminologists would be willing to endorse this Panglossian picture of criminology. Indeed, although there is widespread disagreement regarding the source of criminology's "problems"—Rosenfeld (2011) points to the neglect of macrolevel explanations, Young (2011) highlights the "banality" of "positivist criminology," and Clarke (2004) sees evidence for a wholesale failure of criminological theory to assist in actually preventing crime—there is something like a consensus that criminology could "do better" in its central task of explaining criminal behavior (see Weisburd & Piquero, 2008) and in using this knowledge to develop more effective public policies for managing crime. As Eskridge (2005, p. 306) sums up in his overview of the state of the field of criminology: "We are not a mature science at this point, and we are not certain how to systematically reduce the severity of crime."

A more plausible explanation for criminology's neglect of evolutionary approaches lies with the ideological outlook of most criminologists (Wright & Cullen, 2012). There is no doubt that biological approaches to understanding human behavior in general, and evolutionary approaches in particular, have a somewhat tainted history in the social and behavioral sciences. As Rafter (2008) documents in her history of biological theories of crime, biological approaches to criminology have been employed to justify eugenic programs and to ignore social solutions to crime. Most contemporary criminologists—indeed most social scientists—are politically liberal (Wright & Cullen, 2012), and research clearly suggests that liberals tend to favor environmental theories of crime that highlight the role of an unfair economic system, lack of educational opportunities, and labeling (Cooper et al., 2010; Walsh & Ellis, 2004). Because biological approaches (including those that draw on evolutionary theory) are perceived as advancing a deterministic view of human nature, many liberal criminologists may reject (or ignore) such perspectives because they believe that such approaches offer a pessimistic view of the possibility of social change. Of course, as Wright and Cullen (2012) clearly point out (and as we shall explore in detail throughout this book), contemporary biological approaches to understanding criminal behavior in no way are committed to a deterministic view of human nature. Indeed, for many evolutionarily-minded scholars, the association of Darwinian theory with the political right is somewhat of a puzzle—and an irritating one at that. The philosopher Peter Singer (1999), for instance, was moved to write *A Darwinian left: Politics, Evolution, and Cooperation*, in which he urged liberals to embrace Darwinian theory, and many have noted that evolutionary scientists are often liberals (Darwin himself foremost among them).

Ideology has almost certainly played some role in the neglect of evolutionary approaches by social scientists in general, and criminologists in particular. A related problem concerns the lack of education or training in biology among criminologists, which inevitably leads to a somewhat limited understanding of evolutionary theory. Evidence for this point of view comes from the survey of Cooper et al. (2010) of members of the American Society of Criminology. They found that the number of undergraduate and graduate classes in sociology, psychology, and biology reported by respondents predicted their support for different causes of crime, including the role of evolution. Specifically, the more classes in sociology that participants took, the less likely they were to endorse evolution as an important cause of crime (although this effect was only significant for liberals). Similarly, in a survey of 7763 academic staff in social science and other departments in UK universities, Perry & Mace (2010) found that disciplinary status was the best predictor of "acceptance of evolutionary approaches to human behaviour," with academics in social science departments significantly less likely to endorse evolutionary approaches. Moreover, among this subset of academics, knowledge of evolution positively predicted, and number of years studying social sciences negatively predicted, acceptance of evolutionary approaches to understanding human behavior. The lack of education in evolution is perhaps even more widespread, as Glass, Wilson, & Geher (2012) demonstrate that even among those scholars who had published evolutionary-themed articles in the journal *Behavioral and Brain Sciences*, the amount of training in evolution was limited.

In sum, there are likely to be a number of reasons why evolutionary approaches have had a relatively negligible impact on the field of criminology to date. The argument that we advance in this book is that the time is ripe for this state of affairs to be remedied. In brief, we suggest that there are at least five good reasons why evolutionary approaches should become incorporated in criminology. First, as noted above, many criminologists have voiced concerns about the state of criminology. That is not to say that evolutionary approaches are the cure-all for what many think ails mainstream criminological thinking. However, we think a greater interdisciplinary focus—including the judicious use of evolutionary theory—can enrich our understanding of crime (and hence the discipline of criminology) in important ways. Second, as we have touched upon above, there is already an extensive literature (mainly influenced by evolutionary psychology) that has explored many topics of interest to criminologists. Although, as we argue in Chapter 3, we think there are problems with some of this work, the presence of this—now substantial—literature means that criminologists do not have to start afresh in their application of evolutionary ideas to criminology. Third, the emerging paradigm of biosocial criminology provides a useful framework for introducing evolutionary ideas into criminology, and although biological approaches in general still tend to be neglected, the rapid advance of research on the biological underpinnings of human behavior means that this situation is likely to change in the near future. Fourth, we think that recent developments in the conceptual foundations of evolutionary biology (see Chapter 2) and related developments in the application of evolutionary theory to human behavior (see Chapter 3) provide an approach that, by recognizing the importance of culture in understanding human behavior, is likely to be more amenable to criminologists and more readily integrated with existing criminological theories. Finally, and perhaps most obviously, humans—like all other species on the planet—are the products of evolution, and thus evolutionary theory must to some degree be relevant for our understanding of human behavior, including the behaviors of interest to criminologists.

We think there are a number of good reasons why evolutionary approaches to understanding human behavior should have a more prominent role in criminology than they currently do. For many criminologists and other social scientists interested in crime, these general arguments may hold little weight, and the bottom line will be what such approaches have to offer the study of crime and our responses to crime. We devote a considerable amount of space to this issue, but we think, generally speaking, that an evolutionary criminology can enrich the study of crime in three important ways.

First, the integration of evolutionary explanations with other theoretical approaches in criminology will provide for richer and more comprehensive explanations of the various phenomena of interest to criminologists. We argue that many of the most important topics of interest to criminologists—including the age–crime curve, the preponderance of male–male violence, and the motivation to punish offenders—cannot be completely and satisfactorily explained in the absence of an evolutionary approach appropriately integrated with existing criminological theories. We term this the *"ontological rationale,"* because the inclusion of evolutionary theory provides a richer, deeper understanding of the nature of human behavior. Second, adopting an evolutionary perspective can open up new lines of inquiry and guide new research questions using new methodologies. In other words, the incorporation of evolutionary theory will help to generate novel research questions and programs of research within criminology. We suggest that this provides the *"epistemological rationale"* of evolutionary criminology. Finally, we suggest that evolutionary criminology can contribute in meaningful ways to the practical task of reducing the harm caused by crime (and our responses to crime). This we refer to as the *"pragmatic rationale."*

AN OVERVIEW OF THE BOOK

This book is divided into three parts. In the first part, an overview of the evolutionary framework that we will be using in the remainder of the book is presented. We begin with a review of the key conceptual ideas in evolutionary biology that are important for understanding the application of evolutionary theory to human behavior. This material may be familiar to many readers, but given the relative lack of formal training in evolutionary biology for social scientists, we think this review is crucial to ensure that key processes and theories such as natural selection, sexual selection, parental investment theory, and life history theory are clearly articulated. We also pay particular attention to recent developments in evolutionary thinking that some scholars argue provide an "extended synthesis" that builds on and extends the core ideas of the modern synthesis in evolutionary biology. Of particular relevance for this book is the recognition that nongenetic mechanisms of inheritance—including culture—are essential in the understanding of evolutionary processes. In the second half of Chapter 2, we offer a brief overview of our current understanding of human evolution, from our split with the lineage that led to chimpanzees to the present. Criminologists often recognize the importance of historical processes in understanding patterns of crime and punishment; in this chapter we simply extend the time horizon of interest back several million years. Exploring the "deep history" of our species is important, because it offers the appropriate context for understanding the evolution of our uniquely human nature and thus provides a grounding for the—often implicit—assumptions about humans that sit within theories of crime and punishment (Agnew, 2011a).

In Chapters 3 and 4, these assumptions are brought to the fore. Chapter 3 reviews the various different approaches that have been employed to explain human behavior from an evolutionary perspective, focusing on evolutionary psychology, human behavioral ecology, and gene–culture coevolutionary processes (Durrant & Ward, 2011). We argue in this chapter that a pluralistic approach that draws from each of these three perspectives provides the most promising avenue for advancing our understanding of the evolutionary underpinnings of human behavior (including criminal behavior and our responses to crime). In Chapter 4, we develop and present a conceptual framework for integrating evolutionary explanations with mainstream criminological approaches to understanding crime and our responses to crime. Central to this framework is the recognition that explanations can be drawn from different levels of analysis, and that one of the key tasks is to successfully integrate theories in ways that improve our understanding of the phenomenon of interest. Tinbergen's (1963) distinction between explanations that focus on evolutionary function, evolutionary history, development, and proximate processes provides an enduringly useful way of understanding how different types of explanation can be employed to understand any given behavioral phenomenon. With some qualification, and a particular role for social-structural and cultural explanations (which, we argue, can be viewed in both distal and proximate terms), we use this framework for organizing the theoretical approaches for understanding crime that are used in the second part of the book.

In part two of the book, we focus on theoretical approaches to explaining crime. We begin in Chapter 5 by focusing our attention specifically on the evolution of cooperation. We think that this topic is absolutely crucial for the subject matter of interest to criminologists, and, as Agnew (2011a) notes, almost all criminological theories have specific assumptions—not necessarily grounded in the relevant literature—regarding our "natural" tendencies to act in a selfish or cooperative manner. As we outline in the chapter, an extensive body of research clearly indicates that although selfishness and conflict will always be features of our behavior, we are in many respects "natural-born" cooperators. Each of the four following chapters in this part of the book focuses on one or more specific levels of analysis as we have outlined them in Chapter 4. Thus, in Chapter 6 we address distal explanations for crime by examining the evolutionary history and function of specific criminal behaviors. Our focus here is largely on violent crime (including sexual violence), but our general analysis has implications for other kinds of offending including drug use, property offending, and white-collar crime. In Chapter 7, we shift to considering the developmental origins of criminal behavior. A central task for any developmental theory of offending is to account for the dramatic increase in the prevalence of offending during adolescence and early adulthood, while also explaining why some offenders are much more likely to desist than others. We demonstrate that current developmental theories of crime, alongside our emerging understanding of normative developmental processes, can be enriched by recognizing both the evolutionary "function" of human-specific developmental trajectories and the way in which adaptive individual differences emerge in different social and environmental contexts. Chapter 8 addresses the proximate causes of crime. These are a somewhat mixed bag of processes including characteristics of individuals (e.g., cognitions), situations, and interpersonal social interactions. We also recognize here the importance of human agency and discuss how this can be reconciled with the evolutionary framework that we adopt in the first part of the book. The final chapter of Part II tackles cultural and social-structural explanations for crime. Although it may seem that evolutionary approaches have relatively little to offer in terms of understanding the cultural and structural processes that influence crime and that can account for differences in offending across time and place, we argue that the gene–culture coevolutionary approach outlined in Chapter 3 can help us to understand the emergence of specific cultural and social-structural contexts and why they influence crime (and our responses to crime) in specific ways.

In talking to friends and colleagues about the value of evolutionary approaches in criminology, many (but by no means all!) are willing to concede that we can improve our understanding of criminological phenomena by drawing from evolutionary theory; however, they remain skeptical about the practical usefulness of this knowledge. After all, if certain behaviors reflect specific evolutionary histories, how can we meaningfully intervene to change those behaviors? In the final part of the book, we respond to this concern by fleshing out the practical value of an evolutionary approach to improving the way that we respond to crime. We begin, in Chapter 10, by considering the evolutionary origins of the human motivation to punish offenders (norm violators) and what this means for the development of a criminal justice system that both resonates with our intuitive notions of justice, and responds to offending in a humane fashion. We argue that an evolutionary approach can help us to recognize that punishment is an essential feature of human societies, yet best serves its evolved function to the extent (in most cases) that it adopts an inclusive approach to the treatment of offenders. In this chapter, we also consider what an evolutionary approach has to contribute to our understanding of crime prevention. More specifically, we demonstrate how a clearer understanding about the causal origins of offending can help us to develop both social and situational crime prevention initiatives that are most likely to succeed in reducing crime. In Chapter 11, we discuss an evolutionary approach to understanding offender rehabilitation and reintegration (Ward & Durrant, 2011a, 2011b). Building on our understanding of human cooperation outlined in Chapter 5, and the need to recognize intrinsic human needs, we argue that a central task of offender rehabilitation and reintegration is to create the internal *and* external conditions that are most likely to foster altruistic behavior.

The first couple of decades of the twenty-first century are proving to be an exciting time for criminologists. Recent developments in our understanding of the biological underpinnings of crime offer to add to our already rich knowledge of the proximate psychological and situational factors that have been identified as playing key roles in offending. A now-extensive body of knowledge regarding the developmental trajectories of offending, and how these relate to normative developmental processes, has significantly improved our understanding of the factors that play a role in adolescent offending and contribute to desistance in adulthood. Ongoing theoretical and empirical work on macrolevel structures and processes continues to inform our understanding of patterns in offending, both within and across state and national borders. The time is ripe, we argue, to recognize the added value that evolutionary approaches can offer to our extant body of knowledge concerning crime and responses to crime. The topics that perennially engage criminologists are also of central concern to evolutionary behavioral scientists. To best advance our understanding of crime and to tackle the crime-related problems that subsequently emerge, therefore, we cannot afford to leave to one side the insights that evolutionary theory has to offer.

PART I

THE EVOLUTIONARY FRAMEWORK

2

Evolutionary Theory and Human Evolution

INTRODUCTION

There are no longer any moas in New Zealand. Despite occasional, always unsubstantiated sightings, the nine species of flightless ratite birds that were New Zealand's largest terrestrial herbivores went extinct within a couple of hundred years of human settlement in the thirteenth century. However, the ghost of the moa lingers on in the shape and form of many of New Zealand's native plants. In particular, there are an unusually large number of "divaricating" plants in the New Zealand flora. These plants contain a "distinctive branching structure with wide-angled, thick, inter-laced shoots bearing many leaves" (Bond, Lee, & Craine, 2004, p. 501). In addition, a number of trees go through a juvenile divaricating stage before reaching maturity (Greenwood & Atkinson, 1977). Because of the large number of divaricating plants in New Zealand, their presence across a range of different, unrelated species, and their relative rarity outside of New Zealand, the most obvious explanation for their existence is that divarication is an adaptation that promotes survival and reproductive success under the specific ecological conditions found in New Zealand (McGlone & Webb, 1981).

What could be the possible function of this leaf structure? Two main hypotheses have been advanced. One possibility is that divarication is a climatic adaptation that arose during treeless periods of glaciation in the Pleistocene, and functions to protect growing points from wind abrasion, desiccation, and frost damage (Howell, Kelly, & Turnbull, 2002; McGlone & Webb, 1981). A second hypothesis is that the dense tangle of interlaced branches and modest offering of leaves characteris-tic of divaricating plants is an adaptation that arose in response to the selection pressures exerted by browsing moas (Atkinson & Greenwood, 1989; Greenwood & Atkinson, 1977). Although the jury is still out on

© 2015 Elsevier Inc. All rights reserved.

this case, a feeding experiment found that New Zealand's divaricating plants suffered less damage from browsing ratites (emus and ostriches), in comparison with mammalian herbivores (goats), suggesting that the widespread presence of divaricating plants in New Zealand may well be due to the selection pressures exerted by moas (Bond, Lee, & Craine, 2004).

Although this example may seem to have little to do with human behavior, let alone the subject matter of criminology, it illustrates some key points that are central to our understanding of evolutionary theory and the application of evolutionary theory to human behavior. First, one of the most important contributions of evolutionary theory is to provide answers to *why* questions (see Chapter 4). Before Darwin, answers to such questions were sought in theology, but in *On the Origin of Species*, Darwin (1859) provided a compelling argument that—using the key principle of natural selection—a fully naturalistic account of the origin of the characteristics of different species was possible. Our understanding of the biological world—including humans—would be incomplete without such approach, and it is fair to say that evolutionary theory is the unifying theoretical framework for the biological sciences. The second point is that often our understanding of the evolutionary function of specific characteristics—like the divaricating branch structure of many New Zealand plants—remains provisional and can provide the impetus for programs of research that allow for the comparative evaluation of different hypotheses. Third, although understanding the evolutionary history of any given characteristics necessitates making claims about the past, this does not mean that such claims are mere idle speculation, as they can be more or less well supported given available sources of evidence.

Understanding the behavior of humans is, for various reasons, more difficult than establishing the adaptive function of certain types of leaf structure. However, humans, like all other species on the planet, have an evolutionary history, and understanding that history can provide valuable insights into the origins and functions of the characteristics that we possess. In order to employ evolutionary theory to understand criminal behavior, as we attempt to do in the second part of this book, we must first review some of the key conceptual ideas that are central to evolutionary biology. Inevitably, our discussion of many of these complex issues is brief, but we highlight the key processes and theories that will feature throughout this book, and note the tentative emergence of a new "extended synthesis" in evolutionary theory (Pigliucci, 2009) that has potentially important implications for the social sciences. We then turn to a discussion of human evolution, tracing the origin of the human species from our split with the ancestors of chimpanzees some five to eight million years ago (mya). Our aim in this section is to emphasize some of the major social and behavioral changes that occurred during this period and have profound implications for our understanding of human behavior.

NATURAL AND SEXUAL SELECTION

The idea that humans, along with all other organisms, are the product of a long history of evolution (in Darwin's terms: "descent with modification") is, to all extent and purposes, true (Coyne, 2009; Dawkins, 2009). Indeed, the existence of biological evolution was accepted by many thinkers even before the publication of Darwin's (1859) landmark book, *On the Origin of Species*. Missing from those earlier accounts of evolution, however, was a plausible account of the *mechanisms* responsible for evolutionary change. Any glance at a modern textbook on evolution (e.g., Futuyma, 2009) reveals a large number of interrelated theories that, in combination, can help to explain the characteristics of organisms, changes in populations over time, the geographical distribution of species, the origins of new species, and so forth. However, central to modern evolutionary thought is Darwin's account of the key mechanism responsible for evolutionary change: natural selection.

Natural selection, given time to work, is an extraordinarily powerful process, yet it can be neatly summarized in terms of three key principles: variation, differential fitness, and inheritance. First, the members of a species vary in the different characteristics that they possess. For instance, some impalas may be able to run faster than others, some desert-dwelling toads may be better at conserving moisture than their fellow toads, and some male baboons may be more physically dominant than others. Second, some of these differences will result in differences in fitness. In other words, some members of a species may be more likely to survive and reproduce as a result of the specific characteristics they possess: for instance, the more fleet-footed impalas are more likely to evade predators, the moisture-conserving toads will be more likely to survive prolonged droughts, and more dominant baboons may gain preferential access to food and mates. Third, and crucially for evolution to occur, these differences must be heritable. In other words, they must be reliably passed on from one generation to another (most typically from parents to offspring via shared genes, but see the discussion below). Over time, given these three processes, the characteristics of a population of organisms will change as more favored characteristics are retained at the expense of less advantageous variants.

Natural selection, then, is the primary process that accounts for evolutionary change. By slowly winnowing out less favorable traits and favoring those that reliably enhance survival and reproductive success, the characteristics of organisms are shaped in ways that promote a "fit" between organisms and environments. These characteristics are known as adaptations. The complex neural machinery underlying echolocation in bats, the ability of chameleons to change their skin color depending on local environments, and the bipedal gait of modern humans are all examples of biological adaptations: traits that owe their existence to their historical success in promoting survival and reproductive success. At this juncture it is worth pointing out that natural selection is not the only agent of evolutionary change, and evolutionary biologists also recognize the importance of chance factors (such as "genetic drift") in shaping the characteristics of populations (Futuyma, 2009). Moreover, the process of natural selection not only generates adaptations, but also results in by-products of adaptations, along with a residue of biological "noise" (Buss, Haselton, Shackelford, Bleske, & Wakefield, 1998; Travis & Reznick, 2009). The notion of by-products is widely invoked but captures a heterogeneous class of entities. Familiar examples are the sound that hearts make when they beat (a by-product of selection for the pumping mechanism of hearts), the white color of bones (a by-product of calcium salts that give bones their hardness and rigidity), and the human capacity for writing (a by-product, in part, of the evolved mechanisms underlying language). The idea of biological "noise" simply captures the idea that variation in traits, if it is selectively neutral, will be retained in organisms without contributing to biological fitness.

The problem of clearly demarcating adaptations from nonadaptations in the biological world is an important one. There is no foolproof method for identifying biological adaptations; however, characteristics that have been shaped by natural selection will often display "special design" features such as functionality, economy, efficiency, precision, specialization, reliability, and adaptive complexity (Andrews, Gangestad, & Matthews, 2002; Williams, 1966). The human eye, to use an oft-cited example, bears all the hallmarks of a biological adaptation: multiple parts (retina, lens, cornea, iris) are coordinated to produce a unitary function (sight) efficiently and reliably and with obvious evolutionary benefits (vision is clearly advantageous and has evolved independently many times over). The evolution of the human eye also illustrates another important aspect of biological adaptations—although eyes may be specialized to perform a specific functional task, their design might not always be optimal. Because evolution, as Jacob (1977) has noted, is a "tinkering" process in which the range of possible "solutions" to adaptive problems are constrained by what has gone before (evolutionarily speaking), we should expect that "suboptimal" design that bears the imprint of the evolutionary history of the characteristic in question. For example, because the vertebrate eye originally evolved as a light-detecting (rather than image-creating) device, humans have a "blind spot" caused by the way the optic nerve is positioned in the retina (Travis & Reznick, 2009).

This means that in our efforts to identify adaptations, we need to take into account the history of the characteristic in question. History is also important because different species share common ancestries. Humans and chimpanzees, for instance, share a common ancestor that lived around five to eight mya; all primates (including humans) share a common ancestor that lived approximately 63 mya; all vertebrates are descended from an ancestor that lived over 500 mya, and so forth (see Dawkins, 2004 for a vivid account of this history). In order to provide a clear account of the adaptive evolution of specific characteristics we therefore need to establish which traits are "ancestral" (they were present in the common ancestor of a particular evolutionary lineage) and which are "derived" (they are unique to the particular evolutionary lineage and therefore reflect selection processes occurring after the split from a common ancestor). These considerations form part of what is known as the "comparative method" in evolutionary biology for identifying adaptations and entail detailed phylogenetic (evolutionary historical) analyses of specific characteristics (Griffiths, 1996; Harvey & Pagel, 1991). The details of this approach need not concern us here, but in practical terms it means that in developing hypotheses regarding the evolution of human characteristics, we need to consider their "deeper" evolutionary history, and studies of chimpanzees and other primates in particular can illuminate this process, as we shall illustrate throughout this book (see Mitani, Call, Kappeler, Palombit, & Silk, 2012).

The concept of adaptation, as George Williams (1966) has noted, is an onerous one and we should be cautious in making claims that specific traits are adaptations in the absence of relevant available evidence. This issue may be of particular importance in the study of human characteristics and traits. For instance, there has been much heated debate over whether human rape can be considered a biological adaptation or is the by-product of other adaptations (Thornhill & Palmer, 2000), and disagreement persists in terms of whether humans have specific adaptations for homicide (Duntley & Buss, 2011; Durrant, 2009). As we shall discuss in our account of evolutionary psychology, defining adaptations is a much easier task than identifying them, especially when they are posited for the psychological and behavioral traits of humans, and sometimes evolutionary psychologists have been somewhat overeager to pronounce some human characteristic an adaptation in the absence of a considered evaluation of alternative hypotheses. However, it is a reasonable strategy to develop provisional hypotheses regarding the adaptive functions of specific characteristics and to accept the current best explanation, while recognizing that this acceptance is always subject to change (Durrant & Haig, 2001).

Although it is fairly easy to recognize how running speed in impalas and moisture-conserving mechanisms in desert-dwelling toads contribute to survival, and hence are likely to be the results of natural selection, many characteristics of organisms appear to offer no such obvious utilitarian functions. Consider the rather aptly named long-tailed widow bird. Males of this sparrow-sized species sport a 2 m long tail that clearly hinders the capacity of the bird to fly. As Darwin (1871) recognized, many characteristics of organisms do not enhance survival, but instead are the products of a process he labelled *sexual selection*. Sexual selection is probably best characterized as a special case of natural selection that is related to mate choice and mating (Andersson, 1994; Clutton-Brock, 2004). Darwin (1871) recognized two main types of sexual selection. The first kind relates to mate choice and is referred as intersexual selection. In short, specific characteristics can be selected for, if members of one sex show a preference for certain characteristics that are possessed by the other. It is likely, for example, that the elongated tail of the male long-tailed widow bird is a product of a long history of females preferentially mating with male birds that have the longest tail (Andersson, 1982). The other form of sexual selection, known as intrasexual selection, relates to competition between members of the same sex for mating access to members of the other sex. The evolution of male weaponry in many animal species in the form of tusks, horns, oversized canine teeth, and the like reflect selection for traits that improve the likelihood of success in (typically, but not always) male–male contests, thus creating more opportunities for mating and greater reproductive fitness (Emlen, 2008).

THE MODERN SYNTHESIS AND MIDDLE-LEVEL EVOLUTIONARY THEORIES

The idea of natural (and sexual) selection remains central to Darwinian evolutionary theory, and although there is some debate concerning the nature, scope, and power of selection processes (Pigliucci & Kaplan, 2006), the importance of selection for evolution has been amply demonstrated in a large number of experimental and observational studies (Futuyma, 2009). Since Darwin, there have also been a number of important additional theoretical developments in evolutionary biology. Although the notion of heritability, as we have seen, is central to the process of natural selection, Darwin had little idea concerning just *how* traits were passed on from parents to offspring. The work of the Moravian monk Gregor Mendel, in the late nineteenth century, provided an answer to this problem by positing that organisms inherit discrete units of information (what were to become known as "genes") that combine to generate the characteristics of offspring (Ruse, 2009). Drawing from these insights, the field of population genetics demonstrated how evolution arises through a combination of mutation and selection that leads to changes in the frequency of genes in populations over time. The fusing of population genetics with new developments in paleontology and systematics in the 1930s and 1940s forged what is typically referred to as the "modern synthesis" in evolutionary thought (Ruse, 2009).

Another wave of theorizing occurred in the 1950s, 1960s, and 1970s, and produced a range of additional "middle-level" theories (Durrant & Ellis, 2013) that served to extend the scope of the modern synthesis, especially in terms of understanding animal (including human) behavior. Of particular relevance for evolutionary explanations of criminal behavior are inclusive fitness theory, parental investment theory, life-history theory, reciprocal altruism, and parent–offspring conflict theory.

Altruism is a puzzle for evolutionary theory. As Darwin clearly recognized, behaviors that increase the success of other individuals of the same species at the expense of the altruistic individual should surely be eliminated by natural selection. Yet, altruistic and cooperative behaviors are rife in the biological world. For example, many squirrel species live in small groups of closely related individuals and post sentinels who emit loud alarm calls if they spot predators in their location. Sentinel squirrels thus help their conspecifics to evade predators, but inevitably draw attention to themselves, thus increasing the chances of predation (Davies, Krebs, & West, 2012). Surely selection should favor squirrels that keep mute and run for the trees if they spot a predator, therefore increasing their own chance of survival. A clear answer to this puzzle was formalized by W. D. Hamilton (1964) in what is variously known as *Hamilton's rule*, *kin selection theory*, or *inclusive fitness theory* (Durrant & Ellis, 2013). In short, phenotypic characteristics such as alarm-calling can be selected for, as long as they increase copies of the genes responsible for the trait. Crucially, the genes do not necessarily have to reside in the individual themselves, but may reside in other individuals of the same species. In most animal species, organisms share (on average) 50 percent of their genes with full siblings, 12.5 percent with first cousins, and so forth. Thus, altruistic behavior will be selected for to the extent that the costs of the behavior are outweighed by the benefits of the behavior to the recipient multiplied by the coefficient of relatedness (formally, altruistic behavior can evolve if $rB > C$). This central idea is neatly captured by J. B. S. Haldane who reportedly quipped "I'd lay down my life for two brothers or eight cousins" (Lewin, 1974, p. 325). Inclusive fitness theory was memorably popularized in Richard Dawkins's (1976) book *The Selfish Gene* and is related to the idea that the gene is the fundamental "unit" of selection (see Chapter 5 for a more detailed discussion of the evolution of altruism and cooperation).

Another important theoretical development in evolutionary theory in the latter half of the twentieth century was parental investment theory (Trivers, 1972). According to evolutionary biologist Robert Trivers

(1972, p. 139), parental investment can be viewed as "any investment by the parent in an … individual offspring's chance of surviving (and hence reproductive success) at the cost of the parent's ability to invest in other offspring." Importantly, Trivers recognized that for most species, there are usually gender differences in the typical amount of parental investment provided. These differences, moreover, have ramifications for the evolution of behavior. In short, the sex that invests relatively more in offspring becomes a limiting resource for the sex that invests relatively less and that will tend to compete for access to the more-investing sex. In the vast majority of species, females invest more in offspring than males. Among mammals, this follows from the fact that females bear the substantial biological cost of gestation, lactation, suckling, and (typically) infant care. In combination with the fundamental assumptions of sexual selection, parental investment theory generates a range of specific hypotheses concerning sex differences and mating behavior that have been widely exploited by both human and nonhuman evolutionary behavioral scientists (see Archer, 2009a; Daly & Wilson, 1988; Puts, 2010). We will revisit this theory in a number of places throughout this book and use it (in a somewhat qualified fashion) to help us to understand gender and age differences in risk taking, aggression, violence, and criminal behavior (see, in particular, our discussion in Chapter 6).

The optimal allocation of energy, resources, and behavioral strategies will, for any organism, depend on specific features of their evolved developmental history and the environment in which they are embedded. As Kaplan and Gangestad (2005, p. 68) summarize, "life history theory (LHT) provides a framework that addresses how, in the face of trade-offs, organisms should allocate time and energy to tasks and traits in a way that maximizes their fitness." How organisms optimally allocate resources can be characterized in several different ways, but they can be neatly captured in terms of three fundamental trade-offs (Kaplan & Gangestad, 2005).

The first trade-off pitches investment in current reproduction versus the allocation of energy and resources into future reproduction. T. S. Eliot concisely, if somewhat bleakly, captured the fundamental dynamic of existence as "birth, and copulation, and death," highlighting the central role that reproductive success plays in the evolution of life. However, organisms also need to extract energy from the environment while allocating resources to growth, bodily repair, the evasion of predators, social relations with conspecifics, and so forth. How organisms allocate these resources depends on species-specific characteristics, their sex, the stage in their life span, and features of the environment in which they find themselves embedded (Kaplan & Gangestad, 2005). The second trade-off relates to the allocation of resources to offspring quality versus investment in offspring quantity. Again, the optimal investment will depend on features of the species under consideration and, within species, will relate to sex, age, and environmental context. Finally, a third trade-off concerns effort put into mating (acquiring and maintaining a mate) versus that invested in parenting (investing resources in offspring). Although, as Del Giudice and Belsky (2011, p. 156) note, these three trade-offs are conceptually distinct, they often cluster together so that life-history strategies can be placed "on a single continuum from 'fast' or *r-selected* (i.e., early maturation and reproduction, quantity over quality, mating over parenting) to 'slow' or *K-selected* (the opposite pattern)."

Life-history strategies are often employed to make distinctions among different species. Some organisms reflect selection for "fast" life-history strategies. For instance, salmon mature rapidly, reproduce, lay thousands of eggs, and make no investment in parenting whatsoever. Other species lie near the other end of the continuum. Royal albatross, for instance, mature slowly, only seek a mate once they are 6–10 years old, pair-bond for life, lay a single egg every two years, and spend eight months raising their offspring until they fledge. Humans, of course, lie more to the K-selected end of this continuum of life-history traits. Importantly, life-history strategies not only capture broad species-specific developmental trajectories, but can also be invoked to explain *within*-species differences in the organization of behavior, as the optimal allocation of resources into current-versus-future reproduction, mating versus parenting, and the quality versus quantity of offspring will depend on specific features of the local environment (Del Giudice & Belsky, 2011; Ellis, Figueredo, Brumbach, & Schlomer, 2009). Some of these differences may be of particular importance for understanding individual differences in criminal and antisocial behavior, as certain environments (in particular, those that are unpredictable and that have high levels of extrinsic morbidity–mortality) may result in an adaptive shift to a relatively fast life-history strategy characterized by early reproduction and the allocation of energy to mating rather than parenting effort (Ellis, Boyce, Belsky, Bakermans-Kranenburg, & van Ijzendoorn, 2011). Investment in current reproduction and mating effort may, in turn, promote (among men at least) a wide range of risky and competitive behaviors including aggression, violence, and criminal activities. We provide a more detailed discussion of these ideas within the broader context of developmental criminology in Chapter 7.

Two final "middle-level" theories that we will discuss briefly here are reciprocal altruism theory (Trivers, 1971), and parent–offspring conflict theory (Trivers, 1974). Although inclusive fitness theory provides a clear explanation for altruistic behavior among kin, many animals, including humans, also behave altruistically toward nonrelated individuals of the same species. Trivers (1971) proposed that in species that are able to recognize specific individuals and can preferentially avoid associating with "cheats" (those that fail to return favors), altruistic behavior can be selected for, if the donor of the altruistic act can expect a reciprocal act of altruism from the recipient in the future. Such quid pro quos are, of course, fairly common in the human world, and evolutionary scientists have unearthed additional examples in other species including baboons, chimpanzees, and vampire bats (Cartwright, 2000). However, the conditions that allow reciprocal altruism may actually be quite rare among animal species, and, as discussed in more detail in Chapter 5, neither reciprocal altruism nor kin selection theory can provide a completely satisfactory explanation for the nature of human cooperation in large social groups. Robert Trivers's extraordinarily fertile run of theorizing in the early 1970s also included his presentation of parent–offspring conflict theory. In short, despite the fact that genetic relatedness among family members tends to promote cooperation, the "interests" of family members (from an evolutionary point of view) are not perfectly aligned. Thus, we should expect conflict to occur in families as the optimal amount of parental investment from a parent's point of view will not always match the optimum amount of investment from the perspective of the offspring. Parent–offspring conflict theory has contributed to an active program of research within behavioral ecology and has some important implications for the understanding of conflict in human families, as outlined in a recent review by Schlomer, Del Giudice, and Ellis (2011) (see also Chapter 6).

THE EXTENDED SYNTHESIS IN EVOLUTIONARY BIOLOGY

The success of the modern synthesis in evolutionary biology is without dispute, and it forms the essential theoretical framework for understanding the application of evolutionary theory to human behavior. However, over the last decade or so, a number of evolutionary scientists have argued that the time is ripe for an "extended synthesis" that incorporates recent conceptual developments in evolutionary biology, particularly as they relate to developmental processes and the relationships between organisms and their environments (Pigliucci, 2009; Pigliucci & Müller, 2010). A number of theoretical developments form a part of this proposed extended synthesis, but the most important element concerns the nature of inheritance. As we noted above, one of the key components of natural selection is heritability: for evolution to occur, organisms must reliably pass on advantageous traits and characteristics to subsequent generations. For the modern synthesis, genes are the exclusive mechanism of inheritance. However, there is now widespread recognition that there are also nongenetic mechanisms of inheritance that have important implications for understanding evolution (Bonduriansky & Day, 2009; Danchin, Charmantier, Champagne, Mesoudi, Pujol, & Blanchet, 2011; Jablonka & Lamb, 2005, 2008; but see Dickins & Dickins, 2008 and Dickins & Rahman, 2012 for a dissenting view on the importance of nongenetic inheritance).

The existence of nongenetic mechanisms of inheritance have led researchers to propose the idea of an inclusive concept of heritability that includes four key mechanisms of inheritance—genetic, epigenetic, ecological, and cultural (Danchin et al., 2011).

Genetic inheritance simply refers to the familiar idea, central to the modern synthesis, that offspring inherit genetic material from their parents. Very briefly, epigenetic inheritance refers to the fact that the expression of genes can be modified during development, resulting in phenotypic variations that in turn can be inherited by offspring (see Bonduriansky & Day, 2009; Jablonka & Lamb, 2010 for a more extended discussion). The idea of ecological inheritance draws from niche construction theory and highlights the active role that organisms play in modifying their environments (Odling-Smee, 2010; Odling-Smee, Laland, & Feldman, 2003). Beavers, to use a familiar example, radically change the ecology in which they (and other species) are embedded, through dam-building activities that transform swift-flowing streams and rivers into a series of sluggish waterways connected by robustly constructed dams that pool water in ways favorable to fishing. Importantly, these modifications are "passed on" to subsequent generations of beavers. In other words, beavers not only inherit genes from their parents, but also inherit environmental changes brought about by the activities of beavers in previous generations. Humans are, of course, niche constructors on a truly monumental scale, radically transforming environments in multiple ways. Humans are thus born into environments that have been substantially engineered by previous generations. The final type of nongenetic inheritance is cultural inheritance. We shall have more to say about cultural evolution in Chapter 3, as this forms a key component of human evolutionary behavioral science, but at this juncture we simply note that beliefs, attitudes, norms, values, institutions, and so forth (i.e., "culture") are transmitted from one generation to another (and between members of the same generation) through social-learning processes. Thus humans, and to a much more limited degree other animal species, inherit cultural traits, and these play an important role in explaining phenotypic variation among populations (Mesoudi, 2011).

Another feature of the extended synthesis is the growing acceptance that selection can be viewed as operating at many levels including genes, individuals, and groups (so-called multilevel selection theory; see Sober & Wilson, 1998; Wilson & Wilson, 2007). The traditional view, as outlined above, is that the gene (or the individual) is the primary "unit" of selection, and that group selection processes are either weak or nonexistent. The standard rationale for this assumption is relatively straightforward: behavior that benefits other group members at the expense of the individual will be selected against (unless they are close genetic kin), relative to rational self-interest. According to some biologists, however, this standard account fails to adequately explain the evolution of the extraordinary level of within-group cooperativeness found in so-called eusocial organisms, where large numbers of individuals cooperate, sometimes with nonkin, in tasks that benefit the group as a whole. Bees, ants, and termites are prototypical examples of eusocial animals (sometimes called "superorganisms"), but many believe that human sociality can also be considered to have made the transition to eusociality (Betzig, 2014; Kesebir, 2011; Nowak, Tarnita, & Wilson, 2010; Wilson & Wilson, 2007). To explain the origin of eusociality, the notion of group selection is invoked. In short, the central idea is that individually disadvantageous characteristics may evolve if they benefit groups in ways that make some groups more successful than others, through a process of between-group selection. As Wilson and Wilson (2007, p. 335) summarize: *"Selfishness beats altruism within single groups. Altruistic groups beat selfish groups"* (italics in original). As discussed below, many scholars think that group selection processes were important in human evolution and can help in understanding the high levels of cooperation that occur within human groups (Richerson & Boyd, 2005), although some remain skeptical of the importance of group selection processes (see Leigh, 2010 for a useful overview of the "group selection controversy").

SUMMARY

In this section, we have provided a summary of some of the key theoretical ideas that inform the field of evolutionary biology. Inevitably, our discussion of some of these important issues is brief, and others have not been mentioned at all. However, an understanding of these key concepts will be important in considering the role that evolutionary theory has to play in our understanding of human behavior, and therefore its role in advancing our understanding of criminological phenomena. We need to consider not only the key theoretical ideas that are at the heart of the modern synthesis (in particular, natural and sexual selection, and the various middle-level theories such as parental investment theory), but also need to recognize recent developments in evolutionary biology that highlight the role of an extended model of inheritance that incorporates ecological and cultural processes.

HUMAN EVOLUTION

In September 2003, a remarkable discovery was made in a cave on the Indonesian island of Flores. A skeleton was uncovered of a hitherto unknown hominin species, subsequently named *Homo floresiensis* (Brown et al., 2004; Morwood & Jungers, 2009). Standing at a little over 105 cm and with an estimated weight of between 25 and 30 kg, this new discovery—as Peter Jackson's film adaptations of the *Lord of the Rings* were screening in movie theaters round the world—was subsequently dubbed "the Hobbit." New fossil discoveries of extinct hominines are remarkable enough, but what made this particular find truly extraordinary was that the skeleton (and other, subsequently discovered remains) have been dated at between 74 and 17 thousand years ago (kya) (Wood & Baker, 2011). This means that this new, small-bodied and small-brained hominin species existed contemporaneously with our species, *Homo sapiens*, for tens of thousands of years.

This find, and the subsequent controversy that it generated among paleoanthropologists, illustrates a number of important points regarding the study of human evolution. First, there is a huge interest in the evolutionary origins of our species. This is apparent not only for specialists in the field, but also among the general public (the "hobbit" discovery was front-page news around the world). This interest is perfectly understandable: once we accept the fact of human evolution then it is unsurprising that we have a fascination with our evolutionary origins just as many people do with their family histories. Second, the discovery of *H. floresiensis* and other recent findings, such as evidence for interbreeding between Neanderthals and humans (Green et al., 2010), illustrates just how fast moving the field of paleoanthropology can be, as new archaeological finds and DNA analyses transform our understanding of our evolutionary history. As the historian Ian Morris (2010, pp. 42–43) remarks: "Their [paleoanthropologists] field is young and fast moving, and new discoveries constantly turn established truths on their heads. If you get two paleoanthropologists into a room they are likely to come up with three theories of evolution, and by the time the door shuts behind them, all will be out of date." Despite the swift-moving nature of the field and the often fragmentary nature of the evidence available, however, there is now an extensive body of research that allows us to provide a clear, albeit always provisional, outline of the origin and evolution of our species (Stringer, 2011).

The lineage that led to our species diverged from the one that gave rise to chimpanzees sometime between five and eight mya (see Figure 2.1). There are several things to note about the evolutionary relationship between humans and other primates. First, humans are clearly a species of primate. Second, humans are most closely related to chimpanzees (indeed, more closely related than chimpanzees are to gorillas). And third, the origin of the lineage that resulted in our species is, in evolutionary terms, very recent. Indeed, we share close to 99% of our DNA with chimpanzees (the Chimpanzee Sequencing and Analysis Consortium, 2005). These points suggest that in order to fully understand our evolutionary origins and the characteristics that we possess, we need to consider the evolution of characteristics in primates and great apes more

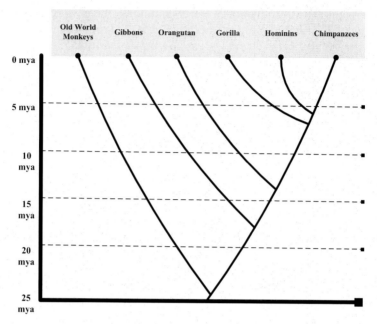

FIGURE 2.1   Phylogeny of primates from 25 million years ago (mya). *Dates from Dawkins, 2004.*

generally. However, despite the substantial similarity between the human and chimp genome, it is impossible to ignore the fact that humans are, in many important respects, *different*.

Strictly speaking, of course, all organisms are unique. However, it is not *just* human hubris to recognize that our species is unusual in important respects. Perhaps the clearest indication of this difference is reflected in our extraordinary success as a species—in evolutionary terms at least. By around 15 kya the human population numbered somewhere in the region of five million, and humans had spread to all parts of the planet (except Antarctica), managing to survive in a diverse range of environments including rainforests, deserts, grasslands, and the arctic (Fagan, 2012). Humans, however, not just survived in these environments—they *flourished*. Although there is substantial evidence for local population declines and the collapse of societies (Diamond, 2005), over the subsequent 15 millennia, the human population rose dramatically, reaching seven billion by 2010. Smil (2011) calculated that the combined biomass of humans (literally our estimated collective weight as a species) in the year 2000 was a staggering 11 times greater than the combined biomass of *all* wild terrestrial mammals. Other analyses suggest that something on the order of 25 percent of all terrestrial net primary production (that is, the available products of photosynthesis) is appropriated for human purposes (Haberl et al., 2007).

What specific characteristics of humans can account for this extraordinary ecological dominance? There is no straightforward answer to this question, but, as a special issue of the journal *Evolutionary Anthropology* (Calcagno & Fuentes, 2012) illustrates, there is considerable agreement on those key characteristics that can account for our "success" as a species, and that help to "make us human." These characteristics include a fully developed theory of mind (the capacity to infer the mental states of others), an enormously flexible open-ended communication system (language), ultrasociality (the widespread cooperation among kin and nonkin alike), and the capacity for high-fidelity social learning that supports uniquely human cultural systems. To these characteristics, we could also add a highly unusual life-history structure with an extended period of juvenile development, cooperative breeding, a postreproductive phase (Hill, Barton, & Hurtado, 2009; Hrdy, 2009), and of course a brain that is approximately six times larger than would be expected for a mammal of our size. Teasing out the causal connections among these various characteristics and their emergence in hominin evolutionary history is no easy task, but in what follows we provide a brief sketch of the key milestones in the evolutionary history of our lineage and some of the important theoretical frameworks that have been developed to account for our unique human characteristics.

An Outline of Hominin Evolution

Sometime between five and eight mya, somewhere in Africa, the lineage that led to our species diverged from that which resulted in chimpanzees. The fossil record for this period is patchy, but there appear to have been a number of hominin species who, like chimpanzees, probably lived in small multimale, multifemale groups, existed on an omnivorous diet, and made relatively rudimentary use of tools (Malone, Fuentes, & White, 2012; McHenry, 2009). Although there is some evidence of bipedalism during this period, clear evidence for the evolution of upright walking appears from around 4.2 mya with the emergence of the australopithecines. *Australopithecus afarensis*, for example, lived roughly between 3.8 and 3.0 mya, and based in part on a remarkable set of fossilized footprints from Laetoli, clearly walked upright. Unraveling the set of selection pressures that resulted in bipedalism remains a matter of some debate among paleoanthropologists, but one important result was the freeing of the hands from their use in locomotion to other purposes such as tool use and the carrying of objects (Stringer, 2011).

Between 2.5 and 1.8 mya, a number of important changes occurred in the hominin lineage. Although the brain size of the various australopithecine species was not significantly different from that of modern-day chimpanzees, the emergence of the genus *Homo* coincided with a dramatic increase in brain capacity. Perhaps not coincidently, the origin of *Homo* is also associated with clear evidence of stone tool manufacture and use, a shift to a more carnivorous diet, an extended juvenile period, and for the first time, dispersal out of Africa (Foley & Gamble, 2009). The next million years or so saw a continuation of these trends: brain size increased, stone tool manufacture became more sophisticated, and hominines penetrated more northerly parts of the Eurasian landmass. Just how many different species of *Homo* existed during this period remains a matter of debate (Wood & Baker, 2011), but by around 200 kya, we see the emergence in Africa of anatomically modern humans—*Homo sapiens*. According to the most widely accepted model, over the next 200,000 years this large-brained hominin, showing evidence of increasingly sophisticated tool use, control of fire, and diverse hunting and foraging strategies, gradually dispersed out of Africa, displacing (either directly or indirectly, and perhaps with a small amount of interbreeding) extant species of *Homo* in Europe (notably *Homo neanderthalensis*) and Asia (*Homo erectus, Homo floresienses*).

Paleoanthropologists often employ the term *anatomically* modern humans to describe the emergence of our species some 200 kya, in order to draw attention to the idea that *behavioral* modernity was a much more recent occurrence, generally dating to about 50 to 40 kya. Around this time, there is abundant evidence for the emergence of modern human behavioral characteristics such as elaborately carved stone tools and artifacts, self-ornamentation, art, and the exploitation of a more diverse range of plant and animal resources. For many, these changes reflect the emergence of modern cognition and an increased capacity for symbolically mediated behaviors. Some scholars suggest that genetic changes at around 50 kya are responsible for behaviorally modern traits observed in the archaeological record from this time (e.g., Klein, 2008), while others point to earlier evidence for such behaviors and suggest that the changes were gradual, perhaps better reflecting changes in population size or interaction with changing local ecologies (see d'Errico & Stringer, 2011; McBrearty & Brooks, 2000; Sterelny, 2011). Regardless of how this debate plays out, by around 12 kya humans had dispersed to all major landmasses except Antarctica, and the existence of settled communities and the domestication of plants and animals became increasingly widespread, ultimately leading to the ecological dominance of humans in the twenty-first century. Although conventional accounts of hominin evolution tend to end with the advent of agriculture around 12,000 kya, it is important to recognize that human evolution has not stopped or even slowed as a result (Powell, 2012).

Indeed, there is now considerable evidence that human evolution continues to occur and may even have accelerated during the last 10,000 years (e.g., Hawks, Wang, Cochran, Harpending, & Moyzis, 2007).

Theoretical Models of Hominin Evolution

There is no shortage of theoretical models that attempt to explain the emergence of uniquely human traits during the course of hominin evolution. One prominent perspective focuses on the role of climate change. In short, it is argued that changing climatic conditions provided the ecological impetus for the evolution of the unique characteristics that make up the hominin lineage. According to Potts's (2012a, 2012b) variability hypothesis, the key climatic factor driving hominin evolution was the rapidly varying climate conditions that prevailed from around 3.5 mya. Potts argues that any given species has three possible "choices" in the face of changing environmental conditions: go extinct, shift to more propitious ecological conditions, or become more versatile. Hominins, it is suggested, "followed" the third option, and, according to this view, environmental unpredictability has been an important selective force that has favored behavioral flexibility and the ability to rapidly adjust to changing conditions (e.g., Potts, 2012a, although see Shultz, Nelson, & Dunbar, 2012).

Although external (or "exogenous") factors such as climatic variability may well have played an important role in the evolution of human characteristics, many scholars point to the role of social factors and emphasize the unique human exploitation of a "sociocognitive" niche characterized by extensive cooperation, language, and cumulative culture (Whiten & Erdal, 2012). In other words, uniquely human characteristics are likely to be the product of adaptations to the social world of early hominins. Although specific scenarios vary greatly in the identification of key selection pressures and processes, and the timing of important developments, central to most accounts of hominin evolution is the increasingly important role of the social group and the demands imposed by cooperation, collective action, cooperative breeding, and the effective management of social conflict (Burkart, Hrdy, & van Schaik, 2009; Dunbar, 2006; Herrman & Tomasello, 2012; Hrdy, 2009; Sterelny, 2012).

One of the important early steps in the evolution of human "ultrasociality" was probably a shift to cooperative foraging, possibly around the time of the emergence of *Homo* (Herrman & Tomasello, 2012; Sterelny, 2012). Truly cooperative resource acquisition—particularly of difficult-to-obtain items such as underground tubers, and the hunting of large game— requires the active coordination of group members to achieve shared outcomes. Selection for motivational, cognitive, and emotional traits that support cooperative activities may also have been enhanced by a shift in life history characterized by cooperative breeding and an extended juvenile period (Burkart, Hrdy, & van Schaik, 2009; Hawkes, 2014; Hrdy, 2009). In particular, pair-bonding and the widespread provisioning of offspring by "alloparents" (e.g., kin and other group members) would select for prosocial characteristics and cognitive traits that support cooperation such as shared intentionality and social learning. The capacity for social learning, in turn, would allow for the accumulation of cultural knowledge—such as how to manufacture tools, how to process food resources, and the best techniques for hunting large game—that would have placed even greater emphasis on mechanisms that enhance cooperation and high-fidelity social learning. In short, uniquely human capacities for cooperation and culture likely evolved through positive feedback loops: cooperative foraging supports a shift in life history involving an extended childhood, which in turn allows for the social learning of important cultural knowledge that further enhances the capacity to successfully obtain resources from the environment (Sterelny, 2012).

An important next stage in hominin evolution, according to Herrmann and Tomasello (2012), involved group-level processes. Successful cooperation involves behavior that benefits members of the group as a whole, even at a cost to specific individuals. This requires the capacity to differentiate in-group from out-group members and the motivation to preferentially cooperate with the former rather than the latter. Groups that were more cooperative—better able to coordinate individual actions to reach collective goals while suppressing selfish behavior—would have been more successful relative to less cooperative groups. Thus, according to Richerson and Boyd (2005), *cultural group selection* was a critical aspect of human evolution, as more successful cultural groups flourished at the expense of less cooperative ones. This process, moreover, would have set up selection pressures for motivational, emotional, and cognitive capacities that support in-group cooperation, such as the motivation to punish those who violate group norms (see Chapter 5), feelings of guilt and shame over transgressions of group norms, and the cognitive mechanisms that allow for the acquisition of group norms, values, and beliefs. At just what point in hominin evolution the transition to modern forms of cultural cognition emerged is a matter of some conjecture, and the evolution of language almost certainly played a key role. However, cumulative cultural traditions are not strongly evident in the archaeological record prior to the evolution of *Homo sapiens,* so it is plausible to suggest that the capacity for fully cumulative cultural cognition emerged at this point in our evolutionary history (Herrmann and Tomasello, 2012).

Once this capacity is in place, the rapidly changing picture of human culture can be largely explained in terms of demographic processes (Powell, Shennan, & Thomas, 2009; Sterelny, 2011). As Sterelny

(2011, 2012) has argued, cumulative cultural evolution depends not only on individual cognitive capacities that support social learning, but also on "adapted learning environments"—in other words, environments rich in learning resources, a range of teachers with expertise, exemplars of tools, and other cultural artifacts—that scaffold learning experiences for the next generation. The larger and more diverse the cultural group, the richer are these resources and the more likely they are to be retained (and possibly) improved upon in subsequent generations. These ideas are consistent with the extended evolutionary synthesis described above: ecological and cultural mechanisms of inheritance play a pivotal role in the human story alongside—and in interaction with—more familiar genetic inheritance mechanisms. From this perspective, the emergence of behavioral modernity—the extraordinary flowering of cultural artifacts that is visible in the archaeological record around 40 kya—was largely the product of changes in population structure and size that facilitated cumulative cultural evolution by providing the kind of learning environments that allowed innovations to be retained, developed, and spread.

We have devoted some space to this (still largely thumbnail) account of hominin evolution for several reasons. First, any attempt to employ evolutionary theory to understand human behavior, including the behavior of interest to criminologists, must recognize the evolutionary origins of that behavior and the context in which its selection may have taken place. Not all behaviors of interest, of course, will have evolutionary "origins" in the last five to eight million years. The capacity for aggression, for instance, is a feature of many animal species and certainly predates the split between the lineages that led to humans and chimpanzees, although the mechanisms underlying aggression (and the social contexts in which it is typically expressed) will have undergone some modification since that divergence. Second, the story of hominin evolution is centrally concerned with the emergence and maintenance of cooperative cultural groups in the face of individual "self-interest." To put this another way, the key features that make us human, and taken together define human uniqueness, are our capacities for large-scale cooperation, language, and culture. Collectively, these capacities account for a good part of the subject matter of criminology: behaviors that cause harm and violate cultural norms ("crime") and the regulation and control of that behavior ("punishment"). The specific account of human evolution outlined above may well be subject to change and revision, but central to understanding human uniqueness, and equally important to the study of crime and our responses to crime, is a recognition that the tendency to adhere to and enforce cultural norms (and a countervailing tendency to seek selfish outcomes) is part of the deep history of our species.

SUMMARY

Humans, like all other species on the planet, are the product of evolutionary processes. Just as the leaf structure of many New Zealand plants has been shaped by a myriad of selection pressures, including the feeding habits of a now extinct guild of flightless birds, so too have our psychological and behavioral characteristics been shaped by the selection pressures exerted (in part) by Pleistocene environments. In this chapter, we have introduced some of the key theoretical concepts that evolutionary biologists employ to understand the biological world, and have offered a sketch of the unique trajectory of hominin evolution over the past seven million years. In the next chapter, we take up the task of using evolutionary theory to understand human behavior in more detail.

3

Evolutionary Behavioral Science

INTRODUCTION

In 1975 the Harvard biologist E. O. Wilson published *Sociobiology: The New Synthesis*, a book that was to become an unusual kind of bestseller. The vast majority of this hefty volume's over 500 pages were devoted to a careful and comprehensive theoretical review of the evolutionary basis of social behavior in nonhuman animals. In the final chapter of *Sociobiology*, Wilson took the logical step of extending this "systematic study of the biological basis of all social behavior" (1975, p. 5) to humans, tackling such topics as aggressiveness, sex roles, religion, and xenophobia. Indeed, one of the explicit goals of sociobiology, as formulated by Wilson, was to absorb the social sciences and humanities into the modern evolutionary synthesis. The ideas developed in this final chapter generated a significant amount of controversy, and the use of evolutionary theory to explain human behavior was variously criticized as deterministic, reductionistic, and ideologically unsound (e.g., Rose, Kamin, & Lewontin, 1984). Wilson himself was subjected to abuse and negative leaflet campaigns, and at a 1978 meeting of the American Association for the Advancement of Science, he was ignominiously doused with a pitcher of cold water by protesters (see Degler, 1991 and Segerstråle, 2000 for historical overviews of the sociobiology debate).

Of course, Wilson was not the first to employ evolutionary theory to understand the behavioral characteristics of humans, and ever since Darwin (1859, p. 373) perspicaciously noted that much "light will be thrown on the origin of man and his history," there have been various attempts to account for the behavior of humans using Darwinian evolutionary theory (Plotkin, 2004; Richards, 1987). As with the work of E. O. Wilson, these efforts have been the subject of a now extensive critical literature. Although as noted in Chapter 1, evolutionary explanations can be said to have penetrated the mainstream thinking of many psychologists, they have had a relatively negligible impact on the social sciences and humanities. In part,

41

© 2015 Elsevier Inc. All rights reserved.

we will argue in this chapter that this neglect reflects a misunderstand-ing of evolutionary theory and evolutionary explanations. However, we also suggest that the failure of Wilson's vision for the social sciences also reflects, to some extent, the difficulty evolutionary approaches have had with advancing our understanding of the phenomena of central interest to many social scientists, particularly those related to social structure and culture. Following Brown, Dickins, Sear, and Laland (2011), we argue that a *human evolutionary behavioral science* can be developed that provides for a more thorough integration with the social sciences, including, of course, criminology (Durrant & Ward, 2011, 2012; Ward & Durrant, 2011b).

It is generally recognized that there are a number of relatively distinct evolutionary approaches to understanding human behavior, includ-ing evolutionary psychology, human behavioral ecology, and cultural evolutionary theory. We begin with a comparative review of these three approaches, outlining their key features and points of difference. We then turn to a discussion of some of the standard criticisms of these approaches. We argue that although many of these criticisms are misguided and reflect a superficial reading of the relevant literature, there are a number of more substantive issues that have yet to be fully resolved. In the final section on "evolutionary behavioral science" we indicate how this might be achieved. This framework will subsequently inform our analyses throughout the remainder of this book.

APPLYING EVOLUTIONARY THEORY TO HUMAN BEHAVIOR

There is no serious disagreement among scientists of all stripes that humans are the product of evolution. Although, as noted in the preceding section, the fossil record of our species is inevitably incomplete, it is clear that like all other species on the planet, *Homo sapiens* has an evolution-ary history. It follows, fairly straightforwardly it would seem, that evo-lutionary theory can and should make an important contribution to our understanding of human characteristics, including our psychology and behavior. Very little is straightforward, however, in the history of attempts to employ evolutionary theory to advance our understanding of human behavior. As we noted in the introduction to this chapter, human socio-biology received a hostile reception in many quarters. Indeed, very few scholars are still willing to label themselves as "sociobiologists," and the program outlined by Wilson in the 1970s (1975, 1978) has been overtaken, with relevant modifications, by at least three separate but overlapping research programs: evolutionary psychology, human behavioral ecology, and cultural evolutionary theory (Brown et al., 2011; Gangestad & Simpson, 2007; Laland & Brown, 2011; Winterhalder & Smith, 2000).

Evolutionary Psychology

The best known, and in many respects most successful, of these three human evolutionary research programs is evolutionary psychology. Over the last quarter century, the field of evolutionary psychology has generated a significant body of research in all areas of psychological science including cognitive, social, clinical, developmental, and forensic psychology (Durrant & Ellis, 2013). There are now dozens of introductory textbooks on evolutionary psychology, evolutionary psychology has become increasingly represented in introductory psychology textbooks (Cornwell, Palmer, Guinther, & Davis, 2005), and articles featuring evolutionary psychological ideas are regularly published in the leading psychology journals such as *American Psychologist*, *Psychological Bulletin*, and the *Journal of Personality and Social Psychology* (e.g., Webster, 2007). In short, evolutionary psychology (although still subject to a relatively extensive body of criticism) to a significant degree has become incorporated within mainstream psychological science. Moreover, although evolutionary psychology has perhaps not provided the revolutionary new paradigm that can serve to unify psychological science as some had suggested (e.g., Buss, 1995), there can be little doubt that it has made significant contributions to our understanding of human cognition and behavior by opening new lines of inquiry, enriching existing bodies of knowledge, and reshaping our understanding of specific domains of knowledge (Durrant & Ellis, 2013).

Evolutionary psychology, in many respects like its forebear sociobiology, draws from the neo-Darwinian synthesis in biology and applies the central assumptions of natural and sexual selection, inclusive fitness theory, and the various middle-level theories (e.g., parental investment theory) to the study of human cognition and behavior. Evolutionary psychologists, therefore, assume that human characteristics can be understood as the product of evolutionary processes. More specifically, it is argued that many of the characteristics of interest to psychologists and other behavioral scientists are adaptations that have been forged during the course of our evolutionary history by the forces of natural (and sexual) selection. In addition to employing the key theoretical developments of the neo-Darwinian synthesis, evolutionary psychologists also typically endorse a number of specific assumptions about the nature of the human mind and the application of evolutionary theory to human cognition and behavior. In particular, evolutionary psychologists argue that psychological mechanisms should be the main unit of analysis and that these mechanisms are likely to be large in number and have evolved to solve specific adaptive problems in our ancestral past (Durrant & Ellis, 2013; Laland & Brown, 2011).

According to evolutionary psychologists, one of the key ways in which evolutionary psychology differs from sociobiology is that the latter tends to focus on the evolution of behavior, whereas, for the former, psychological mechanisms are the main unit of analysis (Cosmides & Tooby, 1987, 2013; Tooby & Cosmides, 1992, 2005). Tooby and Cosmides argue that psychological mechanisms should be the focus of study, because this is the level at which species-typical invariances occur. Behavior, in contrast, is much more variable because it reflects the interaction of universal evolved psychological mechanisms with variable environments. Psychological mechanisms are viewed as psychological adaptations that have been selected for during our evolutionary history, because they successfully solved adaptive problems. As summarized by Confer et al. (2010, p. 111): *"Psychological adaptations* are information-processing circuits that take in delimited units of information and transform that information into functional output designed to solve a particular adaptive problem." Collectively, it is argued that the core set of psychological mechanisms identified by evolutionary psychologists represent our shared "human nature" (Tooby & Cosmides, 2005).

The second assumption widely accepted by evolutionary psychologists is that the human mind comprises a large number of these evolved psychological mechanisms. This is often referred to as the "massive modularity hypothesis" to reflect the idea that these psychological mechanisms are domain specific, and although functionally integrated with one another, are designed to process specific types of information in specific ways, and thus are to some extent modular in nature (Barrett & Kurzban, 2006; Cosmides & Tooby, 2013). The primary logic behind the idea of domain specificity is straightforward: simply put, specific adaptive problems are best solved by specific adaptive solutions. Thus, just as the body comprises a number of specific physiological organs and systems (e.g., heart, lungs, pancreas, kidney, and liver) that have evolved to solve specific adaptive problems, so too—it is argued—we should expect the mind/brain to be replete with an array of domain-specific psychological mechanisms and processes that have been selected to address the commensurately broad range of adaptive problems faced by our hominin ancestors (Confer et al., 2010). Evolutionary psychologists, therefore, propose a large number of specialized domain-specific mechanisms—from fear of snake "modules" (Öhman & Mineka, 2003) to mechanisms underlying mate choice (Buss, 1989).

A third assumption that is largely accepted by evolutionary psychologists is based on the idea that biological adaptations are the product of past selective forces. If we accept—as most evolutionary psychologists do—that evolution is a relatively slow and gradual process, then our attempts to delineate the functional properties of the human mind need to consider how psychological mechanisms successfully solved adaptive problems in ancestral (rather than modern) environments. The historical environment in which a particular characteristic evolved is usually referred to as the *environment of evolutionary adaptedness* (EEA) (Tooby & Cosmides, 1990).

Because many of the interesting and unique characteristics of our species evolved during the Pleistocene and before the advent of agriculture, the EEA for our species is often located during this time period. Evolutionary psychologists, therefore, when developing hypotheses about the nature and function of human psychological adaptations, often consider how these mechanisms would have successfully solved adaptive problems faced by Pleistocene hunter-gatherers, not modern humans. Indeed, mechanisms that promoted reproductive success in ancestral environments may not be adaptive in the modern world—witness how our evolved taste preferences for food high in fat and sugar can lead to serious health problems in a world of abundant, readily available and highly processed food sources (Confer et al., 2010).

Evolutionary psychology can thus be characterized as a field of inquiry that draws on the neo-Darwinian synthesis in evolutionary biology alongside a cluster of special assumptions that serve to apply evolutionary theory to the study of human cognition and behavior. Evolutionary psychologists also typically employ a specific methodological approach to their research, as clearly summarized by Gangestad and Simpson (2007, p. 402):

> (1) A researcher first identifies an *adaptive problem* that recurred in ancestral human groups; (2) the researcher performs a *task analysis*, which asks what kind of computations (information acquisition and processing) would have effectively and efficiently solved the problem in an ancestral world, typically in a domain-specific manner; (3) the researcher tests the hypothesis that modern humans possess these computational procedures.

For example, an extensive body of research has explored the topic of male sexual jealousy (Daly, Wilson, & Weghorst, 1982; Schützwohl, 2005). The psychological mechanisms underlying male sexual jealousy, it is argued, have evolved to solve the adaptive problem of paternity certainty in a species that forges relatively long-term sexual and romantic relationships: males who experienced jealousy when confronted with the sexual infidelity of their partner (or cues to that infidelity) and responded in ways that reduced the likelihood of infidelity occurring would have been more likely to invest in offspring who were their own and thus the mechanisms underlying jealousy (and their sensitivity to relevant environmental cues) have been selected for. This hypothesis has been the subject of extensive research, using standard research methodologies in psychology, and has received a considerable amount of empirical support (Sagarin et al., 2012).

Human Behavioral Ecology

Evolutionary psychology may be the best known of the three approaches that we consider here, but human behavioral ecology is another perspective that emerged around the same time (if not earlier) and is also firmly rooted in the neo-Darwinian synthesis in its attempt to provide evolutionary explanations for human behavior (Laland & Brown, 2011). Human behavioral ecologists typically employ the same toolbox of methods, concepts, and models that are employed by behavioral ecologists studying other species (Nettle et al., 2013a). They have therefore developed an extensive program of research using mathematical models to test whether the foraging behavior of hunter-gatherers conforms to the prediction of optimal foraging theory, in a similar fashion to results from research on nonhuman animals (Kelly, 2013; Winterhalder & Smith, 2000). A key focus of research by human behavioral ecologists relates to the extraordinary flexibility and diversity of human behavior. For human behavioral ecologists, this reflects the fact that humans have the capacity to adaptively adjust their behavior to variable ecological circumstances in a way that will maximize reproductive success (Smith, Mulder, & Hill, 2001). As summarized by Nettle et al. (2013a, p. 1032): "Selection favors various mechanisms for plasticity, such as individual and social learning, exactly because they allow individuals to acquire locally adaptive behavioral strategies over a range of environments."

There is now an extensive body of research that has been carried out within the human behavioral ecology approach on a diverse range of topics including foraging, mate choice, parental investment, sexual division of labor, cooperation, and social structure (see Nettle et al., 2013a; Winterhalder & Smith, 2000 for reviews). Nettle et al. 2013a argue that the human behavioral ecology approach possesses a number of key strengths including broad scope, methodological rigor, ecological validity, and vitality.

Evolutionary psychology and human behavioral ecology share a number of fundamental assumptions. Perhaps most importantly, adherents to both approaches recognize the fundamental importance of using evolutionary theory (in its neo-Darwinian guise) to advance our understanding of human behavior. There are a number of differences between these two approaches, however, although these have perhaps been somewhat exaggerated. The most straightforward difference reflects different institutional backgrounds: evolutionary psychologists are largely trained as psychologists, and human behavioral ecologists typically have academic training in anthropology. This difference often manifests itself in the use of different research methods with different populations: human behavioral ecologists are more likely to focus on hunter-gatherer populations or small-scale human societies using ethnographic research; evolutionary psychologists typically study modern Western populations using standard psychological research methods (although as the analysis of Nettle et al., 2013a suggests, these differences are in no way absolute). In addition to these institutional and methodological differences, there are also a number of more substantive points of difference.

One prominent difference concerns the proposed structure of the human mind. As we have seen, evolutionary psychologists are largely committed to the idea that the mind is composed of a large number of domain-specific psychological mechanisms that have evolved to solve specific adaptive problems. Human behavioral ecologists, by contrast, typically view the human mind/brain in more domain-general terms—rather than a bundle of specialized mechanisms and processes, the human mind has evolved to respond adaptively to a wide range of different ecological contexts. In part this difference reflects a different emphasis on what needs to be explained: evolutionary psychologists argue that psychological mechanisms are the main unit of analysis, whereas human behavioral ecologists focus more on behavior. This leads evolutionary psychologists to a focus on universal characteristics that collectively reflect our human nature, whereas human behavioral ecologists see behavioral flexibility and diversity as the key characteristic of our species.

A second issue concerns the favored approach to studying psychological and behavioral adaptations. Because human behavioral ecologists stress the flexible nature of human behavior and our capacity to adjust behavior to reflect local ecological contexts, they argue that it is appropriate to measure current reproductive fitness as a means to test hypotheses about the evolution of human behavioral characteristics (Mulder, 2007). Evolutionary psychologists, in contrast, emphasize the fact that contemporary environments are significantly different from the environments that we evolved in, and hence current reproductive success may be a relatively poor guide to identifying adaptations.

Despite some substantive differences between the evolutionary psychology and human behavioral ecology camps, there is a significant overlap between the two approaches. Moreover, as Brown et al. (2011) note, there have been a number of attempts to integrate—or at least reconcile—the two perspectives and in many respects they can be viewed as complementary approaches. Before we consider how this might be achieved, we need to consider the third major approach to applying evolutionary theory to human behavior: cultural evolutionary theory.

Cultural Evolution Theory

In their book, *Not by Genes Alone: How Culture Transformed Human Evolution*, Richerson and Boyd (2005) make a compelling case for the importance of culture in understanding human behavior. They open their account with an example that should be of interest to criminologists: Nisbett's (1993) culture of honor thesis. According to this idea, Southern white men adhere to a "culture of honor" that prescribes the use of violence in response to insults, threats, and other slights to an individual's status and prestige. These beliefs, values, and norms in turn, it is argued, have their origin in the settlement of the Southern region of the United States by predominantly Scottish and Irish immigrants who came primarily from herding communities in the British Isles. Because the wealth of herders resides in their—highly mobile and easily rustled—stock, and because they historically lived in environments with little effective rule of law, it paid for them to adopt belligerent attitudes to potential threats from others and to believe in the appropriateness of violence to settle disputes. Children who develop in these environments will, in turn, come to adopt this particular set of norms, values, and beliefs. Southern men have therefore inherited their "culture of honor" from their parents (and parents community), who inherited it from their parents, and so on. The higher incidence of dispute-related homicides in the American South, according to the culture of honor thesis, can be explained by the ongoing socialization of children within this particular cultural milieu (see Lee & Shihadeh, 2009).

Most social scientists, of course, regardless of how they view the culture of honor thesis in particular, will not need to have their arms twisted to accept the importance of culture; cultural and social-structural explanations have a central role to play in disciplines such as sociology and criminology. Richerson and Boyd (2005), however, along with other scholars (e.g., Laland, Odling-Smee, & Myles, 2010; Mesoudi, 2011a, 2011b; Mesoudi, Whiten, & Laland, 2006), make a case for a *Darwinian* approach to understanding culture and cultural evolution. For example, the perspective advanced by Richerson and Boyd (2005) is known as "gene–culture coevolutionary theory" (or "dual-inheritance theory") and rests on three fundamental assumptions (Henrich & McElreath, 2007; Richerson & Boyd, 2005). First, the capacity for human culture is itself a biological adaptation that has been selected for during the course of our evolutionary history, because it successfully advanced reproductive success. Second, this capacity for cultural learning provides the foundation for cultural evolution— a truly Darwinian process that forms a second inheritance system alongside standard genetic inheritance. Third, these two forms of inheritance interact with one another—genes and culture coevolve. More generally, the cultural evolutionary approach to understanding human behavior can be viewed as part of the extended synthesis in evolutionary biology discussed in Chapter 2 that—among other ideas—emphasizes the importance of nongenetic mechanisms of inheritance.

Social learning is not unusual in nature. In many animal species, crucial information about the world is obtained through social interaction with conspecifics (Laland & Galef, 2009; Thornton & Clutton-Brock, 2011; Whiten & van Schaik, 2007). This makes good biological sense: social learning allows developing organisms to obtain valuable information about the environment in which they are embedded without going through the potentially costly process of individual learning. The food choice of rats, for example, is guided in part by what they smell on the breath of other rats—if they are eating the food in question and are still standing then it probably means that the food is not poisonous. Cultural *traditions* are somewhat rarer in the (nonhuman) biological world, although researchers have now identified a number of distinct practices among chimpanzee groups, such as nut cracking and termite fishing, that appear to persist in some but not other populations (Laland & Galef, 2009). Uniquely among animal species, humans not only have robust cultural traditions but also demonstrate the capacity for *cumulative* cultural evolution (Mesoudi, 2011a; Tennie, Call, & Tomasello, 2009). In other words, humans have the capacity to acquire information from conspecifics and to modify that information in adaptive ways so that it is in turn acquired by other members of the group. The ecological dominance of our species, noted in Chapter 2, is largely the product of this ability combined with specific demographic and ecological factors (Boyd, Richerson, & Henrich, 2011; Foley & Lahr, 2011). There is no widespread agreement on the key psychological mechanisms that are responsible for cumulative cultural evolution, but they are likely to involve some combination of the capacity for imitation, active pedagogy, strong prosocial tendencies, a fully developed theory of mind, and a robust symbolic communication system (language) (Dean, Kendal, Schapiro, Thierry, & Laland, 2012).

The psychological mechanisms underlying the capacity for cultural learning are, it is argued, biological adaptations (Richerson & Boyd, 2005). The selective advantages of these capacities are not too hard to figure out, and gene–culture coevolutionary theorists have devoted a considerable amount of time to developing models that clearly show how cultural learning is favored under conditions of environmental variability. When the environment is subject to change (but not *too* rapid change) cultural learning is adaptive, because the information obtained in prior generations can be passed on to future generations, therefore reducing the costs of purely individual (trial and error) learning. A crucial feature of our capacity for cultural learning, therefore, is that it enables us to obtain adaptive information about the world in an efficient and less costly fashion, especially when what counts as adaptive information may change rapidly over time (therefore making purely genetic responses obsolete). In this respect, what individuals learn depends very much on the social environment in which they are embedded. However, cultural learning is not an entirely content-free process, and cultural evolutionary theorists argue that such learning is guided by a number of both *content* and *context* biases (Henrich & McElreath, 2007). Content biases refer to the idea that individuals are more likely to socially acquire beliefs, values, norms, and practices that are consistent with either evolved psychological motivations or other cultural beliefs, ideas, or norms. Context biases reflect the fact that cultural learning is guided by cues in the environment that are likely to be associated with the most adaptive outcomes.

Thus, Richerson and Boyd (2005) argue that social learning is influenced by the nature and status of the model (preferentially learn from those who are similar, successful, and have high status), and how frequent the behavior is (preferentially acquire practices that are more common) (see Rendell, Fogart, Hoppitt, Morgan, Webster, & Laland, 2011, p. 71 for a detailed taxonomy of social learning strategies).

The evolved capacity for high-fidelity cumulative cultural learning provides the basis for cultural evolution. This can be viewed as a truly Darwinian process (Mesoudi, 2011a, 2011b; Mesoudi, Whiten, & Laland, 2006; Richerson & Boyd, 2005). As we outlined in Chapter 2, natural selection can be conceptualized as the outcome of three key principles: variation, differential fitness (or competition), and inheritance. These three preconditions can also be employed to describe cultural as well as genetic evolution. First, there are clearly cultural variants. Indeed, many social scientists have devoted their careers to tracking the way that people in different cultures vary in terms of their beliefs, values, norms, traditions, and institutions. There is also competition among these cultural variants, with some more likely to be transmitted than others. Finally, cultural traits are inherited through the social learning processes outlined above. Cultural evolution then, like biological evolution, is a Darwinian process. However, as Mesoudi (2011a) notes, there are important differences between cultural and biological evolution. Perhaps most obviously, cultural evolution involves the transmission of variants through a different set of processes that are more fluid and subject to the intentional actions of human actors. Whereas genetic transmission is channeled vertically from parents to offspring, people acquire cultural variants (beliefs, values, norms, traditions, etc.) from parents, siblings, community members, and—in an age of global media—from almost anyone on the planet. Moreover, whereas genetic inheritance is a nonintentional process (people do not choose the genetic material they inherit from parents), the acquisition of cultural variants can be actively guided and is thus subject to human agency. These differences, Mesoudi (2011a) argues, suggest that although cultural evolution is a Darwinian process, it is not a *neo-Darwinian* process, and therefore there is a need to clearly outline the important microevolutionary processes that give rise to cultural evolution and that differ from those that underpin genetic evolution. Cultural evolutionists have begun to sketch out these processes, and there is an emerging body of research that demonstrates the value of this approach for understanding such diverse topics as inheritance practice, language evolution, violence, and the historical spread of monogamous marriage systems (Currie, 2013; Henrich, Boyd, & Richerson, 2012; Mace & Jordan, 2011). From this perspective, a strong case can be made that human beings have the capacity to establish and utilize cognitive systems that extend beyond the mind–brain, and in this respect capitalize on what Sterelny (2012) calls epistemic engineering or niche construction.

Cultural evolutionary theory has also been employed to understand the emergence of large-scale complex societies of the kind that now dominate the world (Morris, 2012; Mullins, Whitehouse, & Atkinson, 2013; Norenzayan, 2013; Turchin, 2009; Turchin & Gavrilets, 2009). Turchin, for example, argues that the transition from small-scale, largely egalitarian societies to large-scale hierarchically structured societies, such as modern nation-states, was a crucial development best explained from the perspective of cultural evolutionary theory. In short, it is proposed, following the work of Richerson and Boyd (2005), that cooperation among group members is sustained through the cultural evolution of social norms and social institutions that favor more cohesive and cooperative groups at the expense of less cooperative groups, through a process of cultural group selection. Larger groups are made possible through the symbolic marking of group membership (allowing the identification of in-group from out-group) and the emergence of hierarchical structures that are culturally selected for, particularly in the context of intergroup warfare and competition for resources (see Morris, 2014 on the role of warfare in the development of large-scale social institutions). In a similar view, Philip Kitcher (2011) recently argued that ethics is a form of social technology that emerged during the evolution of human beings to stabilize social cooperation and coordination (see Chapter 5 for further details).

Both cultural and genetic evolutionary processes are crucial to our understanding of human behavior. However, these two processes are not independent from one another: *genes and culture coevolve* (Richerson & Boyd, 2005). As we noted in Chapter 2, all organisms modify their environment to some extent, and these modifications in turn can exert selection pressures for the evolution of specific characteristics and traits. For humans, these niche construction activities occur on a monumental scale and are largely driven by cultural evolutionary processes. Cultural evolution, in turn, transforms the selective environment of humans in ways that will favor certain genetic variants over others (Laland et al., 2010; Richerson & Boyd, 2010). The most well-studied example of gene–culture coevolution is the evolution of lactose tolerance over the last 10,000 years. Although the consumption of milk is a defining mammalian feature, humans are unusual in that they continue to consume milk and milk products beyond weaning and into adulthood. However, the ability to digest lactose, the sugar in milk, is not a universal feature of human populations. Indeed, for many adults, milk consumption is accompanied by unpleasant symptoms such as diarrhea. Researchers have identified that the capacity to digest lactose into adulthood is due to an allele that is significantly more common in human populations that have had a long history of cattle domestication and dairying. This strongly suggests that a cultural practice (dairying) has selected for a gene that promotes the adult consumption of milk, presumably because the bearers of the gene were more likely to survive and reproduce than their counterparts who did not possess the gene (Gerbault et al., 2011). Although this is the best studied and well supported example of gene–culture coevolutionary processes, there are likely many other instances of cultural practices that have shaped human genetic evolution (see Chiao & Blizinsky, 2010; Gintis, 2011; Laland et al., 2010; Miller, 2010; O'Brien & Laland, 2012; Wade, 2014 for further examples and discussion).

The third broad approach to applying evolutionary theory to human behavior focuses on processes that are of central interest to social scientists in general, and criminologists in particular: culture, social institutions, and social structure. A cultural evolutionary approach emphasizes the importance of recognizing that the capacity for culture is itself the result of a number of psychological adaptations that shape how beliefs, values, norms, and practices are acquired. Culture itself, from this perspective, can also be viewed as the subject of Darwinian selection, and thus forms an important component of evolutionary approaches to understanding human behavior. The likelihood that culture and genes have coevolved creates a further layer of complexity that has the potential to further our understanding of important human characteristics.

THE CRITICAL LITERATURE

As we have already noted in several places, evolutionary approaches to understanding human behavior have been subjected to a substantial body of criticism. Before we provide a more detailed discussion of how the three broad approaches outlined above can be integrated to form an evolutionary behavioral science, it is worth briefly examining some of the main criticisms that have been directed at evolutionary approaches. Although we believe there are a number of substantive issues that have yet to be fully resolved—which we will discuss in more detail in the context of presenting an integrated evolutionary behavioral science—there are also a number of relatively enduring criticisms of the evolutionary approach that we argue hold little weight, yet continue to be invoked. Prominent among these criticisms are the ideas that evolutionary explanations are: (1) untestable and unfalsifiable; (2) deterministic; and (3) ideologically suspect.

Evolutionary Approaches to Human Behavior Are Untestable and Unfalsifiable

For philosopher of science Karl Popper (1959), whether a theory was in principle falsifiable was a key defining characteristic of scientific theories and an effective way to demarcate scientific from nonscientific practice. If we are unable to hold a theory up to the world and clearly state under what conditions it may be rejected, then according to Popper we are left with little more than pseudoscience. Criticisms of sociobiology often centered on the claim that the specific hypotheses forwarded by sociobiologists were both untestable and unfalsifiable (Rose et al., 1984). Two issues are of concern to critics. First, if evolution is a historical process that plays out over the reach of time, then how is it possible to test hypotheses concerning the evolutionary origins of a given trait or characteristic when, in the absence of time travel, we are unable to observe the relevant processes at work? Second, and related to the first concern, critics point out that many evolutionary-minded behavioral scientists, when faced with an evolutionary hypothesis that fails to be supported, simply concoct another plausible evolutionary account. In short, it is claimed that specific hypotheses can be neither adequately tested nor subject to falsification.

How much weight do these criticisms hold? It is certainly the case that evolutionary-minded social and behavioral scientists have on occasion been overly speculative in their attempts to explain the evolutionary origin of human characteristics (see Kitcher, 1985a in particular, on "pop" sociobiology). Gould's (1989) claim that sociobiologists are spinners of unfalsifiable "just so" stories with "virtuosity in invention replacing testability as the criterion for acceptance" (p. 530) therefore has some merit. However, it would be inappropriate to tar all evolutionary explanations for human behavior with this brush. Indeed, as Ketelaar and Ellis (2000) argue, evolutionary psychologists and others largely employ the same approach to evaluating specific hypotheses as do other social and behavioral scientists: specific predictions are derived from evolutionary theory (and related middle-level theories) and subjected to empirical testing and potential falsification. For example, Daly and Wilson (1988, 1996) drew on inclusive fitness theory to predict that stepchildren will be more likely to be victims of homicide than biological children, because they share fewer genes with their parents and hence stepparents are less likely to display parental solicitude compared with biological parents. This particular hypothesis was clearly amenable to test, and various studies have largely supported the idea that stepchildren are at greater risk of homicide compared with biological children (Harris, Hilton, Rice, & Eke, 2007; Weekes-Shackelford & Shackelford, 2004). If the numbers had not held up (or if future research finds flaws in the results), then clearly it would be reasonable for Daly and Wilson to either reject or amend their original hypothesis. Indeed, as Confer et al., 2010 note, there have been a number of specific evolutionary hypotheses that have been discarded. The rejection of any given evolutionary hypothesis, however, does not constitute a refutation of evolutionary theory (Ketelaar & Ellis, 2000). Rather, it suggests that the specific hypothesis drawn from evolutionary theory was not supported given the available evidence.

As Durrant and Ward (2011) note, the identification of adaptations is a challenging task, and inevitably some specific accounts will be more speculative and underdeveloped than others. However, as we elaborate in more detail below, when we discuss the comparative evaluation of adaptation hypotheses, specific claims about the evolutionary origins of given traits are amenable, in principle, to rigorous evaluation in terms of the specific epistemic criteria that scientists employ for evaluating any particular hypothesis. Among these criteria are the empirical adequacy of the specific claim: are the empirical patterns found in the world consistent with the underlying claims of the hypothesis and the theory or theories from which it is drawn? However, consistent with contemporary thinking about methodology in the social and behavior sciences (Haig, 2014; Manicas, 2006), we think that there is more to theory evaluation than predictive success, a point we take up in more detail shortly.

Evolutionary Approaches to Human Behavior Are Deterministic

If humans are the product of evolutionary processes, and our specific characteristics and traits have been sculpted by the forces of natural and sexual selection over many millions of years, then surely it follows that human nature is essentially "fixed" by our genetic heritage, as successful genetic variants have been sifted from those that have proven less efficacious in promoting survival and reproductive success. This vision of human nature, according to critics, suggests that our traits are genetically determined, leaving little or no room for the role of the environment, let alone the capacity for human agency (Rose et al., 1984). This crude version of genetic determinism is clearly a straw man argument and readily refuted (Kurzban & Haselton, 2006) through an examination of a now-extensive body of research that has explored how all human characteristics arise through the complex and dynamic interplay between genes and all aspects of the environment (see Walsh & Bolen, 2012 for examples relevant to criminology).

As Pinker (2002) notes, there is a tendency to conflate certain types of causes with a naive conception of determinism, where to say that something is "determined" is to imply that a given outcome is absolutely *certain* given prior states or conditions. Thus, to say that aggression has been selected for in humans (that is, caused by natural selection) can be viewed as saying that humans are *inevitably* aggressive and will engage in aggression at any given opportunity. Clearly this is not the case, and like virtually every other explanation in the social and behavioral sciences, to say that a given trait is caused by something (whether it be genes or features of the social environment) is simply a claim about the probabilistic linkages (if any) between prior and current variables. However, it is worth noting that people in general seem to have a strong tendency to equate genetic explanations with deterministic outcomes (Dar-Nimrod & Heine, 2011).

Dar-Nimrod and Heine argue that this arises through a more general tendency for people to "*essentialize* certain entities that they encounter" (p. 2,
italics added). This process leads people to perceive such entities as having
underlying, irreducible essences that make those entities what they are.
These psychological tendencies tend to be enacted when people encounter
genetic explanations for given traits or characteristics (perhaps because
genes are natural "placeholders" for immutable essences), leading them
to be more likely to view the development of these traits as natural, inevitable, and largely immune to environmental influence (Dar-Nimrod &
Heine, 2011; Gould & Heine, 2012). Of course, just because people seem to
naturally equate genetic explanations with deterministic outcomes does
not mean that such explanations *are* deterministic, although it may suggest that biologically-minded criminologists may need to work especially
hard to counter such biases.

   Although we think crude claims that evolutionary explanations are
genetically deterministic can be readily discarded, we are sensitive to the
lingering concern, perhaps harbored by many social scientists, that an
evolutionary approach to human behavior is incompatible with a view
that places emphasis on the power of human agency. This concern strays
into murky philosophical waters and perennial debates over the human
capacity for free will. We argue in Chapter 8 that folk psychological explanations of human action that explain the actions of agents in terms of
motivations, desires, beliefs, and choices have an irreducible role to play
in the explanation of behavior, and that they are not compromised by an
acceptance of the idea that our behavior has been shaped by our evolutionary history. Indeed, as Dennett (2004) and others have argued, our
capacity for free will is itself a product of (and explicable by reference to)
evolutionary processes. We discuss some of the important issues related to
human agency in more detail below.

Evolutionary Approaches to Human Behavior Are Ideologically Suspect

   Concerns over the putatively deterministic nature of evolutionary explanations are perhaps particularly troubling to social scientists,
because such explanations might serve to legitimize the social and political status quo and promote morally malign outcomes (Rose et al., 1984).
In Segerstråle's (2000) comprehensive history of sociobiology, the importance of debates concerning moral and political values is at the forefront.
The emergence of new approaches to applying evolutionary theory to
human behavior—such as evolutionary psychology—has generated similar worries. Nelkin (2000, p. 24), for example, suggests that "Evolutionary psychology is not only a new science, it is a vision of morality and
social order, a guide to moral behavior and policy agendas." Any attempt

to advance evolutionary explanations for topics of interest to criminologists such as aggression, homicide, rape, and war are likely to raise similar concerns. In particular, it is argued that if rape, war, or homicide (or the mechanisms that underpin these acts) have been selected for because they advanced reproductive success, then perhaps that might serve to legitimize these acts, and even more seriously, result in the moral and legal exculpation of offenders.

Evolutionary psychologists and other evolutionary-minded social scientists are well practiced in rejoinders to these putative concerns. An obvious response is to point out that *we should not equate explanations with exonerations*. In other words, to say that a given behavior is explained by evolutionary history (or by childhood experiences, or by a patriarchal social structure) should not lead to the conclusion that the behavior is morally acceptable (Pinker, 2002). After all, all behaviors have (putative) explanations, and social scientists are largely in the business of developing explanations for behavior. Similarly, while the fact that a child sex offender was abused as a child is explanatorily useful, on its own it does not excuse or justify the offender's actions in any way. The second response is to invoke the naturalistic fallacy—that is, it is logically unsound to derive normative conclusions from factual premises. To say, for example, that violence has been selected for, does not warrant the claim that it is *therefore* morally acceptable: you cannot get from "is" to "ought." Normative conclusions require normative premises—in addition to factual premises—to warrant any such claim.

We think these defensive moves can allay some concerns. However, as Durrant and Ward (2011, p. 365) point out, "the naturalistic fallacy only tells us that we *shouldn't* derive ethical values from facts of the world; it doesn't mean that we will not or that normative considerations should not be based on facts about human nature." The finding that people have a tendency to engage in genetic essentialism, whereby they equate genetic (and by extension evolutionary) explanations with outcomes that are immutable, determined, and natural (Dar-Nimrod & Heine, 2011) suggests that simply invoking the naturalistic fallacy may not prevent people from *thinking* that evolutionary explanations serve to legitimize certain socially undesirable acts. Indeed, a study by Dar-Nimrod, Heine, Cheung, and Schaller (2011) found that compared with university students who read a social-constructivist account of rape, those who read an evolutionary account of rape perceived that rapists had less control over their behavior, evaluated them less harshly, and believed that they should be punished less punitively (although there was no difference in punitiveness between the evolutionary condition and a control condition, suggesting that reading an evolutionary account did not make participants *more* sympathetic towards the rapist than they would have otherwise been). We hasten to point out that we are not arguing that somehow evolutionary behavioral scientists are *responsible* for the kinds of attributions that people tend to make about evolutionary explanations, or that we should desist from making claims about the evolutionary origins of human traits because some individuals are likely to equate such explanations with diminished moral and legal culpability. It does suggest, however, that care needs to be taken in the way that evolutionary explanations are formulated and presented. Moreover, an approach that recognizes the important role of nongenetic evolutionary processes (as highlighted in our discussion of the extended synthesis) is likely to foster a more nuanced understanding of the evolutionary origins of human behavior that perhaps can sidestep—or at least mute the effects of—the strong human tendency to think in essentialist terms.

We think it is also clear that the facts of the world, as we understand them, have some *relevance* for moral reasoning (Wilson, Dietrich, & Clark, 2003). In other words, *ought* implies *can*: is a person *capable* of acting in the way required? To say that a given act is morally wrong is to make a claim about the nature or consequences of that behavior, and to assume that the person(s) concerned possess the capacity and intentions to engage in the relevant actions. Some acts, such as sex with nonhuman animals, are deemed morally impermissible by most people because of their nature, regardless of the consequences, whereas other acts—for example, violence—may be morally acceptable or nonacceptable depending on specific outcomes that are embedded in particular social contexts (e.g., the use of violence to defend oneself from attack that results in serious injury to the attacker may be acceptable, whereas the use of the same level of force to enact a robbery might not) (see Haidt, 2012; Joyce, 2006). Our conceptions of what is morally right or wrong are thus in need of explanation in their own right, and an account of the origins of moral beliefs will be drawn, in part, from an understanding of our evolutionary history (see Chapter 5). In other words, we still need to make a clear distinction between descriptive and explanatory accounts of human acts on the one hand (e.g., how people behave, why they behave in this fashion, and how they make ethical decisions), and the evaluation of actions (i.e., what makes certain acts right or wrong and how) on the other, so it is important not to conflate normative and factual considerations. However, because moral reasoning and ethical decision making are the outcome of human agents having an evolutionary history, we need to be aware of how this history may influence our moral justifications for given acts or behavior.

EVALUATION AND INTEGRATION: TOWARD AN EVOLUTIONARY BEHAVIORAL SCIENCE

Attempts to compare different evolutionary approaches to understanding human behavior often end up focusing on points of dispute and disagreement. There is also a tendency to draw clear demarcating lines between the different perspectives. As Laland and Brown (2011) point out, however, the differences among these three approaches (evolutionary psychology, human behavioral ecology, and cultural evolutionary theory) have perhaps been exaggerated at times, and it is not always possible to clearly align a given researcher or piece of research with a particular perspective. Indeed, there are both points of similarity *and* difference among the three approaches. In this section, we focus on what we consider the most substantive issues that need to be addressed by any viable evolutionary approach to human behavior, and how these issues might be addressed by an integrated evolutionary behavioral science that draws from each of the three approaches outlined in this chapter.

The Nature, Scope, and Identification of Human Adaptations

In a classic paper, the biologists Stephen Jay Gould and Richard Lewontin (1979) invoked the architectural notion of a "spandrel" to describe features of organisms that may appear to be products of natural selection, but are actually *by-products* of evolutionary processes. Spandrels, like those found at St. Marks Cathedral in Venice, Italy (aka St. Mark's Basilica), are necessary by-products of mounting a dome on rounded arches, leaving a series of triangular spaces—often ornately decorated—that have no obvious function (although see Dennett, 1995). A casual observer, Gould and Lewontin suggest, on viewing the richly illustrated spandrels at St. Marks, might conclude that they were the product of design rather than an accidental outcome of architectural necessity. By analogy, the spandrels suggest that many characteristics of organisms are similarly by-products of evolutionary forces, with no obvious functions. Evolutionary biologists in general, and evolutionary accounts of human behavior in particular, they suggest, have been too eager to label the many phenotypic characteristics of organisms as adaptations, when many will have no evolutionary function and are merely by-products of adaptive design. This critique identifies two hotly debated issues within the human evolutionary behavioral sciences. The first concerns how we view the architecture of the human mind: does the mind comprise myriad special-purpose modules or mechanisms, each with specific adaptive functions as evolutionary psychologists tend to claim, or is the mind better viewed as a largely general-purpose organ with relatively little adaptive specificity, as many human behavioral ecologists and cultural evolutionary theorists tend to suggest? The second issue is of a methodological nature: how do we effectively proceed in demarcating adaptations from nonadaptations, and is this task possible in human evolutionary research?

The first of these issues is important because it has implications for the salience of evolutionary explanations. If human behavior is largely the consequence of a handful of domain-general learning processes—say the classical and operant conditioning processes studied by behaviorists, and general social-learning mechanisms—then there is relatively little explanatory value in evolutionary theory for explaining human characteristics. Yes, we can concede that the learning mechanisms are themselves adaptations, but if they are largely content free, then features of the learning environment inevitably become more explanatorily salient. An extreme form of this perspective can be comfortably rejected (Pinker, 2002), and decades of behavioral research have demonstrated that both operant and respondent learning are shaped by a range of species-specific biases that have clear evolutionary origins (Seligman & Hager, 1972). Despite the finding of a number of functionally specialized cognitive systems, such as the ones that underlie facial recognition, an extreme form of the "massive modularity hypothesis" is also unlikely, although this perspective remains the default position for many evolutionary psychologists (Cosmides & Tooby, 2013). The enormously flexible nature of human cognition, and the importance of cultural learning in shaping adaptive behavior, strongly suggests that in addition to various domain-specific psychological mechanisms, the human mind also possesses more domain-general processes that operate across functionally distinct tasks (Fedorenko, Duncan, & Kanwisher, 2013; Peters, 2013). Indeed, as Barrett (2012) has argued, there is no reason to necessarily *choose* between a domain-specific and domain-general view of the human mind, and evolutionary considerations suggest that the mind is populated with a heterogeneous collection of mechanisms that are more or less domain specific.

Even if we accept that the human mind comprises both general-purpose and domain-specific mechanisms, we are still faced with the seemingly formidable methodological challenge of identifying which of these characteristics are evolutionary adaptations with a selective history, and which are best viewed as by-products of adaptations (Durrant & Ward, 2011). For many critics this challenge is the Achilles' heel of evolutionary approaches in the social sciences. Gould (1978), Lewontin (1979), and others (e.g., Rose et al., 1984) argued that sociobiologists were mere storytellers, spinning unfalsifiable narratives about the adaptive functions of various characteristics with little epistemic credibility. More recent critics have made similar claims regarding evolutionary psychology (Buller, 2005; Lewontin, 1990; Lloyd, 1999; Richardson, 2007): in the absence of detailed information about our ancestral environments and the specific selection pressures that hominins faced, we are relegated to making largely unsubstantiated claims about the evolutionary design of the human mind. As the evolutionary biologist George Williams (1966) pointed out in his landmark book *Adaptation and Natural Selection*, the identification of adaptations is an onerous task. However, we suggest that the difficulty in identifying human adaptations should not be viewed as an insurmountable barrier to the development of evolutionary accounts of human behavior.

Indeed, we can employ a number of different criteria to identify adaptations in humans, as outlined in Table 3.1 (Andrews, Gangestad, & Matthews, 2002; Simpson & Campbell, 2005). First, adaptations are often

TABLE 3.1   Criteria for Evaluating the Explanatory Value of Adaptation Explanations

General criteria	Specific criteria	Presence (yes, no)
Does the characteristic have special design features?	Economy, efficiency, complexity, precision, specialization, and reliability	
Does the characteristic have properties that would have led to its selection?	Evolutionary benefits outweigh evolutionary costs	
Does the characteristic emerge reliably in human development and is it universal (or near universal) among human populations?	Reliable emergence during development, and cross-cultural universality	
Do other species have similar characteristics that emerge under similar ecological contexts?	Analogous traits in other species (i.e., not shared due to phylogenetic history alone)	

characterized by so-called special design features such as economy, efficiency, complexity, precision, specialization, and reliability. In other words, if the characteristic or trait appears to be "designed" to fulfill a highly specific function, then it is more plausibly viewed as an adaptation, rather than a by-product. Second, characteristics that emerge reliably during human development and which are more or less universal in human populations are also more likely to be adaptations than functionless by-products of evolutionary processes (although the presence of variation does not preclude the possibility of adaptive design, and universality by itself does not prove that the trait is an adaptation). Third, evolutionary adaptations will have functional properties that, given relevant environmental inputs, will result in benefits (in the currency of reproductive success) that outweigh potential costs. Finally, comparisons with other species can be made that allow us to tease out the relevant phylogenetic pathways that give rise to specific characteristics or traits, and demonstrate how similar ecological pressures can generate similar adaptive characteristics in different species (see Durrant & Haig, 2001).

None of these approaches for identifying adaptations in humans is definitive. However, if used in combination, they can be employed to critically evaluate alternative hypotheses in terms of which one *best* accounts for the sum total of available evidence (Andrews et al., 2002; Durrant & Haig, 2001). In other words, although we may never be able to claim with absolute certainty that a given characteristic is an adaptation with a specific evolved function, we should be in a position to make claims about what is the best explanation for a given trait given the available evidence. Moreover, the development of alternative adaptation explanations for given characteristics promotes comparative theory appraisal and the development of empirical research programs that can provide information better allowing us to evaluate the relative value of the different accounts. In Chapter 6, we illustrate how this approach enables us to evaluate claims about the putative evolutionary origins of rape and homicide.

The concept of adaptation is central to each of the three evolutionary approaches to human behavior discussed in this chapter. We think that a viable integrated account needs to recognize that humans possess both relatively domain-general and relatively domain-specific adaptive mechanisms, with the details to be worked out in subsequent empirical research rather than to be decided a priori (Brown & Richerson, 2014). An integrated account also needs to recognize the formidable challenges in identifying adaptations and be willing to promote comparative theory appraisal as a way of adjudicating between alternative hypotheses about the nature and function of specific human characteristics and traits. The existence of cultural adaptations alongside those that have arisen through genetic selection processes creates additional complexities but also opens up new possibilities for explanation and analysis. The role of culture in accounting for human similarities and differences, however, remains another point of contention among human evolutionary behavioral scientists.

Understanding Human Diversity: The Role of Culture and Development

In Donald Brown's (1991) widely cited book *Human Universals*, an account of the "universal people" is provided that enumerates the many cross-culturally universal characteristics of humans. The idea of a universal human nature underpins much of evolutionary psychology and makes a good deal of intuitive sense: if we are all one species, subject to the same set of historical selection pressures, then apart from some differences that might be sex-linked, we should all share a similar set of cross-culturally universal characteristics. Yet, as social scientists in general and cultural anthropologists in particular point out, there is a substantial amount of human *variation* across cultures (and historical time periods) that seems to undermine the idea of a universal unvarying human nature. Understanding this variability is a prominent concern of both human behavioral ecologists and cultural evolutionary theorists, who tend to emphasize the highly flexible nature of human development.

As illustrated in Figures 3.1 and 3.2, in addition to various species-specific characteristics there are also variations in human characteristics that occur both within and between groups. Some within-group variation is nonadaptive: unique genetic shuffling, genetic mutations, and gene–environment interactions inevitably produce, by chance, phenotypic variation (some people are taller than others, some people have higher IQs, and so forth). Some within-group variation is adaptive and reflects

FIGURE 3.1 An evolutionary taxonomy of within-group differences.

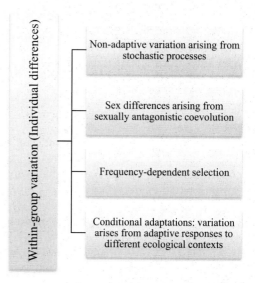

FIGURE 3.2 An evolutionary taxonomy of between-group differences.

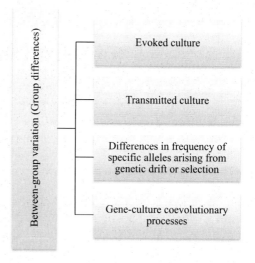

different selection pressures on males and females, a phenomenon known
as sexually antagonistic coevolution. It is also possible that some within-
group variation in characteristics is maintained by frequency-dependent
selection. In short, different characteristics are favored by natural selection
depending on the frequency (rarity versus commonality) of other characteristics. Some within-group variation can also be viewed as the adaptive
calibration of behavior (conditional adaptation) to reflect different social
and ecological circumstances—a suggestion we take up in detail with relevance to criminology in Chapter 7. We should point out here that there

is still significant debate among scholars regarding the relative importance of these different mechanisms for generating individual differences among humans, and this is an active area of research (see Buss & Greiling, 1999; Gangestad, 2010; Miller, 2010; Nettle, 2006). There are also, quite clearly, significant differences *between* human groups on a wide range of human characteristics. How these differences arise is also a matter of contention, and a number of different (non-mutually exclusive) possibilities have been proposed as outlined in Figure 3.2.

Evolutionary psychologists often draw a distinction between "evoked" and "transmitted" culture (e.g., Gangestad, Haselton, & Buss, 2006; Tooby & Cosmides, 1992). Evoked culture captures the idea that cultural variation largely arises through the interaction of evolved psychological mechanisms with local ecological and social environments. In this view, cultural differences are merely local variations on underlying themes. For instance, linguistic diversity simply reflects the operation of evolved mechanisms underlying language acquisition developing in local contexts where different forms of language are spoken. For evolutionary psychologists, the concept of evoked culture does much of the heavy explanatory lifting in terms of explaining cultural variation. The parasite stress model of values and sociality provides a recent example (Thornhill & Fincher, 2014). According to Thornhill and Fincher, infectious diseases have been an important source of human morbidity and mortality throughout our evolutionary history and hence a powerful selection force that has shaped various human characteristics, including our values and patterns of social behavior. The prevalence of infectious disease, however, varies across geographic and ecological contexts, and thus between-group differences for many characteristics reflect evoked cultural responses to the differential prevalence of pathogens. However, as advocates of cultural evolution highlight, a substantial amount of cultural variation arises through the cultural transmission of beliefs, values, norms, practices, and institutions that are replicated within social groups as a result of cultural learning (Mesoudi, 2011a; Richerson & Boyd, 2005). In other words, a significant amount of cultural variation arises through *transmitted culture*. As Brown and Richerson (2014, p. 115) summarize:

> For Cultural Evolutionists, culturally transmitted information has played a vital role in the ability of ancestral human populations to adapt to, and regulate, unpredictably varying environments, and any explanations of human behaviour that fail to take cultural evolutionary processes into account will provide only an incomplete understanding.

Between-group variation, therefore, reflects a combination of both evoked and transmitted cultural differences, with much debate among scholars regarding the relative importance of these processes. In addition, we need to recognize that some between-group variation may be due to differences in the frequency of alleles between groups as a consequence of genetic drift and between-population variation in selection pressures over time (Miller, 2010; Wade, 2014). Finally, as an extension of this possibility, differences among groups may also arise through gene–culture coevolutionary processes, whereby cultural differences (that arise either via evoked or transmitted culture) set up selection pressures that favor certain combinations of alleles over others.

Understanding how genetic and cultural evolutionary processes interact remains one of the fundamental challenges for human evolutionary behavioral science and is critical for understanding the full range of human behavior. Many evolutionary psychologists talk about culture being in some respect restrained by our evolved human nature, and there seems to be something right about this analysis: evolved predispositions tend to channel cultural learning along relatively narrowly circumscribed routes that, in turn, make the cultural acquisition of specific beliefs, desires, attitudes, and practices more likely. Yet at the same time, cultural evolutionary forces can shape sets of beliefs, practices, and institutions in ways that seem, at first blush, startlingly at odds with our evolved nature: celibate priests who believe in an omniscient supernatural entity provide a ready example (see Richerson & Boyd, 2005 for a more detailed discussion of how culture can be maladaptive). We think that a viable integrated evolutionary behavioral science (1) needs to recognize the importance of both genetic and cultural evolutionary processes; and (2) needs to construct explanations that carefully delineate the way that genetic and cultural evolutionary processes interact with each other over time.

Finding a Place for Human Agency

Our epistemological perspective (see Chapter 4) stresses the relevance of a levels-of-explanation framework in accounting for human functioning and the significant roles of agency and intentionality in guiding individual and social actions. According to this perspective, mental states (e.g., beliefs, desires, wishes, intentions, hopes, values, and plans) are irreducibly part of human functioning and cannot be reduced to other levels of explanation (upward or downward). While agency emerges from biological and cultural processes, it is not reducible to either of them; it represents a valuable explanatory perspective level rooted in a unique constellation of capacities. Furthermore, the level of personal agency and its associated concepts of intentions, plans, desires, beliefs, and norms is viewed as indispensable to understanding how culture operates and impacts on the social and physical environment. Agency-constitutive capacities include the ability to learn from others, reflect on the self and the world, set goals and form plans, and evaluate actions.

In our view, the *capacity* for psychological agency evolved through natural selection, while the subsequent development of personhood is dependent on social and cultural learning, and is thus subject to cultural evolution. Human beings are born into social and physical environments comprising innumerable practices (i.e., interlinked actions that involve social cooperation and revolve around central goals or purposes) that in many respects shape the kind of persons they become. However, by virtue of their first-person perspective and capacity for agency, they in turn shape their environments in line with their intentions and plans. In a comparatively recent paper that is consistent with this view, Hooker (2009) outlines a comprehensive biological view of learning via environmental interaction based on the capacity for autonomy. In his model, the ability to utilize internal self-regulation processes in interaction with the environment enables organisms to adapt to changing contingencies, survive, and ultimately flourish. According to Hooker, in complex social organisms such as human beings, these capacities are "graded up" to include the use of language and cognitive cultural institutions such as science and education in the pursuit of personal goals. Hooker states (p. 523):

> Entities with a distinctive wholeness, individuality and perspective in the world, whose activities are willful, anticipative, deliberate, adaptive and normatively self-evaluated, are properly treated as genuine agents. Autonomous systems are inherently all of those things.

The capacity for agency (i.e., the ability to form and implement actions) and the subsequent emergence of personhood (i.e., the particular value commitments and the associated practices in which a person invests) are consistent with an evolutional behavioral science perspective. There is something irreducibly valuable about a first-person perspective that cannot be captured by genetic, neuronal, or social levels of analysis. But, and this is a crucial point, individuals emerge from biological and cultural processes that, ultimately, are evolutionary in nature. However, an adequate explanation of why people do what they do, and what it means, requires an appeal to persons and their capacity for agency.

SUMMARY

E. O. Wilson's (1975) vision of the thorough "Darwinization" of the humanities and social sciences has not yet come to pass. Most social scientists, including criminologists, pay relatively little heed to the role of evolutionary explanations in their discipline. However, in the 40 years since the publication of *Sociobiology: The New Synthesis*, a body of theoretical and empirical work in the three main progenies of sociobiology—evolutionary psychology, human behavioral ecology, and cultural evolutionary theory—has significantly and substantially advanced our understanding of the evolution of the human mind and human behavior. Although these three approaches differ in some (more or less important) respects, we have argued in this chapter that there is substantial scope for the development of an integrated evolutionary behavioral science that recognizes the important role of both genetic and cultural evolutionary processes in understanding and explaining human behavior. How such an approach might be fruitfully integrated with mainstream theoretical explanations in criminology is the subject of the next chapter.

Levels of Analysis and Explanations in Criminology

INTRODUCTION

We are not revolutionaries. We do not seek to instigate a "paradigm shift" in Kuhn's (1970) sense of transforming the discipline of criminology by demonstrating how existing ideas and concepts are "incommensurable" with those imported from evolutionary biology. Nor do we make a case that we are at the dawn of a conceptual revolution (Thagard, 1992) that will see the overthrow of existing theories and models in criminology, and their replacement with those drawn from evolutionary theory. Although the title of this book may suggest otherwise, our goals are more modest. We argue that criminology as a discipline can no longer afford to neglect evolutionary theory. As outlined in Chapter 1, we suggest that evolutionary ideas can advance our understanding of criminological phenomena, guide research in productive ways, and contribute to our responses to offending in ways that can reduce the harm caused by crime. In this chapter, we argue that the way to realize these goals is through the integration of evolutionary theory with existing criminological theories, models, and approaches.

We assume that human beings are evolved organisms who possess a cluster of psychological and social properties that reliably emerge in certain cultural contexts. These capacities include the ability to learn from others, reflect on the self and the world, set goals and form plans, and evaluate actions. This type of emergent materialism accepts that there are *distinct levels of analysis* corresponding to the different systems that constitute human beings and that sustain their functioning. Thus there are genetic, molecular, neurological, psychological, social/cultural, and historical levels of analysis that ought to be factored into any general explanation of human functioning. The relevance of each of these levels, and the processes that are apparent at each level, depends on the specific explanatory

Evolutionary Criminology
http://dx.doi.org/10.1016/B978-0-12-397937-7.00004-5 © 2015 Elsevier Inc. All rights reserved.

question. Overlooking the stratified, dynamic-systems nature of human beings and their functioning is likely to result in limited effectiveness in intervening in the causes of crime and in planning intervention strategies (Ward, 2013).

We begin this chapter with a brief summary of the state of play in criminological theorizing. We conclude, uncontroversially, that criminology is blessed—many would say cursed—with a rich abundance of theories, models, perspectives, and approaches, each of which makes some contribution to our understanding of criminological phenomena (Agnew, 2011a). Indeed, much of the debate over theory in criminology, we suggest, concerns the relative importance of different theoretical approaches. In order to address this question, however, we need to be clear about the explanatory *scope* of criminological theories—that is, what do we want them to explain?

We then turn to a discussion of three conceptual frameworks for organizing the different theoretical approaches that we find in criminology. The first framework addresses ontological concerns about the fundamental structure of humans and human social relations. Here the issue concerns *levels of organization* and how criminological theories can be located within a hierarchical scheme that runs from cellular process to individuals, communities, nation-states, and the world system. The second framework addresses epistemological concerns and focuses on the *kinds* of questions we can ask of any given behavior. We adopt here a modified version of Tinbergen's (1963) four well-known and widely employed explanation types (evolution, function, ontogeny, and causation) and argue that this framework can serve the useful purpose of organizing *explanation types* in criminology, just as it can in the behavioral sciences more generally. Finally, our third framework is also an epistemological one, but focuses on which theory-development *strategies*—rather than types of causes—are reasonable in light of the fundamental structure of the world and human beings; this is called integrative pluralism or interlevel theory development. We argue that criminology, as with the social and behavioral sciences more generally, is best served by a version of integrative pluralism that emphasizes the importance of achieving consistency among theories, while pursuing typically small-scale local integrations. All three frameworks are conceptually linked in the following way: the fact that the world and human beings are characterized by complex, dynamic systems means that explanations should (1) be responsive to different *types* of causes, including historical and developmental ones and (2) seek to construct *interlevel* explanations of crime that span different processes across different compositional levels.

In the next section of the book, we illustrate the value of the overall framework developed in this chapter for advancing our understanding of the causes of crime. In Chapter 6, we explicitly focus on how evolutionary approaches that address issues of function and evolution can advance our understanding of criminological phenomena (by addressing specific questions) in ways that other theoretical approaches are not able to. In Chapters 7, 8, and 9, we focus on how evolutionary approaches can inform theory and research (fostering integrative pluralism) to address questions of development (Chapter 7) and proximate causation at micro (Chapter 8), and macro (Chapter 9) levels.

THE STATE OF CRIMINOLOGICAL THEORY

The annual *American Society of Criminology* presidential address, published in the journal *Criminology*, often provides a forum for the president to present his or her vision of where they believe the discipline of criminology should be heading, what perspectives have been neglected, and what approaches need greater attention. Richard Rosenfeld (2011), for example, in his 2010 presidential address, argues that criminology is currently dominated by "microlevel" theories and approaches that focus on individuals and their immediate social environments (families, peer groups, schools, etc.), while "big-picture thinking is largely absent from contemporary criminology" (Rosenfeld, 2011, p. 2). Criminology, Rosenfeld suggests, needs to pay more attention to macrolevel explanations and processes that focus on the structure and function of social institutions. Robert Sampson (2013), in his 2012 presidential address, also confesses to "worries about the individual-level narrowness of much current scholarship" (p. 2) and argues for the importance of context, especially neighborhoods, in understanding criminological phenomena (see also Sampson, 2012). Messner (2012, p. 6) also notes the "epistemological imbalance in our discipline with respect to levels of analysis" in his 2012 presidential address, while arguing for the more fruitful development of multilevel theorizing in criminology.

Beyond the mission statements presented in the American Society of Criminology presidential addresses, criminologists have variously championed the need to focus more on developmental and life course processes (Laub, 2006), and the situational determinants of crime (Clarke, 2004; Wikström, Oberwittler, Treiber, & Hardie, 2012). Others have argued that criminology has for too long been dominated by sociological approaches to understanding crime, and urge the incorporation of biological and biosocial processes in criminological theorizing (e.g., Walsh, 2009; Walsh & Bolen, 2012). Raine (2013, p. 8), for instance, argues that:

> The dominant model for understanding criminal behavior has been, for most of the twentieth century, one built almost exclusively on social and sociological models. My main argument is that sole reliance on these social perspectives is fundamentally flawed. Biology is also critically important in understanding violence, and probing through its anatomical underpinnings will be vital for treating the epidemic of violence and crime afflicting our societies.

It is not our intention to chastise criminologists by noting the persistent way that they have claimed that "their" perspective or approach has been neglected and is worthy of more attention—after all, we are making the very same claim in this book for evolutionary explanations! Moreover, most of the authors cited above are more than happy to recognize the importance and value of other levels of analysis to the ones that they champion. However, implicitly or explicitly there is a tendency among criminologists to claim explanatory primacy for their favored theory or theoretical approach. We think, therefore, that it is crucial to provide a clear framework (or linked set of frameworks) for understanding how different types of explanations are related to each other and the phenomena that they attempt to explain.

Although criminologists may not be able to agree on what is the most important or relevant approach to understanding crime, there is probably at least one issue on which there is consensus: criminology as an academic discipline is characterized by theoretical diversity. Agnew (2011a, p. 2) notes that "criminology is a divided discipline," with broad fissures that separate not only "mainstream" from "critical" criminologists, but also divides mainstream criminologists from each other. Wikström et al. (2012, p. 3) agree that criminology is a "fragmented and poorly integrated" discipline, while Eskridge (2005), in his survey of the state of the field of criminology, suggests that criminology is not a "mature science" and has failed in its attempt to reduce crime. In principle, empirical testing may be able to sort some of the chaff from the wheat, and allow us to winnow out some of the least promising theoretical alternatives. However, as a rash of recent meta-analyses by Pratt and colleagues suggest (Pratt & Cullen, 2000, 2005; Pratt, Cullen, Sellers, & Gau, 2010), although some theoretical approaches have more empirical support than others, most approaches find some level of support, and taken as a whole there is much progress to be made in explanations for crime (Weisburd & Piquero, 2008). Agnew (2011a, p. 191) nicely captures this state of theoretical "attrition" in criminology:

> Most theories appear to have *some* merit, explaining a portion of the variation in some crime. Criminologists also attempt to integrate certain of these theories. But none of the integrations has attracted wide support; partly because they reflect the divided nature of the field, combining a small number of related theories and ignoring others. And, perhaps most commonly, criminologists set up shop in their own corner of the discipline; mostly ignoring the work of criminologists in other areas, but occasionally drawing on or attacking it.

We suggest that a crucial starting point for thinking about different types of explanations in criminology is to first make it clear what the explanatory scope of criminology as a discipline is. That is, we need to establish just what we want to explain (Durrant, 2013a). As illustrated in

Figure 4.1 we think there are three broad domains of interest that concern criminologists: crime causation, responses to crime, and intervention. We should note here that we are using the term "crime" as shorthand for all of the phenomena that criminologists are interested in explaining (e.g., crimes, norm violations, and harmful acts) as outlined in Chapter 1.

In each of these three broad domains, there are a large number of more specific explanation seeking "why" questions, which criminologists need to address. As we depict in Figure 4.1 for crime causation, these include the very general—but important—question about why it is that crime occurs, and relatedly, why crime often does *not* occur. Criminologists are also interested in explaining patterns of crime as they relate to significant demographic correlates such as age, gender, ethnicity, and socioeconomic status. For instance, we need to account for why men are much more likely than women to engage in most types of criminal behavior, and for why rates of offending tend to peak during adolescence and young adulthood. We also need to account for spatial and temporal variations in offending. That is, we need to explain why crime rates vary across neighborhoods, communities, and nation-states, and how these differences change over time. A large body of research and theory has also addressed individual variations in offending: why are some people more likely to commit crimes than others? We also need to account for intraindividual variation

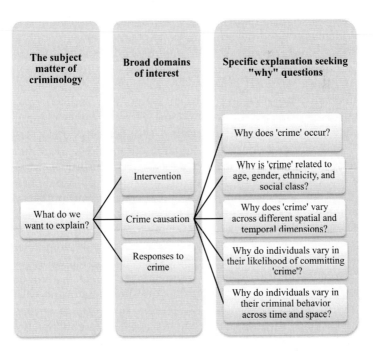

FIGURE 4.1 The explanatory domain of criminology.

in offending: what specific person–situation interactions account for how an individual's likelihood of offending varies across time and space? The questions that we provide in Figure 4.1 are clearly just a sample of the population of such questions that criminologists ask, and we can add a further layer of more fine-grained questions as we address specific types of crime (fraud, sexual offending, homicide, arson, drug use, genocide, and so forth), and even specific "etiological pathways" *within* types of crime (e.g., for child sexual offending—see Ward, 2013; Ward & Siegert, 2002).

We can carry out a similar exercise for the other two broad domains of interest. For many criminologists and others interested in understanding crime, the main focus of interest is not on the causes of crime, but on *responses* to offending. Thus, at a very general level, we want to explain why it is that certain acts (and not others) are subject to informal and formal sanctions, and the nature of the psychological and social processes that give rise to punishment. We also want to explain the variations in responses to crime as they manifest at individual and social levels of organization. A great deal of scholarship, for instance, has been directed at explaining cross-national differences in imprisonment rates, and similar work has explored changes in punishment over time (see Chapter 5). Finally, because criminology is an applied discipline, there are a host of further questions addressing appropriate ways of intervening that can reduce the harm of crime (and the harm caused by our responses to crime). We will want to ask, for instance, whether rehabilitation is effective in reducing reoffending, and how best to reintegrate offenders into the community. More generally, we will want to know how to develop effective policies and programs to reduce crime and the harm that it causes (Chapters 10 and 11).

Our analysis here is clearly not exhaustive. However, there are two key messages that we want to drive home. First, a central task for criminology, like all other scientific disciplines (be they physical or social), is explanation: we want to be able to appease our epistemic need to understand the world (or, to employ Kitcher's (1985b) terminology, to reduce our "ununderstanding") by addressing particular explanation-seeking "why" questions. Furthermore, of particular concern for applied sciences like criminology, we want to use this understanding to improve social outcomes (to reduce the harm caused by crime and our responses to crime). Second, a consideration of the range of questions that we want to address can assist in the evaluation of different criminological theories. Specifically, different theoretical explanations are more or less *salient* for answering different explanation-seeking "why" questions. Before we elaborate on this point, however, we need to consider how best to organize the range of theoretical accounts that have been offered to explain crime and our responses to crime.

LEVELS OF ANALYSIS AND LEVELS OF ORGANIZATION

We think two key distinctions are useful for organizing theoretical explanations in criminology (and in other social and behavioral sciences). The first distinction concerns ontological considerations about the structure of the world, and in particular the human world. Here we use the term *levels of organization* to capture the idea that explanations in criminology (and other social and behavioral sciences) often are focused on specific levels of organization. The second distinction addresses epistemological concerns about the *kinds* of explanations that we employ to advance our understanding of the world. We use the term *levels of analysis* to refer to these different types of explanations. Additionally, the theory-construction strategy that follows, from the structure of the world and the causal types required to explain phenomena, is that of integrative pluralism (i.e., interlevel theory construction). An overview of the various theoretical distinctions is provided in Figure 4.2, and we elaborate on each of the key distinctions in detail in the remainder of this chapter.

Ontological Considerations—How is the (Human) World Structured?

The idea of *levels of organization* is generally considered to refer to part–whole relationships between hierarchically structured entities. As such, it refers to the way the world is organized (Simon, 1962). Potochnik and McGill (2012, p. 120) provide a nice summary of this idea:

> Subatomic particles compose atoms, which compose molecules; cells compose tissues, which compose organs, which compose organisms; interbreeding organisms compose populations, which compose communities, which compose ecosystems; and so on.

In the classic conception of levels of organization, it is generally recognized that levels are discrete, clearly bounded, and nested, so that higher-level entities are composed of lower-level entities (Potochnik & McGill, 2012). Although in the physical, and to some extent the biological, sciences (although see Potochnik & McGill, 2012), this characterization may be effective for understanding the organization of matter, in the social and behavioral sciences levels are sometimes—but not always—conceived in more fluid ways. It is important to note that we are not suggesting that the causal direction between higher-level and lower-level properties is always in one direction, namely from lower-level processes such as biological processes to higher-level psychological and social processes. We think that Sandra Mitchell is correct in arguing for part-to-whole and whole-to-part

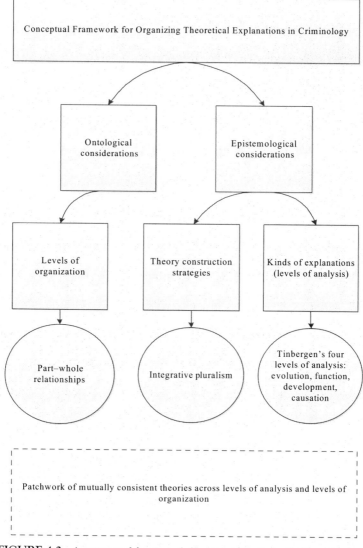

FIGURE 4.2   A conceptual framework for organizing theoretical explanations.

interactions. For example, the specific roles that honey bees adopt within a hive in part depend on the properties of the hive as a whole rather than individual bees' innate, hardwired dispositions (Mitchell, 2009).

In Table 4.1, we provide a rough sketch of how different levels of organization are conceived in different fields of inquiry in the social and behavioral sciences. There is nothing definitive about our organization here, and others may disagree about exactly where specific boundaries lie. Nonetheless, we think the scheme presented here is informative. Criminologists

TABLE 4.1 Levels of Organization in the Social and Behavioral Sciences

	Criminology—selected theories	Anthropology	Other social sciences	Neuroscience	Psychology
Macrolevel	Institutional anomie theory; classic strain theory		Global system, the planet		
			Cross-national entities/Continents		
		State	Empires		
		Chiefdoms	Nation-States Cultures		Intergroup relations
	Social control theory; collective efficacy; subcultural theory	Tribe	States/Regions		
		Band	Districts/Suburbs		
			Neighborhoods/Communities Subcultures		
Microlevel	Differential association; social learning theories; developmental theories	Kin/Extended families	Peer groups		Family and peer groups
			Families		
	Rational choice theory; self-control theory; situational action theory		Individuals	Central nervous system	Persons
	Prefrontal dysfunction theory; reward dominance theory			Brain regions and structures	Various cognitive, emotional, and motivational systems and subsystems
				Cells	
				Intracellular structures and processes	

and sociologists often make the broad distinction between microlevel and macrolevel explanations. Microlevel theories are usually considered to be those that focus on the level of the individual (and various intraindividual processes). Examples include self-control theory, rational choice theory, and theories that focus on neurobiological processes. Developmental theories and approaches that focus on local interindividual social processes are also often considered to be microlevel theories, although this is not always the case. Macrolevel theories, in contrast, focus on structures and processes outside of the individual such as neighborhoods, communities, nation-states, economic systems, and so forth. Anomie/strain theories, social control theory, social disorganization theories, and subcultural theories provide ready examples. In our view, the *specific* distinctions between levels drawn in different academic disciplines are largely methodological ones and reflect the cognitive interests of the theorists rather than natural divisions of the world and human beings.

Thus, the nature and focus of organizational levels depends on the specific field of inquiry and the specific interests of researchers within that field. In neuroscience, organizational structure is relatively straightforward. Cells, such as neurons, comprise various intracellular structures and processes. Cells in turn combine to form tissues that organize into various brain structures such as the amygdala and hippocampus, which are parts of larger systems such as the limbic system. Various other brain regions and systems can be identified that in turn make up the central nervous system (Carlson, 2014; Walsh & Bolen, 2012). Within neuroscience, then, organizational levels relate largely to intraindividual processes. These are also often the focus of psychology, although psychological approaches also encompass the role of family, peer, and intergroup relations. Clear part–whole relations, however, are harder to make in psychology. Certainly, we can draw on a range of explanations that focus at the level of the individual. The human capacity for agency and our enduring tendency to employ folk psychological explanations (couched in terms of beliefs, desires, intentions, values, hopes, and so forth) suggest that this level of organization is an important one. Indeed, most theories in criminology assume implicitly or explicitly that humans make decisions based on their thoughts, beliefs, attitudes, and so on. At intraindividual levels in psychology we can posit various cognitive, emotional, and motivational systems and subsystems that may or may not operate outside of conscious awareness. Many cognitive and social-cognitive theories of offending, for instance, assume the role of perceptual and motivational subsystems involving scripts, schemas, and perceptual biases, and approaches that focus on psychopathology typically invoke the idea of dysfunctional psychological processes.

The relationship between psychological explanations and neurobiological explanations cannot be clearly conceptualized in terms of part–whole relations. That is, we cannot say that neurons are parts of, say, schemas.

Certainly, a rejection of Cartesian dualism necessitates the idea that all mental states are accompanied by physical processes operating in the brain. However, despite some efforts to reduce, or eliminate the psychological level in favor of physical descriptions (e.g., Churchland, 1989), we endorse the mainstream position in the philosophy of mind, that mental state explanations are best conceived of being *instantiated* or realized by physical processes operating in the brain just as—to use the favored metaphor in cognitive science—the running of computer programs is instantiated by the physical hardware that makes up the computer (Sterelny, 1990).

When we turn to the social sciences more generally—economics, political science, sociology, and so forth—it is possible to discern levels that tend to focus either on social relations, geospatial entities, or some combination of these. The lowest level typically considered is that of the individual, with little interest typically directed at intraindividual processes. At higher levels, family and peer groups are important focuses of study, especially in sociology. As we aggregate up to higher levels, the picture becomes somewhat more complex. Many theoretical approaches in both sociology and criminology have an interest in neighborhood and community levels of analysis (e.g., Sampson, 2012). There is probably no widespread agreement about just what constitutes a neighborhood or a community (and how the two are related—see Sampson, 2012 for a discussion), but this level tends to focus on geographically localized entities that involve individuals who in principle (if not always in practice) can interact on a face-to-face basis. Interestingly, the idea of neighborhood appears to be a fairly enduring feature of human cities, clearly identifiable in the archaeological record (Smith, 2010). As we aggregate up to higher levels, larger spatial units can be identified with varying degrees of precision, from districts or suburbs through to nation-states, "empires," and geopolitical regions. These are roughly related to different cultures with their associated collections of values, norms, practices, and institutions. Many criminological theories, including institutional anomie theory and classic strain theory, can be located at these levels of analysis, along with many critical criminological perspectives. Finally, we have the global system and the planet as a whole. Although relatively little criminological work has focused on this level of organization, it is clearly important for understanding transnational crime and global environmental harm (Agnew, 2011c).

It is easy to take the nature of the human social world for granted. However, it is worth pausing for a moment to reflect on the fact that both the scale and complexity of human societies are unparalleled in the rest of the biological world (although social insects provide an interesting point of comparison). Anthropologists (see Table 4.1) recognize the importance of pair-bonds, families, and extended kin groups in human social organization. Humans also form larger groups consisting of multiple family units, called bands, that range in size from about 35 to 80 individuals (Grueter,

Chapais, & Zinner, 2012). Bands, in turn, can be combined to form tribes of less regularly interacting but connected bands numbering from a few hundred to a few thousand individuals (Moffett, 2013). Bands and tribes have important features that set human societies apart from those of other vertebrates. Importantly, they involve substantial cooperation and division of labor among kin and nonkin. Thus, human societies are not just aggregates of individuals, but have complex organizational structures that involve integration of action among individuals, a sense of shared identity or common fate, and—crucially for our understanding of criminological phenomena—processes that enable the resolution of conflicting interests in favor of the group (Kesebir, 2012; Moffett, 2013; for the evolution of human social organization see Chapais, 2013; Grueter et al., 2012; Kaplan, Hooper, & Gurven, 2009). It is likely that these three levels of social organization—family, band, and tribe—were present throughout much of the late Pleistocene and certainly since the evolution of *Homo sapiens*. From around 12,000 years ago, however, the emergence of larger social entities can be discerned in various parts of the world as small-scale, largely egalitarian societies transitioned to increasingly hierarchically organized large-scale social units—chiefdoms, states, and empires (Turchin, 2009; Turchin & Gavrilets, 2009). We shall have more to say about the implications of this transition for criminology in Chapter 9.

The human world, and attempts to explain portions of it, can thus be (variously) ordered in spatial terms, from intracellular processes to global systems. A fundamental ontological feature of our world is that it is also temporally or historically ordered (or, so we perceive): events that occur in the past influence outcomes in the present, which in turn can shape what happens in the future. Our explanations in criminology (and other social and behavioral sciences) can also be organized in terms of their temporal level; that is, we can organize our criminological theories in terms of whether they focus on very proximate processes or whether they direct their attention to more distal causal processes (what Wikström et al. (2012) like to call the "causes of the causes of the causes"). Putting together the spatial and temporal dimensions that structure human life, we can locate some of the more prominent criminological theories in terms of their spatiotemporal location. We have attempted to illustrate this in Figure 4.3, in which a small selection of criminological theories are located along two axes, one capturing the spatial dimension and the other representing the temporal one. Thus, social-control theory is a proximate individual-level theory, social learning theory can be viewed as more distal in focus while emphasizing individual and interindividual processes, and institutional anomie theory focuses on larger-scale social-structural and cultural processes with more distal origins. We also indicate where the different levels of explanation, in terms of Tinbergen's framework, fall within this scheme (see below). Again, there is nothing definitive about our placement of the

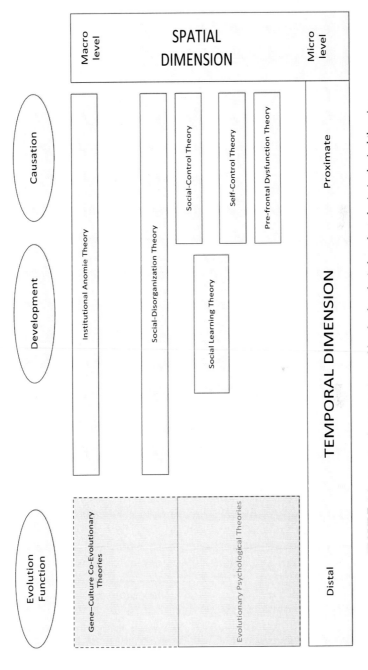

FIGURE 4.3 Levels of organization and levels of analysis for selected criminological theories.

different theoretical perspectives in this figure, and it needs to be recognized that the locations reflect the *primary* focuses of the different theoretical approaches.

Epistemological Considerations—What Kinds of Explanations Do We Seek?

Why do many birds, such as starlings, start singing at the onset of spring? Behavioral biologists recognize that there are a number of distinct ways of explaining this phenomenon. In other words there are distinct epistemological strategies for answering the question of why birds start singing in the spring. The two most widely employed distinctions are between "ultimate" and "proximate" explanations (Mayr, 1961) and between explanations that focus, respectively, on function, evolution, development, and causation (Tinbergen, 1963). Typically, ultimate explanations are associated with questions of function and evolution, whereas proximate explanations are associated with development and causation.

The distinction between ultimate and proximate explanations is usually credited to the evolutionary biologist Ernst Mayr (1961), although as Mayr (1993) himself notes, the recognition of different types of causal processes has a long history in biology. Ultimate explanations are those that explain *why* a given trait exists in terms of the historical process of natural (and sexual) selection. In other words, an ultimate explanation provides an answer that refers to the evolutionary *function* of a given characteristic. An ultimate explanation as to why starlings start singing at the onset of spring is that singing attracts mates and therefore increases reproductive success. In short, singing is the product of natural selection operating in past environments that favored starlings that sing at the start of spring (Davies, Krebs, & West, 2012). Proximate explanations, in contrast, refer to the various causal processes that bring about the phenomenon of interest. That is, a proximate explanation addresses *how* a given behavior or trait is generated. One proximate explanation as to why birds like starlings sing at the onset of spring is that changes in the length of day alter hormonal mechanisms that lead to the various physiological processes that bring about singing (Davies et al., 2012). Scott-Phillips, Dickens, and West (2011, p. 38) capture the key distinction between ultimate and proximate explanations by noting that "proximate explanations are behavior generators, whereas ultimate functions explain why those behaviors are favored."

In a classic paper published in 1963, the ethologist Niko Tinbergen argued that behavioral biologists need to address four major "problems" (each associated with a particular level of analysis): evolution, survival value (or function), ontogeny (or development), and causation. The first two of these problems roughly correspond to Mayr's "ultimate" explanations: survival value refers to how the trait in question contributes to survival and reproductive success and hence was favored by natural selection, whereas questions of evolution concern how the trait in question evolved over time from earlier forms (that is, its phylogenetic history). The last two problems largely reflect issues of proximate causation. Questions of development refer to how the behavior in question developed or emerged over the life course of the organism, while causation refers to the physiological (and psychological—see Sherman, 1988) mechanisms that bring about the behavior.

Another example will help to clarify how these four different levels of analysis can be employed to explain a given biological phenomenon (this example is adapted from Durrant, 2013a, pp. 11–12). Why do the vast majority of humans avoid having sex with their siblings? Perhaps the most obvious explanation for this finding is that most people will find the thought of sex with their siblings both physically and morally unpalatable. These are clearly proximate causal explanations, because they refer to the psychological and social processes that bring about sibling incest avoidance. However, this explanatory story is incomplete, because we want to explain *why* it is that most people find sexual activity with their siblings morally and physically unappealing. An ultimate explanation focuses on the deleterious effects of inbreeding on reproductive fitness. In short, those individuals who were less likely to have sex with their siblings were less likely to have offspring with harmful characteristics and hence would have been reproductively more successful than those individuals without an aversion to sibling incest. The function of the proximate mechanisms that lead individuals to avoid having sex with their siblings is incest avoidance, and these mechanisms have a specific evolutionary history (that is, they have evolved from earlier forms). Finally, we need to consider how it is that individuals become disgusted at the thought of having sex with their siblings, as this is not something present at birth. One plausible developmental explanation is that individuals who group up in close physical proximity to one another (as siblings typically do) develop a natural aversion to sexual relations with one another (Cartwright, 2000). Each of these levels of analysis is clearly important for accounting for sibling incest avoidance in humans, and each provides a part of the overall explanatory picture required to understand this phenomenon.

The value of recognizing different levels of analysis or types of explanations in the behavioral sciences is widely appreciated by biologists (Alcock & Sherman, 1994; Barrett, Blumstein, Clutton-Brock, & Kappeler, 2013), evolutionary psychologists (Buss, 2012), and even some criminologists (e.g., Walsh & Bolen, 2012). Of particular importance is the idea that explanations from all four of the different levels of analysis identified by Tinbergen are necessary to provide a comprehensive explanatory account of any given phenomenon. However, explanations at different levels of analysis should not be viewed as competing accounts (they provide different non–mutually exclusive answers to specific explanation-seeking why questions), although ideally they should be consistent with each other (MacDougall-Shackleton, 2011). We think that Tinbergen's framework—with some minor modifications that we outline below—is ideal for addressing the various phenomena that criminologists are interested in explaining, and we organize the second section of the book accordingly. However, it is important to note the recent debate concerning the value of the proximate–ultimate distinction. Some scholars have taken exception to the term "ultimate," as it appears to connote a more important cause (Sober, 2000), and prefer the term "distal" to capture the role of function and evolution. We think that this change in terminology is appropriate and will follow it in the remainder of this book. Laland and colleagues (Laland, Odling-Smee, Hoppitt, & Uller, 2013; Laland, Sterelny, Odling-Smee, Hoppitt, & Uller, 2011) have also argued that proximate processes, in particular development, play an important role in ultimate (distal) outcomes (selection), and hence a clear distinction between ultimate and proximate explanations should be discarded in favor of the notion of "reciprocal causation." The issues involved here are complex and are the subject of a lively debate in the literature (see Laland et al., 2013 and commentaries). However, there appears to be some agreement that Tinbergen's framework is still important, as long as we recognize interactions among the different levels of analysis.

An issue of greater significance for the social and behavioral sciences (and for our use of Tinbergen's framework) is how best to address cultural and social-structural explanations. Most explanations in the social sciences (including criminology) focus on what appear to be developmental and proximate explanations. Many of these explanatory accounts are indeed clearly proximate: they refer to neurobiological, cognitive, and interpersonal processes that give rise to a given phenomenon. The idea that crime is largely a function of low self-control, for example, is clearly a proximate explanation. Explanations that focus on the influence of the family, neighborhood, social institutions, culture, and so forth can also be viewed as proximate accounts, as they outline how these factors may shape or influence criminal behavior. However, consistent with the extended evolutionary synthesis outlined in Chapter 2, in which the concept of inheritance encompasses both genetic and nongenetic factors, we agree with Laland et al. (2013) (see Scott-Phillips et al., 2011 for a dissenting view) that cultural and social-structural factors can also be viewed as ultimate (distal) explanations, as we need (historical) accounts of how particular social institutions or sets of cultural norms, values, and attitudes come about. In other words, individuals not only inherit genes from their parents; they also inherit families, neighborhoods, social institutions, and other social-structural and cultural features of the environment (e.g., see Mare, 2011; Mesoudi, Blanchet, Charmantier, & Pujol, 2013; Sharkey, 2008). Furthermore, if we accept the key tenets of gene–culture coevolutionary approaches to understanding human behavior (described in Chapter 3), then cultural and social-structural processes can also be viewed in terms of functions (cultural adaptations) that have a (cultural) evolutionary history (Mesoudi, 2011a). In sum, we think that a modified version of Tinbergen's framework is of value for criminology (and other social sciences), recognizing that there are four different but related explanation types that can be employed for any phenomenon of interest, while accepting that social and cultural processes and structures can be viewed in both proximate and distal terms.

Interlevel Theories: What Are Our Explanatory Targets?

The main point of our discussion in this section is to clearly illustrate how each criminological theory can be represented in terms of the level of organization that is its main focus, and the primary type of explanation it offers (in terms of its level of analysis). In part, this level of analysis depends on the nature of the systems that constitute and affect human beings, and the unique properties that emerge at different organizational levels (Mitchell, 2009).

Before we proceed to a discussion of how best to conceptualize the *relationship* between different theoretical approaches, we want to introduce another distinction that we think is important. We take as a starting point that one of the most important overarching aims of criminology, like other sciences, is to provide a complete explanatory account of all of the phenomena that fall within its scope. All criminological theories, models, and approaches are therefore *relevant* to the extent that they contribute in some nontrivial way to this complete explanatory account. However, different theories, models, and approaches will differ in terms of their *salience*, depending on the specific explanatory target under consideration (see Durrant & Ward, 2012; van Fraassen, 1977; Salmon, 1989; Ward & Durrant, 2011). Thus if we want to explain cross-national differences in homicide then different levels of analysis will be more salient than if we are interested in explaining individual differences in offending. We provide a more detailed elaboration of these examples and others in Chapters 5, 6, 7, and 8, but it is crucial to remember here that although some theories or approaches may be more salient for answering specific explanation-seeking "why" questions, other explanations are also *relevant*, and they can, in principle, make an important contribution to the overall explanation. For instance, although social-structural explanations are more salient for addressing cross-national differences in homicide rates, we will also need to be able to elucidate how these shape the processes that operate at the level of the community and the individual.

INTEGRATION AND ISOLATION

As students slog their way through criminological theory after theory, engaged or disengaged as the case may be, with Lombroso, Anomie, the Chicago School, Control Theories, and so forth, some of the more alert among them want to know—reasonably enough—why we do not just integrate them all into a grand theory of criminology and be done with it (Unnever, 2012). Our preceding analysis provides an initial answer to this question: different theoretical approaches provide different explanations and focus on different levels of organization, such that they are more or less salient for addressing specific explanation-seeking "why" questions. However, this answer does not address the issue of how to best relate the different theoretical perspectives. There are a number of possibilities of how to construe the relationships among different theoretical approaches in criminology. We will consider four potential options in this section: epistemological reductionism, isolationist pluralism, and integrative pluralism.

Epistemological reductionism (also referred to as methodological reductionism) is the idea that theories referring to entities and processes at higher levels can be reduced to theories referring to lower-level entities or processes, thus effectively eliminating the need for the higher-level theoretical accounts. Within psychology, the typical focus has been on the explanatory reduction of psychological processes to neurobiological processes, whereas in the social sciences reductionism has typically entailed the reduction of macrolevel processes to microlevel ones that reside at the level of the individual. There is no doubt that epistemological reductionism has a certain elegance and has its conceptual roots in a stratified picture of the world: if the world is really organized in terms of part–whole hierarchies as we suggest, then surely much is to be gained by explaining higher-level processes in terms of those operating at lower or more "fundamental" levels. However, despite the allure of reductionist approaches in science, there is little evidence that they are likely to be fruitful in advancing our understanding of the nature of the world. Crucially, phenomena at different levels of analysis have emergent properties such that explanations at one level of organization cannot be "translated" to explanations at another level without losing valuable information (Dupre, 2012; Jepperson & Meyer, 2011). The concept of inequality, for example, and a description of the macrolevel processes that give rise to and maintain inequality, cannot be adequately captured at the individual level (individuals can only be unequal in *relation* to one another), even though all social groups are composed of individuals.

If theories at higher levels of organization cannot be effectively reduced to theories at other, lower levels, then perhaps we can simply allow that theories can proliferate at will, with no conversations between theories constructed at different levels of organization. One version of this approach, advocated by Feyerabend (1975), is *epistemological anarchism*, which allows for an "anything goes" approach to theory development and explanation: all theoretical accounts are as good as another. Some recent postmodern approaches to science endorse a similar idea. Less radically, we could accept a version of *isolationist pluralism* (Mitchell, 2004), and simply accept that theories at the same level of organization may compete with each other, but remain screened off from theoretical approaches constructed at different levels of organization. Mitchell (2004, p. 85) clearly argues that none of the approaches we have canvassed thus far in this section are satisfactory:

> I find both the advocacy of retaining all, possibly inconsistent, theories that emerge from a community of investigators and the insistence that any collection of analyses of the same phenomena must be reduced to a single theory equally unacceptable. The challenge is to define clearly the middle ground: How can a diverse, well-confirmed, but irreducible set of theories be used collectively to achieve a more complete understanding than any of the theories taken in isolation?

The most viable alternative, according to Mitchell (2004), in a position that we strongly endorse, is some version of *integrative pluralism*.

Integrative pluralism captures the idea that theories at different levels of organization and at different levels of analysis can neither be reduced nor stand in isolation if we are to advance our explanatory understanding of the world. Instead, we should seek to develop fruitful integrations across different levels of analysis and organization. This is unlikely to lead to a single grand theoretical edifice, but rather should be viewed as an attempt to construct a "coalition of friendly theories" (Ward, 2013) that are mutually consistent and can successfully address a range of explanatory targets. This will involve active efforts to create links across all levels of analysis (evolution, function, development, and causation) and levels of organization (part–whole relationships). The idea of a friendly coalition of theories may strike many as unduly generous, as not all theories are likely to be of the same explanatory worth. Unlike the Dodo's caucus-race in *Alice's Adventures in Wonderland*, where all were winners and received prizes, the history of science is littered with a trail of discarded, falsified, and forgotten theories. We certainly do not want to imply that integrative pluralism necessitates a rejection of comparative theory appraisal. Indeed, the active competition of theories should proceed at intralevel contexts, while attempts to integrate theoretical approaches across levels provide strong "selection pressures" to ensure theoretical consistency across levels of organization and analysis (McCauley, 1996). Certainly within each level, and also arguably across levels, theories can be evaluated and compared using epistemic criteria such as simplicity, explanatory depth, external and internal coherence, fruitfulness, and so on (Hooker, 1987; Thagard, 1992).

SUMMARY

Criminologists are no strangers to the idea of theoretical integration. Indeed, integrative criminology is a thriving cottage industry in its own right (see Barak, 1998), with Henry and Einstadter (2006) identifying at least 16 integrated theories currently in play in criminology. Theorists in criminology also recognize a range of different integration theories including various forms of propositional and conceptual integration (see Henry, 2012; Muftic, 2009 for details). Muftic (2009) argues that the integration of microlevel and macrolevel theoretical approaches in criminology has been relatively unexplored, although recent efforts by Messner (2012) to integrate institutional anomie theory (a macrolevel theory) with situational action theory (a microlevel theory) suggests that multilevel theoretical integration is a fruitful area for further work in criminology, as it is in other academic fields (e.g., Jepperson & Meyer, 2011; Thagard, 2012). As Agnew (2011a) notes, however, no integrated theory in criminology has achieved much recognition; he argues that this is largely because there are ongoing disputes about the foundational assumptions on which theories are constructed. For example, different criminological theories vary in their views on whether humans: (1) can be said to possess agency or behavior that is fully determined; (2) are purely self-interested actors or largely community-minded and altruistic; (3) live in societies that are largely consensual or riven with conflict (Agnew, 2011a).

We agree with Agnew that it is essential to ensure that the underlying assumptions of different theoretical approaches are consistent with each other, and suggest that the evolutionary approach that we advocate in Chapter 3 provides some valuable resources to ensure that this is the case. Importantly, it provides the basis for understanding what kind of organisms we are (Chapter 5) and how our evolutionary history (both biological and cultural) has shaped the "nature of our nature" and the social and ecological contexts in which we are embedded. Our task in the remainder of this book is to demonstrate that this perspective, in conjunction with integrative pluralism, has value for criminology as a social science. Our vision for the study of crime is thus a revisionary one. We see little promise in the idea that there is one grand integrated theory of crime just waiting to be discovered (or, rather, constructed) and certainly do not want to argue that evolutionary theory provides the unifying theoretical framework that has so long been missing in criminology (and other sciences interested in the explanation of crime). Rather, we argue that clear thinking about explanation types (with due attention to evolution, function, development, and causation) and interlevel explanations (from intracellular to macrosocial processes) will encourage the development of mutually coherent and mutually informed theories that are more or less salient for addressing specific explanation-seeking "why" questions. The complex, dynamic nature of the world with its interlocking systems that interact across time, requires the adoption of a nuanced epistemological framework. In this chapter, we have suggested that Tinbergen's evolutionary typology of causes, supplemented by Mitchell's interlevel theory-building strategy (i.e., integrative pluralism) provides this framework.

PART II

EXPLAINING CRIME

The Evolution of Altruism, Cooperation, and Punishment

INTRODUCTION

Are humans insectan apes (Crespi, 2014)? Eusocial insects, including many species of bees, ants, and termites cooperate on a scale that has long fascinated and puzzled biologists (Nowak, Tarnita, & Wilson, 2010). Many ant species, for instance, live in huge colonies where there are substantial divisions of labor—workers, soldiers, carers—and the vast majority of individuals suppress their own reproduction to support the reproductive capacity of one or a few other individuals (the queen or queens) (Hölldobler & Wilson, 1990, 1994). In many respects, ant colonies and beehives can be viewed as "superorganisms," where the interests of individual group members are subordinated to the overriding concern of the group as a whole (Kesebir, 2012; Seeley, 1995). The extraordinary amount of altruism and cooperation that is routinely found among eusocial insects reaps substantial evolutionary dividends: ants alone, for instance, are estimated to account for over half of the combined biomass of all insects and their total biomass equals that of humans (Hölldobler & Wilson, 1990; Nowak et al., 2010). Humans, as we noted in Chapter 2, have also achieved an extraordinary level of ecological dominance, funneling a quarter of the sun's energy (via the products of photosynthesis) for our own purposes (Haberl, Erb, Krausmann, Gaube, & Bondeau, 2007). We are also an "ultrasocial," group-living species (Richerson & Boyd, 2005) of "supercooperators" (Nowak & Highfield, 2011) that cooperates widely with both kin and nonkin in a diverse range of contexts including the rearing of offspring (Hrdy, 2009). For these and other reasons, many scholars have argued that humans have also breached the "eusocial threshold" (Betzig, 2014; Foster & Ratnieks, 2005; Wilson, 2012), and that an understanding of human nature necessitates that we comprehend how we have evolved to become, as Crespi (2014) suggests, "the insectan apes."

Evolutionary Criminology
http://dx.doi.org/10.1016/B978-0-12-397937-7.00005-7 © 2015 Elsevier Inc. All rights reserved.

Although not all social scientists will be particularly enamored with the idea of comparing humans to ants, bees, and termites, we certainly think that a clear understanding of the evolution of altruism and cooperation in our species is important for the study of crime and our responses to crime. Two key issues stand out. First, as Agnew (2011a, 2013) has argued, almost all theories of crime have embedded assumptions about human nature that are rarely explicitly articulated. In order to be able to build a comprehensive framework for understanding criminal behavior, one that draws on a range of criminological theories, we need to be clear about our fundamental "nature." This does not, of course, commit us to a rigid or deterministic account of the kind of animal that we are. Indeed, a fundamental characteristic of our species is our extraordinary phenotypic plasticity (see Chapter 3). However, the human species unique evolutionary trajectory has shaped our psychological characteristics in ways that have important implications for our theories of crime. More specifically, although humans may (under certain circumstances) be willing to cheat, steal, and harm one another, we are fundamentally a strongly prosocial, cooperative species that is powerfully invested in the maintenance of social cohesion and social order. This investment has both normative (i.e., value-laden) and descriptive (i.e., factual) components reflecting the gene–cultural coevolutionary process that has helped to determine our nature and ongoing functioning. Understanding the evolution of altruism and cooperation, therefore, can inform the foundational assumptions of many criminological theories by virtue of this unique combination of explanatory and normative elements.

The second issue concerns how cooperation can be maintained in human groups when the temptation to cheat is ever present. This is currently a hot topic in the social and behavioral sciences, as evidenced by the flurry of recent books on the topic (Bloom, 2013; Boehm, 2012; Bowles & Gintis, 2011; Greene, 2013; Haidt, 2012; Hoffman, 2014; Norenzayan, 2013). The answer to this evolutionary conundrum is not straightforward, but one important line of argument emphasizes that the motivation and capacity to engage in third-party punishment has played a pivotal role in the (genetic and cultural) evolution of cooperation in our species. In short, it is a willingness to incur costs to punish individuals who violate group norms that has in part been responsible for the high levels of cooperation routinely in evidence in human societies. We think that this literature has important implications for the understanding of punishment as it is administered in the criminal justice system, and that it can address (in part) a number of key features of punishment that need to be explained. There are also implications for the development of penal policy and correctional practices, which are teased out in the final section of the book.

THE UNDERLYING ASSUMPTIONS OF CRIMINOLOGICAL THEORIES

Are humans naturally selfish, self-interested utilitarian maximizers of their own needs and desires, or are we naturally altruistic and prosocial with a tendency to put the interests of others before ourselves? A third option is that we are essentially blank slates and that whether we are selfish or altruistic depends entirely on how our natures are shaped by the environment. As Agnew (2011a, 2013) argues, criminological theories often draw on one (or more) of these three different options that in turn have different philosophical roots and reflect more enduring discussions about the nature of human nature (see Table 5.1; see also Wheeldon, Heidt, & Dooley, 2014).

Most criminological theories assume—to a lesser or greater extent—that humans are inherently selfish, self-interested actors who are generally motivated to pursue their own self-interests even at the expense of others (Agnew, 2013). This assumption undergirds—either explicitly or implicitly—rational choice theory, routine activities theory, deterrence theory, and control theories (both self and social). Gottfredson and Hirschi's (1990) *General Theory of Crime*, for example, is based on the underlying assumption that humans have an innate tendency to seek pleasure and self-gratification: "We want money without work, sex without courtship, revenge without court delays" (Gottfredson & Hirschi, 1990, p. 89). Humans are therefore assumed to naturally gravitate toward activities that result in immediate gratification (many of which may involve the commission of crime), and it is only our capacity to recognize the long-term negative impact of offending for ourselves and others that—assuming we have the requisite capacity for self-control—restrain us from criminal acts.

TABLE 5.1   The Underlying Assumptions about Human Nature and Their Roles in Criminological Theories

Assumption	Philosophical roots	Criminological theories
Naturally selfish, and self-oriented	Hobbes, Bentham	Self-control theory; rational choice theory; routine activities theory; social control theory; deterrence theory
Naturally altruistic, and other-oriented	Rousseau	Strain theory; neutralization theory; subcultural theories
Blank slates	Locke	Social learning theory; differential association theory

Agnew (2011a, 2013).

It is assumed that humans are predisposed to pursue the benefits that can accrue from criminal acts, and it is only the presence of relevant alternative economic or self-gratifying opportunities, and the consideration of potential costs (in terms of either formal or informal sanctions), that restrain criminal behavior. Hirschi (1969, p. 10) captures this point succinctly when he notes: "The question remains, 'Why do men obey the rules of society?' Deviance is taken for granted; conformity must be explained." In sum, most contemporary theories of crime assume that humans are Hobbesian beasts who are by nature selfish and self-oriented (although to varying extents), and hence the task for criminologists is to explain how our natural inclinations for criminal acts are restrained, and how the criminal justice system can create environments in which such restraint is maximized.

Other criminological theories are predicated, however, on what might appear to be a diametrically opposed assumption: humans are naturally altruistic and other-oriented, and hence special situations or circumstances must lead some individuals to engage in criminal acts in contradiction of this innate proclivity. Strain theories, in both their classic and contemporary formulations, largely assume that humans have a tendency to conform and will engage in criminal acts only when they experience significant strain as a result of their particular social environments (Agnew, 2011a). A number of other theories also focus on processes and mechanisms that enable individuals to engage in harmful and criminal acts, on the assumption that we are "normally" prosocial moral agents who are reluctant to inflict harm on others. Matza and Sykes (1961) and Sykes and Matza (1957), for instance, outline various techniques of "neutralization" that allow feelings of guilt over criminal acts to be suppressed, and various contemporary theories of harmful behavior emphasize the need to explain how humans overcome natural inclinations to avoid harming others (e.g., Bandura, 1999, 2002; Collins, 2009). Arguably, subcultural theories of crime are also predicated on the idea that humans are strongly inclined to adhere to social norms and values, although the emphasis is on how norms and values develop within subcultures that may be at odds with mainstream society. For some criminologists then, humans are Roussean organisms whose otherwise "gentle" nature is corrupted by the nature of society.

A final assumption that features prominently in some criminological theories is the idea that humans are largely blank slates, and hence whether we engage in criminal behavior depends crucially on our specific developmental trajectories and the social contexts in which we find ourselves. Social learning theory (Akers, 1977) and differential association theory provide the clearest examples of this perspective (Agnew, 2011a). Although the importance of social learning is central to most theories within the social sciences, the idea that humans are largely shaped by the environment and by their association with others occupies center stage for both differential association and social learning theory. Aker's (1977) social learning theory, for example, is based on the idea that individuals learn criminal behavior and attitudes that are supportive of crime through individual (reinforcement and punishment) and social (observation and imitation of others) learning processes. From this Lockean perspective humans are neither naturally selfish nor naturally other-regarding, but instead are malleable creatures whose characters are largely shaped by their specific developmental trajectories.

Criminological theories, like all theories of human behavior, are based on assumptions regarding human nature. Although our characterization of the different theories and the assumptions on which they are based clearly lacks nuance and rides roughshod over some important fine-grained distinctions, we think that Agnew's (2011a, 2013) suggestion that such assumptions are important for criminological theories is noteworthy. From our perspective, the most relevant point is that virtually none of the theories outlined in Table 5.1 actually draws on what we know about our evolved nature in any meaningful way. Of course, many of the important advances in our understanding of human altruism, cooperation, and moral behavior have emerged over the last decade so it is understandable that this research does not feature in many earlier criminological theories. However, given our current understanding of human evolution, the time is ripe to reconsider how valid the underlying assumptions of criminological theories are, and how a more complex picture of our "human nature" can be constructed in ways that are relevant for our understanding of crime. We turn to a discussion of this literature shortly, but first we want to consider a second important area in criminology where we think that this literature can be pressed into service—our understanding of punishment.

PUNISHMENT

Until it was finally abolished in 1837, the pillory was a popular way of punishing offenders in England (Hitchcock & Shoemaker, 2006). With head and hands trapped between planks of heavy wood, the offender would be subject to the ridicule and anger of an assembled crowd who would hurl not only verbal insults at the offender, but also an assortment of less than pleasant objects—rotten eggs, rocks, and even dead cats. The pillory is no longer extant, but punishment remains a central—perhaps *the* central—component of dealing with serious normative violations in modern nation-states. Indeed, the existence of the willingness to impose punishment on group members who transgress important social norms is arguably a universal feature of all human societies (Boehm, 2012; Hoffman, 2014).

A reasonably clear working definition of punishment is provided by Miller and Vidmar (1981, p. 146) who suggest that "punishment is a negative sanction intentionally applied to someone who is perceived to have violated a law, a rule, a norm, or an expectation." There are three important elements to this definition: (1) punishment must involve the imposition of harm ("negative sanction"); (2) punishment is typically directed at another individual, although there is also scope to consider punishment directed at specific groups such as families, companies, and nation-states as long as they can reasonably be said to represent discrete entities; and (3) the negative sanction must be imposed in response to a perceived wrongdoing of some sort (which we will summarize as "norm violations," while recognizing that not all norm violations are punished, and some punishable acts are not strictly norm violations—see Horne, 2009). Our main focus will be on punishment that is administered within the criminal justice system—in other words, punishment that is sanctioned by the state. However, punishment occurs in a myriad of contexts where rules or norms are violated (including workplaces, schools, and families), and as anthropological research suggests (Boehm, 2012; Wiessner, 2005), the imposition of punishment also occurs in the absence of formal criminal justice systems.

There is an enormous literature on the use of punishment both within and outside the criminal justice system, and we will make no attempt to comprehensively summarize this material. However, as illustrated in Table 5.2, we suggest that five questions (or rather, distinct clusters of questions) are central to a comprehensive understanding of punishment.

The existence of punishment is almost certainly a cross-culturally universal feature of all human societies (Boehm, 2012; Brown, 1991). Historically, the existence of formal systems of punishment is recognized in some of the earliest written records (Hoffman, 2014). In modern Western societies, punishment is a ubiquitous and central feature of criminal and civil

TABLE 5.2   The Nature of Punishment: What Needs to Be Explained?

1. Why are humans motivated to punish individuals who violate particular laws, rules, norms, and/or expectations?

2. Why are certain human acts (or omissions) punished, and not others? And what accounts for similarities and differences in punishable acts in different social and cultural–historical contexts?

3. What accounts for the nature and intensity of punishment that is imposed on different acts? And why does the nature and intensity of punishment vary in different social and cultural–historical contexts?

4. What specific features of punishable acts and punishable actors influence the nature and intensity of punishment?

5. What accounts for individual differences in the nature and intensity of the punishment deemed appropriate for punishable acts? And what accounts for individual differences in the scope of punishable acts?

law and occurs in numerous other contexts where norms, rules, or expectations are perceived to have been violated. There is also abundant evidence that humans are strongly *motivated* to punish norm violations. The literature on economic and public goods games has clearly demonstrated that people, across a wide range of different cultures, are willing to incur costs to punish others whom they perceive to be acting unfairly (Henrich, Boyd, Bowles, Camerer, Fehr, & Gintis, 2004; Henrich et al., 2006). Moreover, people experience a sense of *injustice* if norm violators go unpunished or underpunished (Darley, 2009). Any comprehensive explanation for punishment must provide an explanation for this enduring human motivation to punish.

The second question addresses the scope of punishable acts. We need to explain why certain actions *constitute* violations of rules, law, norms, or expectations, and therefore are perceived to deserve punishment. It may seem self-evident that certain acts, particularly those that involve the intentional infliction of physical harm, the taking of property, and deception in social exchanges deserve to be punished (e.g., Jones & Kurzban, 2010; Robinson & Kurzban, 2007), yet we still need to account for why acts of this kind are widely recognizable as punishable, whereas others are not. Clearly the scope of punishable acts also varies in significant and substantial ways, historically and cross-culturally. A core set of offenses can be roughly described that tend to be punished in all human societies. However, a list of acts that have been punished (and punished severely) at one time or place but not in another would be both lengthy, and seemingly, quite arbitrary. Any comprehensive explanation for punishment needs to explain why, for instance, homosexuality, apostasy, infidelity, and the sale of heroin have all been punished with death at one time or place while they have been unpunished at others (Braman, Kahan, & Hoffman, 2010; Robinson & Kurzban, 2007).

Research that has asked participants to assign punishment for different acts demonstrates that humans possess quite nuanced punishment responses in terms of the nature and intensity of punishment imposed (e.g., Robinson & Kurzban, 2007; Rossi & Berk, 1997). Moreover, there is often a fairly high level of agreement among respondents for most types of punishable acts, at least in the ordinal ranking of such acts in terms of punishment severity (Kugler, Funk, Braun, Gollwitzer, Kay, & Darley, 2013; Robinson & Kurzban, 2007). Most people recognize (either implicitly or explicitly) that punishment responses should be proportionate to the seriousness of the norm violation, where seriousness is determined largely by some combination of harmfulness and wrongfulness (Alter, Kernochan, & Darley, 2007; Oswald & Stucki, 2009; Stylianou, 2003; Warr, 1989). However, there are often substantial cross-cultural and historical differences in the perceived acceptability of certain acts and in the nature and severity of the punishment that those acts are thought to merit (e.g., Braman et al., 2010; Robinson

& Kurzban, 2007). A challenge for theories of punishment, therefore, is to explain both the similarities and differences in punishment responses that are found, and the various factors that appear to be included with these responses.

Modes of punishment have varied both historically and cross-culturally, but it is possible to organize punishment responses in terms of three broad categories:

1. Permanent exclusion from the community (e.g., death, life in prison without parole, permanent exile, deportation, or ostracism).
2. Temporary exclusion from the community (e.g., fixed prison terms, temporary deportation, exile, or ostracism).
3. Punishment within the community (e.g., fines, shaming rituals, corporal punishment, community service, or restitution).

Understanding preferences for different types of punishment for different types of norm violations is an important task for any theory of punishment. Moreover, clearly both the nature and intensity of punishment deemed appropriate for any specific punishable act vary in significant respects both cross-culturally and historically. Sociologists of punishment, for instance, have written widely on the decline of certain types of punishment (e.g., corporal punishment, shaming rituals, and other public forms of punishment) in Western society (e.g., Garland, 2001), and their partial resurgence in some contexts (Pratt, 2000). Explaining the putative increase in punitiveness in many, but not all, Western countries—especially the United States—over the last few decades of the twentieth century, and cross-national differences in punitiveness has also become a major cottage industry for criminal justice scholars (e.g., Cavadino & Dignan, 2006; Pratt, 2008; Pratt & Eriksson, 2012; Ruddell & Urbina, 2004; Tonry, 2009; Whitman, 2005). Comprehensive accounts of punishment need to account for these variations in both the type and intensity of punishment that are found cross-culturally and historically.

Punishment responses may be broadly matched to the perceived seriousness of certain acts, but they are also influenced by a raft of quite specific features of the punishable acts and of the punishable actor (which themselves may impact perceived seriousness). Attempts to develop sentencing guidelines, for instance, recognize the importance of a wide range of aggravating and mitigating factors, and many of these factors appear to influence people's punishment responses (Hoffman, 2014). These include aspects of the punishable act such as degree of planning, provocation, and victim impact, and features of the offender such as age, prior criminal record, a guilty plea, and expressions of remorse. A good deal of attention has also been directed at the potential influence of so-called extralegal factors such as social class, ethnicity, age, gender, and even attractiveness, on the punishment responses in both experimental and real-world contexts (e.g., Crow & Johnson, 2008; Mitchell, 2005; Robinson, Jackowitz, & Bartles, 2012; Sporer & Goodman-Delahunty, 2009). Any comprehensive explanation for punishment needs to account for why punishment responses are influenced by specific features of the punishable act and punishable actor.

Any discussion of "people's" punishment responses not only needs to take into account cross-cultural and historical differences, but also individual-level differences in punishment responses among people in the same community. A good deal of research has highlighted how a wide range of individual difference factors such as political orientation, personality characteristics, specific beliefs about crime, and demographic characteristics can influence the nature and severity of punishment responses, and even prescribe the scope of punishable acts (e.g., Koster, Foudriaan, & van der Schans, 2009; McKee & Feather, 2008; Payne, Gainey, Triplett, & Danner, 2004; Schans, 2009; Spiranovic, Roberts, & Indermaur, 2012).

We have summarized here what we believe to be the key aspects of punishment that need to be explained. Consistent with the model that we introduced in Chapter 4, it is clear that providing comprehensive, ontologically satisfying answers to the questions posed in Table 5.1 requires a wide range of different theoretical perspectives, from those that focus on the proximate psychological and neurobiological characteristics of individuals (e.g., Buckholtz & Marois, 2012) to accounts that attend to the broader social and cultural features of societies (e.g., Pratt, 2008; Pratt & Eriksson, 2012). In the following section, we suggest that an evolutionary perspective cannot only shed light on some of the assumptions that criminological theories often take for granted, but it can also help us understand the nature of human punishment. Indeed, we make the case that although humans—like all other animals—have the capacity to engage in selfish and harmful actions, we are in many respects "naturally" prosocial and cooperative organisms, and punishment has played a key role in the evolution of our other-regarding motivations and preferences. Understanding punishment requires grasping that it is part of human beings' normative regulation equipment. In this respect, it is subject to strong social and cultural influences, as well as being dependent on innate psychological mechanisms including emotions, theory of mind abilities, and the capacity to make causal attributions.

THE EVOLUTIONARY ORIGINS OF COOPERATION AND PUNISHMENT

We are in many respects a Jekyll and Hyde species. As Mr. Hyde, we fight, maim, kill, rape, torture, steal, lie, cheat, and destroy. We inflict harm on others in ways both small and large, from casual deceit to wide-scale genocide. We are in many respects the worst of animals: we have the capacity to inflict harm on a staggeringly monumental scale, arguably unparalleled by any other species on the planet (see White, 2011). This is of course the stuff of criminology, and explaining why we engage in such acts is a central task for criminologists and the primary focus of this particular book. It is easy for this picture of human nature to dominate, for perhaps we are naturally more fascinated with bad than with good (see Baumeister, Bratslavsky, Finkenauer, & Vohs, 2001). However, for much—if not most—of the time, we are more like Dr. Jekyll than Mr. Hyde: we cooperate with one another in ways both small and large, we invest time, effort, and money to help those in need, and the vast majority of our social interactions are prosocial. At those times, we are in many respects the best of animals, with the capacity to cooperate with one another in staggeringly complex ways that are arguably unparalleled by any other species on the planet. Whether we are "natural-born killers" is a matter of dispute, but without doubt we are "natural-born cooperators."

The evidence for our altruistic and largely cooperative nature is all around us. Life among thousands of anonymous strangers in modern cities would simply not be possible without large-scale cooperation. Of course, it could be argued that institutions such as police and legal systems keep our Hydean nature at bay with the ever-present threat of sanctions; yet, although punishment is an important factor in understanding human altruism and cooperation, much altruistic behavior occurs without threat of sanction and often with very little in the way of reward. Moreover, various "natural experiments," in which groups have found themselves isolated from the effective threat of legal institutions (e.g., after shipwrecks, during episodes of armed conflict, and in the wake of natural disasters), suggest that in many (if not all) cases, cooperation typically ensues despite the temptation to exploit or victimize others (see Robinson, 2013 for a fascinating set of examples). Of course, for most of our evolutionary history we have lived in small, mobile, egalitarian, and highly cooperative foraging groups without the benefit of police officers or law courts. Many scholars have argued that cooperation in such groups is maintained through a combination of our "natural" prosocial propensities, and via the sanctioning of group members who violate social norms (Boehm, 2012; Matthew & Boyd, 2014).

Two other lines of evidence are often pressed into service to demonstrate the strong human tendency to cooperate and the role of punishment in maintaining cooperative behavior. The first source of evidence comes from a large number of studies that have employed behavioral experiments to explore cooperation, trust, and punishment among humans in both Western and non-Western societies (see Balliet & van Lange, 2013; Henrich et al., 2001; Henrich et al., 2006 for reviews). Although space precludes a detailed analysis of this literature, the key findings from this research can be readily summarized. First, and perhaps most importantly, participants in these games are not entirely self-interested. Rather, they appear to be sensitive to considerations of fairness and reciprocity. There is also a general tendency to cooperate with others and to distribute resources in a relatively nonselfish way. Second, individuals appear to be strongly motivated to punish those that act in an "unfair" fashion even at a cost to themselves, and even when they are uninvolved third parties. Third, the overall amount of cooperation is substantially increased when there is scope to punish noncooperators. And finally, although these findings emerge in a diverse variety of cultures, there is also substantial cross-cultural variation in the amount of cooperation and the willingness to punish noncooperators, which appears to covary with the specific economic and social features of the culture (Baldassarri & Grossman, 2011; Gürerk, Irlenbusch, & Rockenbach, 2006; Henrich et al., 2001; Henrich et al., 2006).

A second line of evidence that speaks to our prosocial and cooperative nature comes from developmental work on the ontogeny of moral behavior in young children (see Hamlin, 2013; House, Henrich, Brosnan, & Silk, 2012; Schmidt & Tomasello, 2012; Tomasello & Vaish, 2013 for reviews). Within the first 18 months of life, children demonstrate their capacity for sympathy by providing comfort to those in distress, will spontaneously assist others at a cost to themselves, and show a strong preference for interacting with prosocial individuals. By the age of two, children recognize that they can work with others to achieve joint goals, are strongly motivated to engage in cooperative activities, and demonstrate commitment to cooperative acts. Young children also appear to be acutely sensitive to the distribution of resources, and expect that participants who work toward a common goal will be rewarded equally, while being strongly averse to receiving both less *or* more than others (Shaw & Olson, 2014; Sheskin, Bloom, & Wynn, 2014). By three years of age, children have a clear understanding of social norms and actively begin to enforce social norms on others, even in situations in which they are not personally involved (Schmidt & Tomasello, 2012). Hamlin (2013, p. 191) provides a clear summary of these research findings:

> From extremely early in life, human infants show morally relevant motivations and evaluations—ones that are mentalistic, are nuanced, and do not appear to stem from socialization or morally specific experiences. Indeed, these early tendencies are far from shallow, mechanical predispositions to behave well or knee-jerk reactions to particular states of the world: Infants' moral inclinations are sophisticated, flexible, and surprisingly consistent with adults' moral inclinations, incorporating aspects of moral goodness, evaluation, and retaliation.

In sum, although culture certainly plays a role in the development of moral behavior (House et al., 2012) and there are clear cross-cultural differences in morality, the developmental literature strongly supports the idea of an "innate moral core" that guides the development and acquisition of morality.

Although the *extent* of human cooperation is extraordinary, altruism and cooperation are surprisingly common in the biological world, and many animal species engage in cooperative behavior (Clutton-Brock, 2009; Clutton-Brock & Parker, 1995; Pierce & Bekoff, 2012; Raihani, Thornton, & Bshary, 2012). If we conceptualize cooperative behaviors as "those that have been selected to provide benefits to recipients" being altruistic "when the recipient benefits at a cost to the actor" (Jensen, 2012, p. 566) then the surprise (for a Darwinian at least) is how such other-regarding behavior could possibly evolve. Surely, if evolution by natural selection is driven by the differential fitness of individuals in a population, then those individuals who have a tendency to incur costs to themselves while benefiting others should be efficiently sifted out of the gene pool. As illustrated in Figure 5.1, social interactions between members of the same species can results in a range of outcomes. Selfish behavior needs no special explanation: behavior that benefits the actor at the cost of the recipient, will—all other things being equal—be favored by natural selection. So, too, will behavior that benefits both actor and recipient and much cooperative behavior among both human and nonhuman animals is mutually beneficial (Clutton-Brock, 2009; West, El Mouden, & Gardner, 2011). However, altruistic behavior remains puzzling from an evolutionary perspective: how can behavior that incurs a cost to individuals, while benefiting others, be maintained by natural selection?

Most cases of altruistic behavior are explained via kin selection. As we discussed in Chapter 2, altruistic behavior can be selected for as long as the benefits experienced by the recipient of the altruistic behavior outweigh the costs to the actor, discounted by the degree of genetic relatedness between actor and recipient. More generally, altruistic behavior will evolve as long as the recipient of the altruistic act shares the genes for altruism with the actor: although the actor may incur fitness costs as a

FIGURE 5.1 The evolutionary outcomes of social behavior. *Adapted from West, El Mouden, & Gardner (2011, p. 234).*

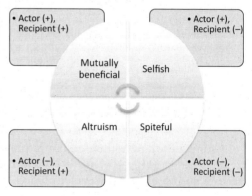

result of such altruism, altruistic genes will spread as long as there are net fitness benefits to the recipient. Kin selection or inclusive fitness theory is capable of explaining a significant proportion of the altruistic and cooperative behavior that is found in the biological world and it is clear that cooperation among kin is a common phenomenon (Kurzban, Burton-Chellew, & West, 2014; Langergraber, 2012; Silk & Boyd, 2010).

Altruistic and cooperative behavior also occurs, however, among unrelated individuals. To explain why this happens, a range of possible explanations have been invoked. Many accounts focus on the role of reciprocal exchanges among unrelated individuals in a population. According to reciprocal altruism theory (Trivers, 1971), altruistic behavior can be selected for if the recipient of the altruistic act reciprocates at some time in the future, thus providing benefits to the actor. This is an example of direct reciprocity: both actor and recipient mutually benefit from the exchange. Other scholars have focused on the role of indirect reciprocity in maintaining altruistic and cooperative behavior. According to this idea, altruistic behavior may not lead to direct benefits from the recipient, but serves instead (or as well) as a means of signaling to others the actor's cooperative nature and thus makes that individual more likely to be trusted in future interactions (Kurzban et al., 2014). Although it is clear that humans do indeed engage in widespread reciprocal relations with others, because transactions are not always instantaneous but instead may involve the exchange of benefits over time, reciprocal exchanges are open to exploitation by free riders who are willing to receive benefits without reciprocating in future interactions.

For many scholars, the solution to this problem is the evolution of "altruistic punishment": if enough individuals within a group are motivated to punish those who free ride on the cooperation of others, then noncooperative individuals will be at an evolutionary disadvantage compared with those who do cooperate, and widespread cooperation can be sustained (Boyd, Gintis, Bowles, & Richerson, 2003; Fehr & Gächter, 2002). In short, human cooperation can be maintained by what Gintis, Henrich, Bowles, Boyd, and Fehr (2008, p. 243) term "strong reciprocity": "A propensity, in the context of a shared social task, to cooperate with others similarly disposed, even at personal cost, and a willingness to punish those who violate cooperative norms, even when punishing is personally costly." Boyd et al. (2003) argue that altruistic punishment has evolved via group selectionist processes. In short, cooperative groups are more successful than noncooperative groups, therefore increasing the frequency of cooperation. Because cooperative groups contain more individuals who are motivated to punish (who serve to reduce the number of noncooperators), the frequency of noncooperators is decreased while the frequency of punishers is increased. In groups containing a large number of cooperators and punishers, the costs of punishment (for the group overall) will be significantly diminished. Although this direct reciprocity model is plausible, we should note that there still remains a considerable amount of disagreement regarding the role of punishment in maintaining cooperative behavior in groups, and many remain skeptical about the role of group selection processes, and hence this topic remains an active area for research (see Baumard, 2011; Krasnow, Cosmides, Pedersen, & Tooby, 2012; Pedersen, Kurzban, & McCullough, 2013).

A number of scholars have argued that the extent and scale of human cooperation requires an explanation that builds on, but also extends, accounts based on kin selection and reciprocity, and embraces the role of gene–culture coevolutionary processes (Alvard, 2013; Chudek & Henrich, 2011; Chudek, Zhao, & Henrich, 2013; Matthew, Boyd, & van Veelen, 2012; Richerson & Boyd, 2005; Richerson & Henrich, 2012). Although the specific details vary somewhat among authors, an overview of the key gene–culture coevolutionary processes is presented in Figure 5.2. Central to this account is the role of social norms and the sanctioning of individuals who violate these norms. Social norms can be defined as "standards of behaviour that are based on widely shared beliefs how [sic] individual group members ought to behave in a given situation" (Fehr & Fischbacher, 2004, p. 185). Kin selection and reciprocity initially shaped early hominin prosocial and cooperative behaviors, as we lived in small, cooperative social groups much like chimpanzees, but perhaps with a greater emphasis on cooperative foraging and alloparenting (see Chapter 2). The evolution of high-fidelity social learning, in which individuals preferentially acquire particular behaviors and ideas due to context and content biases, provided the platform for cultural evolutionary processes. With the emergency of symbolically marked cultural groups, those groups that possessed social norms favoring social cohesion and cooperation, and that punished norm violations, were likely to be more successful than groups lacking such social norms (and the punishment of norm violators), and hence they spread at the expense of less successful groups. These cultural processes transformed the social, and hence selective, environments of human societies: psychological traits and characteristics (what Richerson and Boyd (2005) term "tribal social instincts") that facilitated the acquisition of, and adherence to, social norms would have been favored by genetic evolutionary processes (see O'Gorman, Wilson, & Miller, 2008). These in turn would have facilitated cultural evolutionary processes, by allowing for large-scale societies and institutions (perhaps including religion—see Norenzayan, 2013, 2014; Slingerland, Henrich, & Norenzayan, 2013; Turchin, 2013) that exploited human tendencies to adhere to social norms, punish norm violators, and preferentially cooperate with group members. This gene–culture coevolutionary dynamic can potentially account for both the extraordinary cooperative nature of human societies and how the social norms that guide and govern human life can vary in important ways, both cross-culturally and historically.

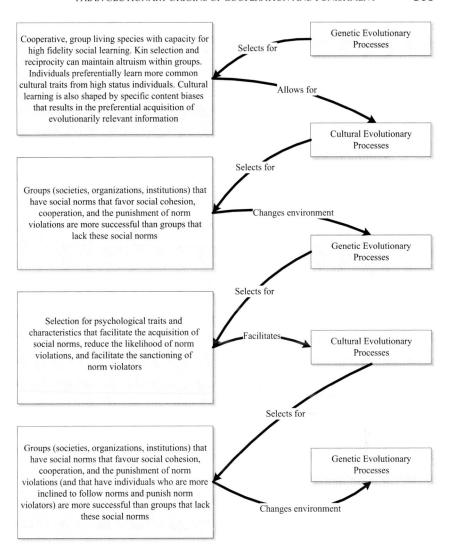

FIGURE 5.2   The gene–culture coevolution of altruism, cooperation, and punishment.

Successful groups are not simply those that have high levels of cooperation per se, but are also highly cohesive socially, relative to out-groups: individuals behave in ways that favor the in-group, adhere to group-held norms, rules, and practices, and are willing in some contexts to place the interests of the group above those of the self or kin. From this perspective, we should expect that some acts such as harm to in-group members, theft, and cheating should be relatively universally punished across groups, because they will reliably undermine the effective functioning of groups (Robinson & Kurzban, 2007). However, acts that are perceived to pose a threat to social cohesion/social flourishing also tend to be punished even if they result in no clear and obvious harm to others. Because punishable acts are simply those that violate certain social norms, a large and diverse range of human behaviors may become subject to sanctions. However, these are likely to fall within a relatively circumscribed range of actions that reflect the recurrent selection pressures posed by life in social groups.

As Haidt and colleagues (e.g., Graham, Nosek, Haidt, Iyer, Koleva, & Ditto, 2011; Graham et al., 2013; Graham, Haidt, & Nosek, 2009; Haidt, 2007, 2012) have argued, there are multiple moral foundations that shape the acquisition of social norms and influence human intuition about what constitutes violations of social norms. Specifically, it is proposed that there are (at least) five moral foundations or moral domains (see Table 5.3). The first two moral domains—care/harm and fairness/cheating—reflect the enduring adaptive challenges of raising dependent offspring and benefiting from social exchanges with others, and are likely to have been shaped by kin selection and both direct and indirect reciprocity. These domains are central to the social life of all human groups, and humans are acutely sensitive to the unwarranted and intentional infliction of harm on others and the violation of reciprocal exchanges. The third moral domain, the authority/subversion foundation, reflects the adaptive challenges of living in hierarchical social groups. Although human forager societies are

TABLE 5.3   The Evolutionary Origins of Moral Foundations

Moral foundation	Adaptive challenge	Original triggers	Characteristic emotions	Key selection processes
Care/Harm	Protect and care for children	Suffering, distress	Compassion for victim; anger at perpetrator	Kin selection
Fairness/ Cheating	Reap benefits of two-way partnerships	Cheating, cooperation, deception	Anger, gratitude, guilt	Direct and indirect reciprocity
Loyalty/ Betrayal	Form cohesive coalitions	Threat or challenge to group	Group pride, rage at traitors, (shame)	Kin selection, reciprocity, gene–culture coevolution
Authority/ Subversion	Forge beneficial relationships within hierarchies	Signs of high and low rank	Respect, fear	Kin selection, reciprocity, gene–culture coevolution
Sanctity/ Degradation	Avoid communicable diseases	Waste products, diseased people	Disgust	Kin selection, gene–culture coevolution

Adapted from Graham et al. (2013, Table 2.1); note that we have added the column "Key Selection Processes."

largely egalitarian (Boehm, 2012), humans still strive for dominance and prestige, and hence we are sensitive to the social status of others. Since the advent of agriculture and the emergence of strongly stratified societies, these—largely suppressed—social motivations for dominance and status, and our responses to status differences, have become more important and likely have been shaped by cultural and (perhaps) gene–culture coevolutionary processes. The fourth moral foundation, loyalty/betrayal, reflects the selection pressures exerted by the need to form cohesive coalitions and to respond to challenges posed by out-groups. Finally, it is proposed that humans are also sensitive to contexts or situations that might have led to the spread of communicable diseases, and that as a result we have developed moral intuitions that shape our attitudes (and associated emotional responses) and behavior toward specific acts and specific individuals who might pose a threat to our immune systems (see also Thornhill & Fincher's (2014) parasite-stress theory of values). It is likely that this domain has become substantially elaborated through gene–culture coevolutionary processes to embrace a wider range of actions and behaviors associated with out-group members and practices. Although moral foundations theory has been met with criticism from some quarters (see Fry & Souillac, 2013; Suhler & Churchland, 2011), it can contribute to our understanding of moral behavior and the punishment of norm violations by highlighting the important moral domains that tend to give rise to social norms and the punishment of norm violators. As illustrated in Table 5.3, moral foundations theory also highlights some of the important proximate mechanisms underlying our moral behavior and that lead to the punishment of norm violations. It is likely that emotions play a crucial role in delineating the moral domains, by making certain features of situations salient and consolidating links between contexts, goals, and actions.

PROXIMATE MECHANISMS AND PROCESSES

In the previous section, we outlined some of the proposed evolutionary processes that can explain the evolution of altruism, cooperation, and punishment in humans. We turn now to a brief overview of the key proximate mechanisms and processes that have been selected to realize these evolutionary functions. We focus first on a collection of other-oriented cognitive and affective processes that include perspective taking, empathy, sympathy, emotional contagion, and compassion. We then discus the role of guilt and shame in motivating prosocial behavior, before turning to a discussion of the emotions that underlie the motivation to punish individuals who violate social norms.

In a recent review of the neuroevolution of empathy, psychologist Jean Decety (2014, p. 128) suggests that "empathy shapes the landscape of our social and moral lives. It can motivate helping others in distress, it plays an essential role in inhibiting aggression, and it facilitates cooperation between members of a similar species." There is widespread agreement among scholars on the importance of empathy for prosocial and altruistic behavior, although there remains substantial disagreement regarding just how to define this and related concepts (see Chapter 11). Maibom (2012, 2014) tackles this contested conceptual domain by first making a distinction between cognitive and affective empathy. Cognitive empathy, or perspective taking, is the capacity to understand the mental states of others and is often referred to as having a "theory of mind." It is possible to experience cognitive empathy (to be aware of another's mental states) without experiencing affective empathy, but arguably the capacity for perspective taking is required for the experience of affective empathy. Maibom then usefully distinguishes among affective empathy, sympathy, emotional contagion, and personal distress. Affective empathy occurs when an individual experiences the same emotion as another individual, as a result of believing that the other individual is experiencing that emotion. For instance, Freddie empathizes with Hubert's feelings of anger at having his prize flute stolen, if Freddie experiences anger *for* Freddie as a result of believing that Hubert feels angry (or imagining being in the same situation as Hubert) due to the theft. Freddie would feel *sympathy* for Hubert if he feels bad that Hubert is upset, without necessarily experiencing the congruent emotional state. Empathy can also be distinguished from the experience of personal distress that may arise from viewing another person's emotional experiences, but that are self rather than other focused. Similarly, individuals can experience the same emotions that others are feeling, but arising from emotional contagion: they occur because others are feeling that way, but they are not felt *for* the other person. In Chapter 11, we argue that psychological altruism plays a more inclusive role in morality, and empathy can be usefully construed as an important, but not necessary or sufficient, component of prosocial action on some occasions.

Regardless of how this family of affective and cognitive processes is conceptualized (others have argued that the term "compassion" provides a more useful concept for capturing the set of affective states that rest upon the concern for others's suffering and that motivates caring behavior (Goetz, Keltner, & Simon-Thomas, 2010), there is widespread agreement that there is an important, albeit complex, relationship between empathy, altruism, cooperation, prosocial behavior, and the inhibition of aggression (Batson, 2011, 2014; Decety & Cowell, 2014; Eisenberg, Eggum, & DiGiunta, 2010; Maibom, 2012). According to Batson's empathy–altruism hypothesis, empathic concern for others is linked to altruistic behavior, and there is a general body of research that supports this relationship (Batson, 2011, 2014; Eisenberg et al., 2010). Moreover, research suggests that lower levels of (especially cognitive) empathy are related to offending (Jolliffe & Farrington, 2004, 2006; van Langen, Wissink, van Vugt, van der Stouwe, & Stams, 2014). However, the relationship between empathy, prosocial behavior, and the inhibition of aggression is perhaps less robust than expected, and not all studies find strong relationships among these constructs (Maibom, 2012, 2014). In part, this is likely due to the fact that empathy is just one process among many that influence prosocial (and antisocial—see Chapter 11) behavior, and our capacity for empathy appears to be flexible and may or may not be extended to others depending on specific cultural belief systems (Hollan, 2012, 2014), as well as aspects of the target (e.g., whether they are members of the in-group (Chiao, 2011; Decety & Cowell, 2014)).

Whether other animals have the capacity to accurately infer the mental states of conspecifics remains a contested issue. However, it is likely that empathic concern, broadly construed (to include personal distress, sympathy, and emotional contagion), has a deep evolutionary history and is linked to the evolution of parental care and other cooperative relations in social species (Decety, 2014; de Waal, 2012). Indeed, research suggests that the neurobiological underpinnings of empathic concern (again, broadly construed) are highly conserved across mammalian species and employ the same neural circuits that underlie pain responses. When individuals are exposed to others in distress, therefore, they experience painful emotional responses that motivate them to do something to alleviate that pain. However, as noted above, this is strongly dependent on specific social and contextual factors (Decety, 2014). Thus, although empathic processes are important for understanding prosocial and antisocial behavior, treatment approaches that aim to enhance empathy may not always be successful (Mann & Barnett, 2013), because antisocial behavior is not necessarily linked to deficits in empathy per se (Ward & Durrant, 2013, 2014). We revisit this issue in more detail in Chapter 11.

Shame and guilt are two other emotional responses that play an important role in understanding moral behavior and can be plausibly conceptualized as evolutionary adaptations that play a functional role in the promotion of prosocial behavior among group members (Nelissen, Breugelmans, & Zeelenberg, 2013; Tangney, Stuewig, Malouf, & Youman, 2013). Guilt and shame are both social emotions, in that they arise when individuals have engaged in behavior that violates social norms, standards, or practices. Although the experience of shame and guilt may co-occur, they can be reliably distinguished from one another: guilt can be viewed as a more "other oriented" emotion that arises from the negative evaluation of a specific *behavior*; shame is more "egocentric," involving a focus on more global negative evaluations of the *self* that arise from specific actions or behaviors (Tangney, Stuewig, & Mashek, 2007).

Most scholars agree on the adaptive functions of guilt. The experience of guilt tends to motivate individuals to repair the harm done by their behavior and prevents them from engaging in future misdeeds. Guilt, then, is a kind of "first-party" punishment (Hoffman, 2014) that plausibly evolved in the context of reciprocal exchanges among humans (Nelissen et al., 2013; Tangney et al., 2013). Consistent with this idea, research has found that guilt-proneness promotes moral and ethical behavior (Cohen, Panter, & Turan, 2012), is negatively related to antisocial and criminal behavior (Stuewig, Tangney, Kendall, Folk, Meyer, & Dearing, 2014), and reduces the likelihood of criminal recidivism (Tangney, Stuewig, & Martinez, 2014). In short, individuals who are more likely to experience guilt tend to behave in ways that reduce the chances of experiencing this negative emotion: they are more prosocial and less antisocial. The evidence for the adaptive function of shame, however, is more mixed: Tangney et al. (2014) found no relationship between shame and recidivism, while Stuewig et al.'s (2014) results suggest that shame-proneness is actually a risk factor for antisocial behavior. Fessler (2007) has argued that shame originally evolved as a means to signal appeasement to more-dominant group members, thus reducing the likelihood of further aggression. This makes sense given that shame tends to be associated with motivations to withdraw and hide from others. As human groups became increasingly egalitarian and cooperation among group members was maintained in part by indirect reciprocity, shame took on the function of signaling to others, in general, that one is still a potentially trustworthy individual who recognizes the social norms of the society (Nelissen et al., 2013).

The final set of moral emotions that we will consider concerns experiences of moralistic anger, disgust, and contempt directed against individuals who violate social and moral norms (Tangney et al., 2007). When individuals are victims of criminal and other harmful behavior, they often experience a strong sense of moralistic anger that can promote retaliation and revenge (Barash & Lipton, 2011). These emotions make good adaptive sense: individuals who are willing to retaliate against others are less likely to be victims of harmful behavior, because they signal to perpetrators (and others) that such harmful behavior has personal consequences. Unsurprisingly, "second-party" punishment (Hoffman, 2014) is a fairly common feature of many animal species. Humans, as we note above, also engage in "third-party" punishment: we appear to be strongly motivated to punish those individuals who violate social and moral norms. Moreover, we experience strong feelings of anger, and other emotions such as contempt and disgust, when we witness or hear about such behavior, even though we have no personal stake in the particular outcome (Darley, 2009).

The experience of these emotions is consistent with a growing body of research that indicates that humans tend to be natural "retributivists"—in other words, we tend to be largely motivated to punish norm violators in relation to the moral blameworthiness of their actions, rather than for other reasons such as deterrence (Aharoni & Fridlund, 2012; Carlsmith, 2008;

Carlsmith, Darley, & Robinson, 2002; Goodwin & Gromet, 2014). Those familiar with the philosophical and criminal justice literature may view this explanation as sidestepping core debates over whether punishment serves primarily deterrent, retributive, communicative, incapacitative, or rehabilitative functions. However, these debates partly are concerned with the *normative* reasons that guide punishment and how rationales for punishment are consciously articulated. From an evolutionary perspective, the distal or ultimate function of punishment is largely consequential in nature: norm violators are punished in order to communicate what is and what is not appropriate behavior and to deter the latter from occurring. However, natural selection has shaped our proximate neural and cognitive machinery so that people's *experience* of responding to punishing norm violations motivates retributive responses (Buckholtz & Marois, 2012; de Quervain et al., 2004; Seymour, Singer, & Dolan, 2007). It is also likely that psychological responses to norm violations and the role of punishment in ensuring group cohesion, directly or indirectly strengthen the norm that all human beings have intrinsic value, a Kantian idea. It is likely, then, that the often powerful emotions we experience when individuals intentionally violate social norms, particularly those involving cheating or the deliberate and unjustifiable harming of others, reflect evolutionary adaptations that promote third-party punishment that serves to stabilize cooperation and prosocial behavior in human groups. In short, we have evolved a set of motivational and emotional characteristics that, taken together, constitute a sense of justice and guide our decision-making when we encounter situations where individuals have violated moral and social norms (Hauser, 2006; Krebs, 2008; Robinson & Kurzban, 2007; Walsh, 2000). Although our focus here has been on the motivation to punish norm violators, a number of scholars have argued that, although punishment may sometimes involve the removal of individuals from society (either permanently or temporarily), we—like other social primates—have also evolved the capacity to engage in forgiveness that motivates the reintegration of individuals into society (see McCullough, Kurzban, & Tabak, 2012; Peterson, Sell, Tooby, & Cosmides, 2010). Arguably, forgiveness and its role in facilitating the repair of relationships damaged by norm violations is the foundation of communitarian responses to crime, such as restorative justice (see Chapter 10).

IMPLICATIONS FOR CRIMINOLOGY AND CRIMINAL JUSTICE

Understanding the evolutionary origins of altruism, cooperation, and punishment has some important implications for criminological theories of offending (Agnew, 2011a, 2013). Clearly, theories that presuppose that humans are naturally selfish and are largely motivated to pursue personal gratification as long as the benefits outweigh the costs need to be rethought in light of the overwhelming evidence that—although we clearly *can* act selfishly—natural selection has shaped our motivational and emotional systems in ways that promote cooperative and prosocial behavior. This understanding promotes a—relatively subtle, but important—shift in the way we think about antisocial and criminal behavior, with the primary task more about explaining *deviations* from altruism and prosocial actions. Criminologists have not entirely neglected this task, of course, and there is an emerging literature that has investigated the role of morality in influencing criminal actions (e.g., Antonaccio & Tittle, 2008). Indeed, Wikström's situational action theory proposes that crime is the outcome of an individual's criminal propensity and criminogenic exposure, where the propensity to commit a crime is jointly dependent on an individual's morality and capacity for self-control (Wikström, 2006; Wikström, Oberwittler, Treiber, & Hardie, 2012). For Wikström, then, crime is construed in moral terms and is influenced by an individual's moral values, moral rules, and moral emotions.

In Figure 5.3, we have outlined how an understanding of our moral nature (including our motivations to punish norm violations), can provide a useful taxonomy for understanding criminal behavior. First, we need to recognize that some offending is likely to arise from the major malfunctioning of evolved psychological systems (e.g., in the context of psychotic disorders and states). Second, some criminal behavior may arise as a result of the "normal" functioning of the evolved mechanisms that underlie altruism, cooperation, and punishment. Perhaps most obviously, individuals can engage in crimes in order to retaliate against those who have wronged them, or wronged others in the community. A functioning criminal justice system that individuals believe is just will serve to

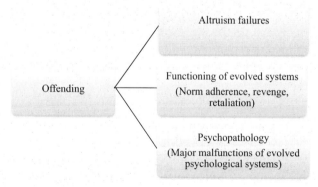

FIGURE 5.3   Offending behavior in relation to our evolved capacity for altruism, cooperation, and punishment.

limit the extent of this type of offending, but individuals have powerful moral emotions that generate feelings of anger that can lead to retaliation in some circumstances. Some offending may also reflect the adherence to particular social norms that *prescribe* actions that are considered criminal in some contexts. For instance, consistent with subcultural perspectives, individuals may believe that it is appropriate to respond with violence in certain contexts, and that to not respond violently represents a violation of the social norms held among group members. The practice of "honor killings" provides an extreme example of how adhering to social norms can result in criminal outcomes (Eisner & Ghuneim, 2013). Finally, criminal behavior can arise as a result of "altruism failures." In other words, our capacity for altruism and prosocial behavior can break down for some individuals in some situations, leading to criminal actions. We provide a more detailed account of how this may occur in Chapter 11, in the context of rehabilitating offenders.

In addition to addressing some of the underlying assumptions of criminological theories of offending, the account that we have offered in this chapter can also help us to address some of the key explanatory questions regarding the nature of punishment (see Table 5.2). Of course, an evolutionary account does not provide us with a *complete* answer to these questions as—consistent with our framework presented in Chapter 4—the distal explanations provided by evolutionary theory need to be integrated with proximal explanations in terms of the neurobiological, psychological, and social mechanisms underlying punishment responses. In addition, we need to recognize the role of social-structural and cultural factors in shaping the nature and form of punishment and how these have changed over time (Durrant & Ward, 2012).

Perhaps most straightforwardly, an evolutionary approach can help us to understand the seemingly universal human motivation to punish those individuals who violate particular social and moral norms. Although there still remains some debate regarding the evolved function of the mechanisms underlying punishment, plausibly these mechanisms are evolutionary adaptations that have been selected for because they enhance biological fitness by promoting cooperation, and thus increasing the likelihood of obtaining rewards for cooperative behavior. Many different acts can be subject to punishment in human societies, but arguably there is a core set of violations—those involving physical harm, the taking of property, and deception in social exchanges—that emerges in all societies and on which there tend to be high levels of agreement about how much such acts deserve to be punished (Robinson & Kurzban, 2007; see Braman et al., 2010, for a critique of this idea and the research that supports it, and the responses by Robinson, Jones, & Kurzban, 2010; Darley, 2010). These core acts are relatively universally punished, and individuals tend to agree on the punishment that such acts deserve because they were likely to have been a recurrent threat to the individual fitness and the effective functioning of social groups. Moreover, the punishment that individuals assign to such acts appears to be calibrated in a nuanced way to the moral wrongfulness of such acts in terms of the *intent* of wrongdoers and the amount of *harm* caused (see Hoffman, 2014, chapter two, for a detailed evolutionary analysis of the basis for the assignment of punishment based on intent and harm).

Of course, humans punish a diversity of different acts in different societies, and the nature and intensity of punishment varies substantially cross-culturally and historically. From an evolutionary perspective, variation in the acts deemed worthy of punishment reflects the evolution of the human capacity to acquire social norms that are prevalent in the local cultural environment. Although certain domains may be more likely to attract the moral attention of human societies, as Haidt's (2012) moral foundations theory suggests, there remains substantial scope for cross-cultural variation in the particular acts that are subject to social sanctions, as through the process of cultural evolution different groups develop distinct collections of values, norms, practices, and institutions that lead to different punishment responses (Henrich et al., 2010). We also think that there is considerable scope for the integration of an evolutionary approach to punishment (in terms of both genetic and cultural evolutionary processes), and the extant literature on the sociology of punishment tends to highlight the role of particular social-structural and cultural factors in explaining cross-cultural and historical variations in punishment (e.g., Cavadino & Dignan, 2006; Garland, 2013; Pratt, 2008; Pratt & Eriksson, 2012; Tonry, 2009; Whitman, 2005). Furthermore, a naturalistic theory of values that incorporates moral norms can be "graded down" to nonhuman organisms and provide standards or goals that promote well-being (i.e., flourishing, and ultimately survival) and reduce the possibility of harm occurring (see Chapter 11).

An evolutionary approach can also potentially shed light on the range of individual factors that tend to influence the nature and magnitude of punishment responses. Such factors include the offender's acknowledgment of guilt, experience of remorse, character and previous record of offending, age, gender, and other demographic characteristics (Robinson et al., 2012). Space precludes anything like a thorough analysis of these (and other) factors, but consider just one important characteristic of offenders that shapes the magnitude of punishment: their previous history of offending. In almost all jurisdictions a record of previous offending is a factor that influences the magnitude of punishment that an offender receives. Three-strikes laws are the most extreme example of the punishment premium that accrues to repeat offenders, but there appears to be widespread agreement in the law and among members of the public that someone who is a repeat offender deserves to be punished more harshly

(Roberts, 2008). Why should this be the case? After all, if two individuals commit the same aggravated robbery of a service station, they are engaging in the same criminal act and should deserve the same punishment even if one has three similar convictions and the other has a blameless record. From an evolutionary perspective, the premium for prior convictions makes perfect sense (which is not to say that it is necessarily morally justified): the best predictor of future behavior is past behavior, and someone who has repeatedly violated important social norms in the past is more likely to violate such norms in the future. That is not to say that we necessarily consider the likelihood of recidivism in coming to a decision regarding punishment (although of course we can); rather, individuals who experience greater moral outrage for repeat offenders are more likely to assign harsher penalties, and hence reduce the likelihood of these individuals transgressing in the future.

Our comments in this section have been necessarily brief, but we think there is substantial scope for integration between evolutionary approaches to punishment and those that focus primarily on psychological and sociological processes. Future work should address the potentially evolutionary underpinnings of our capacity for forgiveness and the implications for the development of therapeutic approaches to justice that focus on restoring offenders to communities (see Chapter 10).

SUMMARY AND CONCLUSIONS

We have covered a lot of ground in this chapter, but an overall survey of the terrain highlights two important conclusions. First, humans are—in many respects—"naturally" prosocial, altruistic, and cooperative. We are by nature normative animals and therefore predisposed to make normative judgments of many kinds, including moral ones centered on social coherence and conflict resolution. Like most other primates we are a highly social species that has "other-regarding" preferences, especially for kin and people who we interact with on a regular basis, but also for non-related individuals. Such other-regarding preferences rely on an evolved collection of emotions and emotional processes including empathy, compassion, guilt, shame, and remorse that function to motivate prosocial, and prevent antisocial, behavior. Central to our capacity for altruism, cooperation, and moral behavior was the evolution of social norms and our capacity to acquire and adhere to them. Any attempt to understand why humans engage in antisocial and criminal behavior needs to take into account what is known about our social nature. In particular, criminological theories should not assume that we are (only) selfish and self-interested organisms, but also need to recognize our inherently prosocial nature and thus explain deviations from our other-regarding preferences.

Second, although moral emotions serve as effective tools for first-party punishment that can prevent antisocial behavior, widespread cooperation, particularly among nonkin, can only be maintained in social groups in which individuals are willing to punish those group members who violate social norms. In short, our motivation to punish norm violators can be plausibly conceived of as an evolutionary adaptation that functions to promote cooperation among group members.

6

Distal Explanations: Adaptations and Phylogeny

INTRODUCTION

Cesare Lombroso, the nineteenth century Italian criminologist, is well known—among criminologists at least—for his suggestion that criminals can be viewed as "biological throwbacks" to an earlier, more primitive stage of evolutionary development (Lombroso, 1884/2006). The idea that the propensity to commit crime reflects the atavistic characteristics of a group of "born criminals" has been widely disparaged by criminologists and makes relatively little sense within the context of the Neo-Darwinian synthesis in evolution. However, if we accept that humans like all other species on the planet are the product of evolutionary processes, then it follows that our behavioral characteristics, including our capacity to inflict harm on others, violate social norms, and transgress against legal codes (i.e., the subject matter of criminology as we have defined it) must *in some way* be related to the selection pressures faced by our ancestors over the course of our evolution. In short, our understanding of criminal behavior can, in principle, be informed by our understanding of the evolutionary functions and evolutionary history of the relevant behaviors and the proximate psychological and neurobiological processes that underpin them. In this chapter, we aim to explore the contribution of *distal explanations* to our understanding of crime. These correspond to Tinbergen's first two levels of explanation: adaptation and phylogeny.

We begin by outlining some key explanatory targets for criminological theories. In particular, we suggest that any comprehensive explanation for crime needs to be able to explain why it is that certain types of criminal acts occur, why they tend to be patterned in particular ways (in terms of the social relationships between offenders and victims), and why it is that males are more likely to commit crimes than are females. We will argue throughout this chapter that the distal level of explanation is the most

© 2015 Elsevier Inc. All rights reserved.

salient for our explanation of these criminological phenomena (although other levels are, of course, *relevant*). We then briefly discuss how evolutionary behavioral scientists tend to conceptualize crime, noting that—unlike Lombroso—most evolutionary psychologists view crime as largely "normal" behavior that reflects the operation of evolutionary adaptations in specific contexts. We then turn to a more in-depth analysis of specific types of offending focusing on violence and sexual offending. Throughout the chapter, we aim to demonstrate that an evolutionary approach that focuses on distal explanations can (1) contribute significantly to our understanding of criminological phenomena (what, in Chapter 1, we referred to as "the ontological rationale") and (2) can lead to productive new lines of research (what we call the "epistemological rationale"). Although we focus squarely on distal explanations in this chapter we also, in the spirit of integrative pluralism (Chapter 4), note points for integration with other levels of analysis that will be explored in subsequent chapters.

KEY EXPLANATORY TARGETS

The nature and prevalence of criminal acts, broadly defined, vary enormously across time and space, but no known human societies exist without them. A fundamental, and somewhat neglected, task for criminological theories is to explain *why* humans (as a species) engage in acts of violence, theft, and so forth. In short, a key set of explanatory targets for theories of crime consist of accounting for the existence of criminal acts. We also need to account for the way that criminal behavior is typically *patterned*: some individuals are more likely to perpetrate crimes compared with others; some individuals are also more likely to be victims of crime compared with others; and some victim–offender relationships are more likely than others.

When all forms of criminal offending are considered, we suggest that patterns of offending and victimization are structured by four main variables: gender or sex, age, social class, and familial relationship. The other major correlate of crime is, of course, race or ethnicity. However, although ethnicity is clearly an important variable for understanding the pattern of offending in most Western countries, it is less relevant for understanding criminal patterns across all societies and in all time periods. Moreover, much (although perhaps not all) of the relationship between ethnicity and offending can be understood in terms of the associations that are found between ethnicity and social class. The relationship between ethnicity and offending is also shaped by the specific cultural-historical trajectories and social-structural dynamics of different countries, so we will revisit this topic in Chapter 9.

For virtually every type of crime (except prostitution where it is criminalized) men are more likely to be the perpetrators compared with women (Daly & Wilson, 1988; Fagan, 2014; Gannon, Rose, & Ward, 2010;

Gartner, 2011). For example, in a total population study of all individuals born between 1958 and 1995 and who lived in Sweden at age 15, 27.8% of men compared with 9.1% of women had received a criminal conviction for any crime (Yao, Långström, Temrin, & Walum, 2014). Moreover, the gender gap in offending tends to be the largest for sexual offenses and for more serious crimes, and much smaller for nonviolent offenses (Gannon et al., 2010; Gartner, 2011; Yao et al., 2014). For example, in the United States between 1980 and 2008, just under 90% of known homicide offenders were male (Cooper & Smith, 2011), and globally men account for 95% of all convictions for homicide (United Nations Office on Drugs and Crime, 2014). Men are also more likely to be the *victims* of violent crime, especially homicide. For instance, based on the latest global study of homicide, 79% of all homicide victims in the world were male (United Nations Office on Drugs and Crime, 2014), as were 77% of all victims of homicide in the United States between 1980 and 2008 (Cooper & Smith, 2011). However, the proportion of male compared with female victims shows substantial cross-cultural variation, and there is a significantly larger relative proportion of female victims in Europe and Asia compared with the Americas (United Nations Office on Drugs and Crime, 2014).

Criminal offending is also strongly patterned by age and social class. Although there are variations in the shape of the age–crime curve by offense type, country, and historical period, the most common pattern shows a sharp increase in the prevalence of offending in adolescence and early adulthood and a decline thereafter. Patterns of offending and victimization are also related to social class with individuals from relatively more deprived socioeconomic contexts more likely to be both the perpetrators and the victims of crime. However, we believe that the developmental level of explanation is the most salient for advancing our understanding of both the relationships between age and offending and social class and offending so we will defer our analysis of these until Chapter 7.

Finally, we need to be able explain how offending and victimization are patterned by familial relationship. Several key themes are important. First, crime occurs among both related and unrelated individuals. Second, whereas males are more likely to perpetrate violent offenses against acquaintances, friends, and strangers, women are more likely to engage in violent offending against family members. Third, men are more likely to be victims of violent offenses perpetrated by nonfamily members, whereas females are more likely to be victims of violent offenses committed by family members. Finally, within the family, the nature and prevalence of offending is strongly related to the relationship between victims and offenders (genetic or nongenetic) and the age of the individuals concerned. We elaborate on these points in more detail in our discussion of family violence later in the chapter.

In Table 6.1, we provide an overview of the key explanatory targets for distal explanations that we have highlighted in this section. It is important

TABLE 6.1   Key Explanatory Targets for the Distal Level of Explanation

Key explanatory targets	
General offending • Humans commit "crimes" • The prevalence of offending is strongly patterned by sex	The existence of criminal acts is a feature of all known human societies. Men are significantly more likely to be perpetrators of crime compared with women for almost all offenses.
Aggression and violence • Humans have the capacity for aggression and violence (including collective violence) • Aggression and violence is strongly patterned by sex and familial relationship	The existence of aggression and violence (including collective violence) is a feature of all known human societies and occurs among both related and unrelated individuals. Men are more likely to engage in all forms of direct aggression, with the gender gap being the largest for the most serious violent offenses (i.e., homicide); women are as, if not more likely, to perpetrate acts of indirect aggression. Men are more likely to be the victims of violent crime in general, especially homicide (although the proportion of male victims varies substantially cross-culturally and historically); women are more likely to be victims of intimate partner violence (although rates may be roughly equivalent in Western countries). Women very rarely engage in physical aggression against other women. Family violence is more likely to occur among genetically unrelated individuals.
Sexual offending • Humans have the capacity for sexual violence, including rape • Sexual violence is strongly patterned by sex	The existence of sexual violence (including rape) is a feature of all known human societies and occurs among both related and unrelated individuals (although the nature and prevalence of sexual violence varies substantial cross-culturally and historically). Men are significantly more likely to be the perpetrators of sexual violence, including rape. Females are significantly more likely to be the victims of sexual violence, including rape.
Other types of offending • Humans have the capacity to commit various types of property-related offending including theft, burglary, fraud, vandalism, and arson • Various other common human behaviors are often subject to criminal sanctions including drug use, gambling, and prostitution • Other types of offending are also patterned by sex	The appropriation (or destruction) of others' material resources (through nonviolent means) is a seemingly inevitable correlate of the existence of private property. Men are more likely to perpetrate property related offending, although the gender gap is relatively muted (and is nonexistent for some offenses in some cultural contexts). Humans appear to have a strong tendency to consume psychoactive substances, engage in games of chance, and to use prostitutes. Men are overwhelmingly likely to be consumers and females the providers of prostitution services.

to note that we are focusing on the most important *general* patterns that are found in the criminological literature as they relate to gender, offense type, and familial relationship. Obviously, there is also substantial variation in the details of how offending is manifested across space and time, and criminologists certainly need to be able to explain this variation. However, we argue that a comprehensive account of crime needs to explain both the existence of criminal acts and the way that they tend to be patterned by gender and familial relationship. To be able to address these explanatory targets in terms of evolutionary function and evolutionary history, we first need to consider the evolutionary context of our social and sexual relationships.

THE EVOLUTION OF HUMAN MATING AND SOCIAL STRUCTURE

Few, if any, introductory textbooks in criminology will devote any space to a discussion of human mating and sexual behavior. Perhaps this is understandable because these topics seem at best tangential to the concerns of criminologists in their efforts to develop theoretical explanations for criminal behavior. We think otherwise: a *complete* understanding of criminal behavior and our responses to that behavior can only be achieved through a consideration of the social and sexual context of human life. Moreover, to understand how crime is related to patterns of human marriage, sexual relationships, and social arrangements, we need to carefully consider how these have evolved during the course of our evolutionary history. No other topic within the human evolutionary behavioral sciences has attracted as much attention as human mating, so our review is by no means exhaustive. Rather, we will focus on the key concepts, findings, and debates within this literature as they are relevant to our understanding of criminal behavior.

In Table 6.2, we provide a summary of the social and sexual arrangements that are found in extant hominids. As illustrated in this table, there is an enormous diversity of patterns found among our extended evolutionary family. Our closest genetic relatives, chimpanzees and bonobos, form what is known as "fission–fusion" social systems with communities comprising both males and females. Communities are relatively stable, but fission into smaller foraging units on a temporary basis. Males are philopatric in both species, with females dispersing from their natal group into neighboring communities on achieving sexual maturity (Malone, Fuentes, & White, 2012; Watts, 2012). Both chimpanzees and bonobos mate promiscuously, with estrous females copulating with multiple males, although higher ranking males can sometimes monopolize ovulating females. As a consequence, there is a high degree of sperm competition among males as the sperm from multiple males may be in the reproductive tract of females

TABLE 6.2 Reproductive and Social Traits of Hominids

Trait	Human	Chimpanzee	Bonobo	Gorilla	Orangutan
Social structure	Multimale, multifemale; mate bonds	Multimale, multifemale; promiscuity	Multimale, multifemale; promiscuity	Unimale (or with two males); harem polygyny	Solitary; males overlapping female ranges
Dispersal	Multilocal marital residence	Male philopatry	Male philopatry	Dispersal by both sexes, with more by females	Emigration by both sexes
Mating system	Monogamy/polygyny	Promiscuity	Promiscuity	Polygyny	Promiscuous polygyny
Male–female sexual dimorphism[a]	1.19, 1.14	1.19, 1.23	1.36	1.63, 2.12	2.21
Mating/paternity	Slight sperm competition	Considerable sperm competition	Considerable sperm competition	Little sperm competition	Little sperm competition
Paternal investment	Considerable provisioning, with some direct care	Little investment	Little investment	Defense	No investment
Mate guarding	Guarding by both sexes, who spend much time apart	Extra copulations for high-ranking males near time of ovulation	Little to no guarding	Guarding by male, who repels all bachelor males	Some chasing off of small males by large males
Sexual coercion	Occasional rape, frequent subtle coercion	Various forms of male coercion	Little or no coercion	Sex only when females solicit	Frequent rape by small males

[a] The figures quoted for sexual dimorphism should be considered indicative only and vary by the specific population sampled (see Marlowe, 2012, for sources). Information derived from Marlowe (2012, p. 470, Table 20.1).

and hence "compete" for the opportunity to fertilize the female's eggs. Perhaps unsurprisingly, given uncertainty over paternity, male chimpanzees and bonobos engage in negligible amounts of paternal investment (Watts, 2012).

The social and sexual arrangements of the other two hominid species—gorillas and orangutans—are markedly different from those found among chimpanzees and bonobos. Gorillas live in small family units with typically one or more males, multiple females, and their male and female offspring who disperse on reaching sexual maturity. Dominant males monopolize mating opportunities with females in their "harem" and vigorously repel intrusions from other males (Malone et al, 2012; Watts, 2012). As a consequence, paternity certainty is relatively high and there is little sperm competition among male gorillas. Uniquely among hominids, orangutans are largely solitary with the range of females (and their immature offspring) overlapping with that of males (Malone, et al., 2012). Large males, with characteristic flanges or cheek pads, attempt to maintain exclusive sexual access to females within their home range, whereas smaller unflanged males appear to adopt a coercive sexual strategy and attempt to forcibly copulate with females while avoiding dominant males (Knott, 2009; Watts, 2012). There is relatively little sperm competition among orangutans and males make no investment in offspring.

How do humans fit into this broader pattern of social and sexual arrangements found among extant hominids? The enormous diversity of human social and sexual relationships precludes a straightforward answer to this question. However, certain modal patterns can be identified and these diverge—often very significantly—from what we find in other hominid species. Chapais (2011, p. 1276) characterizes human societies as "multilevel, nested structures of alliances." The typical pattern found among hunter-gatherers (and thus probably representative of our deeper evolutionary history) involves societies that are comprised of multifamily groups with largely monogamous pairs and their dependent offspring (Gructer, Chapais, & Zinner, 2012). Either males or females (or both) may disperse from, or remain in, their natal groups generating highly variable residence patterns in which brothers and sisters—uniquely among vertebrates—often co-reside (Hill et al., 2011). Multifamily groups form small bands of individuals who, in turn, combine periodically to form larger tribes, with further social aggregations possible (Grueter et al., 2012; Kelly, 2013). The large-scale societies that emerged in the past 10,000 years or so are further characterized by social stratification and increasingly nonegalitarian social relationships (Kaplan, Hooper, & Gurven, 2009; Turchin & Gavrilets, 2009).

Humans exhibit a diversity of different mating arrangements cross-culturally, including monogamy, polygyny, and polyandry. However, there is generally widespread agreement that the modal sexual arrangement involves a relatively enduring, largely monogamous, pair bond involving one male and one female that often (but, not always) exists alongside polygynous sociosexual units involving one male and two or more females (Chapais, 2011, 2013; Fletcher, Simpson, Campbell, & Overall, 2015; Gray, 2013; Marlowe, 2012; Walker, Hill, Flinn, & Ellsworth, 2011). In addition, both males and females engage in short-term sexual relationships that might occur before, during, or after longer-term sociosexual alliances. The existence of polygynous mating and the tendency for males more than females to seek short-term sexual relationships is reflected in the greater reproductive variance typically exhibited by males compared with females (Marlowe, 2012). In other words, males vary more than females in their number of offspring (Betzig, 2012). Moreover, the sexual dimorphism that exists in humans in size and other physical characteristics suggests a history of male–male competition for sexual access to females (Puts, 2010). Broadly speaking then, and consistent with parental investment and sexual selection theory, there are reliable sex differences in the nature and intensity of intrasexual competition (which is greater among males; Puts, 2010), and the preference and willingness to engage in short-term sexual relationships (which is also greater among males; Schmitt et al., 2012).

However, as Stewart-Williams and Thomas (2013) have persuasively argued, it is tempting to exaggerate the sex differences that are found in humans. Furthermore, they argue that evolutionary psychologists, in their presentation of research findings, have sometimes given in to this temptation and this has led to a somewhat distorted picture of sex differences in human mating behavior. Perhaps the most important point to recognize here is that monogamous pair-bonding is the typical sociosexual relationship that is found across human societies and it is highly likely that various characteristics (such as "romantic love") have been specifically selected to facilitate long-term relationships among adult males and females (see Fletcher et al., 2015). Unlike all other hominids, human males also invest significantly in their offspring and this investment makes a real difference in the likelihood of offspring surviving, especially among hunter-gatherer societies, although mothers remain more important to the well-being of offspring compared with fathers (Geary, 2000; Hill & Hurtado, 1996; Winking, Gurven & Kaplan, 2011; although see Sear and Mace, 2008). The existence of enduring pair bonds and the importance of males to offspring survival leads to the conclusion that intersexual competition for access to the most desirable mates is an important feature of both human males and females, although the nature of the competition is likely to vary.

One central question for evolutionary anthropologists is how the rather unusual mating arrangements of humans, involving pair bonding, substantial paternal investment, and a distinct division of sexual labor, evolved from the common ancestor of humans and chimpanzees. It is generally argued that this common ancestor had a social structure similar to that found among chimpanzees and bonobos: multimale, multifemale social groups with promiscuous mating (Chapais, 2011, 2013). Chapais argues that the most likely evolutionary scenario involves a transition from promiscuous mating to a society of multiple polygynous mating units (one male and two or more females). Given the likely magnitudes of sexual dimorphism found among Australopithecines (Dixson, 2012), it is likely that such a social arrangement was in place by 2–4 million years ago. The reduced dimorphism found among *Homo erectus*, along with other lines of evidence, suggests a shift to multilevel communities of largely monogamous mating units (although with some residual levels of polygyny), and ultimately a greater involvement of males in the care and provisioning of offspring (Chapais, 2011, 2013; Fletcher, Simpson, Campbell, & Overall, 2013; Walker et al., 2011). Complicating this evolutionary scenario is the potential role of cultural and social-structural factors in influencing human mating patterns and social arrangements. For instance, in many cultures throughout the world and throughout history, parents have played a pivotal role in the marriage arrangements of their offspring (see Apostolou, 2014) thus potentially influencing the traits that are sexually selected for (although Fletcher et al., 2015, argue that the mate preferences of parents and offspring are actually quite aligned). In addition, cultural belief systems can influence the nature of mating relationships in important ways. For instance, many indigenous populations in lowland South America believe in the idea of partible paternity where it is accepted that there can be multiple fathers for any particular offspring because all the men that a women has sex with during pregnancy help create the fetus (Walker, Flinn, & Hill, 2010). The emergence of large-scale hierarchical societies can also transform the nature of sexual and social arrangements and, as documented by Betzig (2012), the degree of reproductive skew (or variance in male reproductive success) is often much greater among agricultural compared with hunter-gatherer societies. Any complete account of human sexual and social relationships therefore needs to consider both genetic and cultural evolutionary processes (e.g., see Henrich, Boyd, & Richerson, 2012).

What does all this mean for our understanding of the evolutionary origins of criminal behavior? As we elaborate in more detail in this chapter, a large proportion of offending (especially violent and sexual offending, but more indirectly, offending of all kind) is intimately related to human sociosexual behavior and the psychological characteristics of males and females that have been shaped by natural and sexual selection. It is important, therefore, to have a clear understanding of the evolutionary origins of human mating behavior. Although there is a fair amount of debate about how best to characterize the highly flexible nature of human mating arrangements we can draw some tentative conclusions based on the analysis that we have provided in this section:

1. Humans are a pair bonding species that form relatively exclusive, relatively enduring, long-term relationships that often involve substantial paternal investment.
2. As such, both males and female compete among each other for access to mates and invest heavily in long-term relationships with one another.
3. Both males and females also engage in short-term sexual relationships before, during, and after long-term relationships.
4. Because of differences in minimum parental investment, reproductive variance, the relative (un)importance of males to offspring survival, and a legacy of polygyny, males more than females are (on average) motivated to pursue short-term sexual relationships and additional long-term sexual partners (when conditions allow).
5. Therefore, although intrasexual competition exists for both males and females it is likely to be stronger among males and take a different form.
6. There are substantial intrasexual differences in mating behavior in humans that are likely to be influenced by a range of genetic, ecological, and cultural factors and that bear on the nature and intensity of intrasexual competition that occurs.

THE EVOLUTIONARY ORIGINS OF "CRIME"

"Who," Lombroso queries, "is unfamiliar with the fascinating descriptions of insectivorous plants by Darwin, Drude, Rees, and Will? No fewer than 11 species…commit true murders of insects…these examples show the dawn of criminality" (Lombroso, 1884/2006). Lombroso's conception of "murder" will be too elastic for many, and the "intentional" killing of one organism by another long predates the evolution of plants; however, Lombroso's discussion of "crime among plants and animals" contains an insightful kernel of truth. Because evolution via natural (and sexual) selection is an inherently competitive process that entails *differential* fitness, then—all other things being equal—any characteristic that advances survival and reproductive success at the expense of the reproductive fitness of conspecifics is going to be selected for. To the extent that crime involves the infliction of harm and the "unfair" appropriation of resources from others then we would expect mechanisms that underlie such behavior to be the target of natural selection. One prominent approach taken by evolutionary psychologists is, therefore, to argue that crime—or the mechanisms that underlie crime—reflects the operation of evolutionary adaptations (Buss, 2012; Duntley & Shackelford, 2008a, 2008b; Kanazawa & Still, 2000; Shackelford & Duntley, 2008; Walsh, 2009). Thus, Duntley and Shackelford (2008a, p. 380) suggest that:

> ...evolutionary forensic psychology recognizes that crimes such as murder, assault, rape and theft are manifestations of evolutionarily recurrent conflicts between individuals. The cost-inflicting strategies that we recognize as crimes may have been favored by natural selection when they have given individuals an advantage in competition for resources.

From this perspective, although crime may be maladaptive in contemporary modern societies with an effective rule of law (although see Nedelec & Beaver, 2012 and Yao et al., 2014 for research linking antisocial and criminal behavior to reproductive success), the traits that underlie criminal behavior may have been selectively advantageous in ancestral environments (Walsh, 2009).

We concur with evolutionary psychologists that it is enormously useful to consider the potential adaptive function of the mechanisms that underlie criminal behavior, and we believe that such an approach can address many of the explanatory targets outlined in Table 6.1. We also believe it is essential to locate the human capacity for criminal behavior within the broader context of our understanding of humans as a largely prosocial, cooperative species that has evolved in the context of group living (see Chapter 5). We have argued that the problems of group living, and the competition that arises among groups, has selected for a suite of psychological processes that facilitate altruistic behavior and mechanisms that enforce social norms through the use of third-party punishment. From this perspective, a great deal of what we call crime (e.g., rape and violence directed against group members, theft, cheating) reflects behavior that would have been costly for most individuals *even in* ancestral environments.

This suggests, consistent with the arguments developed by most evolutionary behavioral scientists (e.g., Figueredo, Gladden & Hohman, 2011; Walsh, 2006), that we need to consider a number of (non-mutually exclusive) ways of considering the relationship between evolutionary adaptations and criminal behavior. As depicted in Figure 6.1, crime, or the mechanisms underlying specific types of criminal behavior, may be the direct product of evolutionary adaptations, or alternatively be the by-product of adaptations. For criminal behavior that reflects the operation of evolutionary adaptations, it is possible that the behavior reflects adaptations operating as they were designed to by natural and sexual selection (even if they may be selectively disadvantageous in some contemporary environments). The mechanisms underlying criminal behavior may also reflect the operation of conditional adaptations that are manifest in some members of the population under specific ecological and social contexts. It is also possible that

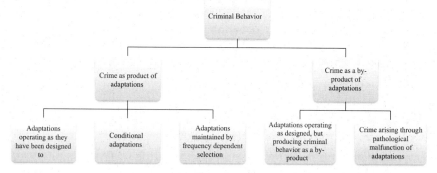

FIGURE 6.1   An evolutionary taxonomy of criminal behavior in relation to adaptive design.

criminal behavior may be the product of frequency-dependent selection so that the mechanisms underlying offending may be maintained in a small number of individuals in a population. We also need to consider the possibility that criminal behavior is the by-product of mechanisms that have been selected for other functions but are otherwise operating as they were designed to do. Finally, crime may reflect the pathological malfunction of one or more evolutionary adaptations. At this stage, we are ignoring the role of cultural evolutionary processes in relation to our understanding of crime, as these will be addressed in Chapter 9.

Although all of these options are, in theory, possible, we think it is crucial to evaluate the relevant evidence on a case-by-case basis. Certainly, offenders are often versatile and hence there may be similar etiological mechanisms underlying a diverse range of offenses; however, it is likely that specific types of offending behavior are related to more specific etiological processes. Moreover, for any given offense type, there may be multiple etiological pathways that need to be considered (e.g., Ward, 2013). In this chapter, we will focus largely on criminal behavior that reflects either the product of adaptations operating as they were designed to or else arising as a by-product of evolutionary adaptations. We think that the role of conditional adaptations in the genesis of offending is important, but will defer a more detailed presentation of these ideas until Chapter 7 in the context of life history theory and the developmental level of explanation. Some criminal behavior also reflects the clear pathological malfunctioning of specific adaptations and we will touch on this issue in Chapter 8 in the context of proximate explanations. Before we begin with a more in-depth analysis of the relationship between specific types of offense and evolutionary adaptations, we will briefly consider the possibility that criminal behavior may reflect the operation of frequency-dependent selection processes such that a small proportion of offenders have been maintained in the population by selection processes.

Frequency-Dependent Selection and Psychopathy

Psychopathy is a clinical construct characterized by a core set of affective, interpersonal, lifestyle, and antisocial features (Hare, 2001; Hare & Neumann, 2008). Psychopathic individuals tend to be callous, lack empathy for others, and display little guilt or remorse for their actions. They also have a manipulative interpersonal style, have a grandiose sense of self-worth, and are impulsive, with a reduced capacity to regulate their behavior. Despite an extensive body of research on psychopathy, there remains considerable debate in the literature regarding the underlying factor structure of psychopathy, with some scholars arguing that it represents a unified construct, whereas others suggest that it is best conceived of as a constellation of traits.

Relatedly, there is also disagreement on whether psychopathy is best conceptualized as a unique taxon (i.e., a distinct subtype of individuals) or whether psychopathic traits exist on a continuum in the population (see Skeem, Polaschek, Patrick & Lilienfeld, 2011, for a review). Despite some disagreement on the best way to conceptualize psychopathy, it is clear that individuals with psychopathic characteristics are at a significantly elevated risk for engaging in a wide range of criminal actions (Neumann & Hare, 2008; Porter & Woodworth, 2006; Salekin, 2008), although it is important not to *equate* psychopathy with offending (Skeem et al., 2011; Skeem & Cooke, 2010).

There is some evidence that psychopathic individuals can be found in a diverse range of cultural contexts (Cooke, 2008), although they make up less than 1% of the general population (of males) (Blair, Mitchell, & Blair, 2005). Given the rarity of psychopathy and the apparently dysfunctional nature of psychopathic traits, it is tempting to conclude that psychopathy must be a form of psychopathology that arises through a combination of genetic and environmental influences that impair the normal functioning of neurobiological and psychological processes. Although this remains a distinct possibility, it is also possible that psychopathy—or, rather, the traits that underlie psychopathy—have been selected for, because of their value in advancing reproductive success for some individuals in some environmental contexts (Glenn, Kurzban & Raine, 2011; Mealey, 1995). As Glenn et al. (2011, p. 372) inquire:

> Might the features of psychopathy coherently be understood as a social strategy that, in ancestral environments, contributed to, rather than detracted from, reproductive success, and was selected for in virtue of the benefits from implementing the strategy.

Psychopathic traits could plausibly promote reproductive success in a number of ways. Psychopathic individuals tend to have a large number of short-term sexual partners, manipulate others to their own advantage, readily use aggression to obtain instrumental goals, and are unconcerned with the infliction of harm on others facilitating a range of exploitative behaviors including rape, cheating, and violence. The problem, of course, for this perspective is that there are substantial *costs* to engaging in this type of behavior—increased risk of mortality, sanctions from group members, and low investment in offspring (Boehm, 2012).

Two main evolutionary hypotheses have been developed that suggest that psychopathy may have been specifically selected for. The first, and most common suggestion, is that the characteristics of psychopathy can be viewed as part of a "fast" life history strategy that promotes certain types of behavior under particular environmental conditions (Barr & Quinsey, 2004; Jonason & Tost, 2010; McDonald, Donnellan, & Navarret, 2012). In other words, psychopathy could be viewed as a conditional adaptation. The second evolutionary hypothesis is that psychopathy is maintained in the population through balancing selection. Under balancing selection, certain traits can be retained in a population when they promote reproductive success in specific environmental contexts. More specifically, frequency-dependent selection can favor traits that might otherwise be disadvantageous when they are statistically rare. The traits that underlie psychopathy thus might be advantageous when they are uncommon as individuals with those traits can successfully exploit others who are largely cooperative and prosocial. As soon as psychopathic traits become more common, they are less advantageous because antisocial individuals are increasingly likely to interact with other antisocial individuals and are less able to reap the benefits of exploitation. Although both of these perspectives are distinct possibilities, as Glenn et al. (2011) conclude, our current state of knowledge does not allow us to say with any confidence that psychopathy has been selected for or whether it is best conceived of as a genuine psychopathology that arises through the malfunction of psychological systems.

AGGRESSION AND VIOLENCE

Day 36. Another attack by Yeroen after repeated provocation by Luit. Yeroen corners Luit in the top of one of the (dead) trees and bites him. This time Luit bites back. Mama, Gorilla, Puist, and Nikkie also play a role in the confrontation. Only Puist actually joins in the fighting, although unfortunately it is not clear whose side she is on. Almost immediately after they have all descended from the tree, Yeroen bluffs over Luit. The two males then kiss each other and lick each other's wounds. Luit's wounds are obviously deeper. *de Waal (1982, p. 110).*

This extract from the primatologist Frans de Waal's (1982) fascinating, although at times disturbing, account of a captive group of chimpanzees at Arnhem zoo clearly indicates the capacity for aggression and violence among chimpanzees. Indeed, decades of field work among chimpanzee communities have provided detailed accounts of the use of both lethal and nonlethal aggression in chimpanzees, at rates that equal or exceed those found in human populations (Wrangham, Wilson, & Muller, 2006). The use of aggression is frequently employed by male chimpanzees in a variety of contexts: to compete among other males for dominance, to obtain resources from group members, and to intimidate females (Muller, Kahlenberg, & Wrangham, 2009). Groups of males also engage in collective hunting, and collective aggression against the members of other chimpanzee groups, with often lethal outcomes (Wrangham, 1999; Wrangham & Glowacki, 2012). Aggression among females is somewhat rarer, but does occur (Pusey, Murray, Wallauer, Wilson, Wroblewski, & Goodall, 2008). Moreover, both males and females may sometimes commit infanticide, killing infants within their groups (Arcadi & Wrangham, 1999).

There is nothing particularly unusual about the use of aggression among our closest genetic relative, the chimpanzee. The capacity for aggression is widespread among animal species and occurs in a diversity of different contexts (Archer, 1988). Predators employ aggression to capture prey, and prey use aggression to resist attack. Aggression is used to negotiate dominance hierarchies and to obtain resources from others. Both males and females aggress against members of their own sex to obtain access to mates, and aggress against each other in the context of mating relationships. Aggression is widely used to retaliate against or punish group members. In many species, both males and females may kill infants. Siblings fight and in some species kill one another. In short, the capacity to engage in aggression is a seemingly ubiquitous feature of the animal world. The evolutionary logic of aggression is straightforward: wherever there is competition among organisms for resources (food, mates, territory, etc.), the use of physical force (and the ability to resist physical force) will be a perennially viable strategy that has the potential to increase reproductive success (Archer, 2009; Campbell, 2005). Thus, it is widely accepted among biologists that animals have specific adaptations for aggression that have been selected for because they increase the chances of survival and reproductive success. However, aggression is also a potentially costly strategy that can result in injury, disability, and/or death. Therefore, as Campbell (2005, pp. 629–630) notes, "Any organism that engaged in it [aggression] in a persistent and inflexible way would be unlikely to survive for long. The contingent nature of aggression and its reliance on net utility are central to an evolutionarily informed understanding of aggression." This means that although many species will have adaptations for aggression, aggressive behavior is highly sensitive to aspects of a species ecology and evolutionary history, specific situational contexts, and features of the individual organism such as age, sex, and physical condition. For instance, although aggression is a common feature of chimpanzee society, it is significantly less common among the closely related bonobo (Furuichi, 2011; Hare, Wobber & Wrangham, 2012). An evolutionary approach to explaining aggression and violence, will, therefore, need to clearly outline both the benefits and costs of aggression and locate these within a species' social and ecological context.

If we take aggression to be "any form of behavior directed toward the goal of harming or injuring another living being who is motivated to avoid such treatment" (Baron, 1977, p. 7) and violence as "aggression that has extreme harm as its goal" (Anderson & Bushman, 2002, p. 29), then it is clear that aggression and violence are not uncommon features of human society. For example, there were an estimated 4.3 million incidences of violent crime in the United States in 2009 (Truman & Rand, 2010), and approximately half a million individuals were the victims of homicide throughout the world in 2012 (United Nations Office on Drugs and Crime, 2014). Aggression appears to emerge early in human development and is present among children younger than 1 year of age and—contrary to a purely social learning explanations—tends to decline after the age of two (Archer, 2009b). Moreover, there is little evidence to suggest that violence is simply a feature of contemporary modern societies as there is an abundance of evidence for its presence throughout history and, prehistory, and in small-scale societies like the ones wherein humans spent the majority of their evolutionary history (Armit, 2011; Boehm, 2011; Keeley, 1996; McCall & Shields, 2008; Nivette, 2011a). Indeed, it seems clear that the rates of violence that are witnessed in contemporary societies are typically much *lower* than those experienced throughout most of human history and substantially lower than rates of violence found among hunter-gatherers and other small-scale societies (Eisner, 2003, 2012; Pinker, 2011; we tackle the explanation for these differences in Chapter 9). The ubiquity of aggression and violence across human societies, its early emergence in development, the existence of specialized psychological and neuro-biological mechanisms for anger and aggression, its clear evolutionary benefits in certain contexts for certain individuals, and its widespread existence across a diverse range of animal species strongly indicates that the capacity for aggression and violence in humans reflects the operation of biological adaptations that have been selected for during the course of our evolutionary history (Archer, 2009a, 2009b; Buss & Shackelford, 1997; Campbell, 2005; Daly & Wilson, 1988, 1997; Goetz, 2010; Liddle, Shackelford & Weekes-Shackelford, 2012).

We think there is strong evidence to support the idea that the capacity for aggression and violence has been specifically selected for in our species. Is it possible, however, that the most extreme manifestation of human violence—intentional homicide—also has a specific evolutionary history? This is the claim made by Duntley and Buss (2005, 2011; Buss, 2005) in their Homicide Adaptation Theory (HAT). According to HAT, humans have specific psychological adaptations for killing that have been selected for because they advanced reproductive success in ancestral environments. In short, Duntley and Buss (2008, p. 43) propose that "humans possess adaptations designed specifically for killing conspecifics." More specifically, it is proposed that humans possess a number of psychological mechanisms that evolved to solve recurrent adaptive problems, including (Duntley & Buss, 2008, pp. 43–44):

(a) preventing the exploitation, injury, rape, or killing of self, kin, mates, and coalitional allies by conspecifics in the present and the future; (b) reputation management against being perceived as easily exploited, injured, raped, or killed by conspecifics; (c) protecting resources, territory, shelter, and food from competitors; (d) eliminating resource absorbing or costly individuals who were not genetically related (e.g., stepchildren); and (e) eliminating genetic relatives who interfered with investment in other vehicles better able to translate resource investment into genetic fitness (e.g., deformed infants, the chronically ill or infirm).

Three main lines of evidence are marshaled to support the central propositions of HAT. First, several animal species appear to kill their conspecifics under specific circumstances and these seem to reflect specific adaptations for killing. Second, homicide—particularly in the foraging societies that characterized most of our evolutionary history—is a relatively frequent occurrence suggesting that it is a behavior that is "visible" to natural selection. And, third, humans seem to regularly engage in homicidal fantasies that involving the killing of others (Duntley & Buss, 2005, 2008, 2011).

Although we think that HAT is a *plausible* evolutionary account of why humans (sometimes) kill one another, given our current state of knowledge, we think it is not currently our *best* evolutionary explanation for homicide. As Durrant (2009, pp. 379–380) summarizes: "Duntley and Buss (2008) have not provided (1) a thorough analysis of the costs and benefits of killing in specific contexts; (2) evidence for 'special design' features for homicide; or (3) a systematic comparative appraisal of the socioecological contexts in which homicide occurs among other species. In the absence of this evidence, the claim that humans possess specific adaptations for killing, suffers in terms of its overall explanatory worth, relative to other evolutionary hypotheses." More specifically, we suggest that although the capacity for aggression and violence is almost certainly likely to have been specifically selected for in our species, it is unlikely that we have specific adaptations for killing our conspecifics. Homicide, therefore, is—given our current state of knowledge—*best* explained as a by-product of evolved mechanisms that underlie the capacity for aggression and violence (Daly & Wilson, 1988).

Distal explanations tackle head on pressing, but often ignore questions regarding the origins of the human capacity for aggression and violence by considering its function and evolutionary history. A distal level of explanation, therefore, adds ontological value in terms of explicating how it is that humans can, under certain situations, aggress against each other. Distal explanations are thus the most *salient* for explaining the existence of aggression and violence in our species. We think that the distal level of explanations is also the most salient for accounting for the pervasive sex differences that are found in the use of aggression and violence.

All the available evidence supports the claim that males are more likely to employ physical aggression than are females (Archer, 2004, 2009a, 2009b). This finding holds up across different cultures, historical time periods, and at different ages of development (Archer, 2004, 2009a; Eisner, 2012; Hess, Helfrecht, Hagen, Sell, & Hewlett, 2010). Moreover, the sex difference in the use of physical aggression is more pronounced for more serious (or risky) forms of physical aggression as illustrated for homicide, which, as we note previously, is largely perpetrated by males. However, there appears to be little difference between males and females in either the experience of anger or the use of indirect aggression (which may actually be more common among females) (Archer, 2004; Archer & Coyne, 2005). Why are males more physically aggressive compared with females? A distal level of explanation suggests that this sex difference arises because there are greater (evolutionary) benefits for males and greater (evolutionary) costs for females in the use of physical aggression to obtain desired outcomes.

We elaborate on these points in more detail later in our discussion of specific contexts in which aggression and violence occur, but the evolutionary logic is relatively straightforward. Because human males, like the males of most species, invest less (on average) than do females in offspring, they are better able to increase their reproductive success through competing among one another for access to additional mates. This results in greater reproductive variance among males compared to females. Hence the (evolutionary) benefits relative to the (evolutionary) costs of intrasexual competition, including intrasexual aggression, are greater for males, compared with females (Archer, 2004, 2009a; Daly & Wilson, 1988, 1997; Puts, 2010). Although most evolutionary behavioral scientists have focused on the greater evolutionary *benefits* of risky and aggressive behavior for men, the work of Anne Campbell (2005, 2013a, 2013b; Cross & Campbell, 2011) emphasizes the greater *costs* (in reproductive terms) that women incur from engaging in behaviors (such as physical aggression) that may lead to disability or death. In short, because women are much more pivotal to the survival and flourishing of their offspring than are men (e.g., Sear & Mace, 2008), we would expect them to be less motivated to put themselves at risk. As summarized by Campbell (2013a, p. 390): "Women's lives are precious commodities. When an ancestral mother risked her life, she risked the lives of her descendants in each of whom she had invested more than any father." At a proximate level of analysis, Campbell (2008, 2013a, 2013b) has persuasively argued that sex differences in the use of physical aggression, and violence are mediated by differences in fear: woman, compared with men, are more sensitive to the possible negative outcomes of behavior (Cross, Copping, & Campbell, 2011), and experience higher levels of fear that in turn result in a decreased likelihood of engaging in risky behavior, including physical aggression. Research suggests that, at the physiological level, differences in fear may be linked to heightened amygdala reactivity and differences in the connectivity between the amygdala and areas of the prefrontal cortex, which in turn are influenced by the activity of hormones, such as testosterone and progesterone (see Campbell, 2013b).

We argue, then, that the distal level of explanation is the most salient for accounting for gender differences in physical aggression and violence. In making this claim, we do not suggest that other types of explanation—e.g., differential socialization into gender specific social roles (Eagly & Wood, 1999, 2009)—are therefore *irrelevant*. Indeed, explanations from various levels of analysis are clearly relevant to our understanding of sex differences in aggression and how those differences might vary across time and space. However, as persuasively argued by Archer (2009a), a social role account fails to explain why sex differences in aggression emerge early in development and why they are so robust across cultures and historical periods (also see Nivette, Eisner, Malti, & Ribeaud, 2014).

It is important to recognize that although violence has an evolutionary basis, this does not in any way commit us to the idea that violence is somehow genetically determined or is an inevitable outcome of specific situations. Indeed, an evolutionary approach, as Buss and Shackelford (1997, p. 611) argue "strongly suggests that aggression is not a unitary, monolithic, or context-blind strategy. Rather, it suggests that aggression is highly context-specific, triggered only in contexts in which the specific adaptive problems are confronted and adaptive benefits are likely to be reaped." In what follows, we examine the role of aggression and violence, and its likely evolutionary origins, in two main contexts: intrasexual competition, and family violence.

Intrasexual Violence

Male–male aggression. Men kill one another much more frequently than women kill other women. In the United States, for example, male-on-male killings accounted for close to 68% of all homicides between 1980 and 2008, whereas the murder of women by other women represented just 2% of all homicides during this period (Cooper & Smith, 2011). Indeed, in a wide-ranging cross-cultural review of 35 studies of same-sex homicide, Daly and Wilson (1988) found that male-on-male homicides accounted for more than 90% of all such homicides in all but one of the samples. Although the figures are most pronounced for homicide, it is clear that there is a substantial gender gap in the likelihood of engaging in same-sex aggression: men physically aggress against other men much more than women physically aggress against other women. Why is this the case? The evolutionary argument that we presented previously provides a clear distal explanation for sex differences in aggression: men have more to gain and women more to lose from engaging in physically risky activities such as aggression. A distal level of explanation can also provide a clear answer as to why male–male aggression is so prominent relative to female–female aggression. To understand why this is the case, we need to consider the main contexts where males aggress against one another.

In his review of the situational dynamics of male–male homicide, Polk (1999) noted that, on most occasions, homicide appears to arise from the escalation of seemingly trivial disputes and arguments between males. Consider the following two examples:

> In a dice game, the victim and offender had a $2 bet, which the victim refused to pay. After both left the game, the offender fired three shots from his car, fatally wounding the victim as he walked along the street. *Wolfgang, 1958, cited in Polk (1999, p. 8).*

> EJF stabbed to death DJC at a notorious Edmonton hotel. They had been drinking. They argued over a glass of beer. They pushed one another prior to the fatal attack. Bouncers separate the two but as EJF was being pulled away from DJC he reached around a corner with his knife and stabbed DJC in the heart. *Silverman and Kennedy (1993), cited in Polk (1999, p. 7).*

In the cold light of day, it seems manifestly absurd to attack, let along kill someone, over something as trivial as a $2 bet or over the price of a glass of beer. Yet, analyses of male–male homicides clearly indicate that they typically arise over arguments and disputes (which may be more or less trivial), often in public spaces in front of bystanders (Daly & Wilson, 1988; Luckenbill, 1977; Polk, 1995, 1999). From an evolutionary perspective, although the content of the arguments may seem trivial they are fundamentally about something far more "important": social status. Social status, in turn, is important because it is reliably linked to reproductive success especially in ancestral environments.

A large body of evidence supports the claim that the tendency for males to engage in physically aggressive acts against other males has been selected for because success in intrasexual competitive conflicts advanced social status and hence reproductive success. First, it is important to note that male–male aggression is a common feature of species that are polygynous, reflecting the steeper gradients in reproductive variance that arises when some males can successfully exclude other males from the mating arena (Archer, 2009a; Puts, 2010). Although pair-bonding and monogamous relationships are central to the mating systems of humans, the evidence that we discussed previously clearly indicates that humans are (somewhat) polygynous and that there is greater variance in male compared to female reproductive success. In polygynous species, it is common for males to be significantly larger and more formidable than females because size and strength are subject to stronger selection pressures among males compared with females. Although human males don't sport any specialized anatomical weaponry such as antlers, horns, or oversized canine teeth, differences in size and strength are broadly consistent with this pattern. Sex difference in height and weight are relatively modest. However, men have 61% more total muscle mass, 75% more arm muscle mass, and 90% greater upper body strength compared with women (Lassek & Gaulin, 2009). In addition, males have stronger bones, larger lung capacity, faster reaction times, and a greater tolerance for risky and dangerous activities (see Sell, Hone, & Pound, 2012, p. 33). In short, although we cannot entirely discount the possible role of other selection pressures in shaping sex differences in size and strength, the most parsimonious explanation suggests that these traits are (largely) the product of sexual selection.

There remains some debate among evolutionary scientists regarding the relative importance of intrasexual (males competing against males) and intersexual selection (females choosing males) in the selection for male–male aggression and the physical characteristics associated with such aggression (Puts, 2010). The currently available evidence suggests that both processes are important. Several studies suggest that, although females do not necessarily favor more aggressive males, they do favor a variety of traits such as muscularity, strength, deep voices, and masculinized faces that are indicators of physically and socially dominant males (Collins, 2000; Fan, Dai, Liu, & Wu, 2005; Frederick & Haselton, 2007; Maner, DeWall, & Galliot, 2008). There is also clear evidence that these characteristics play an important role in intrasexual contests and that males are particularly sensitive to the formidability of other males as indexed through their size and strength (Fessler, Holbrook, & Snyder, 2012; Sell et al., 2010; Puts, Apicella, & Cárdenas, 2011; Sell et al., 2012). Moreover, experimental research has highlighted how mating contexts tend to promote greater intrasexual aggression among males (Ainsworth & Maner, 2012; Gallup, O'Brien, & Wilson, 2011; Griskevicius, Tybur, Gangestad, Perea, Shapiro, & Kenrick, 2009) that, in the real-world, appears to lead to greater reproductive success (Frederick & Haselton, 2007; von Rueden, Gurven, & Kaplan, 2011). In sum, the evidence is consistent with the idea that human males have been "designed" to engage in physical aggression against other males (Sell et al., 2012).

Given our discussion so far, it might actually appear odd that males don't fight one another *more* often than they do. Aside from a few, largely inconsequential, school yard scuffles, the two authors of this book have never been in a physical fight with another male and we are sure that many (but, not all!) male readers of this book could report a similar fight-free personal history. Three points are important here. First, rates of violence (and particularly male–male violence) are substantially lower in most contemporary modern societies than among contemporary foraging societies and in the historical and prehistorical past (Eisner, 2012; Pinker, 2011). We think this is an extremely important point, and the fact that overall rates of violence in a society seem to be driven by levels of *male–male* violence is especially relevant. We take up this topic in detail in Chapter 9. Second, as criminologists are well aware, rates of male–male violence vary in important ways by social class. In other words, there are important individual differences in the tendency to aggress against other males that reflect (in part) exposure to different social and environmental conditions. Again, this is an important topic, but we defer a more detailed exposition of the reasons why this might be the case until Chapter 7. Finally, variations in the use of physical aggression to obtain status are likely to reflect the fact that—among humans—status is not only achieved through the use of physical dominance, but it can also be realized through alternative routes.

According to the dominance–prestige model of human status, the negotiation of social hierarchies in our species is carried out via two distinct, but equally viable, strategies: dominance and prestige (Cheng & Tracy, 2014; Henrich & Gil-White, 2001). Dominance hierarchies are common among social primates and effectively involve the use of force, or threat of force, to obtain social rank and the benefits that accrue to high-ranking individuals. Dominance as a strategy therefore involves the deference of lower ranking individuals based on fear and intimidation. In contrast, although prestige is an equally viable approach for obtaining social status, it entails the freely conferred deference to others based on their skills, knowledge, and success. Whereas dominance is a phylogenetically older strategy for the attainment of social status, Henrich and Gil-White (2001) argue that prestige became an important route to social status in human evolution due to the central role of cultural learning in our species. More specifically, it is argued that humans have social learning biases that lead them to preferentially attend to individuals with the skills, knowledge, or success that suggests that they are good "models" to focus on for the acquirement of culturally valued traits. Such individuals are therefore able to acquire social status and wield social influence through the deference that others afford them.

Various lines of evidence provide support for the dominance–prestige model. First, several studies support the underlying contention that dominance and prestige can be equally viable (but not necessarily mutually exclusive) strategies to obtain social status in both Western (Cheng, Tracy, Foulsham, Kingstone, & Henrich, 2013), and non-Western populations (von Rueden, Gurven, & Kaplan, 2008, 2010). For instance, among the Tsminae, a forager–horticulturalist society who inhabit areas of lowland

Bolivia, both dominant (men rated as better able to win dyadic physical fights) and prestigious (men rated as having greater community-wide influence) individuals had higher levels of fertility, more extramarital affairs and tended to be more likely to remarry (von Rueden, Gurven, & Kaplan, 2010). This suggests that both strategies of obtaining social status are linked to reproductive success. Second, an emerging literature highlights how the two different pathways may be related to different psychological, affective (Cheng, Tracy, & Henrich, 2010), and neuroendocrine (Johnson, Burk, & Kirkpatrick, 2007) profiles suggesting that they are two distinct strategies (see Cheng & Tracy, 2014, for a review). Third, and perhaps most important for our purposes, there are individual differences in the tendency to "adopt" either a dominance or a prestige-based strategy. For some individuals in some social contexts, dominance will be a more viable route to social status: they have the psychological characteristics (e.g., assertiveness, Machiavellianism) and physical attributes (size, strength, and fighting ability) that are likely to prove successful in obtaining high rank in the social environments (those in which such traits are valued and/or in which physical aggression and intimidation are less likely to be suppressed) in which they are embedded. For other individuals, in other environments, high social rank can be better obtained through an alternative route that involves prestige: they have the psychological traits (e.g., agreeableness, altruism) and locally valued skills, knowledge, and abilities that tend to make them viable targets for respect from others, particularly in environments where the opportunities to obtain status via physical aggression and intimidation are limited (Cheng & Tracy, 2014). Thus the dominance–prestige model of social status suggests that individual tendencies to employ aggression in intrasexual contexts will depend, in part, on the specific characteristics of individuals and the environments in which they are embedded. However, it is important to note that the two pathways are orthogonal, rather than mutually exclusive, and therefore are best conceptualized as alternative strategies (rather than alternative types or individuals) that may be more or less likely to be deployed (Cheng et al., 2013).

Female–female aggression. Explanatory accounts of criminal behavior often neglect—or sometimes downright ignore—female perpetrators. Given the preponderance of male offenders, this is perhaps not too surprising. However, females do commit crimes and—although they do so much less frequently than their male counterparts—also engage in intrasexual aggression. Given that males can seemingly benefit more from engaging in costly behaviors such as the use of aggression and violence, why do women also have the capacity to aggress against other women and in what contexts is this most likely to occur? From an evolutionary perspective, the existence of intrasexual competition among women should not be surprising. Because humans develop enduring, largely monogamous, pair-bonds sexual selection is likely to have favored female characteristics that enable them to compete effectively against other females to obtain the best long-term relationship partners—those partners who are most likely to invest in the relationship and in offspring in ways that advance inclusive fitness. In short, females should compete among one another in ways that make them more likely to be chosen as long-term mates (and thus exclude other females) by males who have the characteristics that are most likely to result in viable offspring (Campbell, 2013a, 2013b; Stewart-Williams & Thomas, 2013).

The nature of this competition sometimes involves same-sex aggression. Moreover, as Campbell (2013a, 2013b; Cross & Campbell, 2011) points out, a significant proportion of female–female violence is related to the mating domain. Fights among girls often involve jealousy over sexual rivals and occur in response to threats to sexual reputation. Moreover, same-sex aggression among females is far more prevalent among young women, typically involves friends and acquaintances, and often occurs in the presence of others (Campbell, 2013a; Hirschinger et al., 2003). This is what we would expect if female–female aggression reflects sexual selection pressures that favor traits that allow women to compete successfully against other women in intrasexual contexts. Of course, the prevalence of female–female aggression is substantially lower than that found among males because the costs of engaging in physical aggression are much greater for females. However, females are just as likely to engage in other, less costly, forms of aggression.

Indirect aggression involves the deliberate intent to harm others by "using others, spreading rumors, gossiping, and excluding others from the group or ignoring them" (Archer & Coyne, 2005). Most researchers conclude that females are as likely, if not more likely, to employ indirect aggression compared with males (Archer & Coyne, 2005). Moreover, the form that indirect aggression takes, particularly in adolescent girls, is often directly related to the mating domain. In particular, girls are likely to target other girls' sexual reputation or appearance (Campbell, 2013a). From an evolutionary point of view, this is unsurprising, as males favor both attractive (as indicators of youth, and hence fertility) and nonpromiscuous females (indicating a lower probability of being cuckolded) in long-term relationship partners. Females may be able to successfully increase their chances of obtaining good mates, therefore, by impugning the sexual reputation of their same-sex competitors (Campbell, 2013a, 2013b). The topic of same-sex aggression among females is, no doubt, underresearched, but a distal explanation can help us to understand why such aggression occurs and the form it takes.

Family Violence

Families are an important part of most people's lives. Indeed, from a distal perspective, the evolution of internal fertilization, lactation, and infant care among mammals has led to the evolution of attachment processes that make family relationships and the mechanisms that promote them central to lives of many species. Although human families share many of the same features that characterize the mammalian lineage in general, they also have some unique or, at least, highly unusual characteristics including stable breeding bonds, extensive paternal investment, lengthy childhood, and a significant contribution of grandparents and other "allomothers" to offspring survival (Flinn, 2011; Hrdy, 2009). The importance of human kinship is clearly recognized by anthropologists who have devoted a significant proportion of their energies into documenting and identifying kinship relationships and patterns in human social groups (Flinn, 2011). Evolutionary scientists will find nothing unusual about the importance of families to human existence. Indeed, according to kin selection theory we should expect that cooperation should be more prevalent among kin than among unrelated individuals (Hamilton, 1964). However, the genetic interests of family members are never perfectly aligned and it is therefore unsurprising that conflict is also a feature of family life (Archer, 2013). Indeed, if we recognize that family violence involves a range of harmful acts that include physical attacks, sexual violence and abuse, neglect, and various forms of psychological and emotional abuse (e.g., Gelles, 2007; Tolan, Gorman-Smith, & Henry, 2006), then it is clear that conflict within families can be a major source of harm in society. In this section, we focus on distal explanations for family violence that can explain why violence can be a feature of family life and why it tends to be patterned in particular ways (Archer, 2013). We examine the literature on intimate partner violence first and then turn to a discussion of violence in the context of parent–offspring relationships, before briefly exploring the topic of sibling violence.

Intimate partner violence. Evolutionary behavioral scientists have a somewhat unromantic view of romantic love. From an evolutionary point of view, romantic love—the emotion that features so prominently in human literature, art, and music—is nothing more (or less) than an evolved adaptation that functions to facilitate commitment among intimate relationship partners so that they are more likely to remain together and contribute to the development of viable offspring (e.g., Fletcher et al., 2013, 2015). In short, the emotion of romantic love has evolved because it increases the reproductive success of both males and females. However, the course of love, as all those books, films, and songs remind us, does not always run smoothly. Conflict is also a feature of long-term intimate relationships. From an evolutionary point of view, the existence of conflict is hardly surprising. Although both men and women have the shared goal of raising viable offspring who themselves will reproduce, because the optimal outcome for males can differ from that for females, we would expect conflict to arise between intimate relationship partners, just as it does in other sexually reproducing species (see Arnqvist & Rowe, 2005; Parker, 2006).

Criminologists, of course, are particularly interested in conflicts that result in intimate partner aggression and violence and there is an extensive literature on this topic. According to the World Health Organization (2002, p. 89), intimate partner violence refers to "any behavior within an intimate relationship that causes physical, psychological, or sexual harm to those in the relationship." If we accept this broad definition, then it is clear that intimate partner violence is not an uncommon occurrence. For instance, in the United Kingdom, approximately 33% of women and 22% of men have experienced intimate partner violence in their lifetime (Robinson, 2010), and within any given year around 4–7% of women and 1–6% of men report being victims of partner violence in contemporary Western societies (see Flatley, Kershaw, Smith, Chaplin, & Moon, 2010; Mayhew & Reilly, 2007; Truman & Rand, 2010). Conflict among intimates can also lead to homicide; in the United States in 2009, there were 1095 female and 241 male victims of intimate partner homicide (Uniform Crime Reports, 2010).

The figures quoted in the preceding paragraph suggest a substantial gender gap in the risk of intimate partner violence: women are more likely to be victims compared with men. However, we need to recognize that, in contemporary Western societies at least, population-based studies (employing a measure known as the conflict tactics scale) suggest that men and women are roughly equally likely to perpetrate violence against their intimate partner (Archer, 2002, Straus, 2008, 2011). Although there is still substantial disagreement among scholars regarding these particular findings (Straus, 2011), we believe that four important results stand out in the literature on intimate partner violence. First, a significant proportion of the population experiences intimate partner violence at some point in the lives (although, of course, many individuals do not). Second, women are more likely to experience severe consequences of intimate partner violence, including being killed by their intimate partner. Third, both men and women perpetrate intimate partner violence, including intimate partner homicide. In the following discussion, we argue that a distal level of explanation can help us to make sense of these findings.

Intimate partner violence has been a topic of perennial interest for evolutionary behavioral scientists (Buss & Duntley, 2011, 2014; Daly & Wilson, 1988; Goetz, Shackelford, Romero, & Kaighobadi, & Miner, 2008; Kaighobadi, Shackelford, & Goetz, 2009; Wilson & Daly, 1996, 2009; Wilson, Johnson, & Daly, 1995), although the almost exclusive attention has been on male perpetrators and female victims (although see Cross & Campbell, 2011; Campbell, 2013a). According to Buss and Duntley (2011, p. 418), "contrary to ideals of romantic harmony, sexual conflict is predicted to be common and pervasive and to occur in identifiable regions or 'battlegrounds' in intimate relationships." What are these "battlegrounds" and how might they have contributed to evolved mechanisms that lead to intimate relationship aggression and violence? Buss and Duntley (2011, 2014) outline a number of contexts in which sexual conflict might emerge between intimate relationship partners, but most of the focus of evolutionary behavioral scientists has been on the role of sexual jealousy and paternity uncertainty.

Human males face a gnarly evolutionary dilemma: commitment to an enduring monogamous relationship can be an effective way of ensuring reproductive success as offspring survival is promoted; however, all that paternal effort will come to naught if the offspring are not actually biologically related to the male. Women are assured that their offspring are their own; men can never be sure. In short, men face the chronic problem of paternity uncertainty. According to Wilson and Daly (2009), the perennial problem of paternity uncertainty has selected for *male sexual proprietariness* that is characterized as an "evolved motivational/cognitive subsystem of the human brain/mind" (p. 275) that functions to motivate behavior that results in the reduced likelihood of partner infidelity and mate desertion. The emotion of jealousy is conceptualized to be a component of this system, which is triggered by the actual or perceived sexual infidelities of an intimate relationship partner. According to this evolutionary logic, men who were sensitive to the potential sexual infidelities of their intimate relationship partner and who engaged in various behaviors to reduce the likelihood of them occurring, would be more likely to have offspring that were their own, and hence the psychological mechanisms underlying these behaviors would have been selected for. More specifically, men who tended to monitor the whereabouts of their partner (what, in the animal literature, is referred to as "mate-guarding"), engaged in various controlling behaviors, and used various tactics including force and the threat of force to limit the risk of infidelity, would have been more reproductively successful than their counterparts. Male perpetrated intimate partner violence, therefore, can be viewed as one manifestation of the male proprietary mindset. It is important to recognize that violence is just *one* tactic that males might employ and the use of violence in this context—as in other contexts—will be sensitive to features of the individuals and the broader social and cultural environment (Buss & Duntley, 2011, 2014). Moreover, we need to recognize that intimate partner homicide is an unintended *byproduct* of male sexual proprietariness (see our earlier discussion of Homicide Adaptation Theory).

Several lines of evidence support—or are at least consistent with—this distal explanation for male intimate partner violence. The presence of male sexual proprietariness and the emotion of sexual jealousy appear to be cross-culturally universal, and occur in specific circumstances, suggesting that this is part of our species wide emotional repertoire (Fletcher et al., 2013). Moreover, men engage in more mate guarding and other types of controlling behavior in circumstances that increase their risk of being cuckolded: when their partner is in the fertile phase of their men-strual cycle (Gangestad, Thornhill, & Garver, 2002), when they are more fecund (e.g., not pregnant or lactating) (Flinn, 1988; Graham-Kevan & Archer, 2009), and when their partner is younger and hence at a greater risk of conceiving (Wilson, Johnson, & Daly, 1995). Furthermore, these fac-tors also increase the risk of intimate partner violence that is often related to jealousy and various types of controlling behavior, and is more likely to be directed at young partners (even after controlling for the age of male partners) (Shackelford, Buss, & Peters, 2000; Shackelford, Buss, & Weekes-Shackelford, 2003; Wilson et al., 1995).

Although a distal explanation can increase our understanding of why males engage in intimate partner violence, a focus on men and the adap-tive problem of paternity certainty has obscured the fact that women also engage in intimate partner violence (Cross & Campbell, 2011). Moreover, whereas the rates of same sex violence differ dramatically—men are much more likely to aggress against other men, than women are to aggress against other women—many scholars argue that rates of intimate partner violence—at least in contemporary Western societies—are roughly similar for both males and females. Furthermore, the research clearly indicates that both males and females experience jealousy in similar circumstances, and that jealousy is an important motivating factor in intimate partner violence perpetrated by females against their male partners (see Archer, 2013 for a review). As summarized by Archer (2013, p. 425): "The findings would support a broader view of mating guarding, where both sexes have a motive for control, men to avoid the risk of raising unrelated children and women to avoid the risk of losing a helper and protector." Given the importance of maintaining stable, exclusive pair bonds for both men and women, it makes evolutionary sense that both male and female partners should be sensitive to threats to the primary relationship, although for slightly different reasons. For men, the primary adaptive problem is to mitigate the risk of raising another man's offspring. For women, the threat of their partner deserting or investing resources into other women (and thus decreasing investment in the primary relationship) is the primary adaptive concern.

Although the use of aggression in not the only—or indeed primary—way of reducing these risks, to the extent that it can be effective it is antic-ipated that both men and women should be willing to use threats and force under certain circumstances. Other factors, including the presence of family support, cultural norms that might support or suppress the use violence, and social–structural contexts (e.g., relative gender empower-ment) are obviously important in accounting for the patterns of intimate partner violence that are found (Wilson & Daly, 2009). A distal level of analysis, however, is the most salient explanation for explaining why such violence occurs and why it is often related to concerns over infidelity and partner desertion. The relative similarity in rates of intimate partner violence between men and women (in contemporary Western societies) can be explained given the evolutionary importance pair-bonding in our species, while the higher rates of male-perpetrated intimate partner homicide and the greater harm inflicted on female partners likely reflects a generally greater willingness to use aggression by males and the physical ability to inflict greater harm (especially of course in cultural contexts where such actions are less likely to be condoned).

Parent–offspring, and sibling violence. Parent–offspring conflict theory (Trivers, 1974) extends the logic of kin selection to conflicts that arise in the family (Salmon & Malcom, 2011; Schlomer, Del Guidice, & Ellis, 2011). As outlined in Chapter 2, altruistic behavior can evolve if the net gain to the recipient multiplied by the genetic coefficient to the donor is greater than the cost experienced by the donor. Cooperation in families is therefore expected as parents and offspring on average share 50% of their genes, as do full siblings. Indeed, altruism is a cornerstone of family relationships. However, the cold logic of natural selection creates a problem: offspring may share 50% of their genes with their siblings and their parents, but they share 100% of their genes with themselves. Therefore, as summarized by Schlomer et al. (2011, p. 498):

> It follows that each offspring is selected to demand a greater (disproportionate) share of parental investment for itself, relative to its siblings, than parents have been selected to give, thus setting the state for parent–child and child–child conflict over the distribution of parental investment.

Moreover, from the parents' point of view, the nature and amount of investment directed toward offspring will vary by their fitness and need. The fitness of an offspring reflects its reproductive value in terms of its likelihood of having future offspring given its current physical condition and stage of development. Older, stronger, and more viable offspring have greater potential fitness. Need refers to how parental investment increases the likely reproductive value of offspring. Young, more vulnerable offspring have greater needs because parental investment makes a greater contribution to their future reproductive success. Finally, it should be noted that—from an evolutionary perspective—parents should be less likely to invest in offspring who are not their own (or who have cues that indicate that they are not genetically related).

Archer (2013) provides a thorough summary of the relevant literature from an evolutionary perspective finding, consistent with parent–offspring conflict theory, that violence directed at offspring is highest in infancy and declines with age, is more likely to be directed at poor-quality infants and when parental resources are scarce, and declines with parental age. Research also consistently finds that stepchildren are at a significantly elevated risk of abuse and death at the hands of stepparents (Daly & Wilson, 1996) because of a lack of parental (typically paternal) solicitude that arises because nongenetic parents are (on average) less "motivated" to direct resources to unrelated offspring. We should note, however, that although research is largely consistent with evolutionary hypotheses, possible confounds cannot always be ruled out (e.g., Temrin, Nordlund, Rying, & Tullberg, 2011). Comparatively little research has focused on sibling violence, although consistent with parent–offspring conflict theory serious conflicts among siblings is relatively rare (given regular close proximity) and most conflicts arise over competition for parental resources (Archer, 2013).

SEXUAL OFFENDING

There is a consensus among researchers that a convincing explanation of sexual offending is likely to be multifactorial in nature and incorporate a number of etiological pathways leading to the onset and maintenance of sexual offending (Ward, Polaschek, & Beech, 2006). These factors should include the identification of cultural and biological inheritable traits that increase the chances of individuals' violating important social norms (Ward & Durrant, 2011b). Thus, an important point is that there are likely to be multiple etiological pathways leading to sexual offending, each reflecting the influence of different causes. For example, some individuals' sexual offending is a function of their emotional deregulation, whereas for others it is primarily associated with intimacy seeking (Ward & Siegert, 2002). In our view, *evolved capacities* such as those constituting emotional regulation and social competence, in conjunction with developmental adversity and proximal social, cultural, and environmental factors, are directly or indirectly associated with the occurrence of sexual offending. In discussing sexual offending–related adaptations, we draw from contemporary theories that have explicitly incorporated evolutionary ideas such as the Integrated Theory of Sexual Offending (ITSO) (Ward & Beech, 2006), and recent theoretical work on rape (McKibbin, Shackelford, Goetz, & Starratt, 2008; Muller & Wrangham, 2009).

General Sexual Offending

The content and functional integrity of a person's psychological system is determined by a combination of biological inheritance and social learning. Once acquired, psychological vulnerabilities are thought to function as a diathesis, making it more probable that an individual will struggle to effectively meet specific environmental challenges and therefore make it likely that he or she will commit a sexual offense at some future time.

These circumstances can be regarded as a more *distal* dimension of risk. An individual's current ecology or physical environment is also an important contributor to the etiology of sexual offending through making available potential victims, and, by creating the specific circumstances that trigger the psychological deficits involved, this is a *proximal* or current dimension of risk. For example, the experience of fighting in a war, being subject to social circumstances such as the erosion of one culture by another, or the death of a partner, may sometimes lead to individuals committing a sexual offense. In these kinds of extreme circumstances, individuals can behave in ways they would not normally consider and may even engage in actions that they would view as unacceptable in their normal environments (see Chapter 8). Most sexual offenses are committed by males—approximately 90%—although there is still surprising heterogeneity in offending patterns displayed by females, indicating the presence of multiple motives (Gannon, Rose, & Ward, 2010).

According to the ITSO, sexual offending occurs through the ongoing confluence of *distal* and *proximal* variables that interact in a dynamic way (Ward & Beech, 2006). Genetic predispositions, developmental processes, and social learning have a significant impact upon brain development and result in the establishment of three interlocking neuropsychological systems, each associated with distinct functions and brain structures, and each linked to psychological and neurological adaptations. The three core psychological systems comprising the ITSO, and that in combination with social developmental and cultural factors are hypothesized to culminate in sexual offending, are: *motivation/emotional; perception and memory;* and *action selection and control.* These psychological systems are essential to the emergence of agency and the subsequent ability of organisms to identify threats to themselves, formulate (often multiple) goals and plans designed to address such threats and promote survival related goals, and, if necessary, engage in the revision of action plans and/or goals (see Chapter 8).

The *motivation and emotional system* is associated with cortical, limbic, and brainstem brain structures. According to Pennington (2002, p. 79), a major function of this system is, "...to allow goals and values to influence both perception and action selection rapidly and to adjust motivational state to fit changing environmental circumstances." Problems in an individual's genetic inheritance, cultural upbringing, or negative individual experiences may lead to defects in the motivational/emotional system. For example, someone who was brought up in an emotionally impoverished environment might find it difficult to identify his or her emotions in an accurate manner and also become confused when confronted with emotionally charged interpersonal situations. Such an individual might become anxious or angry and act in an antisocial manner on occasions. Another type of problem could be related to the range of needs or goals sought by a person. Impoverished early learning experiences could lead to an individual lacking the skills necessary (internal conditions) to establish strong interpersonal relationships and result in social isolation and further psychological and social deficits that could lead to sexual offending, such as intimacy problems (Marshall, 1989) or attachment problems (Beech & Mitchell, 2005; Ward, Hudson, & Marshall, 1996). These deficits in interpersonal functioning are the kinds of problems that researchers regard as a type of stable dynamic risk factor for sexual offending, i.e., causal psychological risk factors (see Chapter 8; Beech & Ward, 2004; Mann, Hanson, & Thornton, 2010). Thus, psychological vulnerabilities that have been described in the sexual offending literature as stable dynamic risk factors can be reconceptualized as disturbances in the motivation/emotional system.

The *action selection and control system* is associated with the frontal cortex, the basal ganglia, and parts of the thalamus. A major function of this system is to underpin individuals' capacity to plan, implement, and evaluate action plans, and to control behavior, thoughts, and emotions in service of higher level goals. The action selection and control system is concerned with the formation and implementation of action plans designed to achieve individuals' goals. It draws heavily upon the *motivation/emotional* system for the goals that effectively energize behavior and the *perception and memory* system (see the following section) for procedural and declarative knowledge (i.e., knowledge about how to do certain things, and relevant facts and information pertaining to a given situation). Problems that might arise from malfunctions in the action control and selection system essentially span self-regulation problems such as impulsivity, failure to inhibit negative emotions, inability to adjust plans to changing circumstances, and poor problem-solving skills (Ward et al., 2006).

Deficits in self-management/general self-regulation are exactly the kinds of problems that in the sexual offending literature have been described as a subset of stable dynamic risk factors (Mann et al., 2010). As we have argued previously, it is possible to view these "vulnerability factors" as essentially disturbances in the action selection and control system—in conjunction with input from the other two neuropsychological systems composing the ITSO.

The *perception and memory system* is associated primarily with the hippocampal formation and the posterior neocortex. A major function of this system is to process incoming sensory information and to construct representations of objects and events and make them available to the other two systems. Problems in the perceptual and memory system can lead to maladaptive beliefs, attitudes, and problematic interpretations of social encounters. A consequence of any impairment in this system is that the persons' experience of the world will be distorted in some way, and the evaluation of reasons for action and subsequent action plans would be more likely to result in suffering for the self and others. The presence of maladaptive beliefs that are chronically activated (i.e., frequently available to guide information processing) is likely to cause the subsequent activation of problematic goals and emotions, which in turn make it difficult for a person to effectively control his sexual behavior. We hypothesize that these cognitive structures can function as preattentive filters biasing the processing of social information and resulting in a variety of personal and social difficulties. These problems may underlie the kinds of offense supportive cognitions that Mann et al. (2010) regard as another particular type of stable dynamic risk factor for sexual offending. What have been termed *cognitive distortions* (Abel, Gore, Holland, Camp, Becker, & Rathner, 1989) is arguably caused by entrenched beliefs and subsequent biased information processing originating in the perception and memory system.

We need to stress that persons are not passive recipients of emotions or goals. Rather, individuals often arrive at reasons for acting in certain ways and can exercise their agency in seeking information, clarifying options, and in modifying aspects of themselves and their environments. In other words, although the exercise of agency depends on intact neuropsychological systems it is not identical with them. As discussed in Chapter 8, emotional, perceptual, and cognitive adaptations, in conjunction with relevant developmental experiences and social resources, enable individuals to acquire the capacities to formulate and implement plans that facilitate survival, and ideally, flourishing.

Rape

In recent years, several theories have been developed to explain rape from an evolutionary psychology viewpoint (e.g., Lalumière, Mishra, & Harris, 2008; Muller & Wrangham, 2009; Thornhill & Palmer, 2000; Ward et al., 2006). McKibbin et al. (2008, p. 104) argue that rape in human beings "must also reflect adaptations constructed over evolutionary time" and maintain that learning-based explanations are insufficient to account for such a complex behavior. In their view, rape is most likely an outcome of an adaptation or is the by-product of specific adaptations. McKibbin et al. opt for the view that rape is best conceptualized as a conditional mating strategy that occurs alongside others such as honest and deceptive courtship—although it seems to us that it follows from their analysis that, although some rapes are related to the mating domain, others are likely to be associated with specific personality traits or other domains such as aggression. McKibbin et al. (2008) hypothesize that there are five types of rapists, with each type associated with a specific suite of psychological modules that generate rape in response to specific environmental cues. First, some males find themselves at a reproductive disadvantage and have little or no legitimate access to female sexual partners. This may be because of their lower social status or simply a lack of mating opportunities. It is asserted that such individuals rape because they have no other realistic ways of having sex. Second, McKibbin hypothesized that there are individuals who have deviant sexual interests and who therefore are not sexually aroused by cues associated with consensual sex. Rather, their desires are elicited in the context of violence and coerced sexual activity. Third, some offenders have access to consenting mating partners but are motivated to take advantage of additional opportunities for sex, even if it involves rape. It is anticipated that such individuals may become disinhibited in certain situations, such as war, and on occasions view the benefits of rape as outweighing the costs. Fourth, there are psychopathic, dominant males who rape because their callousness and lack of empathy and concern for the well-being of others means there is no reason why they would not—in certain circumstances at least. For this type of rapist, the psychological mechanisms associated with rape are those that have (arguably) evolved as part of a psychopathic personality disorder (see the previous section). Finally, McKibbin et al. (2008) conjecture that men who are deeply insecure may rape their partners within the context of relationship problems. It is likely that in this situation, rape represents a conditional relationship strategy for dealing with conflict or perceived rejection.

Concerning the four types of biological explanations outlined earlier, it is apparent that for McKibbin et al., the *function* of rape is to secure access to copulation opportunities and therefore it has *evolved* within the context of mating or as another expression of a predatory personality style. The mental modules (*mechanisms*) generating rape behavior are thought to contain conditional decision rules based on partner availability, personal circumstances, and a range of specific mating strategies. The proximal causes will vary within the context of each type of rapist and are likely to result from different life histories or *developmental* factors. For example, as argued by Gao, Raine, Chan, Venables & Mednick (2010), a history of childhood neglect and abuse may cause some men to adopt a predatory, psychopathic style of interacting with other people that under certain circumstances could manifest in the form of sexual aggression.

When using niche construction to explain rape, greater attention is paid to the causal and independent role of culture and the physical and social environments in which individuals develop (Sterelny, 2012). There is less emphasis on discrete mental modules and more on the facilitative influence of social and cultural capital. The three types of inheritance—genetic, cultural, and ecological—are hypothesized to make independent contributions to mating behavior and the underlying mechanisms that generate specific sexual tactics. An illustration of a genetic predisposition might be males' hypothesized tendency to seek impersonal sex and to attempt to control females (Ellis, 1989). An example of a relevant cultural process might be the portrayal of females as sexual objects and males as sexually entitled to have sex when and where they want (Ward & Casey, 2010). A possible ecological process could be the physical segregation of males and females at school and the workplace leaving men with minimal opportunities to acquire more realistic understandings of women's needs and preferences. Thus an individual could enter the mating domain with several possible combinations of the above sets of three factors, resulting in varying degrees of rape-proneness (Sanday, 2003). For some males, the genetic predisposition (*origins*) toward sexual promiscuity (i.e., males consistently look for copulation opportunities while females are more oriented toward choosiness and long term mate selection) might interact with a mating learning environment (life history *or developmental cause*) in which females are routinely ridiculed and presented as inferior, and a culture in which they are not valued and are underrepresented in positions of power and influence. In this situation, a male could hold a schema portraying woman as always sexually available (proximal *mechanism*).

Although it is plausible to suggest that rape might have been specifically selected for (i.e., is an evolutionary adaptation), we think that our current best evolutionary explanation is more consistent with the view that rape is a by-product of other evolved adaptations, in combination with particular developmental and ecological contexts. Specifically, a greater tendency for men (relative to women) to seek impersonal sexual relationships, to dominate and control the sexual behavior of women (especially their partners), and to employ force for instrumental purposes, means that for some men, under certain circumstances, the likelihood of perpetrating sexual offenses is increased. As illustrated in Table 6.2, sexual coercion is not uncommon among extant hominid species, although it is not the *primary* mode of obtaining sexual access to females in any of the species with the possible exception of orangutans. This suggests that the use of force to obtain sexual access to females reflects more general male tendencies to dominate and control females for reproductive purposes, rather than specific adaptations for rape.

SUMMARY AND CONCLUSIONS

In this chapter, we have focused on Tinbergen's first two levels of explanation: adaptation and phylogeny. We have argued that, by taking a distal level of explanation, we can provide *salient* explanations for a number of key explanatory targets in criminology (Table 6.1). Very generally, an approach that draws on our understanding of the evolutionary function and evolutionary history of human behavior can help us to understand why humans commit crimes and why the prevalence of offending is strongly patterned by sex. We suggest that this level of analysis is essential for providing an epistemically satisfying account for these explanatory targets. We have further argued that the distal level of explanation can explain why humans have the capacity for aggression and violence, including sexual violence, and why these types of interpersonal crime are strongly patterned by gender and familial relationship. Explanatory accounts at other levels of analysis are of course relevant for understanding these phenomena, but are incomplete. An evolutionary approach, therefore, can add ontological depth to our understanding of particular types and patterns of offending and can, consequently, direct and guide research in important ways.

We have focused in the chapter exclusively on evolutionary approaches to understanding interpersonal violence. There were several reasons for this choice. First, there is simply more relevant research that is closely linked to evolutionary theory for this type of offending. Second, understanding interpersonal violence in its various manifestations is a central task for criminological theories and therefore a good place to consider the role of distal explanations. Finally, although our focus has been on interpersonal violence many of the arguments that we present here—for example, gender differences in rates of offending—hold for other types of crime as well and are likely to be explicable using the same set of theoretical assumptions. To briefly take two contrasting examples, both collective violence and drug addiction are likely to reflect the operation of evolved adaptations, but in different ways. For collective violence—a seemingly ubiquitous feature of human societies that also occurs among chimpanzee groups—it is plausible to suggest that our capacity to engage in intergroup aggression has been specifically selected for (Gat, 2009; van Vugt, 2009; Wrangham, 1999; Wrangham & Glowacki, 2012), although the evidence remains somewhat inconclusive (Durrant, 2011). For substance use and abuse—again, a seemingly near-ubiquitous features of human societies (Durrant & Thakker, 2003)—it is clear that the mechanisms that underlie our motivation to seek out and consume psychoactive drugs have *not* been specifically selected for, but rather reflect the action of drugs on evolved motivational–emotional systems (reward pathways) that have evolved for other reasons (see Durrant, Adamson, Todd, & Sellman, 2009; Nesse, 1994).

Although we have argued that distal explanations are *salient* for understanding the phenomena we consider in this chapter, the explanations they provide are clearly not complete. Importantly, we have to link distal explanations with developmental, proximate, and social-structural/ cultural explanatory accounts to provide a complete picture. Moreover, other levels of analysis are more *salient* for addressing other specific explanatory targets. In the next chapter, we turn to the developmental level of explanation and focus on how the insights of developmental criminologists can be integrated with those of life history theorists to provide explanations for patterns of offending by age, social class, and other individual difference factors.

7

Development

INTRODUCTION

Life on Earth has existed for approximately 3.5 billion years. Precisely how living entities emerged from inorganic matter remains a contentious topic, but it is generally agreed that the first organisms were simple, single prokaryotic cells. Indeed, multicellular life only emerged approximately 1.2 billion years ago, flowering into a multiplicity of complex shapes and forms during the so-called Cambrian explosion some 500 million years before the present (Levin, 2013). Some find the idea that the dazzling diversity of life that we can see today—from aardvarks to zebra fish—evolved from a common, single celled ancestor as manifestly absurd: how could such a primitive ancestor be transformed into something as large and complex as a horse, humpback whale, or a human? The vast expanse of geological time and the inexorable logic of natural selection provides the answer, but a more flippant—but no less veritable—response is to note that we all seem to manage it, and in 9 months no less. All humans begin life as a single, fertilized cell that rapidly divides and develops as organs take shape, the head emerges, and the skeletal system appears. At approximately 9 months, we are fully formed (although far from developmentally complete).

It is increasingly recognized that development plays a critical role in the evolutionary process (see Chapter 2). Furthermore, the idea that development simply reflects the deterministic construction of an organism based on a genetic "blueprint" has been largely supplanted by the view of development as a complex interactive process in which genes may provide a "recipe" but where the final outcome is contingent on the dynamic interplay between genes and all of the characteristics of an organism's environment (Bjorklund & Blasi, 2012). Organisms, therefore, may have characteristic, species-specific developmental trajectories (an aardvark raised in a human family is still an aardvark), but the interplay among genetic and environmental processes also generates substantial within-species diversity that is not purely predicated on the package of DNA nestled inside the organism's cells. In short, for many

© 2015 Elsevier Inc. All rights reserved.

evolutionary biologists (and, indeed, evolutionary behavioral scientists), development has moved to center stage in their explanatory narratives. The same could be said for a growing number of criminologists who recognize that antisocial and criminal behavior can be understood by locating individuals in their broad developmental context (Farrington, 2003; Laub, 2006). Buoyed in large part by the rich flow of information obtained from a large number of longitudinal studies, developmental and life course criminologists look to developmental processes to understand the emergence, persistence, and desistance of criminal behavior. Laub (2006), for instance, argues that life-course criminology represents the "soul of criminology" and a guiding paradigm for the discipline as a whole.

In the previous chapter, we explored how focusing on distal explanations, in terms of evolutionary function and history, can significantly advance our understanding of criminological phenomena. In the present chapter, we address Tinbergen's third level of explanation: ontogeny, or development. We first outline the key explanatory targets for developmental criminology. We highlight here the importance of explaining the overall shape of the age–crime curve, individual differences in the rate and prevalence of offending, and the factors that lead to desistance from crime. We then turn to a review of criminological explanations for these key explanatory targets, highlighting the most prominent developmental theories or models of offending. Recent advances in our understanding of the biosocial processes underpinning development provide a useful complement to these theories and we discuss some of the key findings emerging from this literature. We then consider how an evolutionary approach can contribute to our existing theoretical understanding of the developmental processes underlying criminal behavior. Drawing from life-history theory, we argue that a better understanding of the patterns of offending that are found can be obtained by considering both our species-specific life-history trajectory and how individual differences may reflect alternate life-history strategies in response to different environmental contexts.

EXPLANATORY TARGETS FOR DEVELOPMENTAL CRIMINOLOGY

There is now a rich body of knowledge concerning the nature and extent of offending across the lifespan. Much of this knowledge has been obtained from a number of longitudinal studies which have tracked individuals over time (see Farrington & Welsh, 2007, for an overview). Although not without their own problems, the value of prospective longitudinal research is clearly outlined by Farrington (2006, p. 123):

The main advantage…is that they provide information about the development of offending over time, including data on ages of onset and desistance, frequency and seriousness of offending, duration of criminal careers, continuity or discontinuity of offending, and specialization and escalation. They also provide information about developmental sequences, within-individual change, effects of life events and effects of risk and protective factors at different ages on offending at different ages.

Some of the key findings that have emerged from longitudinal studies and other types of research on offending across the lifespan are summarized in Table 7.1 (Farrington, 2003; see also Farrington, 2014; Piquero, Hawkins, & Kazemian, 2012). Although these findings are generally robust, as Farrington (2003) notes, it is important to recognize that most research has been conducted on Western populations, focuses on males, and concerns

TABLE 7.1 Key Explanatory Targets for the Developmental Level of Explanation

	Key explanatory targets
General life course patterns • The prevalence of offending is strongly patterned by age	The prevalence of offending peaks in late adolescence (aged 15–19)
	Onset of offending typically occurs between age 8 and 14 and desistance typically occurs between age 20 and 29
	Offending is more likely to occur with others during late adolescence (and individually in early adulthood and beyond)
	Reasons given for offending are highly varied in late adolescence whereas in adulthood utilitarian motives dominate
Offender- and offense-related patterns • There are individual differences in offending • Offending is part of a broader spectrum of antisocial behavior	A small percentage of the population commit a large percentage of all offenses
	An early age of onset typically predicts a longer and more active criminal career
	There is a continuity of offending from childhood to adulthood
	Offenders tend to be versatile rather than specialized
	Offending behavior is part of a broader pattern of antisocial behavior
	Different offenses have different life course trajectories
Factors relating to offending and desistance from offending	The main individual, family, school, and community risk factors for offending are well-recognized
	The main life events that are associated with desistance from offending in adulthood are well-recognized

Farrington (2003, pp. 223–225).

more common offenses such as theft, burglary, violence, and drug use and thus these patterns may not generalize to other populations or for other offense types.

General Life Course Patterns

It is widely accepted that the prevalence of offending is strongly related to age. The characteristic age–crime curve, first recognized by Quetelet (1833, cited in Loeber, 2012), describes a bell-shaped relationship between age and offending: prevalence rises sharply during late childhood and early adolescence, peaking during late adolescence (ages 15–19), and declining thereafter (Loeber, 2012; Loeber & Farrington, 2012; Piquero et al., 2012). The relationship between age and offending is robust. It is found in both cross-sectional and longitudinal studies and therefore does not reflect cohort effects. It is also uncovered in studies that employ both self-report measures of offending and official records and thus cannot be viewed as an artifact of features of the criminal justice system. Nor, as Brown and Males (2011) have recently claimed, is it the spurious outcome of age differences in economic status (Shulman, Steinberg, & Piquero, 2013). Indeed, Hirschi and Gottfredson (1983) boldly claimed that the age–crime curve is a universal and invariant feature of human populations. The shape of the curve, however, does vary somewhat depending on the type of offense examined (property offending peaks earlier than violent offending), gender (the curve peaks earlier and is lower for females), and socioeconomic status (the curve peaks earlier and is higher for individuals from disadvantaged neighborhoods) (Fabio, Tu, Loeber, & Cohen, 2011; Loeber, 2012, see also Greenberg, 2008). However, despite some minor variations in the shape of the age–crime curve, it is clear that adolescents are significantly more likely to commit offenses than individuals from other age groups, and thus one important task for developmental theories of offending is to explain this finding.

Young people are not only more likely to commit criminal offenses; the nature of their offending also varies (on average) compared with older individuals. One important finding that has been replicated in a number of studies is that co-offending (crime committed with others) is more common for younger compared with older offenders (Andresen & Felson, 2010; McCord & Conway, 2005; Stolzenberg & D'Alessio, 2008; Van Mastrigt & Farrington, 2009; Warr, 2002). For example, Van Mastrigt and Farrington (2009), looking at a sample of 61,646 offenders in the north of England between 2002 and 2005, found that 36.5% of individuals aged younger than 18 years committed offenses with others, compared with just 16.8% of offenders aged 18 and older. Co-offending is also more common for certain offenses such as burglary, robbery, theft, and arson compared with other types of crime. Some evidence also suggests that the reasons that young people give for offending are more likely to focus on such things as boredom, excitement, and emotions such as anger compared with older offenders who may offend for more obviously utilitarian reasons (Farrington, 2003).

Offender and Offense-Related Patterns

Several other, fairly robust, findings have emerged from research on criminal careers. One clear finding is that, although the overall prevalence of offending tends to peak during late adolescence, some individuals are more likely to engage in persistent serious offending compared with others. Indeed, many studies have found that a relatively small group of individuals commit a large fraction of all offenses (Farrington, 2003; Moffitt, 1993; Piquero, Jennings, & Barnes, 2012). Moreover, these individuals tend to have an earlier onset of offending, have higher rates of offending, and have longer criminal careers (Farrington, 2003). A good deal of effort has been exerted among researchers who investigate criminal careers to try to identify groups of offenders who vary in their trajectories of offending (Jennings & Reingle, 2012). Much of this research is largely consistent with Moffitt's (1993) dual developmental pathway model in which two main groups of offenders have been identified by their offending trajectories. One group—life course persistent offenders—is characterized by an early onset of problem behaviors, marked continuity in offending, and persistent offending across the life course. The other group—adolescent limited offenders—largely limits their offender career to adolescence and tends to desist from offending during early adulthood. It should be noted, however, that more complex taxonomies, with anywhere up to seven separate trajectory groups, have been proposed, and there is significant interest in both abstainers (those that do not offend at all) and adult-onset offenders (Jennings & Reingle, 2012).

Another important finding for our understanding of age-related offending patterns is that, generally speaking, offenders tend to be versatile, rather than specialized (Farrington, 2003; Piquero et al., 2012). In other words, offenders who engage in violent offenses are also more likely to perpetrate property and public disorder offenses and other types of crime. Indeed, individuals who are more likely to commit criminal offenses are also more likely to engage in a broad range of risky and antisocial behavior including drug use, heavy drinking, reckless driving, truancy, and sexual promiscuity (Farrington, 2003; Jessor, 1987). However, different offense types do tend to have different developmental trajectories, with the prevalence of property offending generally peaking before violent offending, and other types of offenses (e.g., fraud) demonstrating different life course trajectories (Farrington, 2003).

Factors Relating to Offending and Desistance from Offending

It is clear that there are marked individual differences in offending patterns across the lifespan. Thanks in large part to the wealth of data generated by longitudinal studies, criminologists have also developed a generally clear understanding of the main risk factors for offending and the key factors that tend to be related to desistance from offending in adulthood (see Table 7.2).

Strong relationships have been found for a number of individual level factors and offending. Low IQ (Fergusson, Horwood, & Ridder, 2005), low self-control or impulsivity (Caspi, 2000; White, Moffitt, Caspi, Bartusch, Needles, Stouthamer-Loeber, 1994), lack of empathy and the presence of callous-unemotional traits (Frick, Stickle, Dandreaux, Farrell, & Kimonis, 2005; Joliffe & Farrington, 2007), and attention deficit hyperactivity disorder (Brassett-Harknett & Butler, 2007) have all been found to increase the

TABLE 7.2   Risk Factors for Offending and Factors Relating to Desistance

RISK FACTORS FOR THE DEVELOPMENT OF ANTISOCIAL AND CRIMINAL BEHAVIOR

Individual	Low intelligence and school failure
	Low self-control/impulsiveness
	Low empathy/callous unemotional traits
	Attention deficit/hyperactivity disorder
Family	Antisocial parents, siblings, and relatives
	Parental conflict
	Child abuse and neglect
	Harsh or erratic parenting
	Lack of parental monitoring
Social	Low socioeconomic status
	Association with delinquent peers
	Poor school environment
	Deprived neighborhood/community

FACTORS RELATING TO DESISTANCE FROM OFFENDING IN ADULTHOOD

	Marriage
	Parenthood
	Meaningful employment

Farrington (2003, 2010).

likelihood of antisocial and criminal behavior. Characteristics of the family in which children are raised also have been found to strongly predict the development of antisocial and criminal behavior. Indeed, the available evidence strongly supports the idea that crime runs in families: having family members—parents, siblings, and other relatives—who engage in criminal behavior strongly predicts the likelihood of individual offending (Beaver, 2013; Farrington, Jolliffe, Loeber, Stouthamer-Loeber, & Kalb, 2001). Other important family risk factors for offending include parental conflict (Farrington & Welsh, 2007), child abuse and neglect (Gilbert, Widom, Browne, Fergusson, Webb, & Janson, 2009), harsh or erratic parenting, and lack of parental monitoring (Farrington & Welsh, 2007; Simons, Simons, Chen, Brody, & Lin, 2007). Finally, features of the broader social environment such as low socioeconomic status, association with delinquent peers, attendance at disadvantaged schools, and growing up in a deprived neighborhood have all been identified as risk factors for the development of antisocial behavior (Agnew, 2009; Farrington & Welsh, 2007).

It is important of course to remember that risk factors are just that: factors whose presence increases the risk for offending (see Chapter 8). A great deal is now known about the most important risk factors in the development of antisocial behavior, but much less is known about how these risk factors are related to offending. In other words, the causal pathways that link risk factors to offending have yet to be clearly elucidated (Rutter, 2003). In Chapter 8, we state why pinpointing the causal role of risk factors has been so problematic. In brief, it is because theorists have failed to grasp that risk factors—especially dynamic risk factors—are *composite constructs* and, as such, do not genuinely refer to real social and psychological processes.

It is probably fair to say that a greater deal more is known about the factors that are associated with the development of offending and individual differences in the risk of offending than is known about why individuals ultimately desist from offending. In part, this is because desistance factors are *protective factors* rather than risk variables (see Chapter 8). Aside from the effects of age itself, most researchers have focused on the role of engagement with prosocial institutions and practices such as marriage, parenting, and work (Horney, Tolan, & Weisburd, 2012). For males at least, marriage has been fairly consistently associated with reductions in offending, although the effect seems to be stronger for men who marry at an earlier age (Theobald & Farrington, 2009, 2010). Research on the impact of parenting on desistance from crime has revealed less clear-cut results, although parenting tends to lead to desistance when parents are more actively involved in raising their children (Horney et al., 2012). Research on the relationship between employment and crime has also generated somewhat mixed results. Obtaining employment does seem to contribute to a reduction in offending, but the nature of the job and perceptions of employment appear to play an important role in moderating this relationship (Horney et al., 2012).

Summary: What Needs to Be Explained?

Four key findings emerge from the literature on developmental and life course criminology. First, there are significant within-individual variations in offending, which means that the overall prevalence of offending tends to peak during late adolescence. Second, there are substantial between-individual variations in the nature and prevalence of offending such that some individuals are more likely to engage in serious persistent offending than others across the lifespan. Third, risk factors for offending (particularly serious, persistent offending) likely reflect the bidirectional interplay between a cluster of individual level characteristics (low self-control, callous-unemotional traits, low IQ, hyperactivity), features of the family (antisocial parents, abusive and neglectful parenting), and wider social environment (deprived neighborhoods, antisocial peers). Fourth, desistance from offending appears to be related to engagement with pro-social institutions such as work, parenting, and marriage, although the patterns are less clear than for risk factors. The task for developmental and life course theories in criminology is to clearly and effectively *explain* these findings. In the remainder of this chapter, we review efforts to account for the phenomena highlighted in this section with a focus on how evolutionary approaches can advance our explanatory understanding.

APPROACHES TO EXPLAINING DEVELOPMENTAL PATTERNS IN OFFENDING

Despite Hirschi and Gottfredson's (1983) claim that no known psychological or sociological variables can account for the age–crime curve, there has been no shortage of effort by criminologists and other social scientists to explain the peak in offending that occurs during adolescence. Similarly, there are a wide range of theories and models that attempt to explain the individual differences that are found in offending and the overall patterns of offending across the lifespan. Rather than provide a comprehensive overview of these approaches (see Farrington, 2003, 2006; Thornberry, et al., 2012, for good overviews; and Sweeten, Piquero, & Steinberg, 2013 for a recent empirical evaluation of developmental explanations for the age–crime curve), we focus in the section on the type of explanation that has typically been offered to account for developmental trends in antisocial and criminal behavior. We first examine approaches that emphasize the role of social and cultural processes, followed by a discussion of approaches that focus on psychological and biological mechanisms and processes, especially as they relate to normative maturational development.

Social and Cultural Processes

A fundamental tenet of much theoretical work in the social and behavioral sciences is that human behavior is strongly shaped by the social environment in which they are embedded. More specifically, humans acquire much of their knowledge of the world through a process of social or cultural learning. Akers' (1977) social learning theory of antisocial behavior is a good exemplar of this view. Drawing on Sutherland's (1947) idea that criminal and antisocial behavior is learned through a process of "differential association," Akers (1977) and Akers and Jensen (2010) maintain that antisocial and criminal behavior (and the cognitions underlying this behavior) arise through social learning processes such as imitation and differential reinforcement. A social learning perspective provides a ready and intuitively appealing explanation for individual differences in offending across the life span: some individuals, by virtue of their family and social environment, are more likely to be exposed to antisocial behavior (differential association), imitate that behavior, and develop attitudes and beliefs favorable to offending through a pattern of differential reinforcement. A social learning perspective can explain why crime tends to concentrate in families with antisocial parents, and why it is more likely to occur in disadvantaged neighborhoods and communities (which have a higher number of antisocial "models"). Social learning theory can also potentially account for the age–crime curve through the increased exposure to antisocial peers during adolescence.

Social learning theorists tend to downplay the role of innate characteristics and assume that crime, as with other kinds of behavior, is largely the result of specific social environments. Strain theorists share a similar view: humans are not "naturally" inclined toward antisocial behavior (indeed, the opposite is usually assumed) and thus intra- and interindividual differences in offending can be explained in terms of differences in the strain experienced by different individuals at different times of their lives (Agnew, 2003, 2006, 2011b; Baron & Agnew, 2014). According to General Strain Theory, the most recent and well-developed articulation within the strain tradition in criminology, "...a range of strains or negative events and conditions increase crime. These strains lead to negative emotions, such as anger, which create much pressure for corrective action" (Baron & Agnew, 2014, p. 118). Relevant strains may include the failure to achieve positively valued goals, removal of positively valued stimuli, and the presentation of negative stimuli. The impact of strains on offending, however, varies depending on the magnitude of the strain, the subjective interpretation of the strain, and the capacity of the individual to cope with strains in noncriminal ways.

Individual differences in offending across the lifespan are readily explained from a strain perspective in terms of individual differences in the exposure to strains that result in criminal behavior. Thus, life course persistent offenders tend to maintain a high rate of offending across the lifespan "because such offenders are more likely to experience strain, interpret such strain as highly aversive, and engage in criminal coping *over much of their lives*" (Baron & Agnew, 2014, p. 120, italics in original). Risk factors for offending such as child abuse and neglect, parental conflict, and low socioeconomic status thus contribute to high levels of strain among certain groups of individuals. Moreover, these individuals tend to have individual risk factors—in particular, low self-control and negative emotionality—that reduce their capacity to respond to strains in less antisocial ways (Baron & Agnew, 2014). The peak in offending that occurs during adolescence is explained by General Strain Theory in that adolescents experience more strains and therefore are more likely to respond to such strains with criminal and antisocial behavior (Agnew, 2003, 2006). Strains increase during adolescence, according to Agnew (2006), because young people have to negotiate an increasingly demanding social world yet have not obtained the status and resources to realize their goals for autonomy and the other privileges of adulthood. Moreover, adolescents are more likely to view such strains as aversive as they tend to be lower in self-constraint and higher on negative emotionality and are likely to respond in an antisocial way taking into account that they are less likely to receive conventional forms of social support (Baron & Agnew, 2014).

A third major theoretical tradition in criminology that has engaged with the issue of life course patterns in criminal behavior is the social control tradition. Sampson and Laub's life course theory of crime provides the most recent and well developed exemplar of such an approach (Laub, 2006; Laub, Sampson, & Sweeten, 2006; Sampson & Laub, 2005). Central to this perspective is the idea that "crime is more likely to occur when an individual's bond to society is attenuated" (Laub et al., 2006, p. 314). Informal social control that arises through attachment to conventional institutions, such as the family, school, work, and marriage, plays a key role in explaining individual difference in offending across the lifespan. In short, continuity in offending across the lifespan can be explained in terms of the persistence of weak social bonding and, therefore, limited informal social control. Desistance from offending is explained in terms of increased social bonding that arises through engagement with prosocial institutions such as marriage, parenting, and work that may serve as "turning points" in the lives of individuals. Sampson and Laub's (2005) theory can thus potentially account for individual differences in offending because of differences in social bonding and provides an explanation for the desistance from offending that often accompanies marriage, work, and parenting. Sampson and Laub (2005) tend to downplay the importance of the adolescent peak in offending by noting substantial variation in individual age–crime trajectories. The social control perspective can, however, potentially accommodate the aggregate age–crime relationship by noting the decline in social control that is experienced by adolescents relative to both children and adults (Agnew, 2003).

Social processes are also highlighted in a number of integrated theories or models that have been developed to explain patterns of offending across the lifespan. In Moffitt's (1993, 2006) widely cited dual developmental pathway model, for example, the high prevalence of offending during adolescence is attributed to the relatively large proportion of adolescent limited offenders whose offending careers are largely restricted to adolescence and young adulthood. Moffitt incorporates elements of social bonding and social learning theory along with important cultural-historical shifts in developmental patterns to account for the offending pattern of this group. Moffitt argues that historical shifts in the length of adolescence in Western societies (puberty begins earlier, and adult roles and responsibilities are deferred until later) creates a "maturity gap" in which young people are biologically mature yet are denied adult roles and responsibilities. Deviant peers, who have seemingly accrued a greater deal of autonomy and the trappings of adult status, become salient role models and subsequently influence the offending behavior of adolescent limited offenders. Farrington's (2003) integrated cognitive antisocial potential model also integrates elements of social bonding, strain theory, and social learning theory to account for between-individual differences in "antisocial potential" that gives rise to differences in offending across the lifespan, whereas within-individual variations in offending are influenced by features of the social environment (deviant peers, alcohol use, routine activities).

Social processes are clearly important for addressing many of the phenomena outlined in Table 7.1. However, these approaches need to be supplemented with a richer understanding of the biosocial processes underpinning development (Walsh & Bolen, 2012). In particular, to understand developmental patterns in offending, it is essential to recognize the way that individual differences can arise through gene × environment interactions, and to understand the normative biological and psychological features of adolescent development that can account for distinctive age-related effects.

A Biosocial Perspective

Adolescence is generally regarded as a biosocial phenomenon that begins with the biological changes associated with puberty and ends with the attainment of adult roles and responsibilities (Dahl, 2004). As such, although there are important biological changes occurring during this period that we outline, in the following section, the nature and length of adolescence as a developmental period varies somewhat cross-culturally and historically (Arnett, 1999, 2000; Moffitt, 1993). Adolescence is generally regarded as a developmental period in which a range of problem behaviors become prevalent. Although adolescence is not always a period of "storm and stress" (Arnett, 1999), it is clear that adolescents are at an elevated risk for engaging in a variety of problem behaviors including risk-taking, drug use, binge drinking, unprotected sex, and criminal offending (Reyna & Farley, 2006). However, research suggests that the elevated risk profile of adolescents does not arise through a failure to *understand* the risks associated with certain behaviors (Reyna & Farley, 2006, 2007). Rather, it appears that normative aspects of adolescent neurodevelopment can potentially account, in part, for the increased prevalence of risk taking (and criminal offending) that occurs during this period.

Puberty involves a cluster of biological changes that are fundamentally concerned with sexual maturation. These include the beginning of menstruation in girls, and the development of secondary sexual characteristics: increased muscle mass, the lowering of the voice, and facial hair in boys, and breast growth and changes in body shape for girls (Walsh & Bolen, 2012; Weisfeld & Janisse, 2005). These biological changes are driven by the reactivation of the hypothalamic-pituitary-gonadal axis that results in dramatic changes in levels of sex hormones, including testosterone and estradiol (Peper & Dahl, 2013; Rosenfeld & Nicodemus, 2003). Although testosterone increases by a factor of ten during this period for boys, most researchers generally agree that it plays an indirect role in influencing aggressive and antisocial behavior in young men (Archer, 2006a; Mazur, 2009), in part through its organizational effects on developing neural systems (Peper & Dahl, 2013). Of more direct relevance to our understanding of the behavioral changes in adolescence that are related to criminal and antisocial activities are important changes that are occurring in the adolescent brain.

According to the dual systems model of adolescent risk-taking, two critical features of adolescent neurodevelopment account for the heightened risk-taking that is found during this developmental period (Steinberg, 2007, 2010; see also Crone & Dahl, 2012; Somerville & Casey, 2010; Spear, 2013). First, it appears that the pervasive attraction to risky behavior that is demonstrated among adolescents can be related to heightened sensitivity in parts of the brain that are implicated in reward processing, including the ventral striatum (Galván, 2010, 2013; Spear, 2013). In short, adolescents, compared with both older and younger individuals, appear to be more motivated to seek out exciting, risky, and stimulating activities in part because of elevated activity in the brain regions related to reward (see Chapter 8 for an in-depth analysis of the relationship between norms, goals, contexts, and action sequences, including antisocial actions).

Second, the mechanisms underlying self-regulation and the inhibitory control of behaviors are not fully developed until the early 20s. More specifically, prefrontal regions of the brain and their connections to other components of the cognitive control system develop in a linear fashion from childhood to adult with incremental improvements in the capacity for self-control during this time period (Casey & Caudle, 2013; Somerville & Casey, 2010; Steinberg, 2007). The picture provided by the dual systems model is, therefore, clear: adolescent risk-taking can be accounted for, in part, due to an imbalance or asynchrony in the developmental timing of neurocognitive systems underlying reward (earlier development) and cognitive control (later development).

Another important feature of adolescent development, with implications for understanding the peak in risk taking and criminal offending that occurs during this period, is the widely recognized heightened susceptibly of adolescents to peer influence. As noted previously, adolescents are significantly more likely to commit offences with other individuals than are adult offenders. Moreover, association with deviant peers is one of the more robust risk factors for adolescent offending (Jacard, Blanton, & Dodge, 2005). Many scholars have worried over whether these findings reflect selection effects (deviant peers are more likely to associate with deviant others) or the direct result of peer influence (socialization) and it is likely that both processes are important (Ingram, Patchin, Huebner, McCluskey, & Bynum, 2007; Monahan, Cauffman, & Steinberg, 2009; Young, Rebellon, Barnes, & Weerman, 2014). However, experimental research clearly indicates that adolescent risk-taking is heightened in the presence of peers (Gardner & Steinberg, 2005; Weigard, Chein, Albert, Smith, & Steinberg, 2014) and that this effect seems to be mediated by enhanced activation in the brain regions underlying reward (Albert, Chein, & Steinberg, 2013; Chein, Albert, O'Brien, Uckert, & Steinberg, 2011). More generally, adolescence is a period that involves heightened sensitivity to social relations and adolescents are particularly sensitive to cues underlying social acceptance and exclusion which appear to be underpinned by developing neurocognitive systems (Blakemore & Mills, 2014; Somerville, 2013). As summarized by Somerville (2013, p. 125):

> Convergent evidence suggests that adolescents display heighted sensitivity to social evaluation at various levels of complexity...these features...appear to be instantiated by robust response properties in neural circuitry important to assigning value to social-affective information during adolescence.

Although the emerging picture of adolescent biosocial development and its relationship to risk-taking and criminal behavior is generally well-supported, it should be noted that the dual systems model of adolescent risk-taking has received criticism from some scholars.

For example, Pfeifer and Allen (2012) argue that it fails to account for the complexity of developmental variation in brain function (Pfeifer & Allen, 2012), whereas others have challenged its value in explaining the actual pattern of risk-taking behavior that occurs (Willoughby, Good, Adachi, Hamza, & Tavernier, 2013), and whether it reflects cross-culturally (Choudhury, 2010) and historically (Feixa, 2011) universal patterns of brain development. More research will, no doubt, help to clarify these issues (Strang, Chein, & Steinberg, 2013) and clearly the broader role of social context is relevant to understanding risk-taking behavior. However, adolescence as a developmental period appears to be cross-culturally universal (Schlegel, 1995; Schlegel & Hewlett, 2011) and, as we discuss in more detail later, is likely to be an evolved feature of the human life history with characteristic functional properties that are linked to features of biological development.

The dual systems model of risk-taking can provide a partial explanation for the peak in offending that is seen during adolescence. However, it is clear that there are significant individual differences in the nature, onset, and duration of offending among individuals. Developmental criminologists widely recognize, for example, that a small number of individuals are responsible for a significant proportion of crime (see Table 7.1). Moreover, there appears to be a marked continuity in antisocial behavior from childhood to adulthood with longitudinal research clearly supporting the idea that personality traits and antisocial behavior in childhood predict offending in later life (e.g., Moffitt, Caspi, Harrington, & Milne, 2002). Finally, there is an abundance of research that suggests that crime runs in families: having a family member who engages in criminal and antisocial behavior is an important risk factor for offending (Beaver, 2013; Farrington & Welsh, 2007). For example, the Pittsburgh Youth Study found that 43% of all arrests in the sample were experienced by only 8% of families (Farrington, et al., 2001). Clearly there are individual difference factors that appear to emerge early in development and that make some individuals more crime prone than others. Although most criminologists have focused on the role of early developmental environments (family, neighborhood) in influencing antisocial behavior, as Boutwell (2014) notes, children not only inherit environments from their parents; they also inherit genes. Understanding individual differences in offending therefore necessitates a focus on the role of both genes *and* environment and how the two interact in the origin of antisocial behavior.

As illustrated in Table 7.2, the early environmental risk factors for later antisocial behavior are generally well recognized. Children who grow up in environments characterized by abuse, neglect, overly harsh and erratic parenting, poverty, and neighborhood deprivation are at an elevated risk for offending in later life (Farrington, 2003, 2010). The psychological characteristics that are related to childhood antisocial behavior are also well studied: children who are impaired on a range of neurocognitive functions, including the capacity to regulate behavior, are at a risk for later offending (e.g., van Goozen, Fairchild, & Harold, 2008; Moffitt, 2000; Raine et al., 2005). Finally, behavior genetic research using twin and adoption designs typically find that around 40–50% of the variation in antisocial and criminal behavior can be attributed to genetic factors (see Baker, Bezdjian, & Raine, 2006; Moffitt, 2006; Rhee & Waldman, 2002). The overarching picture that these various lines of research suggest is one in which neurocognitive factors underpin many of the important individual differences in offending and that these factors are influenced by both the genes and the environments in which children inherit from their parents. As van Goozen et al. (2008, p. 227) conclude: "It is likely that the origin of antisocial behavior in young children lies in this combination of a difficult temperament and a harsh environment in which there is ineffective socialization."

This picture might suggest that genes and the environment are both important but have *separate* effects on the development of antisocial behavior. However, there is a growing recognition of the importance of gene–environment *interactions* in explaining individual differences in a wide range of characteristics, including antisocial behavior (see Manuck & McCaffery, 2014, for a review). As Beaver, Nedelec, Schwartz, & Connolly (2014, p. 127), succinctly note:

> …gene–environment interactions refer to the idea that the effects that genes have are contingent on the presence of certain environmental stimuli and, conversely, that the effects that environments have are contingent on the presence of certain genetic factors.

A pivotal study demonstrating the role of gene–environmental interactions for the development of antisocial behavior was carried out by Caspi et al. (2002). This research demonstrated that the effect of exposure to maltreatment in childhood on antisocial behavior in later life was moderated by genetic factors. Specifically, children who had a genotype that coded for low MAOA activity (an enzyme that functions to metabolize neurotransmitters) were at a significantly greater risk for antisocial behavior later in life compared with children with a genotype for high MAOA activity. For children who were not exposed to maltreatment, there was no difference in the risk for antisocial behavior in later life for the two groups. A recent meta-analysis of the role of MAOA and childhood maltreatment on antisocial behavior (Byrd & Manuck, 2014) largely supports the gene–environment interaction revealed in the study by Caspi et al. (2002), and there is now a significant body of research supporting the role of gene–environment interactions in the ontogeny of antisocial and criminal behavior (see Beaver & Connolly, 2013, Beaver et al., 2014).

This research has underlined the *plasticity* of genetic influences on behavior and how features of the environment play a critical role in the regulation and expression of genetic effects—a process known as epigenetics (Walsh & Yun, 2014; see discussion on the extended evolutionary synthesis in Chapter 2). Two main models have dominated attempts to understand the interaction of genes and environments: the diathesis stress model and the differential susceptibility model (Beaver & Connolly, 2013; Bakermans-Kranenburg & van Ijzendoorn, 2015).

According to the diathesis–stress model, negative outcomes (such as antisocial behavior) arise through the pairing of genetic risk factors (vulnerable genotypes) with environmental adversity: individuals dealt a poor genetic hand will only experience adverse outcomes when located in risky environments that "trigger" or "release" the latent risk posed by their genetic potential. The differential susceptibility model, in contrast, proposes that there are individual differences in the *susceptibility* to environmental influences. Some individuals, by virtue of their genotype, are more responsive to environmental influences "for better or for worse": in adverse environments they are more likely to display negative outcomes and in more supportive environments they are more likely to experience enhanced functioning (Belsky & Pluess, 2009, 2013; Ellis & Boyce, 2005, 2011; Ellis, Boyce, Belsky, Bakermans-Kranenburg, & Ijzendoorn, 2011). Several studies provide support for the differential susceptibility hypothesis and it seems that some individuals, by virtue of their genes, are more responsive to environments in ways that can lead to outcomes that increase the likelihood of antisocial behavior in some contexts and increase the likelihood of *prosocial* behavior in others (Bakermans-Kranenburg & van Ijzendoorn, 2011; Belsky & Beaver, 2011; Simons & Lei, 2013).

It is likely that both the diathesis stress model and the differential susceptibility model can account for the gene–environment interactions that are found in research and both processes are likely to be in play. In addition, Pluess and Belsky (2013) propose—in what is in many respects the mirror image of diathesis stress—that some individuals may have genotypes that make them more responsive to positive experiences, a phenomenon they term "vantage sensitivity." Further empirical research will help to disentangle these different gene–environment interactions as more detailed linkages are made between genes, neurobiological and psychophysiological processes, and behavior. However, this body of research is important for our understanding of how antisocial behavior develops because it begins to tackle an enduring puzzle in developmental criminology: why do some individuals who grow up in criminogenic environments go on to become persistent offenders while others do not (Beaver et al., 2014)? There are also potential implications for prevention efforts that we will touch on in Chapter 10 (see Bakermans-Kranenburg & van Ijzendoorn, 2015).

Summary

An approach that integrates biological, psychological, social, and cultural factors can make significant strides toward addressing the explanatory targets outlined in Table 7.1. The importance of social processes in understanding patterns of criminal and antisocial behavior across the lifespan is clear. There seems little doubt that social learning processes are essential for understanding the development of antisocial and criminal behavior (Pratt, Cullen, Sellers, & Gau, 2010) and can play a role in accounting for individual differences in offending. Individuals, by virtue of their social environment, are exposed to different models and their behaviors are subject to different contingencies of reinforcement. Because antisocial and criminal behavior essentially involves the violation of shared societal norms (see Chapter 4), it is also clear that the extent to which an individual invests in and is socially bonded to conventional institutions and groups will influence offending. Attention to biological processes can enrich this picture in important ways. First, understanding the normative maturational changes that occur during adolescence can assist us to further understand why this period is one that involves heightened risk-taking, particularly in the company of peers. A consideration of genetic factors and gene–environment interactions can also help to account for individual differences in offending across the lifespan and how these are influenced by environmental factors. In short, we believe that a biopsychosocial perspective on human development is *salient* for addressing the key explanatory targets presented in Table 7.1.

In the remainder of the chapter, we make the case that an evolutionary perspective is *relevant* for understanding developmental patterns in offending and that it can enrich our understanding of the biological, psychological and social processes that we have outlined (ontological depth), in ways that can promote productive lines of research (epistemological worth). There is some scope, for example, to extend the social learning perspective by considering insights from the evolutionary literature on cultural learning. In particular, a recognition that social learning is shaped by specific content, model-based, and frequency dependent biases (Mesoudi, 2011a; see Chapter 3) may help to develop a more fine-grained understanding of how specific social learning contexts shape antisocial behavior. Variables associated with social learning theory—particularly association with antisocial peers, gang membership, and peer pressure—can also potentially account for the overall shape of the age–crime curve as peers become a more powerful source of social influence during adolescence.

However, missing from a social learning perspective is an account of *why* peer influence increases its salience during adolescence and declines thereafter (Agnew, 2003). A social learning perspective is also less informative about the processes that result in desistance from offending during adulthood. A social bonding perspective, although valuable, also needs to account for the developmentally recurrent differences in social bonding that occur across the lifespan and *why* they should be related to criminal behavior. An evolutionary perspective can also help us to understand the neurodevelopmental literature by considering how the developmental changes associated with adolescence may reflect selection pressures on developing brain systems in the service of reproductive outcomes. More broadly, situating human development within a life history framework can assist us in making sense of both how and why different environmental contexts lead to different developmental outcomes and why these might be moderated by individual differences in susceptibility to rearing.

EVOLUTIONARY APPROACHES

Humans, like all other species, have a characteristic life history that reflects the recurrent selection pressures faced by our ancestors. Development does not involve a simple scaling up of babies into adults, but rather a series of developmental stages characterized by key transitions that involve "the strategic allocation of an organism's energy toward growth, maintenance and reproduction" (Hochberg & Belsky, 2013, p. 2). As we discussed in Chapter 2, life-history theory concerns how developing organisms make tradeoffs between investment in growth, body maintenance and learning (i.e., *somatic effort*), and *reproductive effort*, including investment in mating and parenting (Del Giudice, Angeleri & Manera, 2009). Different stages of the human life history will involve a relative different focus on these central developmental tasks. The key life-history stages and periods of human development are outlined in Table 7.3 with important biological milestones contrasted with those of chimpanzees.

The human life history is somewhat unusual: we are a long-lived species with a truncated gestation time, a lengthy period of juvenile development, and a postreproductive stage. We also experience relatively low mortality rates and have high rates of fertility (Gurven, 2012; Kuzawa & Bragg, 2012). Human infants typically wean at around 24 months of age, which is half the age of weaning in chimpanzees. Unlike chimpanzees and other primates human development is characterized by a childhood period in which individuals are weaned, but still highly dependent on the care of others (mothers and alloparents) for their nutritional needs. Researchers suggest that childhood evolved around the time of *Homo habilis* and

TABLE 7.3 Life History Stages and Periods of Development in Humans (and Chimpanzees)

Periods of development[a]	Developmental stages[b,d]	Key biological milestones[c] (humans)	Key biological milestones[c] (chimpanzees)
Prenatal period (conception to birth)	Prenatal period	Gestation: 269 days	Gestation: 228 days
Infancy (birth to 18–24 months)	Infancy (birth to 2–3 years)	Weaning: 24 months[e]	Weaning: 48 months[e]
Early childhood (2–5 years)	Childhood (2–3 to 7 years)		
Middle and late childhood (6–11 years)	Juvenility (7 to 10–12 years)	Adrenarche: 6–8 years[b]	
Adolescence (10–12 to 18–21 years)	Adolescence and early adulthood (10–12 to 18–24 years)	Weaning to menarche: 12.9 years	Weaning to menarche: 5 years
Early adulthood (20s–30s)	Mature adult	Menarche to first reproduction: 4.1 years	Menarche to first reproduction: 3 years
Middle adulthood (40s–50s)	Postreproductive (females)	Life expectancy at age 15: 52.7 years	Life expectancy at age 15: 29 years
Late adulthood (60s–70s to death)		Maximum life span: 121 years	Maximum life span: 66 years

[a] Santrock (2012, p. 14).
[b] Del Giudice, Angeleri, & Manera (2009).
[c] Gurven (2012).
[d] Del Giudice & Belsky (2011).
[e] Thompson (2013).

served a number of functions, including enhanced fertility (by freeing mothers from direct provisioning, it shortened interbirth intervals), the promotion of brain development and learning, and an extended "assessment period" in which local ecological conditions could be evaluated and subsequent behavioral strategies could be adaptively mapped to key features of the environment (Del Giudice, Angeleri & Manera, 2009; Kuzawa & Bragg, 2012; see our discussion in the following section). After childhood is a period labeled "juvenility" (or what developmental psychologists term "middle and late childhood") beginning at around the age of 7. This period involves physiological changes such as the secretion of androgens from the adrenal glands ("adrenarche"), a growth spurt followed by deceleration of growth, the emergence of the first molars, and the brain reaching its adult size (Hochberg & Belsky, 2013).

II. EXPLAINING CRIME

After juvenility is adolescence, which is an extended period in humans characterized by rapid growth, a cascade of sex-differentiated physiological changes, and the direction of energetic resources into mating effort and related tasks, such as the negotiation of social hierarchies. As Ellis et al. (2012, p. 599) summarize:

> ...adolescence is fundamentally a transition from the pre-reproductive to the reproductive phase of the life span. The developing person reallocates energy and resources toward transforming into a reproductively competent individual. From an evolutionary perspective, a major function of adolescence is to attain reproductive status—to develop the physical and social competencies needed to gain access to a new and highly contested biological resource: sex and, ultimately, reproduction.

From an evolutionary perspective, the heightened risk taking that is seen during adolescence (and the associated increase in the prevalence of offending), the greater importance of peers and social relations with others, and the increase in the intensity of intrasexual aggression reflect the developmental importance of adolescence as a time for attracting and maintaining mates and for establishing social status (Bjorklund & Hawley, 2014; Ellis et al., 2012; Kruger & Nesse, 2006; Wilson & Daly, 1985).

The various biological, psychological, and social changes that occur during adolescence, therefore, can be viewed as characteristics that have been selected for because of their role in advancing reproductive success. Thus the increase in sensation seeking and risk-taking that is linked to heightened activity in the brain's reward circuitry that emerges during mid-adolescence (whereas cognitive control systems are not yet fully mature) is not simply an accidental by-product of neural development, but is likely to reflect design for enhanced risk-taking during this period. Similarly, the finding that risk-taking is enhanced in the presence of peers (and that co-offending is significantly more common during adolescence) is because the primary evolutionary function of risk-taking and both intra- and intersexual competition is to obtain social status and to signal to others one's reproductive value—performing dangerous stunts in the privacy of your own bedroom makes little sense. Consistent with our analysis in Chapter 6, although risk-taking, sensation seeking, and intrasexual aggression increase for both boys and girls during adolescence the magnitude of these changes is significantly greater for boys as reflected in the sharp rise in the ratio of male to female mortality during adolescence, peaking at three male deaths for every female death during the 20- to 24-year age range (Kruger & Nesse, 2006, see also Shulman, Harden, Chein, & Steinberg, 2014).

Although humans, like other species, have a characteristic species-specific life history, a life-history framework is also valuable for understanding important *individual differences* in life-history strategies (with implications for antisocial and criminal behavior) and how these are related to features of the developmental environment. Because ecological conditions might change from one generation to the next and thus affect how individuals should best negotiate the social and physical world, it is argued that a degree of phenotypic flexibility in life-history behavior is an evolved feature of humans, perhaps arising in part because of the rapidly fluctuating nature of environmental conditions during the Pleistocene (Kuzawa & Bragg, 2012; Wells, 2012). From an evolutionary developmental perspective, there are four plausible pathways that can account for individual differences in antisocial and prosocial behavior (Figures 7.1 and 7.2). As depicted in Figure 7.1, individual differences may be predominantly genetically based (model A) and arise through either stochastic processes (i.e., are nonadaptive) or else are the product of frequency dependent selection (see the discussion in Chapter 6). Individual differences may also arise because of exposure to extreme environmental contexts (model B) that lie outside of the "normal" range that humans would have experienced during their evolutionary history. Such environments are likely to lead to psychopathology that may also be linked to antisocial outcomes. Although these two models are likely to capture some of the individual variation in antisocial behavior that is found in human populations, we will mainly focus on the two models that are illustrated in Figure 7.2. We first outline how natural selection may have shaped life-history strategies to facultatively adjust to different environmental conditions (model D), and then consider how differences in susceptibly to environmental influence may also have been selected to generate reproductively advantageous outcomes (model C).

As we outlined in Chapter 2, life-history theory concerns how organisms make tradeoffs in the allocation of resources to various life-history tasks, with life-history strategies arrayed on a continuum from "faster" to "slower." Life-history theory predicts that there are individual differences *within* species in terms of the life-history strategy that is "pursued" because the most adaptive behavioral patterns will depend on specific features of the environment. As illustrated in Table 7.4 for humans, faster life-history strategies entail more rapid rates of development, earlier puberty, more casual sexual relationships, earlier reproduction, more offspring, a shorter time horizon, and a tendency to seek out immediate gratification. Slower life-history strategies entail the opposite patterns (Bjorklund & Ellis, 2014; Ellis et al., 2012). We should also note here that the most important components of these life-history strategies are different for men compared with women. Because of differences in parental investment and thus the potential rate of reproduction, it is expected that males more than females will be motivated to pursue fast life-history strategies focused on successful intrasexual competition that results in an increase in reproductive opportunities. Because females cannot significantly increase their reproductive success by obtaining access to more mates, a faster life-history strategy for women is likely to involve faster development, earlier onset of puberty, and

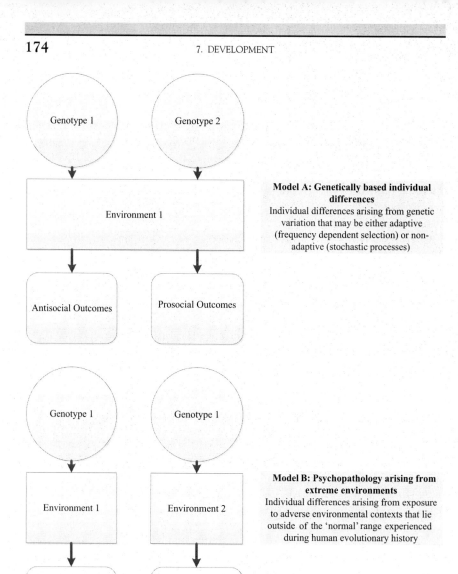

FIGURE 7.1 Evolutionary developmental models for understanding individual differences in antisocial and prosocial behavior: the role of genetics and environment.

earlier age of reproduction (Bjorklund & Ellis, 2014). In sum, it is argued that natural selection has favored *adaptive phenotypic plasticity* so that developing organisms adjust their behavior in ways that are likely to best serve their reproductive interests (which also depend on their sex) in the environments in which they are embedded (West-Eberhard, 2003).

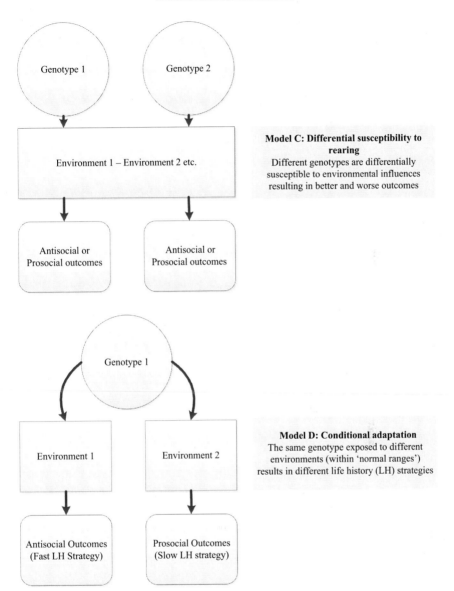

FIGURE 7.2 Evolutionary developmental models for understanding individual differences in antisocial and prosocial behavior: adaptive phenotypic plasticity.

There are a number of different models of life-history development in humans that largely converge in terms of their underlying assumptions (Belsky, 2012). However, probably the most fully realized current model of life-history strategies in humans is the Adaptive Calibration Model (ACM) developed by Bruce Ellis, Marco Del Guidice, and

TABLE 7.4   Faster and Slower Life Histories

	Slower life history	Faster life history
PHYSIOLOGY		
Rates of development	Slower	Faster
Onset of puberty	Later	Earlier
Biological aging	Slower	Faster
MATING		
Sexual debut	Later	Earlier
Sexual partners	Less	More
Relationships	Pair-bond	Casual
PARENTING		
Age of reproduction	Later	Earlier
Number of offspring	Fewer	More
Investment in offspring	Higher	Lower
ECONOMIC PSYCHOLOGY		
Time horizon	Long	Short
Immediate gratification	Delay	Seek
Risk losses for big gain	Avoid	Take

Ellis et al. (2012), Figure 7.1.

colleagues (Del Giudice, 2009; Del Giudice & Belsky, 2011; Del Giudice, Ellis, & Shirtcliff, 2013; Ellis & Del Giudice, 2014). Central to the ACM is the idea that humans make shifts in their life-history strategy at key periods or "inflection points" in development in response to prevailing life-history conditions. Ultimately, the function of these shifts is to better match behavioral strategies to the likely environments that will be experienced during adulthood. Three critical aspects of the early developmental environment are argued to play a key role in this process: (1) resource availability; (2) extrinsic morbidity/mortality (harshness); and (3) unpredictability (Ellis, Figueredo, Brumbach, & Schlomer, 2009). In environments characterized by very low resource levels (e.g., malnutrition, extreme energetic stress), it is argued that slow life-history strategies are likely to be entrained with slower growth and later reproduction. However, given an adequate level of nutrition to support growth and development, faster life-history strategies are likely to emerge in environments characterized by higher levels of extrinsic morbidity and mortality (i.e., higher levels of violence, disability, and death) and greater environmental unpredictability (i.e., more changes in residence, family structure, and resource availability). The evolutionary logic of this model is relatively straightforward: when the environment provides cues that indicate that premature mortality is more likely, or that future environments cannot be predicted it pays the developing organism to shift to life-history strategies characterized by earlier puberty and sexual debut (for women) and greater risk-taking, intrasexual competition, and mating effort (for males). In short, life-history strategies are developed to increase the likelihood of successful reproduction in environments that are more likely to lead to earlier death or disability. Thus, according to the ACM, humans have evolved to facultatively adjust their life-history strategies to match critical aspects of the developmental environment.

We should make it clear here that although we have talked of life-history "strategies," the ACM does not suggest that humans *consciously* readjust their behavior to match features of the environment. Rather, the stress response system (SRS) is argued to play the key mediating role. The SRS comprises three main physiological systems: the sympathetic nervous system, the parasympathetic nervous system, and the hypothalamus-pituitary-adrenal axis, with its primary function to "coordinate the organism's physiological and behavioral responses to environmental threats and opportunities" (Del Giudice et al., 2013, p. 29). The SRS thus takes in critical information about the environment and uses that information to coordinate physical and behavioral responses on a wide range of life-history-relevant traits. In dangerous or unpredictable environments, it is argued that a more responsive SRS develops to facilitate vigilance to environmental threats that, for males, involves the development of an agonistic behavioral pattern with heightened sensitivity to threat-related cues. In environments characterized by extreme stress (e.g., serious trauma, exposure to persistent and high levels of violence), the SRS becomes hyporesponsive, leading to a highly unemotional pattern of stress responsivity and, for males, a fast life history characterized by high levels of competition and risk taking. Ellis et al. (2012, p. 600) provide a clear summary of the model:

> The evolutionary model posits that natural selection shaped human neurobiological mechanisms to detect and respond to the fitness-relevant costs and benefits afforded by different environments. Most important, these responses are not arbitrary but function adaptively to calibrate developmental and behavioral strategies to match those environments...Thus, stressful environments do not so much disturb development as direct or regulate it towards strategies that are adaptive under stressful conditions.

Important "switch points" in human development that lead to changes in life-history strategy are hypothesized to include pre- and early postnatal development, juvenility (adrenarche), and puberty, although potentially life-history strategies are open to change throughout the life course (Del Giudice & Belsky, 2011).

Life-history models of human development, including the ACM, have now generated a significant body of research that largely supports the underlying assumptions of life-history theory. Many of the early research findings focused on pubertal timing in girls, finding that exposure to environmental cues that indicated a likely lack of paternal investment (e.g., father absence) predicted earlier puberty (Belsky, Steinberg, & Draper, 1991; Ellis, 2004; Tither & Ellis, 2008). More generally, both cross-sectional (Del Guidice, Ellis, Hinnant, & El-Sheikh, 2012; Griskevicius, Tybur, Delton, & Roberstons, 2011; McCullough, Pedersen, Schroder, Tabak, & Carver, 2012) and longitudinal (Belsky, Schlomer, & Ellis, 2012; Dishion, Ha, & Véronneau, 2012; Gibbons et al., 2012; James, Ellis, Schlomer, & Garber, 2012; Sheppard, Garcia, & Sear, 2014) research has largely supported the contention that exposure to harsh and/or unpredictable environments significantly predicts the development of fast life-history strategies characterized by (in males) an increase in mating rather than parenting effort and greater risk-taking and antisocial behavior. For example, Simpson, Griskevicius, Kuo, Sung, and Collins (2012) reported on findings from the Minnesota Longitudinal Study of Risk and Adaptation, which has tracked a sample of 165 individuals from birth through to their early 20s. Harshness in this study was indexed by socioeconomic status (ages 0–5 years) and unpredictability was derived from a composite based on changes in employment of parents, changes in residence, and changes in cohabitation status (ages 0–5 years). The study found that unpredictability (but not harshness) at ages 0–5 predicted number of lifetime sexual partners, and aggressive, delinquent, and criminal behavior at age 23. In other words, those individuals who were exposed to more environmental unpredictability in their early years were likely to have more sexual partners and to engage in greater levels of aggressive, delinquent, and criminal behavior later in life.

Of particular interest to criminologists is the idea that a life-history perspective can help us to understand the enduring relationship that is found between social class and a wide range of negative health and social outcomes including criminal and antisocial behavior. A large body of research has clearly demonstrated that socioeconomic disadvantage predicts negative health outcomes, and individuals who experience socioeconomic disadvantage not only die at a younger age, but also perceive that they will not live as long as those who are relatively more advantaged (Adams, Stamp, Nettle, Milne, & Jagger, 2014; Braveman, Egerter, & Williams, 2011; Dow & Rehkopf, 2010; Nettle, 2009). Socioeconomic status is also a major predictor of antisocial and criminal behavior with individuals from more socially and economically deprived backgrounds more likely to engage in a wide range of criminal and antisocial behaviors (e.g., Fergusson, Swain-Campbell, & Horwood, 2004). Moreover, individuals from deprived backgrounds tend to begin offending at an earlier age and are less likely to desist from offending during early adulthood than are individuals from more socially and economically advantaged environments (e.g., Fabio et al., 2011). However, socioeconomic status *per se* does not directly cause the development of antisocial and risky behavior; rather, socioeconomic disadvantage tends to be associated with a large number of other risk factors (e.g., physical abuse, frequency of family changes, weak parental attachment) that are likely to play a more important causal role (Fergusson et al., 2004). A life-history framework provides a useful way of understanding and organizing these findings. Socioeconomic disadvantage is strongly related to increased environmental harshness (cues to higher rates of morbidity and mortality) and unpredictability (more frequent changes in social and ecological conditions) that lead developing children to "expect" that their lifespan is likely to be shorter. This results in a coordinated shift to a faster life-history strategy characterized by earlier sexual maturation, a greater number of sexual partners, and an increase in risk-taking and intrasexual aggression that is likely to facilitate (or would have in ancestral environments) greater opportunities for reproductive success in environments in which individuals are less likely to survive.

A life-history perspective can help us to understand individual differences in offending and the idea that these differences are linked to the conditional development of alternative life-history strategies (Figure 7.2, model D), has enormous explanatory potential. However, the story—as is usually the case—is likely to be more complex. First, we need to recognize that individual differences arise in part from genetic differences and the impact of extreme environmental conditions (Figure 7.1, models A and B), including those characterized by exposure to novel toxins (e.g., chemicals, high pollution). We also need to be cognizant of the fact that although humans demonstrate adaptive phenotypic plasticity, there are also likely to be individual (genetic) differences in susceptibility to environmental influences (see our earlier discussion; Figure 7.2, model C). From an evolutionary perspective, individual differences in susceptibly to environmental influences represents a form of "bet-hedging": because future environments are inherently unknowable, natural selection has maintained a variety of strategies, some that involve conditional shifts depending on environmental influences and others that are relatively impervious to environmental context (Belsky & Pluess, 2009; Ellis et al., 2011). Second, consistent with the extended synthesis in evolutionary theory (Chapter 2), we need to recognize that the impact of environmental factors on developmental outcomes occurs across a variety of timescales (Kuzawa & Thayer, 2011). There is now abundant evidence that earlier developmental experiences (including those experienced in utero) can affect future developmental outcomes, plausibly in an adaptive fashion. However, research on the role of epigenetic processes suggests that there are also *transgenerational* influences of the environment on downstream developmental outcomes. For instance, it seems that the experiences of mothers (e.g., exposure to stress during *their* childhood) can influence the intrauterine environments of their developing offspring (Chung & Kuzawa, 2014; Kuzawa & Sweet, 2009). Finally, a life-history perspective in no way precludes an analysis that focuses on the role of either human agency (see Chapter 8) or cultural and social-structural factors, a point we take up in more detail in Chapter 9.

SUMMARY AND CONCLUSIONS

In sum, we think that an evolutionary perspective is *relevant* for addressing some of the key explanatory targets outlined in Table 7.1 and can be effectively integrated with explanations that focus on proximate psychological, neurobiological, and social processes. The prevalence of offending is strongly patterned by age because a significant proportion of criminal behavior is related to risk-taking and status-seeking behaviors that increase during late adolescence and early adulthood because this is the developmental period in which individuals exert the most effort toward obtaining social status and attracting and retaining mates. To realize these evolutionary functions, neurocognitive systems have been designed to promote the seeking of rewards—especially in the presence of peers—whereas self-regulatory systems remain relatively immature. As individuals transition into adulthood, long-term intimate relationships are being forged and effort is directed more toward parenting rather than mating, with concomitant changes in the salience of risk-seeking and intrasexual aggression. However, changes in relationship status may lead to related changes in intrasexual competition consistent with recent research that suggests that, in males, levels of testosterone decline when they get married (Booth & Dabbs, 1993; Gray, Ellison, & Campbell, 2007) and become fathers (Gettler, McDade, Feranil, & Kuzawa, 2011; Gray, Kahlenberg, Barrett, Lipson, & Ellison, 2002), but increase again if they get divorced (Mazur & Michalek, 1998).

An evolutionary perspective is also relevant for understanding individual differences in offending, why offending appears to be part of a broader spectrum of antisocial behavior, and why certain risk factors are associated with antisocial and criminal outcomes. Individual differences in offending from an evolutionary perspective can be explained (in part) from adaptive shifts in life-history strategies that are initiated by exposure to specific environmental experiences during critical periods in development. Offending tends to be part of a broad spectrum of antisocial behavior because life history strategies direct resources toward greater risk-taking, intrasexual competition, and mating effort that themselves are linked to a variety of criminal behaviors (physical and sexual violence, drug use, property offending, etc.). Indeed an evolutionary life-history perspective extends its analysis to theoretically relevant characteristics (e.g., earlier puberty, sexual debut, number of sexual partners) that are less readily comprehensible from the perspective of mainstream criminological explanations (e.g., anomie-strain theory; see Walsh, 2011; Chapter 9). Finally, a life-history perspective can help us to understand what features of early environments are likely to play critical roles in the later development of antisocial and criminal behavior and can thus tease out genuine causal process from the raft of risk factors identified by developmental criminologists. The idea that an evolutionary life-history perspective on the developmental origins of antisocial and criminal behavior can add ontological depth to our understanding of the findings in life course criminology as well as direct research along epistemically profitable lines, is nicely captured by Simpson et al. (2012, p. 684):

> An evolutionary life history perspective can appreciably increase and broaden our understanding of how exposure to different dimensions of stress shapes important developmental outcomes later in life. The application of life history thinking not only clarifies and contextualizes why certain experiences or events encountered earlier in life prospectively predict certain development outcome later on; it can also steer researchers toward novel hypotheses not anticipated by traditional theories of social development.

One of the many intriguing findings from a comprehensive citation analysis of scholars in criminal and criminal justice journals between 1986 and 2010 is the prominence of researchers who have a strong interest in developmental processes (Cohn, Farrington, & Iratzoqui, 2014). The prominence of development criminologists is understandable given what we know about the importance of developmental experiences for criminal behavior and the shaping of life course offending trajectories. We think that there are substantial gains to be made by integrating insights from life-history theory with those from developmental criminology and this should be a fruitful avenue for further research (see Boutwell, Barnes, Deaton, & Beaver, 2013; Wiebe, 2012, for recent findings).

Proximate Explanations: Individuals, Situations, and Social Processes

INTRODUCTION

As discussed in Chapter 4, Tinbergen stated that scientists typically invoke explanations that focus on (1) adaptations or evolutionary function: what contribution has a trait made to survival and reproductive success? (2) Phylogeny, or evolutionary history: how has that trait evolved over time? (3) Developmental processes: how does the trait in question develop over the lifetime of the organism? (4) Proximate mechanisms: through what psychological, social, cultural, or biological mechanisms is the trait expressed and how do these mechanisms generate behavior? In this chapter, we intend to concentrate on the fourth type of causal explanation, that dealing with proximate mechanisms operating at the time the offense occurs. In our view, because proximate causes are temporally and causally linked to offending and recidivism, it makes sense that they should be one of the primary targets of policy and therapeutic interventions.

In line with the focus of this book, an important question we set out to answer in this chapter is *why* individuals choose to engage in crime, and by doing so, transgress strongly endorsed social and moral norms. A related question concerns how the process of normative guidance falls apart and what kind of psychological and contextual processes enable this to happen. We are also interested in explaining why some individuals rather than others are more likely to commit crimes, and also what accounts for intra individual differences in offending that make offending more likely in some contexts rather than others.

In selecting the proximate mechanisms to discuss in this chapter, our intention is to focus on those that have been linked to the onset and

Evolutionary Criminology
http://dx.doi.org/10.1016/B978-0-12-397937-7.00008-2 © 2015 Elsevier Inc. All rights reserved.

reoccurrence of offending, and can be plausibly conceptualized as adaptations or by-products of adaptations. In addition, they need to currently be a focal point of theoretical and empirical research in the forensic and correctional domains. We suggest that work on dynamic risk factors meets these requirements and can be reasonably construed (after some conceptual reworking) as proximate causal factors that are related to evolved traits. For example, the dynamic risk factor of intimacy deficits can be conceptualized as arising from the need of human beings to form close social relationships. In the case of intimacy failure, the person concerned lacks the necessary psychological and contextual resources to meet this need in prosocial and personally fulfilling ways. As a consequence of the absence of the required personal and social capabilities to establish and maintain intimate relationships, some individuals commit sexual offenses (Ward, Polaschek, & Beech, 2006). Other types of dynamic risk factors can also be theoretically traced back to motivational, cognitive, and behavioral adaptations such as the capacity for self-regulation (or agency), emotional identification and control, social learning, causal and inductive (generalizing) reasoning, group identification, status and resource seeking, and identity formation.

The four major groups of dynamic risk factors evident in the sexual offending area are emotional dysregulation/internalizing difficulties, deviant sexual interests, intimacy/social relationships, and offense supportive norms, attitudes, and beliefs. Interestingly, these risk domains coincide with four major systems comprising human agency: cognition, emotion, social context, and physiological/motivational. Every human action, including criminal actions, will reflect aspects of each of the four systems. We will point to these connections in the relevant parts of this chapter. According to the gene–culture coevolution model cultural and social factors also evolve and exert selection pressure on genes as well as directly on normative attitudes, beliefs, social practices, and behavior.

The problem with basing the (proximate) explanation of crime on dynamic risk factors in their typical form is that such an account fails to adequately reflect human agency and the goal-directed nature of action. What you typically end up with is a list of factors that predict recidivism and little or no understanding of how they actually cause offending in part or collectively. This is because criminal justice researchers tend to become preoccupied with risk assessment and prediction and therefore heavily favor psychometric models of offending over causal ones. In our view, this is a mistake and likely to lead to theoretical and practice dead ends very quickly; additionally, it conflates psychometric relationships with causal explanation (Ward, 2014). A more fruitful strategy is to flip the research focus around and concentrate instead on the goal-directed nature of human functioning and the constituents of human agency. The question then becomes: what types of goals (and their motivational and cognitive underpinnings), strategies, plans, and contexts are associated with the violation of significant social and moral norms?

In this chapter, we first outline the concepts of dynamic risk factors, criminogenic needs, protective factors, and desistance processes. The ability of these concepts to function as explanations of crime is critically evaluated and their relationships to adaptations explored. A major problem identified is that dynamic risk factors are *composite* constructs and are summaries of psychosocial and social characteristics and processes. Because of this hybrid nature, they do not actually refer to real factors at all. In short, dynamic risk factors do not actually exist. A similar problem holds for protective factors although the issue here is more one of vagueness than failure to genuinely refer. Second, the Agency Model of Risk (AMR) is systematically outlined and its grounding in biological and cultural processes is discussed. Third, we demonstrate how dynamic risk factors and protective factors once distributed across the components of human agency contribute to the occurrence of crime. Finally, we conclude the chapter with a discussion of some research implications of our model.

DYNAMIC RISK FACTORS, PROTECTIVE FACTORS, AND DESISTANCE

Dynamic Risk Factors

Researchers in the correctional and sexual offending fields have paid considerable attention in recent years to the development and validation of risk assessment measures and protocols (Mann, Hanson, & Thornton, 2010; Ward, 2014). It is fair to say that the identification of risk factors and risk assessment has been prioritized in the field and, increasingly, practitioners and researchers have used them to explain sexual offending and to guide treatment. In brief, risk assessment is the process of using risk factors (i.e., any variable that is measurable and predictive of harmful outcomes) to estimate the likelihood of a person committing another offense in the future (Cooke & Michie, 2013). The process of risk assessment may differ in terms of its degree of structure and reliance on professional judgment and/or a set of explicit rules. The nature of the risk factors used in research and clinical assessment varies in a number of ways, including their degree of changeability (static versus dynamic), duration (stable versus acute), content (e.g., relational style, attitudes, and biomarkers), form (risk versus protective), and function (causal, contributing, or contextual).

Dynamic risk factors in general terms are conceptualized as "enduring factors linked to the likelihood of offending that can nevertheless be changed following intervention" (Beech & Craig, 2012, p. 170). A subset of dynamic risk factors has been called *criminogenic needs*, essentially offender or social characteristics that are causally related to individuals' criminal behavior and that, if modified or managed in some way, result in lower reoffending rates (Andrews & Bonta, 2010). In an important recent article, Mann et al. identified a number of what they called *psychologically meaningful* risk factors that were considered to be prima facie causes of sexual offending and validated predictors of recidivism. The list of supported meaningful risk factors for child sexual abuse included sexual preferences for children, emotional congruence with children, general self-regulation problems, emotional deregulation, offense supportive attitudes, poor cognitive problem-solving, and lack of adult intimate relationships. Mann et al. (2010, p. 210) concluded that:

> Assessment and treatment for sexual offenders should focus on empirically established causal risk factors. In this review, we propose a definition of psychologically meaningful causal risk factors as propensities and outline the types of evidence required to identify them. Although the causal role of such factors has yet to be established, we believe that the causal factors for sexual recidivism will ultimately be drawn from variables similar to those included in our list. We believe that it is these variables that should be emphasized in treatment.

Formulating the concept of a dynamic risk factor more specifically: reduced amounts of a characteristic x is associated with O being less likely to commit further crimes at $t2$. According to Mann et al., a subclass of dynamic risk factors may be psychological causes.

Protective Factors

The concept of protective factors has been imported from the child maltreatment area to forensic and correctional contexts to shift the emphasis in risk assessment from that of estimating the likelihood of inflicting harm on others to characteristics that may buffer or moderate the impact of an adverse event on children. Child maltreatment theorists have argued that it makes sense from therapeutic and policy perspectives to understand why certain individuals are less affected by traumatic or stressful experience, whereas others go on to develop a number of psychological and social problems. In the child maltreatment area, Afifi and MacMillan (2011, p. 268) define protective factors as: "A protective factor may influence, modify, ameliorate, or alter how a person responds to the adversity that places them at risk for maladaptive outcomes."

However, in the criminal justice domain, there has been a noticeable shift in the meaning of the concept of protective factors, especially in terms of what is considered to be the protected object, the source of the potential harm, and the time frame concerned. The offender undergoing risk assessment is viewed as the source of the harm and the protected object is the community or certain groups of potential victims such as children or adult women. According to de Vries Robbé (2014), protective factors are:

> factors that can compensate for a person's risk factors […], characteristics of an offender, or alternatively, his environment or situation, that reduce the risk of future violent behavior […].

Thus protective factors in sex offender assessment are those factors that reduce the chances of recidivism occurring. More specifically: greater amounts of characteristic x are associated with O being more likely not to commit an offense at $t2$. Simply put, a dynamic risk factor is a characteristic that is associated with a reduced likelihood of reoffending. The interesting thing to note about this definition is that the temporal focus is extended and any aspect of an offender's characteristics or environment may be a protective factor as long as it is risk-reducing. The difficulty with broadening the range of the concept of protective factors so much is that it makes it harder to distinguish between protective factors, maturational effects, and therapy-induced change or desistance events. Thus it is no longer clear that it is protection from harm that is being referred to rather than simply change processes that reduce the possibility of harm occurring in the future (see the following section).

Desistance

Alongside the primarily psychometrically driven research into risk and protective factors there has been a parallel strand of work examining aspects of the person and the environment that help offenders desist (protect) from further offending. This research tradition has been labeled as desistance research. Desistance theory and research is primarily descriptive and seeks to understand the change processes that are associated with individuals turning away from lives of crime and becoming reintegrated into the community (McNeill, Batchelor, Burnett, & Knox, 2005). Thus, desistance from criminal behavior is considerably more than simply stopping. As the desistance process advances, there may be intermittency, a combination of pauses, resumptions, indecisiveness, and ambivalence, all of which may finally lead to termination. Desistance is often defined as a termination point, or "the last officially recorded or self-reported offense" (Kazemian, 2007, p. 9). However, it is more properly seen as a dynamic, ongoing process. In essence, it is the state of stopping and staying stopped that we refer to as "desistance" (Maruna, 2001).

It is possible to identify three strands in desistance theory, those that stress the importance of *maturation, agency,* and *social relationships* (Maruna, 2001; McNeill et al., 2005). Theorists have sometimes contrasted objective desistance factors (e.g., a job or marriage) (Giordano, Longmore, Schroeder, & Seffrin, 2008; Laub & Sampson, 2003) with a subjective sense of meaning, arguing for the primacy of one over the other. More recent theoretical work has emphasized the interaction between all three sets of desistance factors and that it is in the interfaces between these variables that desistance exerts its effect (McNeill, 2006; Porporino, 2008).

Dynamic Risk Factors, Protective Factors, and Desistance: Adaptations?

Our aim in this book is to develop a gene–culture coevolution theoretical framework that can provide a comprehensive, multidisciplinary perspective on the onset and maintenance of crime. We argue that explaining the onset or cessation of offending by reference to dynamic risk factors in conjunction with protective factors and desistance is a theoretical dead end. It misconstrues the conceptual structure of dynamic risk factors and fails to result in interlevel, comprehensive explanations. However, despite their conceptual thinness we agree with Mann et al. (2010) that dynamic risk factors appear to track causal processes in some way, and if the argument of this book is correct, are likely to display some connections with psychological adaptations. But what are they?

In his recent monograph, de Vries Robbé (2014) attempted to match aspects of healthy psychological functioning (protective factors) with dynamic risk factors identified in sex offenders—essentially, the adaptive pole of a dimension. In our view, the healthy end of the dimension can be plausibly linked to evolved traits and their proximate expressions. To give four examples, de Vries Robbé (2014) hypothesized that:

1. The healthy factor of a moderate intensity sex drive and associated preferences for sex with someone you are emotionally attached to could be related in a dysfunctional way to the dynamic risk factor of *sexual preoccupation.*
2. The adaptive preference for consenting, reciprocal sex with sexual partners of adult age could be related in a dysfunctional way to the dynamic risk factor of *deviant sexual interests* and preference for sex with children.
3. The adaptive need to form emotional intimacy with adults could be related in a dysfunctional way to the dynamic risk factor of *emotional congruence with children.*
4. The adaptive capacity for self-regulation of action and self-control could be related in a dysfunctional way to the dynamic risk factor of *impulsiveness and recklessness.*

Each of the adaptive ends of the dimension or pole can be viewed as an adaptation or the by-product of an adaptation. First, possessing a moderate sex drive should enable individuals to procure mates and to acquire the resources they need to function well in the social environment they find themselves. The ability to work, acquire food, sustain relationships, create and cement social alliances, and so on requires the availability of energy and time. A sexually preoccupied individual is likely to struggle to be able to do this and therefore will be vulnerable to experiencing distress and acting in harmful ways. Second, having preferences for sexual relationships with adult partners is more likely to result in personal survival of individuals, any offspring, and genes, and to conform with cultural norms concerning the nature and functioning of intimate relationships. The absence of such adaptive sexual preferences could result in social ostracism or punishment, and ultimately an impoverished quality of life. Third, having the emotional, social, and cognitive capacities to establish and maintain romantic, familial, and strong social relationships with conspecifics will help groups create cohesive functioning and lay the platform for the emergence of normative codes. The ability to accurately infer mental states in others and to use these formulations to explain and predict persons' actions is an essential skill and its absence can severely cripple individuals' social and psychological functioning. The presence of this set of capacities in non-human primates strengthens the case for theory of mind abilities (including empathy) being adaptations (Andrews, 2012). Fourth, all of these adaptive traits and outcomes rely to some degree on the possession of intact self-regulation (or agency) capabilities. The ability to translate needs and emotions into goals, to create plans that translate these goals into action sequences, and then to be able to effectively implement and evaluate such plans is essential for adaptive functioning in most social contexts and likely would have been directly selected for. In fact, organisms are arguably characterized by their ability to actively seek and acquire the physical and social/cultural resources they need to sustain their physical functioning, to repair damage, and to modify their environments in ways that assist in this process (Christensen & Hooker, 2000).

Some theorists have taken these dynamic risk factors and deconstructed them into their causal and attribute features and applied the resulting multilevel theories to domains such as sexual offending (Ward & Beech, 2014). For example, Beech and Mitchell's (2005) theoretical work on intimacy deficits in sexual offenders denotes mechanisms at different levels and across varying explanatory domains in an attempt to build a comprehensive understanding of intimacy deficits. They refer to the neurobiology of attachment behavior as well as specifying the psychological mechanisms constituting attachment strategies. Beech and Mitchell explicitly incorporate the agency or commonsense level of explanation by referring to issues of trust and perceptions of safety. There are also references to environmental processes and developmental variables in their attachment theory.

Critical Comments

Although the use of dynamic risk factors for *risk prediction* purposes is perfectly acceptable there are significant problems employing them to explain offending, individually or collectively. Furthermore, this difficulty is compounded when they are incorporated into clinical case formulations. There are two major difficulties in our view: (1) Dynamic risk factors are actually psychometric, *composite* constructs and therefore a mixture of causal elements and clinical attributes; and (2) because they are composite factors, they do not actually exist or genuinely refer to psychological and social processes (Ward & Beech, 2014). And, because they strictly do not exist, it is meaningless to investigate their relationship with protective factors and other risk and offense-related variables. This is a radical claim and completely undermines the correctional field's current preoccupation with constructing explanatory and case formulation models based on dynamic risk factors. We will examine each of these problems in turn.

First, dynamic risk factors are composite factors in at least three distinct senses. They are frequently discussed in the literature and appear in psychometric models as a *type* of construct, whereas in fact they are a collection of dynamic risk factors; thus, the general category label is simply a placeholder. For example, de Vries Robbé (2014) unpacks the general category of dynamic risk factors evident in sex offenders into such elements as sexual preoccupation, deviant sexual interests, offense-supportive attitudes, emotional congruence with children, impulsiveness, poor cognitive problem-solving, grievance/hostility, and lack of concern for others (pp. 43–44). The difficulty is that later in his monograph, he outlines a proposed explanatory model that uses the general term *risk factors* in which he explores their relationship to violence and protective factors (p. 152). At best, the use of this term is misleading, whereas at worse it conflates levels of constructs. A further problem related to the composite nature of dynamic risk factors is that each specific factor is typically broken into further features, some of which causally exclude each other. For example, in his recent summary of risk and protective factors in adult male sexual offenders, Thornton (2013) listed sexual violence and sexual interest in children as subdomains of the general dynamic risk factor of sexual interests. The problem is that the "umbrella," so to speak, of deviant sexual interests consists of qualitatively different variables, which arguably refer to distinct causal processes and their associated problems. Finally, the description of dynamic risk factors is vague and seems to include both trait and state aspects. For example, the stable dynamic factor of general self-regulation includes negative emotionality (a mental state) and poor problem-solving (a trait or enduring psychological feature). Thus dynamic risk factors are really psychometric instruments that contain heterogeneous features and in this sense are summaries or composite constructs.

Second, the problem of dynamic risk factors' composite nature has serious implications for its usefulness in both theory construction and clinical case formulations, once their construct validity status is evaluated. We argue that taking into account their composite nature, and the mixture of causal elements and clinical attributes or "symptoms," they do not genuinely refer to processes and structures in persons and the world and therefore do not exist. Dynamic risk factors are of instrumental value in risk assessment contexts, but once they are incorporated into explanations and clinical case formulations they exceed their existential warrant, so to speak. They then become fictitious entities. Because dynamic risk factors do not strictly exist, it is meaningless to investigate their relationship with protective, other risk and offense-related variables. Borsboom (2005, p. 158) captures this issue nicely when he asserts:

> If a term is treated as referential but has no referent, then one is reifying terms that have no other function than that of providing a descriptive summary of a distinct set of processes and attributes. For instance, one then comes to treat a name for a group of test items as if it were a common cause of the item responses. That of course is a mistake.

> If no attribute answers the referential call the test is not valid for measuring that attribute no matter how useful the test may be for prediction, selection or how well it may fulfill other functions.

The problems associated with the concept of protective factors in the criminal justice domains resides less with its construct validity status and more with issues of vagueness and the violation of its conceptual boundaries. As stated previously, the concept of a protective factor used in the criminal justice field has been imported from the child maltreatment domain and extended beyond its original use to refer to *any* characteristics of offenders, their situation, or intervention programs that decrease their chances of reoffending. The original meaning of the possession of features that protect a person from the short- and long-term negative effects of an adverse event have been lost. In fact, the concept of protective factors cannot retain the original child maltreatment meaning in forensic and correctional contexts as this would entail the conceptually muddled implication that the offense would not have occurred. In the child maltreatment literature, there is interest in why children exposed to adverse events do not develop subsequent psychological and behavioral problems. The equivalent scenario for offenders is to ask why offenders do *not* commit an offense; that is, what protects them against this outcome? If you reply that what we are interested in is recidivism, the focus has then shifted from a failure to develop an initial set of problems to the *reoccurrence of harm*—to others. Furthermore, if the concept of protective factors refers to any feature of the offender and his situation at any point that reduces the chances of an offense reoccurring, then it collapses into discussion of etiology: why did *x* reoffend when *y* did not? This is simply a form of causal analysis and introducing the concept of protective factors adds nothing and simply muddles the picture. Finally, because dynamic risk factors lack construct validity and therefore do not genuinely refer to real psychological and social processes, there is little point investigating their relationship to protective factors, outside of a risk prediction context. In the context of risk prediction, pragmatic considerations can override those of truth and explanatory robustness. However, this is not the case when it comes to the construction of etiological explanations and their subsequent application in treatment planning (Ward & Beech, 2014).

AGENCY MODEL OF RISK

It is time to take stock of the argument so far. The psychometric concepts of dynamic risk factors and protective factors have been increasingly used beyond risk assessment and management contexts to explain the onset of offending and to guide interventions with offenders. Even though there are serious theoretical problems with both sets of concepts, it seems likely that dynamic risk factors, in particular, track at least some of the causal processes that underlie and constitute offending. Otherwise, it is hard to account for their success in predicting recidivism rates and in guiding some aspects of treatment. Furthermore, it is reasonable to assume that constituents of dynamic risk factors exert a causal influence and are in part at least proximate explanations of crime. There is also a case to be made that they are causally related to adaptations and, in this respect, reflect the evolutionary history of human beings.

We seem to have arrived at an impasse: although dynamic risk factors do not appear to genuinely refer to real psychological processes, they are markers for crime-related processes. They excel in risk prediction contexts but in their traditional form are not good candidates for causal explanations of offending and therefore should not be used—unmodified—in clinical case formulations. The trouble is that they are currently used in both of these ways. The problem as we see it is that researchers and clinicians have no viable alternative. They want to hang on to the benefits of a dynamic risk factor framework, and protective factors to a lesser extent, but are unclear how to resolve the theoretical problems outlined previously. We believe the answer resides in stepping outside a purely risk assessment and management lens to focus on the components of human agency. *Agency* refers to a person's capacity to effectively manage multiple and sometimes competing goals in ways that enable him or her to sustain functioning, repair any damage (often at a biological level through internal physiological processes), avoid harm and threats, and to implement plans that are cohesive and responsive to any relevant contexts—social, physical, and cultural (Christensen, 2012; Christensen & Hooker, 2000). In our model (see Figure 8.1), the components of agency are goals, formation of plans and selection of strategies, plan implementation and evaluation,

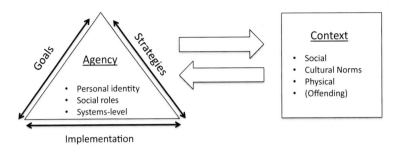

FIGURE 8.1   The agency model of risk (AMR).

and the subsequent revision of goals if required. The interaction between agents and their environments is dynamic and bidirectional, and agents have the capacity to actively construct their social, physical, and cultural knowledge contexts as well as be shaped in turn by such environments. Once a simplified conceptual model of agency has been constructed, it is relatively easy to demonstrate how dynamic risk factors can be distributed across the model and therefore provide a conduit between risk assessment, etiological explanation, and treatment.

Dynamic risk factors in the correctional and forensic domains are intended to predict harm related to reoffending, typically to victims and the community. Protective factors are features that lessen the chances of risk factors having this effect; or more generally, if present they reduce the likelihood of offending occurring. As stated previously, it is a good idea to *flip* things around and start with the personal and contextual factors that both dynamic risk factors and protective factors refer to. In our view, they refer to the components of agency: goals, plans and strategies, implementation and evaluation, and the subsequent revision of goals and plans. Furthermore, in our model, there are three levels of agency, each associated with its own distinct set of goals, plans, and strategies, and each capable of influencing the others types of agency (see the following section): system level, social role, and personal. As proposed earlier, dynamic risk factors do not exist other than as summaries of different variables, and because protective factors are defined in terms of harmful (risk associated) outcomes, they do have not conceptual meaning aside from this context.

Thus, risk factors once broken down into their causal elements can be viewed as psychological and social processes (i.e., those associated with goals, plans, strategies, and action implementation) that impair normal functioning and hence disrupt persons' internal and external relationships to their social, cultural, and physical environments. This disruption can be at multiple levels and even be confined to incorrect actions within a single practice (e.g., relationship repair). Protective factors, once broken down into their core elements, work in multiple ways across the various levels of agency to inhibit and/or disrupt dysfunctional systems and to restore normal functioning. Sometimes the constraints exerted by protective factors may be external, such as the construction of supportive social networks around high-risk offenders. Strengths are conceptualized as internal and external capacities that enable offenders to flourish in certain environments, which can be used also to motivate them, and which can also be recruited to function as protective factors in some situations.

The theoretical roots of the AMR are diverse and draw from dynamical systems theory (Christensen & Hooker, 2000), gene–culture coevolution theory (e.g., Odling-Smee, Laland, & Feldman, 2003), cognitive neuroscience (e.g., Maise, 2011), philosophy (e.g., Sterelny, 2012), psychology of action (e.g., Huang & Bargh, 2014), criminology (e.g., Walsh & Bolen, 2012), and forensic psychology (Andrews & Bonta, 2010). In drawing from this body of theory and research, we have formulated three general theoretical assumptions concerning the nature of human beings and the role of values in explaining human action. These assumptions provide the overall theoretical justification for the AMR.

First, we argue that emergent materialism is a powerful and persuasive view of human functioning, with its commitment to multiple, nonreductive levels of analysis and its insistence that psychological capacities such as agency play a crucial role in promoting survival, and flourishing. According to emergent materialism, there are *distinct levels of analysis* corresponding to the different systems that constitute human beings and that sustain their functioning. There are ontological (i.e., the nature of human beings and other organisms) and epistemological (i.e., knowledge about human beings and other organisms) strands to this view. From an ontological perspective, each system affects the others and yet has its own unique set of processes that contribute to the overall functioning of the organism: organisms are dynamic, complex systems embedded within social, physical, and cultural environments. From an epistemological viewpoint, knowledge concerning the processes constituting each system level offers a valuable insight into the organism's functioning. The salience of the level of explanation will in part depend on the relevant question and therefore the problem at hand. Agency-level explanations of human interaction, including crime, with their reference to personhood and intentional mental states, provide a unique and irreducible explanatory perspective. Attention to individuals' experiences, values, beliefs, and social/cultural contexts should be explicitly taken into account when developing theories of normative and dysfunctional human behavior.

Second, we acknowledge the pervasiveness of normativity in the natural world as well as in human culture. The influence of values is evident in the norms that govern the functioning of different action sequences such as predator behavior, workings of biological systems, the application of human moral systems, and primate social relationships. In speaking of the ubiquity and essential roles of norms in biological and social systems, Christensen (2012, p. 104) views "normativity as inherent in the organization or form of living systems, specifically in the form that generates their unity and hence explains their existence". Normative principles are natural in the sense they specify the functional parameters of biological systems and social practices and have their origin in the development of agency in organisms of all types. Norms are reflected in action goals and the strategies selected to further these goals are evaluated against these norms, typically in a fluid, dynamic, and immediate manner, in "real time." In complex animals such as human beings the capacity to flexibly adjust goal directed strategies and plans in response to changing environmental contingencies is in part due to cognitive capacity and to the availability of social and cultural resources (Sterelny, 2012).

Third, internal psychological processes, such as emotions, cognitions, drives, and needs, underpin goals and can influence subsequent action unconsciously or consciously (Huang & Bargh, 2014). Goals are activated or selected in response to external contexts and their cues such as the presence of a prey or threats, and by internal cues such as hunger, fear, sexual desire, or anger. In describing these cues, Christensen and Hooker (2000, p. 11) state:

> We shall term the signals which a system uses to differentiate an appropriate context for performing action the system's explicit norm signals. For example, hunger signals differentiate blood sugar levels and act to initiate and focus food search activity. Explicit norm signals provide information about appropriate action because they differentiate more and less discrepancy between some current system condition and a reference condition, the norm satisfaction state, which modulates subsequent performance.

Emotions, hunger, and other motivational states function as signals that the organism needs to deal with relevant challenges, whether they are threats, opportunities for rewards, or physical needs. One of the notable features of highly complex organisms such as primates, and especially humans, is that they have to balance multiple goals at any one time and construct plans and strategies intended to realize them to guide action (Huang & Bargh, 2014). Such models enable the organism to anticipate or predict environmental outcomes and the norms (which set standards of performance and specify desired outcomes) associated with their constituent goals help to correct action if there is a discrepancy between outcomes and norms (Christensen, 2012). Higher order cognitive systems, language, and normative codes expressed within language are capable of creating more abstract, symbolic cues that can activate goals and their subsequent plans. Furthermore, adaptations such as social learning (via modeling, imitation, etc.) can facilitate this process and create external contexts that scaffold the acquisition of complex skills. For example, in a criminal justice context, individuals sometimes acquire offending skills from fellow offenders and through reflection on their own offending experiences (Bourke, Ward, & Rose, 2012).

We will now describe the AMR in more detail (see Figure 8.1). In the AMR, there are two major sources of causal influence: the agent and the context (environment). We have used the term *agent* to better capture the self-regulation of persons and the term *contexts* because it more adequately reflects the fine grained nature of environments that activate, and are responsive to, the agent's goals. In the AMR, there are bidirectional relationships between the agent and the environment, which is intended to convey their dynamic interactions and reciprocal causation. The temporal scale may reflect real (immediate) time processes and ongoing contact as well as portraying extended sequences of interactions. It is also a feature of the AMR that both partners in an interaction sequence respond to and also shape or construct each other. This is similar to the niche construction component of the gene–culture evolution model that we outlined in Chapter 3. In other words, we argue that the most scientifically defensible way of conceptualizing human beings and their relationship with the environment is in dynamic, interactional terms.

We will start with the agent side of the relationship and make a few general comments to begin with. The first thing to notice is that there are three primary components involved in the initiation of action: selection of goal(s) (What is the purpose of the action? What outcomes does the agent desire to achieve?); the construction of a plan and selection of the strategies required to realize the plan (this will involve norms that specify effective strategies and how best to integrate goals, strategies, and norms within a coherent action sequence); and the implementation and evaluation of the plan (Did the plan result in the desired outcomes? If not, why not? How can it be revised in the light of its failure to achieve the desired result?). Second, the three components of the action sequence have bidirectional relationships with each other. Third, there are three levels of agency within the AMR: systems level, social roles, and personal identity, each conceptually linked to distinct sets of goals, strategies, and implementation practices.

The Agent

In the AMR, proximate causal factors in the AMR are the result of developmental experiences and ultimately have their origin in adaptations and their by-products. The capacity for agency is inherent in all living things; however, in human beings the level of sophistication is ratcheted up several notches because of their ability to intentionally structure learning and physical environments (i.e., niche construction). The origins of this enhanced agency capacity arguably resides in the possession of language and cognitive plasticity. A consequence of this suite of competences is that human beings can engage in mental time travel (i.e., think counterfactually about their past and possible future) and regulate action through the application of complex mental models and the acquisition of cultural cognitive and behavioral tools. According to the AMR, basic human needs and their elaboration into explicit norms and their accompanying strategies create an array of scripts and action templates. Emotions function as fast appraisal systems that inform the organism about its current goal status and progress, and therefore can function as effective action organizers and prompts. Furthermore, norms are linked to specific emotions, which are usefully viewed as internal cues indicating that things are going well or badly. For example, a sex offender may have an insecure attachment style and feel anxious when in the presence of adults. The activation of feelings of anxiety or fear could cause that person to feel vulnerable and to seek out children for support. As a consequence of this goal state, he or she may engage in the sexual abuse of a child but view this as a caring and mutually beneficial encounter. Thus there is a close causal connection between attachment-related beliefs, emotions and needs, current environmental cues, and the formation of a plan to sexually abuse a child. The activation of a goal can unconsciously affect an offender's subsequent behavior and result in a complex sequence of actions that lead to high-risk situations. The goal-dependent actions are represented in long-term memory in the form of cognitive scripts and contain information that guide the offending behavior. They specify the conditions under which an offense plan can be enacted, including the creation of access to possible victims and the use of strategies to groom and subdue them. These scripts can be enacted without conscious intention and with minimal awareness of the overall goal.

Thus, at times, goals can be automatically activated and embedded within action plans or offense scripts that come with prepackaged strategies. However, on other occasions, offenders will construct new plans in response to unique motivational states and environmental cues, once they have formulated their goals—although the initial goal formulation may not be explicit (Huang & Bargh, 2014).

The implementation of a plan always occurs within a particular environment in response to internal and external cues, and in this respect is ecologically sensitive. In other words, offenders do not simply come up with general plans that ignore the context in which they live and overlook the various social and physical affordances inherent in these contexts. Once plans are constructed, individuals carry them out and evaluate the degree to which they are successful in achieving their goals. According to Bourke et al. (2012), child sex offenders vary in their ability to reflect on the success of their offending plans and in the degree to which they are able to revise them in the light of varying circumstances and their own needs. For example, some child sexual offenders possess cognitive structures and competencies related to their offending that have become deeply entrenched. These competencies facilitate their ability to detect offense opportunities and to seamlessly navigate their way past the various constraints and barriers designed to protect children from exploitation and abuse.

The bidirectional causal relationships depicted in the AMR rests on the assumption that each component of the action sequence can influence the others, both during and following the completion of the action and its subsequent evaluation. For example, if an individual is experiencing trouble constructing a workable plan, he or she may adjust goals or, partway through the execution of an offense, might abandon the original plan and refine it. In other words, although we have conceptually divided the sequence into three major components in actuality, they are seamlessly integrated.

The final key feature of the AMR is the existence of levels of agency. For purposes of illustration, we have included three agency levels in the model but readily acknowledge that this is more for didactic purposes and we are not committed to there being only three—or even these particular three. The important point is that each level is associated with different types of action sequences in response to varying internal and environmental cues. The level of *system agency* is meant to deal with threats to the physical nature of agents, for example when feeling threatened or when intoxicated or unwell. We suggest that the activation of this level of agency will determine the types of goals and plans constructed, and itself is likely to be triggered by unique contextual cues, for example the presence of a threat to safety. The agency level *of social roles* is associated with particular social institutions and contexts. For example, a sex offender might be working as a therapist and in this role blurs the boundaries between professional and personal interests. He takes advantage of a patient and sexually assaults her, possibly rationalizing it as part of therapy. Another example is that of rape in wartime. A soldier might see victims as the enemy and incorrectly justify his sexually abusive actions as legitimate acts of war. In other words, in both examples, the offense-related goals, strategies, plans, and implementations are strongly connected to specific social contexts and identities. The *personal* level of agency concerns individuals' overall sense of identity and their core normative commitments. It seeks to fashion connections between global (implicit or explicit) plans for living and individuals' most heavily weighted values. For example, an offender might conceive of himself as a sensitive, somewhat empathic person who is distrustful of adults. He seeks the company of children because they are perceived as less rejecting and more considerate. This could provide an emotional and social context for sexual offending to occur, in the presence of normal human needs for sex and intimacy. Another example is a man who views himself as a "fighter," someone determined not to be "pushed around" by what he perceives as "bossy females." Such an individual is predisposed to mistakenly interpret assertive behavior by women as deliberate snubs and worthy of violent retaliation (e.g., rape). In all of the three levels of agency, there are possible interactions and any one individual could move between them depending on the external contexts and their motivational state.

The Context

The AMR is a dynamic interactional model of human action and states that sometimes the initial causes of offending may be external such as the presence of offending opportunities (Smallbone & Cale, in press). Other examples include being a member of a gang, part of a pedophilic network, or the loss of a romantic partner. However, on its own, the presence of contextual cues will not be enough to initiate offending. In addition, there is likely to be a corresponding shift in the agent's goals, and before this, his motivational state and cognitive functioning. The individual will need to interpret what is happening around him and form some type of offense-related goals. Following the setting of goals, he requires the construction of a plan and strategies that will enable him to overcome any conflicting personal motivations and that give access to a potential victim and means of overcoming resistance. On the other hand, desistance factors such as the presence of social support, employment, intimate relationships, and being afforded the chance to "knife off" an offending identity and lifestyle can decrease the chances of recidivism.

A unique feature of the AMR is its implication that at times environments may effectively override a person's inhibitions against harming others, for example because of the presence of powerful emotional states in threat situations or because of the social framing of a situation by other people (e.g., racial riots). Given human beings' strong, arguably innate, need for social connection and responses to threats, they may be especially susceptible to malign influences in certain kinds of contexts. In addition, subcultures that strongly promote norms that dehumanize or alienate individuals could also create external contexts that increase the chances of crime occurring. The tendency for people to seek out and create environments that resonate with their interests and attitudes is likely to facilitate such an effect.

Thus from the viewpoint of the AMR, social and cultural environments/contexts can either activate individuals underlying crime supportive attitudes, beliefs, and goals or in some cases actually *create* them. The rejection of certain ethnic subgroups or people with certain characteristics by a community may alienate and insulate them from prosocial influences and create enormous resentment and norms that endorse antisocial behavior. What starts out as primarily an environmental explanation of crime ends up shaping and entrenching cognitive and behavioral characteristics that predispose individuals to harm others.

But, and this is a crucial point, irrespective of where the causal influences originate, the commission of an offense requires the presence of *both* an agent(s) and an external context that supports criminal actions. The degree to which one or the other dominates in a subsequent explanation is a function of the presence of conflicting goals, persistence of offense supportive or unsupportive attitudes and beliefs, and contexts that either encourage prosocial behavior, or funnel individuals in to adopting offending lifestyles.

Dynamic Risk Factors, Protective Factors, and the AMR

In summary, we argue that rather than develop explanations based on dynamic risk factors and protective factors it makes more sense to focus on action and its core components. The major reason for this suggestion is that there are significant theoretical problems with both concepts that make them unsuitable for explanatory purposes. From the viewpoint of the AMR, dynamic risk factors can be deconstructed into psychological and social processes that are distributed across components of the action sequence; i.e., they *exist* as components of action not as things in themselves. Protective factors are simply action components that function as *brakes* or *eradicators* of problematic action components, although strengths refer to any prioritized goals and capacities of persons and contexts and thus do not need to be specifically mentioned in a causal risk model. We will now attempt to make our analysis more concrete by taking the dynamic risk factor of socioemotional difficulties in child molesters and demonstrate how the psychological and social elements comprising this broad risk factor can be located within the AMR.

Socioemotional Difficulties and the AMR

The cluster of dynamic risk factors variously labeled socioemotional problems, intimacy deficits, or the relational style domain (Thornton, 2013) consists of a collection of psychological and social attributes that have been associated with offending. Beech and Craig (2012, p. 174) describe the risk factors constituting this domain in the following way:

> This domain relates to interpersonal difficulties, particularly characterized by a lack of emotional intimacy in relationships. Either a lack of intimate partners or the presence of conflicts within an existing relationship is predictive of sexual reoffending… For men who sexually abuse children, the presence of emotional over-identification (emotional congruence) with children interferes with their ability to establish healthy adult relationships…; and is a powerful predictor of sexual recidivism.

The dynamic risk factor of intimacy deficits is not a homogeneous construct (see the previous section) and furthermore contains distinct types of psychological and social processes belonging to different parts of an action sequence dedicated to the pursuit of intimacy-related goals. To make the example as clear as possible, somewhat artificially, we concentrate on one facet of this risk factor, *emotional congruence with children* (see Figure 8.2). In brief, an individual has a history of attachment difficulties and has subsequent problems trusting adults in the context of close relationships. As a consequence of this distrust and fear of intimacy, such individuals fail to develop mature intimacy skills and view children as less rejecting and more emotionally rewarding to relate to. In our AMR example, the primary goal is to establish intimacy with a child. The plan and intrapersonal strategies associated with this goal are to spend time with a child and prepare her for a sexual and "intimate" relationship (what has been referred to as *grooming*). In seeking to create the opportunity for a sexual encounter, the individual plans to gradually encourage the child to share her feelings with him and to reciprocate. His profession of schoolteacher puts him into daily contact with dozens of children and guarantees him authority and respect from them. He also intends to give the selected child gifts and ask her to play computer games at his place. This plan is put into place and the offender strikes up conversation with a child he has been teaching at school, one that seems socially isolated and possibly neglected by her caregivers. Things do not go as well as planned and the child resists his attempts at establishing a friendship and refuses to talk about her feelings or to go to his place to play computer games. The offender reevaluates his plan and decides to target another child, this time a boy. He proposes to set up an after-school computer club and believes this will prove an attraction to this boy and other children. The relevant contextual factors for the offender's grooming behavior and subsequent sexual abuse of a child is the physical layout of his classroom, a subculture consisting of associates who share his interest in sex with children,

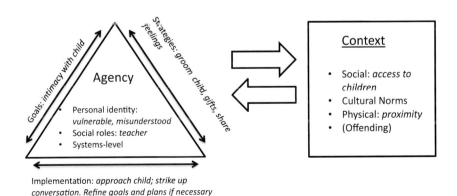

FIGURE 8.2 Using the AMR to explain intimacy deficits.

and a social position in which his authority and his motives for spending extracurricular time with children are not questioned. There is a dynamic interaction between these contextual features, and his goals, strategies, plan, and its implementation. Relatedly, underlying his goal of establishing a sexual relationship with a child are a number of unmet needs for intimacy, fear of rejection, and long-term attachment difficulties. In this case, the role of teacher constitutes the relevant level of agency, although the boundaries with his ongoing personal identity issues are somewhat porous. Certainly, one justification for his grooming of a child for sex is that he is teaching him or her about life and relationships, and it is simply an extension of a teaching role.

In this example, one aspect of the dynamic risk factor of intimacy deficits has been broken down into its action components. It is clear that there are emotional, sexual, cognitive, behavioral, and contextual features of this risk factor that are causally interconnected and that reinforce and shape each other's expressions. It is not too difficult to construct a more general model that incorporates all facets of the intimacy dynamic risk factor, or even construct an integrated action model of all risk factors operating in a particular case or across a subgroup of offenders. It simply requires accepting the possibility of individuals holding multiple goals, and that one of the evolved functions of agency is to construct dynamic models containing multiple goals coherently organized in an action plan.

RESEARCH IMPLICATIONS

The AMR provides an account of how dynamic risk factors could be causally related to the occurrence of crime and by extension to the initial onset of offending. That it is built upon the concept of agency and action components underlines the importance of goal directed behavior for both biological organisms and for persons. The relational aspect of the model acknowledges the important causal role of the social, cultural, and physical environment in facilitating and shaping offense-related proclivities while also pointing to the way human beings' niche construction abilities create offense-supportive contexts.

The AMR is a conceptual model of dynamic risk factors and protective factors transposed into components of human action and provides a useful way of thinking about the link between risk and explanation. It can help researchers analyze the relationships between person and contextual variables and points to the dynamic, interactional nature of offending (and all human action). The traditional formulation of dynamic risk factors—and protective factors—is theoretically problematic and unable to explain the onset and reoccurrence of offending. What is lacking is an understanding of how the causal processes that constitute dynamic risk factors (criminogenic needs) exert an influence on individuals and their environment. The AMR can clarify this.

How does the AMR fit within an evolutionary approach? We have argued that dynamic risk factors and protective factors can be conceptualized as proximate causes once they have been deconstructed into their psychological and social constituents. The central role that agency plays in the AMR is consistent with evolutionary theory concerning the survival advantages that social learning and culture confer on human beings. Having the ability to intelligently organize goals and strategies within flexible action plans means that organisms can learn quickly from each other and adaptively respond to changing environmental challenges. The capacity to develop agency is an adaptation, one we share to some extent with all organisms, especially primates. Furthermore, the cognitive and motivational architecture underpinning agency is inherited and aspects of this fundamental equipment is evident in dynamic risk factors. Adaptations such as the need for intimacy, the ability to think causally and to form folk psychological explanations, the presence of emotional responsiveness and empathy, and the ability to imitate others and to think strategically can all develop in dysfunctional ways. Dynamic risk factors are one such form; once conceptually reworked, the processes referred to by risk-related constructs are plausible, proximate causes of offending.

CONCLUSIONS

The forensic and correctional psychology field has become fixated on dynamic risk factors and their function in assessment and the management of offenders (Gannon & Ward, 2014). Alongside this preoccupation has been a recent tendency to rely on dynamic risk and protective factors to explain offending and as a consequence of this extension of their original use, to use them to formulate clinical cases and guide interventions with offenders (Ward, 2014). In this chapter, we critically examined these concepts and concluded that, although they are useful in risk prediction and to a lesser degree risk management, they are ill-equipped to play any sort of explanatory role, either in research or therapeutic contexts. In short, dynamic risk factors do not exist. Our solution to this problem was to develop the AMR, which is based on the concept of agency and has a strong grounding in biological and psychological theory. In our view, the AMR is able to make room for the causal aspects of dynamic risk factors while demonstrating how they are distributed across the action cycle and function as proximate causes of offending. Furthermore, once dynamic risk factors have been conceptually reworked in the AMR their links with gene–culture coevolution theory is more obvious and defensible.

CHAPTER

9

Social-Structural and Cultural Explanations

INTRODUCTION

Prediction is a risky business. If you get it right, you can bask in the knowledge that, through your understanding of the relevant causal dynamic processes involved, your have somehow transcended our inability to foresee the future. If you get it wrong, you look like a fool. In the mid-1990s, several social forecasters got it spectacularly wrong in their forecasts of future crime rates: writing as homicide victimization rates in the United States reached 10 per 100,000, and homicide offending rates for young people (age 14–24) breached 30 per 100,000 (Cooper & Smith, 2011), several authors predicted a continuing expansion in homicide among young people over the next decade, with dire consequences (see Zimring, 2014 for a discussion). With the benefit of hindsight we know, of course, that they were way off the mark. Crime began falling in the United States in the early 1990s and kept on falling. Moreover, crime declined seemingly just about everywhere in the Western world from the mid-1990s. For historians of crime, the recent fall in offending reflects a much longer trend in Western societies toward a decline in violent offending since at least the Middle Ages (Eisner, 2003; Pinker, 2011). In short, crime rates demonstrate substantial temporal variation: they are significantly higher during some historical periods compared with others. There is also substantial *spatial* variation in the rates of crime. Whether the ecological unit of analysis is neighborhoods, communities, cities, states, regions, or nation states the prevalence of crime varies from places to place, often in a dramatic fashion. A central task for criminological theories is to satisfactorily explain these findings: why do crime rates vary so much across time and space?

In this chapter, we first provide an overview of the nature of this variation and identify the main criminological explanations that have been developed to account for the patterns that are found. Our focus is, therefore, on cultural and social-structural explanations. We begin with an overview of historical trends in crime, focusing on both the long-term trends in Western society since

Evolutionary Criminology
http://dx.doi.org/10.1016/B978-0-12-397937-7.00009-4

© 2015 Elsevier Inc. All rights reserved.

the Middle Ages, then turning to a discussion of the international crime drop that began in the early 1990s. We then provide an overview of ecological variation in crime rates at various levels of spatial aggregation: neighborhoods, cities, regions, and countries. Much of the work in this space has been devoted to an elucidation of the various factors that can predict the ecological variation that is found, but there also have been various attempts to account for the findings drawing on mainstream criminological theories that focus on social-structural and cultural processes. We therefore outline various explanations for these temporal and spatial patterns focusing on social-structural changes, changes in routine activities, and cultural changes. Although we are far from a complete explanation of the historical and ecological variation in offending, mainstream criminological accounts are, we suggest, *salient* for addressing this variation. In the final section of the chapter, we argue that an evolutionary perspective is, however, *relevant* for understanding the findings that we present and can add explanatory value to existing theoretical accounts.

HISTORICAL TRENDS

Over the past decade, criminologists, historians, and other social scientists have made substantial strides in our understanding of temporal patterns in criminal offending. Two main historical focal points have dominated this research. Building on early research by Gurr (1981), who identified a substantial decline in homicide in Europe from the Middle Ages to the present, there is now an emerging body of research that has begun to provide an increasingly nuanced portrait of this decline, largely focusing on rates of homicide in Europe (Eisner, 2003, 2014; King, 2014; Mares, 2009; Pinker, 2011; Spierenburg, 2008) and to a lesser extend in the United States (Roth, 2001, 2009, 2012; Turchin, 2012). The second focal point zooms into a more restricted chronological frame, illuminating the significant, substantial, and seemingly international decline in crime that has occurred since around the mid-1990s (van Dijk, Tseloni, & Farrell, 2012). Again, there has been a focus on homicide rates, but the more detailed criminal statistics available for more recent periods has allowed for a more expanded analysis of the crime drop that takes in a range of different types of offense (Farrell, Tilley, & Tseloni, 2014). There are numerous explanatory accounts for these temporal patterns, but—understandably—they have mainly directed their attention to changes in social-structural and cultural factors that are plausibly linked to propensities and opportunities to commit crime.

The Long View

Who would be a king? In an effort to capture rates of violence in periods that predate detailed quantitative records, Eisner (2011) examined the frequency of regicide in Europe over a 1200-year time span, from 600 to 1800. The choice of regicide was dictated by the fact that, although "garden-variety" homicides did not make their way in to the historical record before around 1200 (and only then in a very patchy way), the killing of kings and queens were inevitably recorded. Two key findings emerged from the research: first, being a regent is a very risky occupation, with just under 15% of the more than 1500 regents murdered during the period of the study; second, rates of regicide dropped precipitously, from close to 2500 deaths per 100,000 rulers years in the seventh century, to less than 200 deaths per 100,000 ruler years in the eighteenth century. The decline in the killing of kings (and queens), according to Eisner (2011), can be viewed as part of a more general fall in violent crime in Europe over the past millennia or more.

Although we have some understanding of the nature of violence in earlier time periods (e.g., Armit, 2011), quantitative accounts of the rate of homicide (presumed to be an index of the rate of violent crime more generally) begin in the thirteenth century in Europe. As can be seen in Figure 9.1, the overall pattern is clear: mean homicide rates across different European regions peak at just over 30 per 100,000 in the early fifteenth century and then fall dramatically to around 1 per 100,000 in the early twentieth century where they have largely remained (Eisner, 2003, 2012, 2014). The overall decline is undisputed, although there is significant regional variation in the timing of the declines that are found. More specifically, declines in homicide began earliest in England and the Netherlands, and

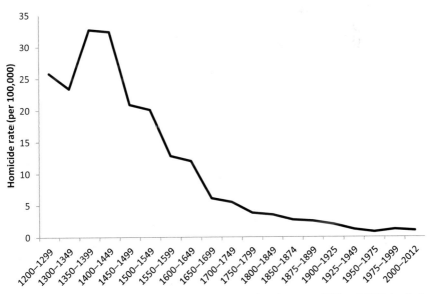

FIGURE 9.1 Mean homicide rates in European regions between 1200 and 2012 (excluding Corsica and Sardinia). *Eisner, (2014, Table 4).*

occurred much later in Southern European countries (see Eisner, 2012, 2014 for details). Eisner (2003) argues that although rates of homicide declined for both female and male perpetrators, the overall declining trend in homicide in Europe since the Middle Ages was largely driven by a significant drop in the frequency of male/male homicides (Eisner, 2014). For example, the ratio of male to female homicide perpetrators in London dropped from 13 males for every female in the early fourteenth century to three males for every female in the late nineteenth and early twentieth centuries (see Figure 9.2). In short, as summarized by Eisner (2014), "any covariates that may explain the long-term decline in homicide must probably focus on the pacification of unrelated male-to-male interactions in public space." Most historical research has focused on Europe, but several scholars have also examined fluctuating patters in homicide in the United States. Roth (2001, 2009), for example, found that rates of homicide in the early seventeenth century were extremely high, especially in some regions, and then declined significantly until the early nineteenth century with substantial fluctuations in the past 200 years. Turchin (2012), in an analysis of politically motivated violent events (e.g., lynchings, riots, terrorism) in the United States from 1780 to 2010, also found dramatic fluctuations during this period with peaks in 1870, 1920, and 1970.

What factor or factors can account for these changes? We will discuss more general theoretical accounts that attempt to explain the temporal patterns in crime rates that follow, but Eisner (2012) provides a useful summary of the main cluster of factors that have been identified by different scholars (see Table 9.1). Although Eisner, Pinker, and Roth differ

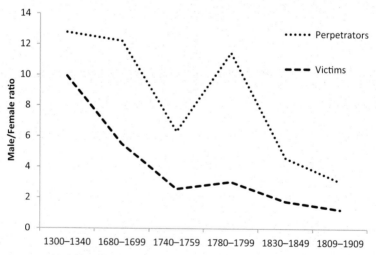

FIGURE 9.2   The ratio of male to female homicide perpetrators and victims in London from 1300 to 1909. *Eisner (2014, Table 5).*

somewhat in the key factors that they believe can explain historical trends in crime, there are clearly some similarities in their views. All three scholars emphasize the importance of changes in the power, scope, and legitimacy of the state in accounting for the long decline in homicide seen in the historical record. Where authority is vested in the state to exact punishment on individuals who commit crimes and when this authority is carried out in a (reasonably) legitimate fashion then the "need" for individuals to resort to violence to redress harms is substantially lessened. All three also emphasize the importance of cultural norms, values, and practices in influencing the use of violence. Eisner (2012, 2014) focuses on the role of institutions (e.g., church, family) and wider cultural values that have increased levels of self-discipline and self-control. Roth (2009) notes the importance of values favorable to the in-group brought about by increases in political solidarity, and Pinker (2011, p. 688) highlights how increases in gender equality and the emergency of "female-friendly" values can lead to declines in violence through a process of *feminization*:

> Several variety of feminization, then—direct political empowerment, the deflation of manly honor, the promotion of marriage on women's terms, the right of girls to be born, and women's control over their own reproduction—have been forces in the decline in violence.

Other factors that are viewed as potentially important include belief in the legitimacy of the social hierarchy (if people believe their position is legitimate they are less likely to resort to violence to obtain social

TABLE 9.1 The Key Factors Identified by Eisner, Roth, and Pinker That Can Account for Historical Changes in Violence

Eisner	Roth	Pinker
Changes in centralized state power	Belief in the stability of government and a fair and just legal system	Coercive power of the (legitimate) state (*Leviathan*)
"Disciplining revolutions"	Patriotism, empathy, and fellow feeling arising from political solidarity	Commerce and reciprocal relations between individuals (gentle commerce)
The legitimacy of state structures	Legitimacy of state structures and officials	Gender equality and acceptance of female values (*feminization*)
Protestantism (cultural values emphasizing self-control)	Belief in the legitimacy of the social hierarchy	*Expanding circle* of moral concern
		Human reason (*escalator of reason*)

status; Roth, 2009), commercial relations among individuals (of importance mainly for understanding declines in collective violence; Pinker,
2011), and the expanding circle of individuals who are brought within
individuals' moral purview (Pinker, 2011). We return to a discussion of
some of these factors later, but alongside research that has focused on
the long decline in violence in Western society over the past millennia
is a more narrowly directed collection of studies that have attempted to
explain the—surprising to many—decline in violence and other crimes
that has occurred since the 1990s.

The Rise and Fall of Crime (1950–2010)

In 1950, Truman authorizes production of the hydrogen bomb, the
cost of a gallon of gas in the United States is 18 cents, Uruguay beats
Brazil by 2 to 1 to win the World Cup, and rates of homicide in many
Western countries are at an all-time, historical low. In the United States
the homicide victimization rate in the 1950s hovered at just over
4 per 100,000 (Cooper & Smith, 2011), and in a sample of 17 European
countries the mean homicide rates was 0.79 per 100,000 (Eisner, 2008).
As Eisner, (2008, p. 305) summarizes for Europe in the late 1950s and
early 1960s: "These rates are quite remarkable. They represent the lowest levels of criminal killing documented in Europe since the start of
the written records 800 years ago and may well be the lowest rates ever
recorded anywhere in the world." These extraordinary low levels of
violence, however, did not last. Beginning in the early to mid-1960s in
the United States, Canada, and most Western European countries, homicide rates began to climb, breaching a rate of 10 per 100,00 in the United
States in the 1980s (Cooper & Smith, 2011). Other crimes were also on
the increase in many Western countries: rates of violent crime, motor
vehicle theft, theft, burglary, and robbery all rose significantly from the
early 1960s through to the early 1980s in the United States, Canada, and
other Western countries (Farrell et al., 2014). The rise in crime during this
period was spectacular, but not entirely universal. For instance, rates
of homicide in Japan peaked just after the Second World War at 3.5 per
100,000 and then declined consistently over the next half a century to
the current rate of 0.3 per 100,000 (Johnson, 2008; United Nations Office
on Drugs and Crime, 2014). The precipitous decline in a wide range of
offending that occurred from the early to the mid-1990s were also widespread, but by no means universal.

Evidence for a decline in crime emerged first in the United States
where the rates of homicide halved between 1992 and 2011 (Smith &
Cooper, 2013). It soon became apparent, however, that the reduction
in homicide in the United States appeared to be part of a much wider
decline in a range of different offenses in a number of countries. The

timing, nature, and scope of the decline, however, varied cross-nationally. Both official statistics and victimization surveys revealed substantial declines in homicide, other violent offending, theft, and vehicle theft for the United States and Canada, from the early to mid-1990s. In Europe, Australia, New Zealand, and elsewhere, declines were reported in some offense types, but not others, and patterns varied depending on the source of statistics employed (official statistics vs. victimization surveys) (see Aebi & Linde, 2012; del Frate & Mugellini, 2012; Baumer & Wolf, 2014; van Dijk & Tseloni, 2012; Mayhew, 2012; Tseloni, Mailley, Farrell, & Tilley, 2010, for further analyses). Taken as whole, however, Farrell et al. (2014) offered the following conclusions:

- "There has been a significant and prolonged 'crime drop' in many industrialized nations.
- The extent and nature of the crime drop appear to be more similar between more similar countries (in Canada and the United States, e.g., there are marked similarities)
- The extent of the evidence means that the likelihood that crime drops in different countries are a coincidence is vanishingly small, which implies a causal link.
- These crime drops were generally preceded by several decades of rapidly rising crime."

Although there is general agreement on the broad contours of offending over the past 60 years or so, there is no widespread agreement on what the primary causal factors and processes are that can account for the changes that have been found. Farrell (2013) lists 15 distinct hypotheses that have been offered to explain the crime drop that range from the legalization of abortion in the United States in 1973, to changes in the demographic structure of the population. Farrell and colleagues (Farrell et al., 2014; Farrell, Tilley, Tseloni, & Mailley, 2010; Farrell, Tseloni, Mailley, & Tilley, 2011) favor an explanation that focuses on how changes in the level and quality of security have driven declining crime rates for both property and personal offending. Others have argued that changes in cultural values can explain both the increase in offending that occurred after 1950 and the subsequent decline in the 1990s (e.g., Eisner, 2008, 2014; Kivivuori, 2014), whereas some scholars argue that economic (poverty, income inequality), and demographic (proportion of young males, ratio of younger to older individuals) factors are most important (Baumer & Wolf, 2014; Jacobs & Richardson, 2008; see also Fox & Piquero, 2003; Lauritsen, Rezey, & Heimer, 2014). Space precludes a thorough analysis of these various hypotheses and the relevant evidence that they explain (or do not explain). We therefore turn to an overview of ecological variations in crime rates before presenting a discussion of how mainstream criminological theories can potentially explain both historical and ecological variations in offending.

ECOLOGICAL VARIATIONS IN CRIME

Rates of crime vary—often dramatically—across different geographical contexts. Homicide rates provide a ready example. As illustrated in Figure 9.3, the rates of homicide vary by a factor of 179 between high homicide countries like Venezuela and low homicide countries such as Japan. Criminological interest in the nature, extent and—crucially—*cause* of this variation is understandable: for example, if the United States had the same homicide rate as Japan, there would be about 13,000 fewer homicide deaths every year. In this section, we focus on the main dimension of ecological variation at different levels of spatial organization—neighborhoods, cities, states, regions, and nation states—and the main factors that have been shown to predict variation.

Criminologists, like most social scientists, don't have much truck with the notion of universal "laws," but if there is anything like the "first law of criminology," it would be that patterns of crime and victimization are not evenly distributed across individuals, families, and communities. In fact, the very opposite appears to be the case: a relatively small number of individuals (and families) are responsible for a significant proportion of crime; a relatively small proportion of individuals experience a significant proportion of victimization; and a relatively small number of neighborhoods or communities

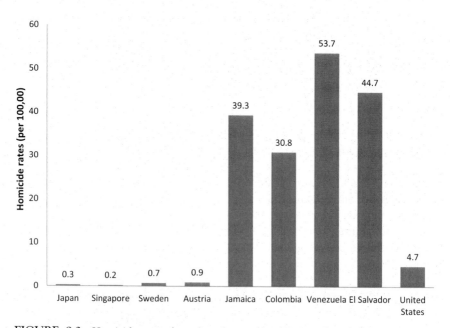

FIGURE 9.3 Homicide rates for selected countries (2012 or latest available). *United Nations Office of Drugs and Crime (2014).*

account for a significant proportion of the overall amount of crime. Criminologists have long been interested in the neighborhood characteristics that appear to be associated with higher levels of criminal offending. Shaw and McKay (1942) noted that levels of crime and disorder varied significantly within Chicago with some neighborhoods having high rates of crime and others experiencing lower crime rates. Moreover, they found that neighborhoods were relatively stable over time in their relative levels of crime, despite changes in residential composition. These general findings have since been replicated many times and suggest that there are certain characteristics of particular neighborhoods that make higher crime rates more likely and that endure over time (Sampson, 2012). Shaw and McKay argued that three main factors were associated with high crime neighborhoods: low socioeconomic status, racial heterogeneity, and high rates of residential mobility. Subsequent research has largely reinforced the idea that neighborhoods characterized by concentrated social disadvantage, and high rates of residential instability, have substantially higher rates of offending than more stable, socially advantaged neighborhoods, although results for the impact of racial/ethnic heterogeneity are more mixed (Bruinsma, Pauwels, Weerman, & Bernasco, 2013; Nieuwbeerta, McCall, Elffers, & Wittebrood, 2008; Sampson, 2012; Sampson, Raudenbush, & Earls, 1997; Sutherland, Brunton-Smith, & Jackson, 2013; Wikström, Oberwittler, Treiber, & Hardie, 2012). Moreover, there appears to be good evidence that the relative rankings of high crime and low crime neighborhoods are stable over time, even as the overall rate of crime in a city undergoes changes (see Sampson, 2012). In short, it appears that some neighborhoods have characteristics that can account for enduring between-neighborhood differences in crime rates.

Changing perspective from local contexts where individuals might interact with each other on a day-to-day basis, criminologists and others have also noted significant *regional* differences in rates of crime. Probably the best known regional difference is the finding that rates of violent crime are significantly higher in the American South than in Northern (and Western) American states (Nisbett, 1993). The evidence base for this finding is relatively secure: rates of violent crime and, more particularly, homicide are higher in Southern states of the United States than elsewhere in the country. More specifically, it is found that rates of dispute-related homicide perpetrated by white males is significantly higher in the Southern states, and where there is a greater concentration of Southern white men (Lee & Shihadeh, 2009; Ousey & Lee, 2010). We discuss possible explanations for this finding in the next section.

Rates of crime also vary substantially among cities, states, nations, and more inclusive geographical regions. The annual United Nations Global Study on Homicide provides a wealth of data on the nature of this variation. In 2012, 437,000 individuals were the victims of intentional homicide resulting in a global average rate of 6.2 individuals per 100,000. However, the rate of homicide varied substantially—from a low of 0.2 in Singapore to a high of 90.4 in Honduras. Homicide rates also demonstrate clear regional patterns with very high rates in the Americas (16.3 per 100,000) and Africa (12.5 per 100,000) and relatively low rates in Asia (2.9 per 100,000), Europe (3.0 per 100,000), and Oceania (3.0 per 100,000) (United Nations Office on Drugs and Crime, 2014). There is now an extensive body of research that has explored the various factors associated with cross-national variations in homicide rates, although most studies focus on a relatively narrow range of, largely Western, countries and are inevitably limited in the range of potential variables that they can include. In a narrative review of 65 studies, Pridemore and Trent (2010) concluded that income inequality was the most reliable and robust predictor of homicide rates, although a large number of different variables, including population structure (percent of young people), sex ratio (male:female ratio), divorce rate, level of urbanization, poverty, and gross domestic product were significant in some studies but not others. A meta-analysis of cross-national predictors of homicide conducted by Nivette (2011b) found a number of significant effects across studies with poverty, income inequality, divorce rate, population growth, female labor participation, and infant mortality (among others) positively related to homicide rates and decommodification (relative spending on social welfare), ethnic heterogeneity, and development negatively related to rates of homicide. Other studies, with different samples, have found relationships between homicide and a range of variables including inequality and infant mortality (Ouimet, 2012), income inequality and low levels of trust (Elgar & Aitken, 2010), political instability (Chu & Tusalem, 2013), and lack of political legitimacy (Nivette & Eisner, 2013). Most research has focused on cross-national variation in homicide rates, but other studies that have examined differences among cities find that measures of deprivation and population structure (especially urbanism and population density) are the most significant predicts of homicide rates (McCall, Land, & Parker, 2010; McCall & Nieuwbeerta, 2007).

Making sense of this literature is no easy task, and many variables (e.g., that relate to cultural attitudes, values, and beliefs) that might potentially influence rates of homicide and other types of offending are simply not available for cross-national comparison. Moreover, as Eisner (2012) argues, a lack of consistency in samples, operationalization of key variables, and interpretation of results has hampered efforts to draw definitive conclusions. Moreover, variables that likely predict rates of homicide and other types of crime may vary depending on the nature of the society (Nivette, 2011a). However, higher rates of homicide (and other forms of offending) seem to be positively related to higher levels of income inequality, economic deprivation, and demographic factors (including ethnic heterogeneity, divorce rate, population growth, percentage of young individuals, and sex ratio), and negatively to indicators of political legitimacy.

THEORETICAL EXPLANATIONS FOR ECOLOGICAL AND HISTORICAL VARIATIONS IN CRIME

We have now clearly established that rates of crime vary—and vary substantially—over time and across different ecological units such as neighborhoods, regions, and countries. We have also touched on a number of "risk factors" that are associated with this variation. Ultimately, however, we will want to provide clear *theoretical explanations* that identify the key causal processes that give rise to the variation that is found. Most of the explanations developed by criminologists focus on macro-level structures and processes (see Table 4.1). This focus makes sense: the most *salient* explanatory accounts are those that can explain the differences that are found and because macro-level structures and processes demonstrate considerable spatial and temporal variability it is likely that they play a key causal role in accounting for variation in crime rates (Pratt & Cullen, 2005). Of course, crime—whether fraud, murder, drug-dealing, or rape—is perpetrated by individuals so a satisfactory macro-level explanation will need to explain how macro-level processes affect individuals in ways that make them more likely to engage in criminal acts in some places and historical periods in comparison with others. Broadly speaking, two main types of explanation are employed. The first focuses on key social-structural processes and institutions, and the second privileges cultural norms, beliefs, attitudes, and values. This distinction, however, is not absolute and many theoretical accounts combine elements of both approaches. We turn, then, very briefly, to an overview of the main social-structural and cultural approaches that have been developed to account for variations in offending.

Social Structural Approaches

Social disorganization theory/collective efficacy. The underlying assumption of social disorganization theory is that neighborhoods characterized by social disadvantage, high residential mobility, and ethnic heterogeneity are socially disorganized: informal mechanisms of social control (e.g., schools, churches, community institutions) are weak, resulting in low levels of social cohesion and a subsequent diversity of values and norms regarding appropriate behavior. Through socialization processes, values that facilitate delinquent behavior are transmitted generationally accounting for stable patterns in crime rates over time (relative to socially organized neighborhoods). The most recent and widely regarded theoretical approach within the social disorganization tradition is Sampson's theory of *collective efficacy* (Sampson, 2012; Sampson et al., 1997). Collective efficacy refers to macro-level properties of communities that relate to levels of social cohesion (shared values, norms, and expectations regarding behavior), and the willingness of residents to intervene to enforce these norms, values, and expectations. Thus Sampson et al. (1997, p. 918) argue that "the differential ability of neighborhoods to realize the common values of residents and maintain effective social controls is a major source of neighborhood variation in violence." The collective efficacy of a neighborhood, in turn, is influenced by concentrated disadvantage and residential mobility: socially disadvantaged and less stable neighborhoods result in lower levels of collective efficacy which, in turn, influence rates of crime.

The idea that neighborhood variations in offending rates relate to differences in collective efficacy has been supported by a number of studies in the United States (Sampson, 2012; Sampson et al., 1997), the United Kingdom (Wikström et al., 2012), the Netherlands (Nieuwbeerta et al., 2008), and Australia (Mazerolle, Wickes, & McBroom, 2010), although not all studies have provided unequivocal support for the theory (Bruinsma et al., 2013; Sutherland et al., 2013). However, it seems clear that differences among neighborhoods in the degree of social cohesion and willingness to enforce social norms can account for some of the variation that is found. Moreover, Sampson (2012) has argued that changes in collective efficacy over time can account for some of the historical trend towards declining rates of violence in the United States since the mid-1990s. Collective efficacy theory has been pressed into less regular service in attempts to explain variations in offending over longer time periods and among larger ecological units (cities, states, regions, and countries). However, plausibly many of the variables that predict higher rates of crime (such as poverty, income inequality, levels of trust) manifest at the more local level as a higher number of neighborhoods with relatively lower levels of collective efficacy. The long-term historical trends in violence are less readily accounted for by collective efficacy theory. Broadly speaking the historical trend has been towards less socially cohesive, more mobile, and more ethnically heterogeneous societies over time although it is unclear how this has played out at the level of individual neighborhoods.

Anomie/strain theory. For Merton (1938), crime was inextricably linked to social-structural and cultural processes. Individuals who are thwarted from obtaining the "American dream" of economic prosperity and success by virtue of social-structural barriers that impede social mobility, resort to "deviant" (i.e., criminal) routes to obtain the status that they are otherwise denied. In short, the tension arising from culturally prescribed goals and an inability to meet them produces a "strain to anomie" that is manifest in criminal behavior. Contemporary work with the strain/anomie tradition also highlights the role of cultural values and social-structural processes. In *Crime and the American Dream*, Messner and Rosenfeld (2013) focus on how the institutional structure of American society privileges the economy above all else, and how this impacts in adverse ways on other important institutions such as the family or the education system. As summarized by Messner, Rosenfeld, and Karstedt (2013, p. 411), Institutional-anomie theory (IAT) can explain high rates of crime as a result of

> ...dominant cultural values that extol the virtues of competitive individual achievement and wealth accumulation at the expense of values that emphasize non-economic forms of achievement, collective solidarity, and the common good.

Although IAT was originally developed with a focus on explaining the high rates of crime found in American society relative to other Western nations, it can also potentially account for historical and ecological variation in offending. Ecological variation in crime can be accounted for by IAT in terms of the relative emphasis that societies place on the economy as the dominant institution and their failure to insulate citizens from the vicissitudes of the market economy. More recently, Messner (2012) has attempted to bridge the macro-micro divide in criminology by integrating IAT with Wikström's situational action theory. The focal point of this integration is morality: certain institutional "configurations" (i.e., the favoring of the economy over all else) lead to higher crime rates because of the related weakening in other important institutions (family, school, and religion) that play a central role in the inculcation of cooperative behavior by facilitating moral development along prosocial lines.

Crime pattern theories. Another theoretical perspective in criminology that has been at the forefront of efforts to explain ecological variation in crime—particularly the historical pattern over the past 50 years or so—draws on how social structural and cultural changes affect the routine activities of individuals in ways that influence criminal decision-making. Routine activities theory notes that for crime to occur three things need to converge in time and space: (1) a motivated offender; (2) a suitable target; and (3) the absence of a capable guardian (Felson, 2008). The first of these factors is simply taken for granted and then largely ignored—there will always be individuals willing to take advantages of criminal opportunities. The second two factors will, inevitably, vary across time and space: in some locations and historical periods, there are more suitable targets and less capable guardians than others, and hence rates of crime will vary accordingly. The rapid rise in rates of offending that occurred in many Western countries in the late 1960s and early 1970s can be attributed, from this perspective, to critical changes in routine activities: suburbanization and the greater entry of women into the workforce removed many capable guardians, and the rise in consumer goods created more suitable targets. This approach has also been employed to account for the drop in crime that has occurred since the 1990s. In particular, according to the "security hypothesis," the dramatic fall in offending was largely driven by improvements in the scope, range, and quality of security measures employed to prevent crime (Farrell et al., 2011, 2014). Although this approach may only seem applicable for understanding changes in property crime, Farrell et al. (2014) argue that property offenses are "keystone" crimes that once suppressed forestall criminal careers and bring about a fall in other kinds of offending as well.

Cultural Explanations

The civilizing process. Norbert Elias was a German sociologist who published his magnum opus, *The Civilizing Process*, in 1939. Although Elias was predominantly concerned with explaining historical changes in "civilized" behavior (i.e., manners and personality), the key processes that he identified have been pressed into service by historians of crime to explain the dramatic fall in homicide rates in Europe since the middle ages (Eisner, 2003, 2008, 2012, 2014; Pinker, 2011; Spierenburg, 2008). As Eisner (2014) summarizes, Elias linked changes in the social structure of society to changes in the psychological characteristics of individuals. Two key social structural changes are identified: the power of the state expanded and its monopolization over the capacity to wield violence (i.e., punishment) became more legitimate, and there was the development of greater economic interdependencies among individuals with the expansion of the market economy. These social-structural changes, in turn, wrought changes in the psychological characteristic of individuals. Starting with elites, the capacity to exert self-control over behavior became increasingly important, and the appropriateness of using physical force to resolve disputes declined. These changes diffused to the wider population and became increasingly entrenched through socialization practices. These key ideas have also been employed to explain the increase in violence from the late 1960s and subsequent declines in the 1990s in terms of changes in cultural values and norms that emphasize hedonism and individual expression in the 1960s, 1970s, and 1980s, and their reversal in the 1990s (see Eisner, 2008, 2014; Pinker, 2011 for details and empirical support for these ideas).

Subcultures and the culture of honor hypothesis. The role of cultural values, norms, and practices is also emphasized in approaches that attempt to explain why certain groups engage in much higher rates of violence than others. The subcultures of violence theory, originally developed by Wolfgang and Ferracuti (1967), explained the high rates of violence that were typical of certain groups in society (lower class males) in terms of a shared set of norms, values, and practices that are conducive to violence. Extending these ideas, Anderson (1994, 1999) argued that certain social environments—particularly those where violence is common and there is a lack of third party enforcement—tend to lead individuals to adopt a "code of the street" where the use of violence is a normative way to resolve disputes and to obtain status. Whereas subcultures of violence theory mainly focused on explaining high rates of violent crime in disadvantaged communities, the "culture of honor" thesis was primarily developed to explain the high rates of homicide in the American South (Nisbett, 1993). Specifically, it is argued that Southern white men adhere to a culture of honor: they believe that the use of violence is the appropriate—even oblig-atory—response to threats to self, family, and social status. The package of values, norms, beliefs, and practices that make up the culture of honor, it is further argued, arose among herding communities in the British Isles as a reputation of responding to threats with violence would have been adap-tive in communities with little rule of law and with wealth (livestock) that are highly mobile and hence relatively easily rustled. These individuals then settled as immigrants largely in the American South where their par-ticular set of values are transmitted to their children through socialization practices. Both the subcultural theory of violence (e.g., Stewart & Simons, 2010) and the culture of honor hypothesis (Baller, Zevebergen, & Messner, 2009; Ousey & Lee, 2010; although see Daly & Wilson, 2010) have received support from the relevant empirical literature, and it seems plausible to suggest that at least some of the ecological variation in rates of violent offending can be attribute to differences in violence-related norms, beliefs, and values.

Summary

Our summary of the main social-structural and cultural theories that have been employed to explain historical and ecological variation in offending has necessarily been brief, and we make no attempt to pro-vide a comparative evaluation of the explanatory worth of these differ-ent perspectives. Indeed, all of the relevant theoretical approaches find some support in the literature (Pratt & Cullen, 2005) and can probably account for some of the variation that arises over time, and among dif-ferent neighborhoods, cities, regions, and countries. We think that these approaches are *salient* for explaining historical and ecological variation in offending and leave it to others to evaluate their relative worth. We do think, however, that the evolutionary approach that we advocate in this book can enrich our understanding of variations in crime and can be successfully integrated with the perspectives presented in this section.

AN EVOLUTIONARY PERSPECTIVE

There is a yet to be told history of crime that extends from the origin of our species to the present. However, despite scattered findings in the archaeological and historical record (e.g., Armit, 2011), we have little in the way of hard quantitative evidence of variations in crime rates until the

Middle Ages—although such variation almost certainly existed. The over-all contours of human history, from 50,000 years ago to the modern era is, however, reasonably well understood and there is a fascinating body of work, making increasing use of quantitative evidence to explain the spread of humans out of Africa from 50,000 years ago, the emergence of agriculture 12,000 years ago, and the subsequent dramatic, although geo-graphically uneven, patterns in social development that have occurred since (e.g., Diamond, 1997; Fukuyama, 2011; Morris, 2011, 2014). There is substantial disagreement regarding just how and why humans in some regions abandoned hunting and gathering in favor of a sedentary agri-cultural lifestyle, but the impact of these changes on human social history is widely recognized. For our purposes, the crucial changes involved the emergence of—often highly—stratified societies from largely egalitar-ian foraging groups. The ability to accumulate wealth, social divisions of labor, and changing population patterns created societies in which steep gradients in social status became entrenched. Large-scale societies cre-ate significant problems for cooperation which evolved in the context of small, egalitarian foraging groups where everyone was known to one another. To maintain social cooperation in such large groups, critical cul-tural changes were necessary, including the effective and legitimate use of force to regulate antisocial behavior. Norenzayan (2013) has also argued that cooperation can be enhanced among societies that adopt certain reli-gious practices because they not only enhance social cohesion through shared values and beliefs, but also belief in moralistic gods who are will-ing and ready to exact divine punishment on wrong-doers would have promoted cooperation and prosocial behavior. Although the importance of within-group social cohesion was important to the effective social func-tion on large-scale societies, one of the key selective forces was probably intergroup conflict and cooperation. In short, as Morris (2014) has recently proposed, warfare played a critical role in building large-scale, socially cohesive societies, although always ones that were potentially subject to fragmentation and collapse perhaps, as Turchin (2006) has argued, in reg-ular secular cycles.

The large-scale historical picture of human social, cultural, and genetic evolution is important not only for explaining historical variation in offend-ing rates, but also for more local variation because differences among ecological units largely arise through historical processes. The emerg-ing literature on "deep" historical processes is, therefore, important for understanding current social practices and institutions and their variabil-ity across geographical regions. We think that there is substantial scope for criminologists to draw on this emerging literature to explain trends in crime across time and space, especially given the greater willingness for social historians to employ quantitative methods to explore historical patterns and changes over time (e.g., Morris, 2011, 2013; Turchin, 2012).

We will, however, largely focus on historical changes in crime over the past 500 years and ecological variability in offending in this section, with the aim to integrate key evolutionary processes with empirically identified risk (and protective) factors and key macro-level explanations.

In Figure 3.2, we indicated that variations in group-level characteristics are typically explained by evolutionary behavioral scientists in terms of four key processes: evoked culture, transmitted culture, genetics, and gene–culture coevolution. To explain historical and ecological variation in offending, we will mainly focus on the first two of these processes before touching on how genetic and gene–culture coevolutionary processes may contribute to our understanding. Two general points are worth mentioning before we engage in this task. First, although the explanatory challenge is to account for *variation* in offending, it is important to recognize that, to account for variation in any phenomenon, it is essential to have a clear understanding of the causal mechanisms and processes that underlie that phenomenon. For example, to account for variation in homicide across time and space, we need to integrate causal theories of why humans engage in homicide with theoretical accounts of how these mechanisms respond to changing social and ecological contexts. Second, although the literature reviewed previously clearly indicates enormous variability in offending rates across time, the patterns that we address in other chapters of this book remain largely unchanged. More specially, men are more likely to engage in violent offending at all times and in all places and homicide is dominated by males killing other males. The relationship between offending, age, and social class are a little more varied but—with some local exceptions—the age–crime curve largely holds across time and space and social class is a consistently robust predictor of offending (although with some interesting historical changes over time).

In Table 9.2 we provide the key evolutionary processes that we think are important for accounting for ecological and historical variation in offending, the link to empirically identified "risk" and "protective" factors and relevant connections to mainstream criminological theories. This table does not exhaust all of the potentially relevant factors and processes, but it does capture the ones that have been most prominently discussed in the literature. As Eisner (2012, Table 1) notes, high homicide societies are characterized by a number of key features: homicides are predominantly between acquaintances and strangers, males are overwhelmingly both the perpetrators *and* victims, and violence can be successfully employed as a viable route to obtain social status. Consistent with this picture we argue that one important, overlapping, set of factors and processes relates to the intensity of male–male competition, effort put in to mating rather than parenting, dominance as a viable route to social status, and the entrainment of fast life history strategies. If, as we argue in Chapter 6, social and sexual arrangements shape the intensity of intrasexual competition

TABLE 9.2   Key Evolutionary Processes That Can Account for Historical and Ecological Variation in Crime

Key evolutionary processes	Link to important "risk (and protective) factors"	Relationship to key macro-level explanations
Factors and processes that increase or decrease: • Male–male intrasexual competition • Mating rather than parenting effort • Dominance rather than prestige as a viable route to social status • The entrainment of fast life history strategies	• Income inequality/relative deprivation • Poverty, infant mortality, harsh environmental conditions • Sex ratio (female biased) • Family environment (divorce rate) • Criminal opportunities	• Anomie/strain theory • Social disorganization/collective efficacy
Factors and processes that increase or decrease prosocial and increase or decrease antisocial behavior: • Values, norms, institutions, and practices that enhance or decrease social cohesion and social connectedness • Levels of informal social control • Levels of formal social control	• Urbanism, residential mobility, ethnic heterogeneity • Cultural values and norms that promote cooperation, self-control, and prosocial behavior • Cultural values and norms that promote the legitimate use of violence • Collective efficacy • Political instability; lack of viable, legitimate third-party punishment • Surveillance and monitoring	• Social disorganization/collective efficacy • Anomie/strain theory • Crime pattern theories • The civilizing process • Subcultural theory/culture of honor hypothesis
Factors that increase the variability among human groups/populations	• Geographical isolation resulting in changes in allele frequency among human groups via genetic drift and selection • Gene–culture coevolutionary processes	

which, in turn, influences the rate of risk-taking, antisocial, and criminal behavior perpetrated by males, then conditions that promote male–male competition will lead to higher rates of a wide range of crimes, including homicide.

What factors tend to enhance male–male competition and why do these factors have this effect? One key variable is inequality. As we have seen, income inequality is one of the most robust cross-national predictors of homicide rates. It is also clearly linked to rates of crime more generally, and even rates of bullying among young people (Elgar, Craig, Boyce, Morgan, & Vella-Zarb, 2009). Moreover, income inequality is a robust predictor of negative health outcomes, and the ratio of male to female mortality (Kruger & Fisher, 2014). In short, in societies characterized by steeper gradients in social inequality there is more crime, and higher rates of a diverse range of health and other social problems (see Wilkinson & Pickett, 2009, for a comprehensive review). How are two macro-level variables like income inequality and homicide rates causally linked? From an evolutionary perspective, income inequality increases levels of male–male intrasexual competition in risk-taking and violence. Ultimately, evolution is about *differential* fitness: reproductive success is not about how "fit" you are per se, but how fit you are relative to your same-sex competitors. It is hardly surprising, therefore, that human behavior is highly sensitive to gradients in characteristics—like the social status that arises with high incomes in modern societies—that are linked to reproductive success. Men, more than women, are likely to be sensitive to these social gradients because, as we elaborated in Chapter 5, they have potentially more to gain by virtue of their social position (Daly & Wilson, 1988; Daly, Wilson & Vasdev, 2001). Thus in environments (cities, states, regions, countries) characterized by higher rates of income inequality, there are relatively more males who receive relatively less of the available status associated with wealth and who hence are more motivated to engage in behaviors that may elevate social status. High rates of income inequality also tend to be related to low rates of social mobility: as societies become more unequal, there are fewer opportunities to ascend the social hierarchy. Drawing from the dominance-prestige model of social status discussed in Chapter 5, this implies that, precluded from opportunities to obtain prestige, relatively more men in unequal societies find dominance a more viable route to social status. This analysis is consistent with the finding that income inequality predicts rates of bullying in adolescence (a marker of the importance of dominance strategies during a developmental period in which social hierarchies are becoming crystallized) as well as female preferences for masculinized faces (Brooks, Scott, Maklakov, Kasumovic, Clark, Penton-Voak, 2011) (suggesting that features relating to dominance become more important in prospective relationship partners in unequal societies).

Other factors that enhance male–male competition include overall levels of poverty, the sex ratio, and rates of divorces (see, in particular the work of Barber, 2007, 2009, 2011). As we have argued in Chapter 7, certain social and ecological conditions tend to entrain fast life history strategies for children during critical stages in their developmental history. High rates of poverty, infant mortality, and harsh environmental conditions are predictors of offending therefore, because they increase the likelihood that individuals will "adopt" fast life history strategies that involve early maturation, effort into mating rather than parenting, and enhanced intrasexual competition. Plausibly the relationship that is found between divorce and homicide rates (although not in all studies and probably of decreasing importance in societies where rates of marriage are declining), can be understood in terms of creating unpredictable social environments that also may entrain fast life history strategies, along with directly increasing overall levels of male–male competition. Concentrated poverty tends to amplify these processes as poverty is intergenerationally transmitted through social and epigenetic processes (see Chapter 7). Moreover, in disadvantaged neighborhoods with high crime rates often a significant proportion of—particularly young—men spend substantial time away from the community as a result of being incarcerated. This, in turn, creates further unpredictability in family relationships along with skewing the operational sex ratio. Although it might seem logical to assume that a relatively greater proportion of men compared with women would lead to higher rates of violence, the opposite appears to be the case. This makes sense from an evolutionary point of view, because when there is an excess of males women have relatively more individuals to choose from and hence can exert their preferences for males who are willing to maintain committed relationships and make long-term investments in offspring. When there is a relative dearth of males, they are better able to exert their own preferences for a relatively large number of short-term relationships, hence enhancing overall levels of male–male competition. Of course, as Schacht, Rauch, and Borgerhoff Mulder (2014) remind us, enhanced mating competition does not *necessarily* equate to higher rates of violence as aggression is just one potential manifestation of intrasexual competition. More generally, the relationship between factors that enhance male/male competition and rates of offending are clearly moderated by ecological factors that influence the range and scope of criminal opportunities. For instance, as Farrell and colleagues have argued (e.g., Farrell et al., 2014) various forms of property offending become less viable in ecological contexts where target hardening initiative successfully make such activities less economically fruitful thus limiting the capacity of a "criminal career" to promote social status. Other changes in social and ecological conditions—e.g., changes in alcohol policy—may also moderate the relationship between levels of male–male competition and crime by providing or limiting opportunity for intrasexual competition to occur. For example, alcohol deregulation increases the availability of alcohol to young people who congregate in social contexts which likely heightens intrasexual aggression and reduces the capacity to regulate behavior (Durrant, 2013b).

We think that there are also clear links between the key evolutionary processes identified in Table 9.2 and important macrolevel theories in criminology. To illustrate, IAT emphasizes the importance of particular cultural values that elevate the importance of economic competition and individual achievement and deemphasize other forms of achievement and institutions that might buffer individuals from economic disadvantage. These values are inextricably linked to levels of inequality in society and are also likely to create a larger segment of individuals exposed to concentrated levels of poverty. In other words, the macro-level changes identified by IAT change the social environment in ways that are likely to promote intrasexual competition, heighten the importance of dominance as a strategy to obtain social status and create conditions that are likely to entrain fast life history strategies. More broadly, our analysis so far has emphasized the importance of evoked culture: universal psychological mechanisms underlying socio-sexual strategies play out differently under different ecological and social circumstances. We also think that transmitted culture has a crucial role to play in explaining historical and ecological variations in offending.

In Chapter 5, we argued that humans are a highly prosocial, cooperative species and that our capacity to cooperate, both with kin and non kin, likely reflects a history of genetic and cultural evolution, along with gene–culture coevolutionary processes. Because crime is, almost by definition, antisocial behavior, it follows that factors and processes that tend to enhance cooperative and prosocial behavior will be related to lower levels of offending. Conversely, factors and processes that tend to weaken the human inclination to cooperate will result in higher rates of offending. Finally, we need to consider how cultural evolutionary processes shape a range of values, norms, and practices among social groups that may enhance or dampen criminal behavior in general and violent behavior more specifically. First, consider a set of classic risk factors that have been linked to higher rates of violent crime: urbanism, residential mobility, and ethnic heterogeneity. Each of these factors has traditionally been related to decreases in social cohesion and social connectedness because individuals, on average, are less likely to share values, norms, and practices with other members of their community. In the absence of shared norms and values regarding appropriate behavior there is inevitably a decline in the levels of both "first-party" punishment as individuals are less clear about the appropriate social norms that guide behavior and therefore may be less likely to self-censure their behavior, along with lower levels of second and third party punishment and hence a decrease in social control. In this respect the evolutionary perspective that we outlined in Chapter 5 is broadly consistent with the key insights of collective efficacy theory: communities that have lower levels of social cohesion and have residents that are less willing to intervene to reinforce social norms will have higher rates of crime. An evolutionary perspective also supports the importance of legitimate third party punishment in regulating rates of—especially violent—crime in society. As we argued in Chapter 5, although humans may be "natural-born cooperators," there is also a tendency to employ antisocial behavior to obtain benefits at the expense of group members and this tendency is—largely—successfully suppressed through the willingness of group members to punish individuals who violate social norms. Both historically and cross-culturally, societies and communities that lack legitimate third-party punishment of antisocial behavior have higher rates of offending. Two main evolutionary processes can account for this finding. First, in the absence of punishment, cooperative behavior declines and antisocial behavior increases as the benefits of the former, and the costs of the latter are diminished. Second, in the absence of legitimate third party enforcement of social norms, individuals respond to such violations by enacting second party punishment—that is, they engage in revenge. Revenge, in turn, tends to set off cycles of retaliation that can substantially inflate rates of violent crime in society (Boehm, 2011; Roth, 2011).

Finally, we need to recognize that between-group differences in rates of crime can be strongly influenced by differences in values, norms, institutions, and practices that arise through cultural evolutionary processes. As advocates of cultural evolution note, our capacity for culture reflects the evolution of social learning mechanisms that enable the transmission of ideas, values, beliefs, practices, and institutions among members of social groups. Humans are powerfully influenced by their cultural environment and their capacity for agency shapes, and are shaped by, the social and cultural contexts in which we are embedded (see Chapter 8). As noted earlier, many scholars believe that essentially cultural explanations have an important role to play in explaining temporal and spatial variation in offending. Shifts in cultural beliefs and values relating to self-control may have been important in the declining rates of violence since the Middle Ages, and specific cultural values may be able to explain community, regional, and national differences in offending. What does a cultural evolutionary perspective add to this literature? We think a cultural evolutionary approach can be fruitfully integrated with other macro-level criminological explanations like the civilizing process, subcultural theory, and the culture of honor thesis and can add value to these approaches. Importantly, a cultural evolutionary framework has developed specific models regarding the way that cultural variants are transmitted. Space precludes a thorough presentation of these ideas, but they involve different mechanisms of transmission (e.g., one to one vs. one to many; vertical [parent to offspring] vs. horizontal [among members of the same generation]), and the role of specific content, model-based, and frequency based biases in social transmission (Mesoudi, 2011a). So, for example, the idea that the decline in violence in Europe in the Middle Ages first occurred among elites and then spread to the general population is consistent with the idea of prestige-based social learning biases that favors the learning of cultural variants from high status individuals. The development of models of cultural learning potentially provides fertile ground for further research that can link cultural microevolution (the processes that cause changes in cultural variants overtime) with cultural macroevolution (the relationship between cultural variants over time, using cultural phylogenetic methods). The willingness of historians of crime to employ diverse sources to explore the way that relevant cultural variants, such as markers of self-control, change over time (e.g., Eisner, 2014; Roth, 2012) opens up substantial scope for theoretical integration of cultural evolutionary ideas with those employed by mainstream criminologists.

We conclude this section by considering whether or not historical and/ or ecological variation in crime might be potentially explained by genetic differences among human populations. This is—to put it mildly—a potentially controversial area of inquiry. For reasons that are entirely understandable given the lamentable history of "race science," this is ground that most social scientists are simply not willing to traverse (Wright & Morgan, 2014). However, given the rapid advances that are being made in human evolutionary genetics (see Jobling, Hollox, Hurles, Kivisild, & Tyler-Smith, 2013; Wade, 2014), it is a topic that cannot be entirely ignored. Moreover, by reason that there are substantial ethnic and racial differences in rates of conviction and incarceration in many Western countries (Piquero, Piquero, & Stewart, 2014), it is a topic that criminologists will, at some point, have to engage with (Walsh & Yun, 2011). First, we need to consider what is meant by the term "race." This is no easy task and there remains considerable, legitimate, scholarly debate about just what constitutes race. From an evolutionary perspective, race simply refers to differences in the frequencies of particular alleles that cluster among certain populations and allow for differentiation between different population groups (Wade, 2014). These differences arise as different populations of humans become relatively or absolutely geographically isolated with each other over time leading to local changes in the frequencies of specific alleles through genetic "drift," and selection processes. Many of these differences as they relate to skin pigmentation and other physiological traits are now well-documented (Jobling et al., 2013). There are also plausible gene–culture coevolutionary processes at work as cultural practices change selection environments that favor some alleles over others (see our discussion in Chapter 3 on the evolution of lactose tolerance in populations with a history of dairy farming).

Our take on the available literature is that, at this point in time, there is *no convincing* evidence of genetic differences in human populations that are likely to have any significant explanatory value in accounting for racial and ethnic differences in offending. We cannot dismiss the possibility that such evidence might emerge in the future, but there are several reasons to believe that this conclusion will not be substantially altered. First, the magnitude of the racial differences in conviction and incarceration rates in countries like the United States, New Zealand, and Australia is staggeringly large but so too are differences in a host of well-known and widely replicated risk factors for offending that are associated with low socioeconomic status. Racial differences in socioeconomic status in these countries are clearly linked to histories of colonialism, slavery, racism, and discrimination. Add the role of potential bias in the criminal justice systems and most (if, perhaps, not all) of the racial variation in arrest and conviction rates can be explained. Second, although there are clearly genetic differences among racial groups that give rise to different physical traits, phenotypic characteristics that relate to brain and behavior are much less canalized than those that give rise to skin pigmentation and other physiological characteristics. In other words, although research may uncover clear racial variation in alleles that play a role in neurodevelopment (Wade, 2014), gene–environment interactions, including epigenetic processes, will make the "direct" effects of these differences on phenotypic characteristics less visible. We have proceeded with this topic in a somewhat cautious manner. However, it is never wise to second-guess what science will produce in the future, and we encourage criminologists to familiarize themselves with the relevant literature as it emerges to enable a reasoned and informed analysis of this topic.

SUMMARY

Crime rates vary. In some populations and in some periods, the prevalence of crime is much greater than in other populations and at other time periods. Accounting for these findings is an enormously important task because if we can understand the causal processes that underlie variation then we may be in a position to enact policy changes that can bring about changes in the volume of crime in society at any given point in time. Criminologists have made significant progress in both identifying the "risk factors" that seem to relate to higher rates of offending and in constructing plausible explanatory theories that can potentially account for the patterns that are found. We have argued that these macro-level theoretical explanations are the most *salient* in understanding why it is that temporal and spatial variation in offending occurs. We have also suggested that evolutionary explanations can contribute to our understanding in important ways and hence are *relevant* for furthering our understanding of the patterns that are found. Indeed, we think that there is substantial scope to build integrated explanatory accounts that incorporate some of the important insights from evolutionary theory—especially those of cultural evolutionary theory—with those developed by mainstream criminologists.

PART III

RESPONDING TO CRIME

10

Punishment, Public Policy, and Prevention

INTRODUCTION

Crime is responsible for a significant amount of human suffering in society. The lives of victims and their families can be adversely affected—often in profound ways. Crime can erode social trust in community and lead to fear among residents. Crime is expensive for police and even more expensive to prosecute and contain. Perpetrators, too, suffer from the effects of their offending as their lives are altered, often permanently, and typically for the worse. In this book, we have made the case that an evolutionary approach is invaluable for advancing our understanding of why crime occurs and what accounts for the main patterns in offending that we observe. Criminology is, however, best conceived of as an applied social science. Thus, it is essential that we employ our best theories of crime to develop interventions that can best reduce the amount of harm caused by crime and by the way that we respond to crime. In the next two chapters, we tease out the implications of an evolutionary approach for punishment, prevention, and public policy (this chapter), and the rehabilitation and reintegration of offenders (Chapter 11).

We begin by considering some important conceptual issues that arise in applying evolutionary criminology to the effective management of crime. We focus first on how an evolutionary approach can contribute to social and situational crime prevention efforts. Drawing from the material presented in Chapter 5, we then consider what an evolutionary perspective has to offer in terms of understanding how we should punish offenders and what potential opportunities there are for restorative justice initiatives. We conclude this chapter by considering the wider public policy implications of an evolutionary approach to crime prevention. In the next chapter, we explore in depth the way that an evolutionary approach can contribute to the effective rehabilitation and reintegration of offenders. Preventing crime (and the harms caused by crime) is no straightforward

Evolutionary Criminology
http://dx.doi.org/10.1016/B978-0-12-397937-7.00010-0 © 2015 Elsevier Inc. All rights reserved.

task and an evolutionary perspective offers no magical solutions. However, armed with a conceptually richer account of why individuals offend, why we punish, and what accounts for variation in offending (and punishment), provides us with an opportunity to help guide the development of effective strategies for managing crime.

APPLIED EVOLUTIONARY CRIMINOLOGY

Advocates of the "paleo diet" suggest that we can employ our understanding of what our ancestors ate to guide us in our nutritional choices in contemporary modern environments. The underlying argument is straightforward: If our body evolved to process certain kinds of food sources, then this is the diet that is likely to provide us with the best opportunity to live a healthy life. Not all evolutionary scholars are so sanguine about the merits of the paleo diet (e.g., Zuk, 2014), and we are personally less than enthusiastic about the joys of consuming bone marrow, a likely importance source of protein for Pleistocene hominins. More generally, there are both merits and potential pitfalls in employing our understanding of human evolution to guide practical choices in the modern world. As advocates of "evolutionary medicine" have argued, understanding our evolutionary history can prove invaluable in enriching our knowledge of health and disease (Gluckman, Beedle, & Hanson, 2009; Nesse & Stearns, 2008). However, we need to be aware of the fact that evolution "cares" nothing about our overall well-being; selection operates by favoring characteristics that increase inclusive fitness. Blindly following the pathways that evolution has laid down, therefore, may not lead us to optimal outcomes for ourselves or for society. Relatedly, we cannot assume that what has been favored by natural selection is necessarily *morally* good in the societies in which we inhabit. However, keeping these general caveats in mind, we suggest that—drawing from work in evolutionary medicine— there are four main evolutionary pathways that can help us to understand problem behaviors—in particular those that are related to criminal offending (Durrant, 2013b). These relate to (1) evolutionary adaptations; (2) conditional adaptations; (3) evolutionary mismatch; and (4) cultural evolutionary processes.

The first pathway suggests that problem behaviors can arise as a result of evolved psychological mechanisms operating as they were "designed" to by natural and sexual selection. A significant amount of male–male aggression, for instance, reflects selection for intrasexual competition among males because success in such contexts advances reproductive success (see Chapter 6 for details). Male–male violence, from this perspective, is something that—although socially undesirable—reflects the operation of evolved adaptations working as they were designed to. Problem behaviors can also arise through the operation of conditional adaptations operating as they were designed to by natural and sexual selection in response to specific social and ecological environments. For example, in Chapter 7, we argued that many life course–persistent offenders can be conceptualized as pursuing fast life history strategies because of their exposure to harsh and/or unpredictable environments during development. The third pathway highlights that sometimes problem behaviors arise, or are exacerbated, because of a mismatch between evolved mechanisms and features of the current environment. For instance, the widespread availability of alcohol and other drugs was almost certainly not a feature of our ancestral environments but because drugs act on evolved motivational and emotional systems, many individuals pursue the use of drugs with detrimental effects for their health and for society (Durrant, Adamson, Todd, & Sellman, 2009). Some drugs—in particular alcohol—play an important role in violence in contemporary societies through their psychopharmacological properties (see Giancola, 2013) that, in combination with drinking environments that often involve large number of similar aged young individuals, promote intrasexual competition while reducing self-regulatory capacities (Durrant, 2013b). Finally, we need to recognize that problem behaviors can arise, or be exacerbated, through cultural evolutionary processes. As discussed in Chapter 9, it is likely that cultural values, norms, and practices regarding violence can undergo dramatic shifts over time suggesting a key role for cultural evolution in understanding (and potentially, reducing) the incidence of certain types of offense.

Before we begin considering specific approaches for preventing crime, we think it is useful to recognize three key general points regarding an evolutionary approach to reducing problems behaviors. First, where possible, programs and policies should work with, rather than against "human nature." Even if we recognize that humans are enormously flexible in their behavioral repertoires, there are likely to be certain practices, policies, and social arrangements that work too crudely against the grain of evolved predispositions and proclivities and hence are likely to be ineffective. Arguably, for example, the large-scale failure of communism as implemented in the Soviet Union under Stalin and in China under Mao reflects (in part) that forced collectivization and the related appropriation of primary production by the state offered no incentives for individuals to adopt effective agricultural practices. A second, related point, is that it can often be possible to effect "workarounds" that act on the same evolved motivations that lead to problem behavior but, instead, channel the behavior along more societally desirable paths. For instance, bullying typically reflects underlying motivations to achieve and obtain social status via dominance. Programs for bullying are unlikely to be effective by simply enforcing "zero tolerance," but are more likely to lead to lasting change by creating alternative, prosocial pathways to obtain social status

(Tybur & Griskevicius, 2013). Finally, it is absolutely essential to recognize that humans are prosocial animals who are geared to learning, adhering to, and enforcing social and cultural norms. There is, therefore, enormous scope to alter ecological and cultural environments in ways that enhance prosocial and cooperative behavior to the benefit of all (Biglan & Cody, 2013; Biglan & Embry, 2013). Evolutionary approaches are increasingly being pressed into service in order to provide guidance to changing problem behaviors and to inform policy decisions (see Biglan & Cody, 2013; Biglan & Embry, 2013; Tybur & Griskevicius, 2013; Wilson & Gowdy, 2013; Wilson, Hayes, Biglan, & Embry, 2014). We think that there is significant scope to use these ideas to address the problems that arise from crime in society.

SOCIAL AND SITUATIONAL CRIME PREVENTION

A widely employed taxonomy in the crime prevention literature draws a distinction between social and situational crime prevention. Social crime prevention typically targets more distal causes of crime such as those that relate to individual characteristics, and the school, family, and community environment. In short, social crime prevention initiatives aim to change individuals and social environments in ways that can lead to reductions in offending. Situational crime prevention, in contrast, targets the more proximate causes of crime with a focus on how specific features of the physical and social environment can lead to reductions in criminal behavior.

Situational Crime Prevention

Police officers can't help but think they have a magical effect on the flow of traffic—all they have to do is to enter a stream of vehicles in a marked patrol car and the cars around them immediately slow down and become more cautious. There is of course no magic involved: human behavior is enormously flexible and will change in predictable ways to different features of the situation as they emerge. Altering the nature of situations, then, is a viable strategy for reducing criminal behavior. Clarke (2008) suggests that there are five key situational crime prevention strategies: (1) increase the effort of offending; (2) reduce the rewards of offending; (3) increase the risk of offending; (4) reduce provocation; and (5) remove excuses. There is now a reasonably extensive literature on the effectiveness of situational crime prevention efforts (see Clarke, 2008; Eck, 2002; Welsh & Farrington, 2006), and our aim in this section is to explore how various strategies might be effective from the evolutionary point of view that we have developed in this book.

The first two of these strategies—increasing the effort and reducing the rewards of offending—are fairly straightforwardly explicable from both a rational choice and evolutionary perspective. If, as we have suggested, a good deal of offending is related to the pursuit (either directly or indirectly) of social status, then changing the reward structure of the environment will alter the relative value of criminal actions as a means to increase social standing. "Target hardening"—better locks, bars, screens, security measures and so forth—simply means that offenders find it harder to obtain the rewards of offending (both in the tangible sense of material objects and in terms of the social status that these bring) and therefore must pursue alternative channels to realize their underlying goals. Although Farrell, Tilley, and Tseloni (2014) have plausibly argued that changes in security measures have been instrumental in the decline in both property and violent offending, from an evolutionary perspective, it is relatively easier to foreclose opportunities for theft, burglary, and robbery than it is for interpersonal violence crimes. More generally, the efficacy of strategies to increase the effort and reduce the rewards of offending will be directly related to the importance (in evolutionary terms) of the specific criminal activities in realizing evolutionarily relevant goals.

Efforts to increase the risk of offending such as the implementation of closed-circuit television, improved street lighting, and better opportunities for natural surveillance have been shown to be effective in reducing certain types of offending (e.g., Welsh & Farrington, 2006). Strategies to remove excuses for offending such as instructions, signs, notices, and techniques for altering the conscience of individuals have been less rigorously evaluated. However, we suggest that both of these situational crime prevention strategies can be effective for largely the same reasons: they provide ecological contexts that enhance prosocial behavior by reinforcing social and moral norms and alerting individuals to the risk of punishment. As we argued in Chapter 5, humans' cooperation is maintained through a combination of internalized social and moral norms and the negative emotional states that violation of these norms instigate (first-party punishment), and the threat of informal (second-party punishment) and formal (third-party punishment) sanctions that might range from social disapproval to a criminal conviction. Any change in the ecological context that leads individuals to believe that they are, or might be, under surveillance from others is likely to enhance prosocial behavior. Consistent with this idea and more formal evaluations of the effect of closed-circuit television and better street lighting on crime, are a number of experimental studies that indicate that prosocial behavior is enhanced when individuals believe that they are being watched (e.g., Zhong, Bohns, & Gino, 2010). Even the presence of subtle cues, such as the presence of "eye-like" stimuli that suggest that people are being monitored, can substantially increase prosocial and cooperative behavior (e.g., Nettle et al., 2013b; Rigdon, Ishii, Watabe, & Kitayama, 2009). From an evolutionary perspective, this suggests that efforts to improve the actual or perceived belief that individuals are being watched are likely to be effective tools in reducing certain types of crime. From a rational choice perspective, it could be argued that this effect occurs simply because the risks of offending in terms of formal punishment are enhanced, but from an evolutionary point of view the broader implications of this research suggest that the creation of environments that enhance prosocial and cooperative behavior involves "working with" our evolved predispositions to be concerned with the negative social evaluation of others and to adhere to social and moral norms.

Several situational crime prevention strategies aim to change social and physical environments to reduce provocation. Examples include the separation of rival sporting fans, the neutralization of peer pressure, and various approaches to regulating the availability of alcohol and public environments where it is consumed. Consider strategies to reduce alcohol-related violence. Graham and Homel (2008) suggest that various situational changes such as a reduction in crowding, the cutting of waiting times to enter bars, improved lighting, the control of temperature and noise, and the effective enforcement of rules can all help to reduce the situational triggers for violence in public drinking environments (also see Forsyth, 2013). From an evolutionary perspective, many drinking environments create the "perfect storm" for the occurrence of intrasexual violence: there are large numbers of young men (and women) in public spaces where apparently minor threats to status (jostles, bumps, eye contact) are likely (and by virtue of alcohol's psychopharmacological effect are likely to be *attended* to; see Giancola, 2013), and where there may be local norms that make violence in such situations either acceptable or even obligatory. Creating barroom environments where the risk of threats to social status are reduced (e.g., less crowding), and where local norms regarding appropriate behavior are clearly set and enforced (e.g., by having bar staff intervene in fights before they escalate) will discourage antisocial behavior and allow individuals to "save face" if threats to status do occur (Durrant, 2013b; Graham & Homel, 2008).

Social Crime Prevention

There are a large number of different social crime prevention programs that have been developed and are subject to formal evaluations. Most of these programs focus on addressing the known risk factors for offending and there is a good deal of evidence that properly developed and implemented social crime prevention programs can be effective in reducing offending (see Welsh & Farrington, 2007 for a review). From an evolutionary perspective, the importance of developmental focused social crime prevention initiatives cannot be emphasized enough. If, as we argue in Chapter 7, developmental environments play a key role in shaping offending trajectories—in part because of their impact on the development of life history strategies—then social crime prevention initiatives that target developmental environments afford opportunities for creating ecological contexts that are likely to best lead to more prosocial and cooperative behaviors. Moreover, to effectively address the peak in offending (and other forms of risk-taking) that we see in adolescence, it is crucial to recognize the evolutionary function of this developmental period. In this section, we draw on the excellent recent review of how an evolutionary approach to risky behavior can inform policy and practice by Ellis et al. (2012), who highlight programs and practices that are (1) likely to be ineffective in changing behavior and (2) those that offer the most promise.

Approaches to intervention that largely focus on merely preventing or stopping risky behavior without any consideration of the *function* of that behavior are not likely to be effective. If, as we argue in Chapter 7, adolescence is a period of heightened risk taking because selection has favored the development of psychological and neurobiological mechanisms to enhance risky behavior and intrasexual competition, then attempts to simply enforce "zero tolerance" (e.g., for bullying), or abstinence only (for sexual behavior) without providing environments that offer alternative routes for realizing evolved goals are likely to ineffective. Similarly, educational approaches that mainly aim to increase adolescents' *knowledge* of the harms of risk behavior (e.g., many drug-education programs) are not likely to result in changes to behavior even if they increase an awareness of the harm involved. Indeed, by making the harm of certain behavior more salient, such programs may actually increase the behaviors they are trying to reduce because it is the potentially *costly* nature of the behaviors that is one of their major draw cards for youth. The crucial point, as Ellis et al. (2012) emphasize, is that attempts to reduce risky and harmful behavior have to recognize the evolved functions of those behaviors (see also Tybur & Griskevicius, 2013).

Given our understanding of the evolved function of adolescence and the role of risky and antisocial behavior in meeting evolved motivations and preferences, what kind of programs are most likely to gain traction with youth? A crucial insight is to recognize that although aggressive and risky behaviors function to advance social status, and hence reproductive success, they are not the *only* routes to status in humans. As we argued in Chapter 6, the dominance/prestige model of social status suggests that for humans there are several distinct, non-mutually exclusive routes to obtaining high social status. An alternative route involves the display of prosocial, altruistic, and cooperative behavior and the development of valued skills, resources, and abilities that confer *prestige* on individuals. Creating ecological environments that facilitate these alternate routes could therefore be a highly promising alternate route to reducing harmful and risky behavior in adolescence (see Biglan & Embry, 2013; Ellis et al., 2012; Tybur & Griskevicius, 2013, for examples).

In Chapter 7, we discussed research and theory that suggests that there are critical inflection points in the human life history that contribute to the development of alternative life history strategies. More specifically, environments that are overly harsh or unpredictable are more likely to entrain the development of fast life history traits which increase the risk for antisocial and criminal behavior. The implication of this literature for social crime prevention efforts is relatively straightforward, as clearly summarized by Ellis et al. (2012, p. 609):

> From an evolutionary perspective, fast LH strategies…constitute reliable development responses to environmental cues indicating that life is short and future outcomes cannot be controlled or predicted. Because these are powerful evolved responses that promoted lineage survival during our natural selective history, Band-Aid interventions (e.g., sex education, birth control, promoting self-esteem, training coping skills, teaching problems solving strategies) are unlikely to effect change at a foundation level…Prevention and treatment programs instead need to address *causative environmental conditions*. (Italics added.)

We think that the key contribution of an evolutionary approach is to helping us to go beyond our understanding of the developmental risk factors for offending to identify the key causal processes that are most likely to be implicated.

From an evolutionary perspective, many extant social crime prevention programs do a reasonably good job at addressing some of these important causal processes and have been shown to be effective in reducing offending (see Olds, Sandler, & Kitzman, 2007; Sutton, Cherney, & White, 2008). Home visitation programs, for example, that provide information about proper prenatal and antenatal care, parenting practices, and health care create less harsh (and, potentially, more predictable) intrauterine and early childhood environments that, in turn, can promote the development of slower life history strategies. Similarly, parent education and preschool enrichment programs that have targeted disadvantaged families may exert their positive effects largely through an amelioration of the harshness of local environments. In short, programs that create environments that are less dangerous and more predictable are likely to entrain the development of slow life history strategies. As our knowledge of the key environmental cues that shape life history strategies and the most important developmental inflexion points advance, there is scope for the development of programs that better target the key causal processes that are implicated.

PUNISHMENT AND RESTORATIVE JUSTICE

Punishment

In his autobiographical account of prison life, Jack Henry Abbott (1981) vividly describes his experiences of life as a prisoner in the United States during the 1960s and 1970s. The book is an uncomfortable read as Abbott recounts his experiences of starvation, violence, forced medication, and solitary confinement. Prisons in most Western countries are not quite as appalling as those described by Abbott, but there is no doubt that imprisonment and other forms of punishment exact significant levels of harm. For offenders, there is often the deprivation of liberty, autonomy, and security. Prisoners are exposed to high rates of physical and sexual violence, experience a high incidence of mental disorders, and have a substantially elevated risk for self-harm, including suicide (Haney, 2003; Irwin & Owen, 2005; Liebling, 2007). Imprisonment and other forms of punishment also have a largely negative, collateral effect on family members and the wider community (Murray, 2005; Murray & Farrington, 2005). Finally, the cost of enforcing punishment in society—especially the maintenance of a prison system—is enormous in financial terms. Given the manifest costs of punishment, perhaps we would be better off without it, or at least we could eliminate the use of imprisonment as a means to punish offenders. Both of these viewpoints have their advocates. For example, Boonin (2008) argues that the harms of punishment simply cannot be justified and therefore it should be abolished, whereas a number of scholars have advocated for the abolition of prison as a form of punishment.

Like most liberal-minded academic social scientists, we have a good deal of sympathy for these views. However, an evolutionary perspective suggests that the existence of punishment is essential for the viable functioning of any society—small or large. Without the existence of the third-party punishment of individuals who violate important social and moral norms, there will almost certainly be a substantial reduction in cooperation and an increase in unsanctioned punishment. The reasons for this are outlined in Chapter 5: humans are strongly motivated to punish those individuals who transgress against social norms and this motivation is associated with powerful emotional responses of anger, disgust, and contempt. We are not simply suggesting here that we *should* punish norm transgressions *because* that is how we have evolved to respond to such transgressions. Rather, any attempt to abolish punishment is likely to have unintended negative consequences given our evolved predispositions and the evolutionary function of punishment. However, although an evolutionary perspective suggests that punishment is an essential feature of society, what is less clear is just *what* acts are worthy of punishment by the state and *how* these acts should be punished.

Research supports the idea that for a core set of offenses that involve the intentional infliction of harm on others there is a good deal of agreement in terms of what should be punished and the relative magnitude of punishment that these acts deserve. As Hoffman (2014) argues, we appear to be sensitive both to the magnitude of the harm that a given act causes and the extent to which the act was deliberate or intentional. Therefore, we punish those acts most severely that involve high levels of harm and that arise from clear intentions to inflict high levels of harm. Acts that involve negligible levels of harm are less likely to invoke punishment responses; and acts that may involve harm, but are not intentional, tend to be viewed as somewhat blameworthy. These distinctions, of course, are largely captured in legal definitions around, for example, homicide. Many acts, however, do not appear to involve any significant amounts of harm—for example, adultery and same-sex sexual relations—and yet have been subject to severe penalties in certain places and at certain times. In many Western countries, drug use (especially the use of cannabis) has become the focus of sustained debate about the appropriateness of state-inflicted punishment. Can an evolutionary approach provide guidance as to whether these acts should or should not be subject to punishment by the state? The short answer is, no: it is not possible—or desirable—to derive what is morally appropriate from our understanding of evolutionary processes (see our discussion in Chapter 3). However, an evolutionary perspective can help us to understand *why* it is that such a diverse array of—apparently nonharmful—acts may be subject to punishment in particular places and times. Haidt's (2012) moral foundation theory provides some useful guidance here as many of the acts that we criminalize are based on our moral intuitions about what is right and wrong and although those intuitions have an innate basis they are strongly shaped by cultural environments. The solution is not necessarily to accept that different people's vision of morality is equally justified or viable, but rather to recognize the evolutionary source of their moral beliefs and to employ our capacity for reasoned debate to reach points of common ground (Haidt, 2012).

Much of the debate around punishment in Western society is concerned less with whether we should punish, or even what acts we should punish, but more with the quantum of punishment that is perceived to be appropriate. There is now an extensive amount of literature that largely argues that many Western, especially Anglophone, countries are overly punitive in their responses to crime. For example, a recent book by Pratt and Eriksson (2012) was subtitled "an explanation of Anglophone excess and Nordic exceptionalism," and many scholars have subjected the precipitous rise in the incarceration of offenders in the United States since the 1970s to sustained criticism (e.g., Gottschalk, 2006). Again, an evolutionary approach cannot provide explicit guidance about how much (and through what means) specific acts should be punished. However, we think that the literature discussed in Chapter 5 is largely consistent with the view that humans intuitively believe that the quantum of punishment should fit the moral wrongfulness of a given act in terms of its harm and the intent of the transgressor. The ratchet of punitiveness tends to move in one direction (toward greater rather than lesser punitiveness) because people respond emotionally to serious offenses (which are the ones that they are most often exposed to in the media and through other channels) and thus have a tendency to demand more severe penalties for those acts (Hoffman, 2014). As work on public opinion suggests, however, when given an opportunity to respond in a more nuanced fashion with a richer amount of information about specific crimes, the public are rather less punitive and suggest punishments that are more in line (or even more lenient) than those that are actually employed (Roberts & Hough, 2005). In short, although the cognitive and emotional systems that underlie our motivation to punish are probably evolutionary adaptations, they can result in a diverse array of responses depending on the specific features of the wider cultural and ecological context.

Restorative Justice

Psychological and behavioral adaptations and cultural practices have evolved in tandem in response to the violation of significant moral norms. One result of this dynamic, evolving interaction of biology and human nature has been a suite of normative systems and institutions specifically designed to prevent, and if necessary, manage serious wrong doing (i.e., crime). The ability to empathize with victims, to feel anger when others or oneself have been unfairly harmed in some way, to punish or to seek revenge on aggressors, and to forgive wrong doers can be viewed as adaptations. There is extensive research evidence that human beings are naturally predisposed to punish norm violators in order to deter them from inflicting what is perceived as unjustified harm on other people (see Chapter 5)—harm, that if unchecked, is likely to damage social cooperation and social networks, with a consequent devastating impact on the survival chances of the group, and individual fitness. Alongside the inclination to punish or seek revenge against aggressors, individuals sometimes choose not to engage in "payback" and instead attempt to preserve what they see as valuable relationships; they may *forgive* the person who has harmed them. McCullough, Kurzban, and Tabak (2013, p. 2) have recently proposed an evolutionary model that attempts to map the cognitive and behavioral mechanisms that generate revenge and forgiveness responses. They state

> …that revenge and forgiveness result from psychological adaptations that became species-typical because of their ancestral efficacy in solving recurrent social problems that humans encountered during evolution (Williams, 1966). Revenge and

forgiveness, we argue, have complementary biological functions: We posit that mechanisms for revenge are designed to deter harms, and that forgiveness mechanisms are designed to solve problems related to the preservation of valuable relationships despite the prior impositions of harm.

A problem with groups or individuals seeking revenge without the mediation of an impartial agency is that it can lead to a seemingly endless cycle of harmful actions and counter actions that destabilize social networks. McCullough et al. (2013) argue that social groups (and later societies) build on human beings' natural predispositions to punish and to forgive, to construct formal dispute procedures, and ultimately, normative systems designed to address serious wrongful actions in more adaptive ways. An example of a biological adaptation that has evolved to deter aggressors is the capacity to inflict punishment and its subsequent cultural development into a formal criminal justice system. The proto-institutional and formal institution of punishment capitalizes on the cognitive and emotional components of a *natural inclination* to punish such as perceptions of unfairness, anger, desire for revenge, and the ability to forgive.

Punishment can be defined loosely as the intentional infliction of sanctions by the state on individuals who have unjustifiably harmed other people (Boonin, 2008). There are numerous normative justifications of punishment evident in the contemporary literature including retributivism (i.e., *backward* looking—inflict justified harm for harm done) consequentialism (i.e., *forward* looking—inflict justified harm to prevent future harm), and communicative (i.e., inflict justified harm to *restore* community relationships). Communicative theory has the ability to incorporate retributive and consequential elements, and is a natural conceptual partner of restorative justice, a community-oriented response to crime and punishment (see the following section). Duff (2001, p. 106) argues that there are three aims integral to the institution of punishment from a communicative viewpoint: secular repentance, reform, and reconciliation through the imposition of sanctions. More specifically, he argues that punishment is:

> a burden imposed on an offender for his crime, through which, it is hoped, he will come to repent his crime, to begin to reform himself, and thus reconcile himself with those he has wronged.

The focus of the communicative justification of punishment on the well-being of a community means that relationships between moral stakeholders are of critical importance and the role of individual entitlements and duties (although important) assumes lesser importance. It is a collectivist approach to resolving disputes between people and in arriving at solutions to ethical problems such as crime. Although restorative justice is a response to crime that asks questions such as: "How can we repair the damage created by an offense? What steps need to occur to restore confidence in a community's norms and to protect victims while holding offenders accountable?" In our view, restorative justice presupposes the validity of a community-oriented or relational ethical theory and meshes well with human beings' desire to punish and also to forgive; it acknowledges human beings' interdependence and the origin of morality in small groups of hunters and gatherers (Boehm, 2012).

The process of reconciliation involves forgiveness and the willingness of individuals and the State to look beyond the imposition of punishment (or vengeance) to the moral task of repairing damaged relationships between offenders, victims, and the community. According to Walker (2006, p. 28), moral repair is "restoring or creating trust and hope in a shared sense of value and responsibility" following the experience of intentional and undeserved harm at the hands of another person or persons. The tasks associated with the repair of damaged relationships include placing responsibility on the offender, acknowledging and addressing the harm suffered by the victim, asserting the authority of the norms violated by the offender and the community's commitment to them, restoring or creating trust among the victims in the relevant norms, and reestablishing or establishing adequate moral relationships between victims, wrongdoers, and the community. The concept of moral repair is implicit in the central assumptions and principles of restorative justice although it is rarely explicitly discussed in this form (Walker, 2006).

According to Walgrave, restorative justice is "an option for doing justice after the occurrence of an offence that is primarily oriented toward repairing the individual, relational, and social harm caused by that offence" (Walgrave, 2008, p. 21). One of the main reasons why restorative justice has become so prominent in contemporary criminal justice discourse is that it is viewed as a fundamentally different, yet viable, approach to achieving justice. Moreover, it is considered to be an approach to crime that sets out to heal damaged communities rather than simply punishing and sending offenders to prisons or community supervision without further thought (Johnstone & Van Ness, 2007; Morris, 2002). Restorative justice is based on a tripartite set of moral relationships between moral agents. The three kinds of relationships are those between: (1) victims and offenders; (2) offenders and the community; and (3) offenders and practitioners (e.g., therapists, restorative justice conference facilitators).

Zehr and Mika (1998) outline three core principles that underpin restorative justice (RJ) initiatives such as victim–offender conferences, sentencing circles, and circles of support, that resonate with the core ideas in this definition. First, criminal conduct damages both people and their relationships with one another. Such violation harms all of the key stakeholders in crime—victims, offenders, and communities—whose needs therefore ought to be actively addressed through a restorative process of some kind. Second, crime results in both obligations and liabilities for offenders. The offender is obliged to take responsibility for the crime and attempt to repair the harm caused. The intention behind holding offenders accountable is to seek reparation rather than to simply punish them, although there is some tension evident between these two conflicting values (see Ward & Salmon, 2009). Additionally, the community is obliged to support both the victim and the offender in dealing with the effects of the crime. Third, the purpose of restorative justice is to facilitate community healing by repairing the harm that results from crime, more specifically, the fractures within relationships between victims, offenders, and the community that inevitably occur following offending. Restorative values such as participation, respect, honesty, humility, interconnectedness, accountability, empowerment, hope, truth, empathy and mutual understanding form the foundation of, and subsequently guide, practice (Zehr & Toews, 2004).

The relation between RJ and offender rehabilitation and desistance is a controversial one with some theorists arguing that RJ practices are likely to facilitate offender reintegration and lower recidivism rates (Morris, 2002), whereas others believe that this is unlikely (Ward, Fox, & Garber, 2014; Ward & Langlands, 2009). In part, this is a dispute concerning the type of normative projects (e.g., punishment vs treatment) associated with RJ and offender rehabilitation as well as reflecting disagreement over the empirical status of RJ interventions (e.g., family group conferences, sentencing circles; Ward et al., 2014). Theorists who support the conceptualization of RJ as a crime-reduction model argue that to the extent that it reduces reoffending it is because the offender acquires empathy (or some related competencies such as theory of mind or psychological altruism) in the process and loses the motivation to reoffend. The subsequent shift in attitudes may signal to others that he is ready to make amends for the harm committed and to actively seek social reintegration and reconciliation.

Reflecting on the theoretical underpinnings of RJ, its unique value arguably resides in providing opportunities for offenders and members of the community to repair the harm to relationships caused by crime. And generally in this framework, as Ward and Langlands (2009) point out, rehabilitation, if it occurs, is an added bonus rather than a central aim. Additionally, the main contribution to rehabilitation for high-risk offenders is likely to be via increased motivation to make amends for the harm inflicted on innocent people. Thus the link with desistance processes is likely to work through the identification of community (ethical and social) norms and an acceptance of their authority for offenders, victims, and members of the community—essentially, moral repair (Walker, 2006). The effects of this acknowledgment, and its translation into improved interpersonal functioning and daily activities, is likely to be reflected in social acceptance in multiple areas such as employment, relationships, educational opportunities, and so on. In our view, the relation between RJ and desistance is normative in nature; it is characterized by norms (i.e., rules that spell out what constitutes obligatory, permissible, and unacceptable actions and outcomes) that specify who has moral status within a community and what can be reasonably expected from its members in light of these norms. These norms will also indicate what kind of repair work needs to occur when norms prohibiting harm to members of the community are violated. Restorative justice can be usefully seen as a subset of these norms primarily oriented around a response to crime that reflects these core, communitarian values. If RJ encounters create a sense of agency and shift in narrative identity in offenders, this is likely to be the result of the acceptance of responsibility for harms committed and the commitment to making amends through reparation and/or personal change. Restorative practices can reinforce the shared norms that offenders have in common with victims and others; a shared sense of values can have a reintegrative effect on offenders. In their recent article on RJ, desistance from offending, and offender rehabilitation, Ward et al. (2014, pp. 40–41) state that it is

> ....helpful to view restorative justice as an overarching ethical umbrella (i.e. the focus on moral repair specifies how crime should be responded to and what kinds of responses should be expected from offenders, victims and the community), offender rehabilitation as a means of creating offender capabilities within this umbrella (i.e. offender programmes have a strong value base that is strongly constrained by the concept of moral repair—and RJ—which is evident in the construction of positive, mutually respectful, pro-social intervention programmes), and desistance processes as ways of cementing initial behavioural and psychological changes into fulfilling and sustainable lifestyles (i.e. rehabilitation programmes are scaffolds that assist the process of re-entry and reintegration....The three conceptual frameworks represent distinct, although linked, levels of analysis: RJ represents the ethical normative, rehabilitation is prudential normative (or capability building), and desistance embodies the social normative level).

The dynamic, interactive conception of agency outlined in Chapter 8 has its conceptual foundation in gene–culture coevolution theory and is consistent with RJ, desistance, and rehabilitation practices. A narrative shift in identity from that of an offender to someone who is "making good" is created by the realignment of personal and social values with contexts that facilitate the possibility of individuals changing. Without social and cultural supports, and the opportunities to engage in meaningful social roles and practices, desistance from offending is almost impossible (Laws & Ward, 2011; Maruna, 2001; Ward & Maruna, 2007). Restorative justice with its roots in natural predispositions to seek revenge, social connectedness, and the willingness to forgive those who have unjustifiably harmed others, can increase the chances of these facilitative processes occurring.

WIDER POLICY IMPLICATIONS

We will conclude our discussion of the role of evolutionary approaches in the development of effective crime prevention efforts by briefly considering some wider implications for public policy. Our discussion will focus here on how changes in individual behavior might be achieved by altering or influencing macro-level social-structural and cultural variables and processes. Inevitably, change at this level is harder to achieve, but an evolutionary perspective that draws on an extended conception of inheritance (genetic, epigenetic, ecological, and cultural) offers some guidance in how we might manage effective change so as to reduce the negative impact of crime and our responses to crime.

Policy efforts to reduce concentrated poverty, decrease income inequality, and facilitate the legitimate, fair, and effective use of law are likely to reap dividends in terms of reductions in crime (along with numerous other social and health related benefits; Wilkinson & Pickett, 2009). We are hardly the first to make this claim, nor does it necessarily require an evolutionary perspective to recognize the benefits that come from such policies. However, an evolutionary approach highlights how poverty and inequality contribute to more antisocial and criminal behavior by narrowing the opportunities for individuals to obtain social status through legitimate means and by heightening, in particular, levels of male–male competition. The human tendency to adhere to locally held social and moral norms, moreover, is likely to be substantially enhanced if the processes and practices that underlie the policing of these norms are fair, transparent, and effective. Translating these aims into effective policy is no easy task, and inevitably they involve sustained political will. However, recognizing the reductions in crime that could arise by reducing poverty, decreasing inequality, and improving the legitimate and effective rule of law is at least a start. It also worth noting that there are multiple routes to realizing these goals that will be more or less viable in different cultural contexts (Wilkinson & Pickett, 2009).

We have emphasized in this book that genetic and cultural evolutionary processes and their interaction need to be understood to satisfactorily explain criminal behavior. We have also highlighted the central role of human agency in directing change. Although it may seem that an evolutionary approach might wed us to a limited array of options for large scale changes in human behavior—perhaps only via directed genetic evolution—a more inclusive understanding of evolutionary processes that incorporate genetic, epigenetic, ecological, and cultural evolutionary processes opens up a much richer array of possibilities. As scholars such as Eisner (2014) and Pinker (2011) have emphasized, the astonishing decline in interpersonal violence in Western countries over the past 500 years can be at least partly (perhaps mainly) attributed to changing cultural values, norms, beliefs, expectations, and institutions. Because humans are a cultural species whose behavior is strongly influenced by social and moral norms and the ecological contexts in which they are embedded, changes in these norms can effect significant changes in behavior that can be sustained through cultural and ecological inheritance. Sustained efforts to support and facilitate the development of pro-social norms and change norms that support or facilitate antisocial behavior are, therefore, likely to be one essential component of efforts to reduce the harmful effects of crime. Changes in legal practices have an important role to play in this context. For example, by redefining certain acts that were not criminalized as offenses (e.g., marital rape) and decriminalizing certain acts that were subject to criminal sanctions (e.g., same-sex sexual relations), the law can provide signals as to the normative boundaries of human social behavior. In a recent article, Wilson et al. (2014) draw on the expanded notion of inheritance that features in the extended evolutionary synthesis (see Chapter 3) to map out a new science of intentional change that is centered on evolutionary processes (see also Biglan & Cody, 2013; Biglan & Embry, 2013). Inevitably, our efforts to effect change should be guided by what works (i.e., it should be evidence-based), and what is morally acceptable. An evolutionary perspective does not provide all the answers. It does, as Wilson et al. (2014) argue, offer a coherent theoretical framework for integrating the basic and applied sciences in a way that can foster the development of a science of intentional change that has implications for our efforts to reduce offending and the various harms that arise from crime and its management.

The Rehabilitation and Reintegration of Offenders

One of us has recently remarked about the conceptual and practical disconnection between explanations of crime and the assessment and rehabilitation of offenders (Ward, 2014). The main problem with this disconnection is that from a conceptual viewpoint there is minimal attention given to providing an explanation for why offending and its associated problems have occurred, and therefore, little understanding of what factors should be targeted in intervention programs. From a practical perspective, clinicians have become preoccupied with risk assessment and pretty much focused intervention entirely on the identification and modification of dynamic risk factors in the absence of any clear understanding of how they originated, and perhaps more crucially, how they interact with each other. Reflecting on the sex offending area, Ward (2014, p. 130) commented:

> Furthermore, the status of theory construction has fallen significantly and there is very little cooperation between researchers working on the conceptualization of risk factors and those seeking to explain the causes of sexual offending. In addition, assessment and case formulation seems to revolve largely around the detection of dynamic risk factors and the classification of offenders and their problems amounts to formulating risk profiles.

In our view, one of the problems facing policy-makers and practitioners in the forensic and correctional areas is a lack of a theoretical framework that can do justice to the research findings on reoffending and risk, and incorporate the multidimensional nature of human functioning. Most theories of crime only address one or two levels of analysis and rarely build biological variables into explanations of the onset and maintenance of crime. In our view, the gene–culture coevolution theoretical framework outlined in Chapter 3, has the resources to provide a comprehensive understanding of crime which can inform the practice of rehabilitation.

© 2015 Elsevier Inc. All rights reserved.

In the remainder of this chapter, we briefly inquire into the nature of offender rehabilitation and the additional value an evolutionary approach can bring. We then summarize the evolutionary behavioral science model developed earlier in the chapter and draw out five major general implications of this perspective for offender rehabilitation. To make this discussion more concrete, we take the example of empathy and altruism and demonstrate how formulating these concepts in ways consistent with a gene–culture coevolution model can provide useful practice directions.

WHAT IS OFFENDER REHABILITATION?

The rehabilitation of incarcerated offenders has multiple phases to it including participation in intervention programs such as social skills or empathy training, initial reentry into the community, gradual social reintegration, and ultimately the adoption of an offense-free lifestyle. From a desistance perspective, the last phase involves the acquisition of social and psychological capital and a fundamental transformation in an offender's self-conception, or what has been referred to as narrative identity (Andrews & Bonta, 2010; Ward & Maruna, 2007). Social learning theories (e.g., cognitive behavioral treatment models) are typically the theoretical basis of best-practice correctional programs and it is assumed that offending is primarily a product of faulty social learning. That is, individuals are hypothesized to commit offenses because their social and self-management skill deficits make it difficult for them to seek reinforcement in socially acceptable ways (Laws & Ward, 2011; Ward, Polaschek, & Beech, 2006). Practitioners are expected to concentrate their therapeutic efforts on managing or eliminating dynamic risk factors. Dynamic risk factors such as impulsivity or offense supportive beliefs are potentially modifiable psychological and environmental variables thought to causally contribute to the onset of criminal events and their successful reduction typically results in lowered reoffending rates (Andrews & Bonta, 2010). The primary causal mechanisms hypothesized to generate offending are social and psychological in nature, although on rare occasions it is acknowledged that individuals' antisocial actions are partly caused by dysfunctional biological mechanisms such as abnormal hormonal functioning in the case of some sex offenders (Andrews & Bonta, 2010; Marshall, Marshall, Serran, & Fernandez, 2006; Ward et al., 2006). In the contemporary criminological and correctional literature, comparatively little attention has been paid to the role of adaptations and their by-products in the creation of crime or crime facilitative circumstances. However, from an evolutionary viewpoint, it is possible to conceptualize the causal factors targeted in correctional problems as proximate mechanisms that represent the downstream effects of development and, ultimately, evolutionary adaptations. For example, the emotional, cognitive, and behavioral mechanisms underlying high risk-taking behaviors could be traced back to an evolved set of adapta-tions that increase the chances of survival in stressful environments (see Chapter 7). In other words, there is no reason why current rehabilitation programs and their associated etiological commitments cannot be theoreti-cally embedded within the framework of evolutionary behavioral science.

Building on the etiological assumptions embedded in contemporary literature, the main goal in correctional programs is to assist offenders to change the way they think, feel, and act and to use this knowledge to avoid or escape from future high-risk situations. The various intervention modules that comprise correctional programs are centered around differ-ent dynamic risk factors, and it is common to find ones dealing with cog-nitive distortions, deviant sexual interests, social skill deficits, impaired problem-solving and cognitive skills, empathy deficits, intimacy deficits, emotional regulation difficulties, impulsivity, lifestyle imbalance, sub-stance abuse, and postoffense adjustment or relapse prevention (Andrews & Bonta, 2010; Ward & Maruna, 2007). In recent years, there has been sig-nificant debate on the utility of incorporating approach goals (i.e., goals that refer to achievement of a specific outcome such as employment skills or social skills) into programs and trying to help offenders capitalize on their strengths and core commitments. Much of this discussion centers on human needs and core interests, emotions, and the fundamental capaci-ties of human beings, and is consistent with evolutionary theory. The evidence from research into what works in rehabilitation indicates that effective interventions should look outward to the broader social and cul-tural environments as well as inward to crime related dispositions and properties (Andrews & Bonta, 2010; Laws & Ward, 2011).

By virtue of the strong causal role allocated to cultural change processes and resources, gene–culture coevolution theories such as niche construction theory are well-positioned to accommodate these requirements while also making room for innate mental mechanisms. According to these dual-focus theories, relatively fixed psychological mechanisms coexist alongside pow-erful social learning opportunities and cultural practices, and crucially, the two sets of inheritance systems interact and modify each other's component processes. In other words, human beings are by nature cultural animals: they have inherited a suite of cognitive, social, and emotional adaptations *and* a set of cultural resources that enable them to adapt relatively swiftly to changing environmental and personal circumstances (Sterelny, 2012).

EVOLUTIONARY EXPLANATORY FRAMEWORK AND REHABILITATION

The construction of theories of crime will hopefully result in robust explanations of the problems and actions associated with specific offenses as well as providing correctional program designers and practitioners guidance on what problems to focus on in their work with offenders. We build theories to understand why certain problems have occurred, how they develop, and what the distal and proximal causes are that create and maintain them. To increase the chances that efforts at theory creation are likely to be successful, it makes sense to be clear about the methodological and empirical constraints that need to be taken into account in this process. These constraints should reflect our most up to date knowledge concerning the world and our place in it, and any strategies for designing useful theories. It is helpful to ask the following types of questions in this process. What kind of creatures are we? Are we material (i.e., entirely composed of matter) organisms with the capacity for agency (i.e., capable of acting on the basis of reasons), or simply biological machines? How do we develop as persons and what kind of minds do we have? Are our minds entirely located within the brain or do they extend into the environment in some way, for example, via the recruitment of cognitive tools and cultural resources? Have we inherited an array of natural desires and a cognitive architecture or is our nature characterized by its plasticity and dependence on cultural scaffolding? Or are we a mixture of both?

It is important to possess an accurate understanding of the nature of human beings if theory construction in the human sciences is to result in deep and fruitful explanations. As stated earlier, we assume that human beings are evolved organisms who possess a cluster of psychological (adaptations—cognitive, social, motivational) properties that reliably emerge in certain cultural contexts under certain conditions. The *cognitive* capacities include: language; the ability to learn from others via social imitation and modeling; being able to critically reflect on the self and the world and to construct models of possible future lives and outcomes (i.e., to engage in mental time travel); having the ability to set (often nested sets of) goals, form plans, and to implement them; and being able to evaluate the outcome of our actions and use the resulting information to revise future actions and aspirations. The *motivational* properties include basic human needs such as the need for warmth, social support and care, food and water; basic emotions such as fear, disgust, and joy that motivate individuals to actively avoid harm and to seek out the resources required to sustain, and even enhance, well-being; and moral emotions such as guilt and remorse that arguably develop from basic emotions, cognitive appraisals, social emersion, and language. The *social* properties include the capacity to use social imitation to participate in and actively support norms that sustain and protect the functioning of the primary social groups encountered by individuals. Also included are the initially informal and later formal codification of social and moral norms to ensure all members have invested in the survival of the group and are able to work on collective projects that will protect the group from predation and other threats. These include tool-making, hunting, conflict resolution, child-rearing, punishment, and "teaching."

We have argued that a gene–culture coevolution conceptualization of human evolution (Chapter 3) alongside Tinbergen's (1963) influential account of explanation (Chapter 4) provides a rich and nuanced account of human functioning than can usefully inform practice. Case formulation in practice involves the construction of a mini-explanatory theory or model of an offender's presenting problems and his or her association with his criminal actions, and provides a causal and normative justification of intervention. A good case formulation incorporates a description of the relevant clinical phenomena a practitioner wishes to explain, an account of the interlocking, multilevel causes that generate the phenomena, and an appeal to the developmental, environmental, and historical factors that helped to shape offender vulnerabilities and identify triggers to the offending. Drawing from gene–culture coevolutionary theories and research in the construction of a case formulation will prompt the practitioner to look beyond a simple cataloging of dynamic risk factors and criminal actions. For example, in the case of rape, asking the following (Tinbergen's) explanatory questions can suggest multiple intervention streams ranging from policy to specific treatment strategies (see Ward & Durrant, 2011a, Ward and Durrant, 2011b). First, an inquiry into the possible adaptations or evolutionary function of rape may point to males' tendency to engage in impersonal sex or to infuse sexual contexts with status concerns. Second, there is the question of how these (hypothesized) traits evolved over the evolutionary history of *Homo sapiens*. Was the tendency to engage in impersonal sex a relatively recent trait (adaptation or by-product of an adaptation) or is it more long-standing? Three, what environmental, cultural, or psychological developmental processes are involved in the formation of rape tendencies? For example, are men who go on to commit rape more likely to be dismissively attached and report a history of parental rejection (Ward et al., 2006)? Finally, what specific psychological, biological, social, cultural, and environmental proximate mechanisms cause rape? Are some cultures more rape-prone because of a tendency to bestow lower social status on children and women? Are men who rape more adversarial in their relationships with females and do they tend to hold extreme gender norms?

Because we are committed to the metaphysical theory of emergent materialism, historical, biological, social, and agency-level explanations all have something to offer in accounting for crime (Baker, 1999). In particular, we would like to stress the importance of *agency-level* explanations (or more strictly, understanding) when identifying the causes of crime and when working with offenders to reduce their chances of reoffending. References to individuals' mental states (e.g., beliefs, desires, wishes, intentions, hopes, values, plans) and their associated commonsense explanations, are irreducibly part of human functioning and do not seem able to be reduced to other levels of explanation (upward or downward). This is in part because most human actions occur within social and relational contexts, and as such, cannot be reasonably reduced to neuronal processes and molecular interactions without losing an essential and explanatorily valuable perspective.

REHABILITATION IMPLICATIONS

We would now like to discuss five general implications of adopting an evolutionary explanatory framework for the rehabilitation of offenders. More specifically, the following factors ought to be taken into account when intervening with offenders: (1) the normative-capacity-building nature of offender rehabilitation, and cultural and biological inheritability and its basis in genetic and cultural inheritance systems; (2) the crucial role of social, ecological, and cultural environmental factors in rehabilitation (reentry, integration, and desistance)—a relational, view; (3) individuals' cognitive and behavioral plasticity and thus the critical role of epistemic niche construction; (4) the extended cognitive system and its role in treatment and desistance; and (5) inherited motivations or natural desires, including emotions. In part, this suggests the need to adopt a naturalistic conception of values, and has implications for grasping the links between dynamic risk factors, protective factors, and strengths. We will briefly discuss each in turn.

Normative-Capacity-Building Nature of Offender Rehabilitation

The rehabilitation of offenders is a normative-capacity-building process that draws from research on the technology of behavioral change and a range of ethical, prudential, and epistemic values. In the correctional arena, values are reflected in ethical principles that spell out the general duties of practitioners toward the community, victims, and the offender, based on the intrinsic worth of all members of the community. The duties of practitioners are intended to protect the core interests of all those affected by crime and to cover agency and well-being interests of individuals and social groups. More specific norms comprise professional codes of practice of the different professions and essentially define the scope of what constitutes acceptable practice—and in turn delineate the boundaries of each role. Thus, ethical, prudential, and epistemic values infuse all aspects of correctional assessment, intervention, and follow-up and are central drivers of change (Ward & Maruna, 2007). They inform professionals about the outcomes or experiences they should be seeking to achieve with clients and which ones they should try to avoid. In brief, values are evident: (1) In the definitions of risk assessment and the goal of crime reduction—to assess the probability of harmful outcomes occurring and to reduce the amount of harm. The numerical range of risk bands (e.g., what reoffending rates constitute low-, medium-, or high-risk bands) are in part dependent on value judgments: how much reoffending is a community prepared to tolerate over a specified period. (2) In intervention targets such as increased empathy, emotional control, or social functioning. In fact, empathy work is viewed in the offending domain as a critical component of the change process *because* it is assumed to directly influence individuals' sense of responsibility and determination to commit themselves to therapy. (3) In the concept of narrative identity that resides at the center of the change and desistance process. Narrative identity is based on individuals' conception of their lives and core commitments, and the implications this has for future lifestyle and actions. It essentially shapes persons' lives, and by doing this, informs them of what characteristics they should cultivate, how to act, and what goals to strive for. Prudential values spell out how best to increase individuals' well-being, whereas epistemic (i.e., knowledge regulating norms) values are crucially involved in the design of treatment programs, especially those aspects that inform offenders how to evaluate their beliefs and attitudes, and solutions to problems. From a gene–culture coevolution viewpoint, values should be viewed naturalistically and their acceptability as norms based on their ability to help agents secure the resources required to sustain their (biological, psychological, and social) functioning and to repair or avoid damage to themselves and others. Thus the source of values is to be sought in basic self-regulatory capacities, and norms are based on markers of possible benefits or harms to organisms (e.g., hunger signals a need for food, whereas fear indicates the need for protection and search for safety. The respective norms indicate the benefits of seeking the former and avoiding the latter). The evaluative component of offender rehabilitation involves a diverse range of norms stipulating such things as what constitutes good relationships, "nondistorted" beliefs and attitudes, healthy emotional management, appropriate and normal sexual fantasies and drives, appropriate responsiveness to other people's desires and interests, and adaptive problem-solving. From a naturalistic perspective, these norms are cognitive tools that enable people to obtain beliefs and avoid harms; the nature of the specific harms is ultimately related to the facts of the body, mind, and social and cultural context (Kekes, 1989).

The *capacity-building* part of correctional rehabilitation draws from empirical research concerning how best to establish the social and psychological resources individuals need to live prosocial and personally meaningful lives (Andrews & Bonta, 2010; Ward & Maruna, 2007). Correctional interventions are necessarily based on values and their associated principles, standards, and norms because it only make sense to design a treatment plan once it is clear what capacities (e.g., skills, attitudes) are required to achieve certain standards (related to norms): the capacity for establishing and maintaining healthy relationships, the capacity to form rational beliefs, the ability to respond in an emotionally appropriate way to threat or stress, etc. A crucial aim of all offender interventions is to improve offenders' perceptions of other people's mental states, especially their needs, interests, and emotions, and by doing so, make it less likely they will behave in harmful ways in the future. This is an emotional/cognitive task as arguably altruistic actions are reliably generated by sympathetic or empathic affective states (Batson, 2011; see the following section).

Role of the Environment: Social, Cultural, and Ecological

Natural selection from a traditional viewpoint exerts an influence on the gene frequencies in populations by selecting for individuals who cope more effectively with adaptive problems such as how to deal with predation threats or food shortages. Organisms that can outmaneuver predators or whose traits enable them to access previously hard to obtain food sources are more likely to survive and reproduce. Once culture is included in an evolutionary explanation, social and cultural practices and humanly created environmental changes such as farming practices also exert selection pressure. In the example of psychopathy, childhood adversity and abuse may result in individuals adopting different life-history strategies, ones that will increase their chances of survival in chaotic, inconsistent, and dangerous environments. In our view, the bidirectional influences that organisms and their environments have on each other underlines the interactional, dynamic nature of human functioning, and the importance of focusing on action (and dynamic person–environment interactions) rather than simply the manipulation of internal representations. In developing their interactivist–constructivist model of human learning, Christensen and Hooker (2000, p. 9) state that "The basic problem of living then is: how to use one's own capacities to manage one's interaction with the world, and within oneself...." By virtue of their niche construction activities, *Homo sapiens* actively transform the knowledge and physical aspects of their environments, which in turn modify their own characteristics and functioning, for better or worse. Learning is anticipative and directed toward the achievement of well-being enhancing goals within specific contexts, and problem-solving typically occurs *on line* to so speak, in the heat of action sequences (or practices) rather than in cool reflective moments. As a consequence, human beings have been shaped by biological and cultural factors to be versatile, agile, socially embedded problem-solvers who actively restructure their environments and themselves in line with their goals. More specifically (Christensen & Hooker, 2000, p. 11):

> Cognitive processes are embedded within an autonomous system involved in organized dynamic interaction processes in a structured environment, and they operate by continuously modulating (rather than controlling) these interaction processes so as to be coherent across multiple constraints and timescales.

Thus a picture emerges of human beings as relational in nature but with a fair degree of autonomy, with distinct biological and psychological boundaries. Cultural knowledge and practices offer resources that can be drawn from as needed (e.g., books, cognitive tools, language, technology, social supports) to achieve prioritized goals or become incorporated into a persons' functional repertoire in the form of skills and knowledge. Innate capacities such as working memory, processing speed, simple causal reasoning, concept formation, attentional control, and motivational biases provide a basic set of resources to initiate, and later entrench and elaborate, goal achievement.

What are the implications of such an interactivist, dynamic view of learning and human functioning for offender rehabilitation? One way of intervening would be to manipulate the nature of individuals' social and developmental environments so they are likely to engage in less socially problematic strategies (see the following section). Once we have a good understanding of the conditional rules associated with specific psychological modules and the norms inherent in cultural practices, it may be possible to predict what cues will activate them and, in principle, work out how best to intervene in ways that make the development of serious antisocial behavior less likely. From a niche construction standpoint, establishing education programs in schools and via the media could promote norms and attitudes that encourage more constructive ways of resolving problems and facilitate greater gender equality. Early intervention programs could also focus on creating community groups and resources to assist individuals who are struggling with social and psychological adjustment issues. At a cultural level, there may be a social commitment to rehabilitation and also changes to the way sexuality is represented, and the way males and females are acculturated. The impact of such a cultural change is likely to be pervasive and alter the context in which males are socialized, thereby possibly lessening the likelihood of developing rape-supportive attitudes and beliefs. Finally, an example of ecological interventions would be to create physical spaces where males and females can interact informally from a young age, so encouraging greater awareness of each other's needs and characteristics.

Cognitive and Behavioral Plasticity

We agree with Sterelny (2012) and Christensen and Hooker (2000) that human beings are characterized by considerable cognitive and behavioral plasticity, and this flexibility has allowed them to design and use cultural and environmental resources to solve problems and enhance the quality of their lives. From the viewpoint of the gene–culture coevolution model, human beings are characterized by a considerable degree of cognitive malleability and are culturally capable and responsive animals (Sterelny, 2012). Thus, prevailing ethical and social norms and the social learning that imparts them significantly influence the acquisition of psychological capabilities. This is what we referred to earlier as the normative-competency building nature of offender rehabilitation.

As stated previously, a lack of built-in solutions to the full range of adaptive problems currently confronting human beings (e.g., the development of rewarding social relationships and the acquisition of status in large-scale, hierarchically organized, and demographically fluid modern societies) points to the importance of acquiring general cognitive strategies and having access to external knowledge and support systems. Although specific domains of expertise are also necessary to meet needs and to function in the modern world, an advantage of possessing a range of general problem-solving abilities, and alongside this, self-reflective capacities, is that solutions to novel problems can be created reasonably quickly when required. From the standpoint of this model, it is imperative to carefully construct the learning environments of offenders and to ensure that social and cultural institutions possess mechanisms to facilitate the reliable transmission of knowledge while participating in programs and when released from custody. What happens after treatment is as important as what occurs during it. Research suggests that desistance from offending is best fostered by investing in social supports, employment opportunities, and in essence, giving people the resources, and opportunities, to fully engage in community life (Laws & Ward, 2011). It is not just a question of simply applying knowledge about the inherited structure of the mind to control or redirect a narrow range of predetermined behavioral possibilities (although such knowledge may play a role in the rehabilitation process). In principle, there are a broad range of behavioral options, guided by ethical and social values, and it is possible to modify deeply held attitudes and proclivities to a significant degree. Interventions for offenders based on a gene–culture coevolutionary approach ought to reflect these important insights and make sure that psychological, social, and cultural learning environments promote the adoption of core skills and values in constructive ways as well as seek to protect the community. In part, this means attending to what is important to offenders alongside what interventions are likely to reduce the risk of further offending. Thus, a significant therapeutic task is to help individuals construct good life plans, which detail their central values and identity, and outline ways of realizing them within particular environments. The internal capacities and external resources required to successfully implement a good life plan will be clearly delineated and the time line for its implementation set out in a step-by-step, graded manner for therapists and offenders to use during the latter's desistance journey. When we discuss the example of empathy and altruism later in the chapter, we will give some concrete examples of how this can be done in specific treatment modules.

The Extended Cognitive System

A recent innovation in the cognitive science literature has been the introduction of the extended mind theory of cognition (EMT), which fits nicely with the relational nature of human beings and their cognitive flexibility (Clark, 2003, 2008; Ward, 2009). In our view, this is a striking feature of the gene–culture coevolution model. The available research evidence indicates that human beings' ability to construct and in turn be shaped by their environments(s), in conjunction with their cognitive and behavioral plasticity and the role of culture and social learning in creating minds, means that it is a mistake to view human nature as biologically fixed and contained inside people's heads. Clark (2003) noted that human beings do not have a set nature with a "simple wrap-around of tools and culture; the tools and culture are as much determiners of our natures as products of it" (p. 86). Johnson (2007, p. 152) makes this point well:

> Finally, meaning does not reside in our brain, nor does it reside in a disembodied mind. Meaning requires a functioning brain, in a living body that engages its environments - environments that are social and cultural, as well as physical and biological. Cultural artefacts and practices…preserve aspects of meaning as objective features of the world.

Thus, human agents have evolved to possess *hybrid* cognitive systems consisting of an integrated combination of internal (brain-based systems) and external components (written materials, language, other people, computers, calculators, etc.) that enable agents to engage effectively in cognitive tasks such as problem-solving. An implication of this viewpoint for offender rehabilitation involves setting up (hybrid) cognitive systems that contain both internal components (e.g., skills for evaluating goals and means to achieve them) and external resources such as access to information, technology, social networks, and other people such as group members (Ward, 2009). Community support initiatives such as Circles of Support (Wilson, 2007) are interesting examples of an extended cognitive system and fit together well with this evolved feature of human beings. One of the functions of Circles of Support is to provide sex offenders with exposure to a group of supportive and engaged individuals who hold prosocial norms and behave in ways that reflect these values. It is reasonable to assume that one of the ways this initiative works (and the preliminary evidence is that it does reduce reoffending in high-risk sex offenders) is by assisting offenders to discover more socially adaptive ways of thinking about themselves and others, within a community setting.

An additional implication of the EMT is acknowledging the importance of treating offenders in an ecologically responsive manner. It is essential to think about individuals' probable release environments when planning treatment and to ascertain the social and cultural contexts that will probably confront them on release (Ward, 2009). Furthermore, therapists, group members, and the various physical and cognitive resources available to individuals in treatment can be considered as part of their (extended) cognitive systems rather than simply as useful supplements to a self that is encapsulated and relatively cognitively immune to external influences.

Innate Motivational Factors

According to the gene–culture coevolution model (in fact, according to all of the major evolutionary models), individuals possess evolved dispositions to seek valued outcomes in the various domains of living; these are evident in their motivations, needs, and emotions (Arnhart, 1998; Kekes, 1989; Ward & Stewart, 2003). The suite of emotional and motivational predispositions can be viewed as explicit *norm* signals that "provide information about appropriate action" in specific contexts by making the discrepancy between reference values and the current condition of an organism salient (Christensen & Hooker, 2000, p. 11). For example, feelings of hunger reflect low glycogen levels prompting the person to seek food to avoid harm and to sustain functioning. Furthermore, more sophisticated normative signals such as feelings of guilt or anger are developed through social learning and exposure to cultural models and serve to enhance well-being and ultimately survival. Kekes (1989, p. 28) does a good job of making the link between motivational states and norms clear when he states:

> The facts of the body, self, and social life constitute part of the foundation of human motivation. For we all want to protect the conditions in which we can obtain the benefits and avoid the harms these human characteristics define. Thus, the facts of the body, self, and social life establish what must be the minimum conditions for human welfare. To jeopardize these conditions is to harm us, and thus it is evil; to protect the conditions is to benefit us, and so it is good.

In our view, the biological and psychological research evidence supports the claim that all people, including offenders, are naturally inclined to seek certain goals or what we call (after Kekes, 1989) *primary human goods* such as relatedness, creativity, physical health, agency, and mastery (Laws & Ward, 2011; Ward & Maruna, 2007). In brief, *primary* goods are states of affairs, states of mind, personal characteristics, activities, or experiences that are sought for their own sake and are likely to increase psychological well-being if achieved (Ward & Stewart, 2003). *Instrumental* or secondary goods provide particular ways (i.e., means) of achieving primary goods. For instance, it is possible to secure the primary good of relatedness by the way of romantic, parental, or personal relationships.

The notion of instrumental goods or means is particularly important when it comes to applying rehabilitation initiatives based on them to offending behavior because it is assumed that a primary reason individuals commit offenses is that they are seeking primary goods in socially and often personally destructive ways. However, there is considerable flexibility in the way basic needs, and the goods they are associated with, can be realized in people's lives. This suggests at least two things: forensic and correctional practitioners need to (1) engage offenders in a dialogue to identify what means of achieving the full range of primary goods are likely to be realistic and also meaningful to the person, and (2) help offenders to become more reflective and self-critical so they can acquire the capability to evaluate what it is they need, what is important, and to arrive at ways of acting that are more likely to result in a fulfilling and crime-free life (Laws & Ward, 2011). A further practice implication is that a good lives plan that is incoherent (i.e., has ways of achieving primary goods that are inconsistent either for each good, or across the different classes of goods (e.g., work at the expense of intimacy)) is likely to result in poor levels of social integration and increased risk of reoffending. This is in part because human beings do not deal well with cognitive dissonance, which a contradictory plan for living is likely to create (Ward & Maruna, 2007). Therefore, practitioners should work closely with offenders to develop rehabilitation (i.e., good lives) plans that revolve around their core commitments, include all the major primary goods, and outline the internal and external resources required to successfully implement the plan in the environments they are likely to be released into.

If you accept that, like all human beings, offenders possess a suite of natural desires (Arnhart, 1998) and core emotions (and their more complex derivatives) that function to direct and organize action, then practitioners should take this into account when designing interventions. Failure to do so may make it difficult to motivate offenders and to construct plans for living that reflect their priorities and increase the chances of social integration and ultimately reduce reoffending. What this means is that the trend of current programs to focus rehabilitation and treatment on the modification of dynamic risk factors is misguided. In part, this is because risk-oriented intervention goals are avoidant in nature and tend to be preoccupied with what offenders should *not do* rather than what specific conditions they ought to aim for—such as specific types of work as opposed to unemployment. Furthermore, the usual practice of listing dynamic risk factors and then allocating offenders to their respective treatment modules can create therapeutic fragmentation, and, more worryingly, overlook the important role of agency and its component idea of narrative identity in the change process. The construction of an adaptive narrative identity is an essential aspect of the effective rehabilitation for offenders. The process of developing such an identity depends on the acquisition of capabilities and resources that will enable an offender to effectively implement a good lives plan in his or her postrelease environment. Primary human goods (and the related processes of needs, interests, and emotions) are a central feature of such a plan, and an important therapeutic task is to align treatment interventions to offenders' valued goals. Offenders' personal strivings express their sense of who they are and what they would like to become. Narrative identities, for offenders and for all people, are constituted from the pursuit and achievement of personal goals, rooted in emotions and core human needs.

EXAMPLE OF EMPATHY AND ALTRUISM

According to Oxley (2011), empathy is "both an act *and* a capacity" (p. 15). Individuals engage in acts of empathy when they imagine how someone else is likely to be feeling in certain situations, or alternatively, anticipate how they would feel in similar circumstances. To act empathically, individuals require cognitive and emotional capacities such as the ability to psychologically decenter, emotional knowledge, and the possession of emotional regulation, deliberation, and perspective-taking skills. Oxley (2011, p. 32) defines empathy as follows (also see Chapter 5):

> Feeling a congruent emotion with another person, in virtue of perceiving her emotion with some mental process such as imitation, simulation, projection, or imagination. (italics in the original)

Several researchers have argued that empathy plays a foundational role in morality and, furthermore, is evident in some degree in non-human animals, particularly primates (de Waal, 2006; Maibom, 2014). In view of the fact that criminal actions clearly override the interests of victims as well as the larger community, it is not surprising that empathy and its related processes are of interest to correctional theorists and practitioners (e.g., Barnett & Mann, 2012). Empathy interventions are a key component of many offender rehabilitation programs and in the case of sex offenders, almost mandatory.

The phenomenon of empathy and its explanation and role in morality has been the subject of controversy and it is unclear to what degree offenders lack empathy or simply fail to exercise it in the case of their own victims. Furthermore, there are contrasting definitions of empathy and little agreement concerning what it actually is. Its relationship to allied concepts such as altruism is disputed and its causal links to ethical (and thus offending) behavior are, therefore, contested (Maibom, 2014; Ward & Durrant, 2013). We will put these concerns to one side for the remainder of the chapter and accept that empathy has an important, although circumscribed, role in promoting prosocial behavior. We argue that in the correctional domain it is best viewed within the context of psychological altruism, as developed in a book by Kitcher (2011). In Kitcher's hands, altruism is a multidimensional concept based on emotional, social, and cognitive processes that have evolutionary origins and also strong cultural and normative components. In our view, altruism (and empathy) is an excellent example of a phenomenon that is best accounted for in terms of gene–culture coevolution theory, with multiple levels of explanation required.

Kitcher's Concept of Psychological Altruism

Kitcher (2011) developed a theory of ethics based on the assumptions of naturalistic pragmatism. According to this perspective, ethics is a form of social technology that emerged during the evolution of human beings to stabilize social cooperation and coordination. He argues that when human beings lived in relatively small groups, cooperation was essential for survival. Foraging for food, dealing with predators, or simply being faced with fluctuations of the environment and weather meant that groups that were motivated to take each other's interests into account were more likely to survive and reproduce. Kitcher points to the crucial role of early *Homo sapiens'* emotional and cognitive capacities in creating strong social bonds within groups. However, the problem with relying on psychological states such as altruistic emotions and social motivations is that they can be unreliable at times, particularly once the population grew substantially and human beings started to live in much larger groups. The cost of altruism failure would be extremely high and most likely result in significant harm to the interests of group members, and the group itself. Kitcher argues that ethical norms were initially constructed to coordinate the actions of group members and were arrived at through a process of consultation and group consensus. Over time these norms were codified into oral language and later in a written form, which made it easier to transmit them to successive generations, thus consolidating cultural practices designed to sustain the group/society. The important point is that according to Kitcher, ethical norms are essentially social tools that were designed to piggyback on human beings evolved (natural) cognitive and emotional capacities. The emergence of ethical norms bestowed an advantage to *human groups* as they functioned to stabilize altruistic responses and also solved the problem of encouraging members of a social group to act ethically when no longer in the line of sight of other members of the group; in other words, they promoted self-control. That human beings are intentional animals capable of accurately inferring the mental states of conspecifics made it easier to acquire the capacity for self-normative guidance though the internalization of a group's ethical norms.

According to Kitcher, *psychological altruism* is concerned with the intentions of an agent and is evident when an individual adjusts his or her actions to take into account the interests and desires of other people. Kitcher (2010, p. 122) states that:

> To be an altruist is to have a particular kind of relational structure in your psychological life – when you come to see that what you do will affect other people, the wants you have, the emotions you feel, the intentions you form change from what they would have been in the absence of that recognition. Because you see the consequences for others of what you envisage doing, the psychological attitudes you adopt are different.

More specifically, Kitcher contends that an individual's altruism profile can be best described by the use of five dimensions: intensity, range, scope, discernment, and empathy. The *intensity* of an altruistic response involves the degree to which persons realign their own desires or interests to accommodate those of another. The *range* of someone's profile refers to the list of people whose desires or interests (could involve all human beings or be restricted to family and friends) he or she normally takes into account when acting. The *scope* of an altruism profile denotes the internal and external contexts in which an individual is likely to act altruistically. For example, a male might usually take his partner's desires into account in their relationship unless he was feeling angry or depressed. An individual's *discernment* refers to his or her ability to identify the consequences of his/her actions for relevant others. Finally, someone's *empathy* skills speaks to the ability to accurately infer another person's desires, or more broadly, relevant mental or physical states. This is similar to the notion of perspective-taking and theory of mind ability. Kitcher comments that typically individuals' altruistic profiles consist of an inner circle of valued people whose interests they almost always take into account when acting in ways that are likely to influence them. However, it is likely that the interests of persons on the periphery or beyond this circle would be overlooked or downplayed.

It is possible to transform the concept of psychological altruism into a theoretical framework capable of guiding theorists and empirical researchers in the formulation of explanations of altruism (and empathy) failures. From the perspective of this framework individuals act in ways that harm others (altruism failure) when: (1) they do not sufficiently modulate their own desires (etc.) to adequately respond to the situation at hand (intensity); (2) they unreasonably exclude certain classes of people or specific individuals from the list of those toward whom they ought be behave altruistically and therefore would not offend against them (range); (3) they fail to behave altruistically in certain contexts because of the influence of cognitive, emotional, physiological, social, or environmental factors (scope); (4) they are incapable of, or fail in certain contexts, to exhibit their capacities to discern the consequences of their actions for the individuals they offend against (discernment); and (5) they lack the capacity to accurately detect the mental states of people they offend against or, if they possess this capacity, they fail to exercise it in certain contexts (empathy skill). Of course, these claims are abstract and overly general but they function as useful indicators of the social, psychological, and physical variables researchers ought to concentrate their efforts on.

Aims of Rehabilitation

The aims of rehabilitation from the framework of psychological altruism is to make it less probable that an offender will experience altruism failure and therefore fail to take the desires and interests of relevant individuals into account in the course of their daily lives. Failure to do so could adversely impact on them and other members of the community in two ways. First, once in a high-risk situation, disregarding the desires and interests of a potential victim makes it easier for an individual to commit an offense. Second, consistently acting in ways that ignore the preferences and interests of other people is likely to impair the social reintegration process because of the adverse effects on offenders' vocational, social, and intimate relationships (Ward & Laws, 2010). Minimizing the likelihood of altruism failures occurring by strengthening the social, psychological, and situational components of psychological altruism through program interventions should also make it easier for offenders to live more fulfilling lives.

Assessment

The aim of the assessment phase of offender treatment is to systematically collect clinically relevant information about individuals' offending, functional life domains, personal characteristics, and developmental and social history. Once an offender's problems have been identified, a case formulation (or mini-clinical theory) is constructed in which the nature of the problems, their onset, development, and interrelationships are outlined. Following the development of a case formulation, clinicians construct an intervention plan in which the various intervention goals, their sequencing, and strategies for achieving them are noted. Focusing on sex offender treatment for convenience, the components of a comprehensive treatment program should include the following types of interventions: cognitive restructuring/offense reflection, sexual reconditioning, sexual education, social skill training, problem-solving, (empathy) perspective-taking/constructing victim biographies/victim impact work, intimacy work, acquiring emotional regulation skills, lifestyle/leisure planning and experience, vocational training, and reentry or adjustment planning, including relapse prevention (Marshall et al., 2006; Laws & Ward, 2011).

When formulating a case, the theoretical framework we derived from Kitcher's altruism dimensions can be used to direct and concentrate clinical attention to certain kinds of problems. Drawing from the assessment data (comprising interview information, psychological measures, archive data, behavioral observations, etc.), practitioners can ask the following questions, each covering one of the five dimensions of altruism.

Range. Are there any individuals or classes of people explicitly excluded from the offender's list of altruism targets? Does he hold certain beliefs or attitudes that effectively disenfranchise persons from a consideration of their interests, for example children or young adult women? Does he lack the skills to communicate openly and honestly with adults?

Scope. Are there any internal contexts in which the offender's ability to act altruistically are compromised in some way? For example, does he find it hard to take account of someone else's interests when feeling angry, sexually aroused, or lonely? What about external contexts? Does the offender struggle to control his sexually deviant desires and preferences when alone with a child or woman? What about if he is in the company of certain groups of friends? Or when he is socially isolated?

Discernment. Does the offender lack an adequate understanding of the psychological and developmental needs of children? Are his problem-solving and inductive reasoning skills of poor quality, making it difficult for him to think through the consequences of acting in sexually abusive or offense reacted ways?

Empathy skills. Does the offender struggle to accurately identify other people's mental states during an interaction? Is he able to adjust his actions in light of his reading of others' mental states?

Intensity. Does the offender possess the general practical reasoning and self-management skills in order to frame other people's situations in ways that accurately describes what is going on for them? Having done this, can he realign his own desires (and other relevant mental states) and actions to respond in an appropriate manner? Intensity is a more global capacity that builds on the skills, etc., aligned to the other altruism dimensions.

It is anticipated that the answers to the above questions will enable practitioners to determine the reasons why a sex offender acted in ways contrary to the desires and interests of his victim. This information can then be recruited in the construction of the case formulation and subsequent intervention plan.

Practice

In discussing the practice implications of the theoretical framework derived from Kitcher's concept of psychological altruism, we will describe briefly four typical sex offender rehabilitation modules and trace their potential for increasing the likelihood of an offender acting altruistically.

Understanding One's Offending/Cognitive Restructuring

The aim of this module is for offenders to acquire an understanding of the psychological and contextual triggers and precursors to their offending, and importantly, to grasp the goals guiding their offense-related actions. With prompting and feedback from the group, often individuals start to question their understanding of their motives and the way they interpreted the actions of other people, including victims. Typically, offenders will complete this phase of rehabilitation with a sense of accountability for their actions (often displaying significant remorse), awareness of the problematic nature of some of their beliefs and attitudes, and a grasp of their own set of risk factors for further offending.

The major clinical focus of this module is individuals' offense supportive beliefs and attitudes and acceptance of responsibility for their abusive actions. It is normal to see the emergence of an awareness of their cognitive and emotional barriers to accepting victims as moral equals (range)—beings who merit equal consideration of their desires, needs, and interests when contemplating sex. Furthermore, clinicians may obtain insight into offenders' knowledge of sex and interpersonal relationships, and obtain a fuller grasp of their particular altruism profile. Finally, it should be possible to ascertain how emotionally competent individuals are and what relationships exist between emotional states and offending (contextual dimension).

The assumption that offenders are predisposed to seek a range of primary goods (valued outcomes) in their everyday lives will prompt therapists to look beyond simple sexual gratification to explain their motivation. The emphasis on practical reasoning and self-regulation, and the need to understand actions from the point of view of the fit between a person and their environment should yield a richer understanding of their offending and also point to intervention strategies that are likely to engage the offender more fully. This is because, according to the gene–culture coevolution model, failing to attend to individuals' "natural desires" (i.e., core interests and needs—what we have called primary human goods) may result in their displaying a lack of motivation, and, importantly, minimal investment in the change process.

Empathy Training

As stated earlier in this chapter, the major aim of the empathy module is to encourage offenders to reflect on the impact of sexual abuse on victims and their families. This is achieved through the use of victim biographies, role plays of the index offense, and the assimilation of information about sexual abuse and its consequences for victims. Offenders often describe this as an emotionally powerful, even traumatic, experience and state that it helped them to grasp the self-serving nature of their behavior and related disregard for the well-being of vulnerable children and unconsenting adults.

Victim perspective taking and appropriate emotional responding are therapeutic targets of this module and are classical components of an empathy response. In the language of psychological altruism, an expectation is that empathetic accuracy is improved, discernment skills are sharpened, and contextual features of high-risk situations that increase the likelihood of sexual crime occurring, are discovered.

Ideally, cultivating the ability to respond empathetically to another person's emotional state will motivate them to act in ways that at least do not undermine their interests. But, as we have noted in a recent article (Ward & Durrant, 2013), this might not be enough to encourage someone to act altruistically when they are strongly motivated to sexually offend. Thus, as part of empathy training, we suggest ensuring that offenders are helped to identify and state the norms governing sexual and close relationships. And alongside this process, be assisted to realize that empathic feelings can be unreliable and undermined by contextual features such as strong emotional states. Understanding the evolution of empathy and its role in establishing social cohesion (and the threats to it) may help to remind practitioners that empathy interventions should be undertaken within an altruism context.

Social Skills and Intimacy Interventions

The social skills/intimacy module seeks to equip offenders with the internal and external capabilities to adaptively manage challenges of the social world and to learn how to establish and maintain intimate relationships. The rationale for such an emphasis is that research has indicated that some offenders commit sexual offenses because of their feelings of loneliness and social isolation (Ward, Mann, & Gannon, 2007). In addition, in this module, there is an emphasis on dealing with social conflicts and learning how to communicate feelings in a range of interpersonal contexts, from work to disagreements in close relationships. Successful desistance from offending requires the cultivation of strong social supports and the ability to communicate needs to others in a constructive way. The impact of offenders' early interpersonal relationships is usually explored and the resulting influence on their internal working models of attachment figures and romantic partners are clearly identified. At this point, problematic attitudes, beliefs, and interpersonal strategies are usually identified and ways of dealing with them in treatment noted.

Offending is an interpersonal event and involves an interaction between at least two people—the offender and the person he sexually assaults. Internal working models of relationships that are characterized by distrust or perceptions of vulnerability may impair offenders' perceptions of children and adults and result in sexual crimes. Problematic beliefs of these types, and the strategies that accompany them, make it difficult for offenders to function in a psychologically altruistic way. There is frequently a problem of range, where the needs and interests of certain people are dismissed as irrelevant, or else are misperceived in ways that promote sexual offending (empathetic skill). There may also be problems of context (e.g., experiencing altruism failure when feeling lonely) that would benefit from therapeutic attention.

The assumption that offenders are (naturally) strongly motivated to establish social relationships, and taking into account the role of relationships in mediating therapeutic interventions, should reinforce the importance of this module to practitioners. In particular, the relational nature of the self, and the need to explain action within a relational context, makes it imperative that the quality of the offender–practitioner relationship is good. Furthermore, active attempts should be made to cultivate a good working alliance, and the regrettable tendency, increasingly apparent in correctional practice, to concentrate entirely on offenders risk factors and to underplay the relational aspects of treatment should be avoided (Gannon & Ward, 2014). In other words, the evolved predispositions of all human beings to need and rely on social contact and learning should be at the heart of practice.

Emotional Regulation

Emotional regulation interventions are based on the assumption that a lack of emotional competence can make it hard for offenders to read social cues accurately and to adhere to social and ethical norms in high-risk situations. Core emotional competency skills include the ability to accurately identify and label emotions in oneself and in others; once the emotions have been correctly identified, knowing how to act in (adaptive) ways prompted by the emotion in question; and being able to manage negative emotional states so they do not overwhelm the person concerned.

Intense emotional states can disinhibit individuals and create immense pressure on them to act nonaltruistically, especially in situations when they experience a strong desire to act in antisocial ways. For example, if an offender is experiencing strong feelings of anger, asserting some degree of self-control could be particularly challenging. Norms directing an offender to attend to his potential sexual partner's desires or preferences may be overlooked and his own desires thought to override all other motivations. Alternatively, another sex offender could use sex as a soothing activity and, when feeling vulnerable, anxious, or depressed, seek out a sexual partner. These kinds of problems are unfortunately relatively common and point to issues with psychological altruism. Perhaps the most obvious issue relates to one of internal context, where failure to effectively modulate certain moods makes it hard for an offender to act in a psychologically altruistic manner; his own desires and needs take precedence in a context when the reverse should be true.

The ability to adjust action in light of changing environmental circumstances and to ensure that important normative signals are attended to require the presence of good self-regulation skills, including emotional regulation and control. Difficulty reading emotional and internal cues adversely affects a person's ability to discern normative signals and increase their chances of acting in harmful ways toward others. Therapists using a gene–culture coevolution theoretical framework will understand and appreciate the crucial role of emotions in normative regulation and use this knowledge to better inform their practice.

CONCLUSIONS

In this chapter, we have explored the practice implications of the gene–culture coevolution model. There were five general practice implications that were applicable to the rehabilitation process in general, all stemming from the relational nature of human functioning and its associated cognitive and behavioral plasticity. To make the discussion a little more concrete, we took the example of altruism and its related concept of empathy and demonstrated how its combination of biological and cultural components could inform practice in novel and potentially valuable ways. The normative–capacity building nature of offender rehabilitation points to the pivotal role of values, and the overlap between punishment and treatment.

12

Looking Forward from the Perspective of the Past

In this final chapter, we would like to identify and discuss important areas for future empirical research and theoretical work arising from the overall argument of this book. Human beings are complex organisms that possess an array of innate biological and psychological capacities that evolve within a cultural matrix. From a biological perspective, they are dynamic, complex systems that use their inheritance of cognitive and social tools to construct life worlds, and over time, even change their nature. It is a theoretical mistake in research to decompose human beings into their components and to try to explain the functioning of the whole simply by analysis of the parts. Psychological and physical properties are distributed across the whole organism and, in an important respect, come into existence in interaction with the environment. It is tempting to view culture and genetic inheritance as two strands of a double helix, linked by bridges that are so tightly interwoven that separation is practically impossible. Whether such a radical holism is true is arguable. However, the key point is that we are creatures of action, and our relationship to the contexts in which we live our lives is dynamic and fluid.

We would like to briefly discuss four major implications of the model of gene–culture coevolution outlined in this book as they relate to the explanation and management of crime: integrative pluralism, physical embodiment, the role of emotion, and the distributed nature of cognition. All of these themes can be traced back to our conception of human beings as materially embodied, dynamic agents.

INTEGRATIVE PLURALISM: A DEEPER ONTOLOGY

According to the agency model of risk outlined in Chapter 8, an adequate explanation of crime ought to encompass multiple levels of analysis and, importantly, privilege the role of agency. Human beings formulate goals based on needs, emotions, and values, and construct

Evolutionary Criminology
http://dx.doi.org/10.1016/B978-0-12-397937-7.00012-4 © 2015 Elsevier Inc. All rights reserved.

plans that seek to realize these goals in particular environments. The formulation of action plans relies on a suite of psychological, physical, and social capacities and is always responsive to environmental cues and affordances. The agency level of analysis is critical to understanding crime because it is the normative space where individuals' experiences, aspirations, history, and abilities to control their world converge. The ability of human beings to effectively take greater control of their lives rests heavily on sophisticated cognitive and behavioral abilities and the existence of cultural resources and scaffolding: we actively use the skills of other people and the advantages provided by social institutions to successfully realize our plans. Biological and cultural evolution are the twin motors that underpin our ability to adapt to environmental challenges and to live meaningful and fulfilling lives. Sometimes things go wrong and people fail to adhere to the social and ethical norms of their community; sometimes, they inflict significant, unjustified harm on other people. In our view, once the complex nature of human functioning is accepted, the explanation of crime should be pluralistic (i.e., consist of multiple levels of analysis) and integrated (i.e., the different levels need to be conceptually linked). A gene–culture coevolution model, in conjunction with Tinbergen's causal framework, can help us to achieve this goal.

Thus, our approach to explaining crime is based on three primary, related, theoretical claims. First, human beings are physically embodied agents and as such, are complex organisms with multiple levels of functioning. Theories of crime and empirical research should be pursued at all levels of explanation embedded within a gene–culture coevolution conceptual framework. We suggest that such a framework is likely to result in a deeper and more integrated understanding of crime and its precursors, and can capitalize on biological, psychological, social, cultural, and physical perspectives. Upward or downward theoretical reductionism needs to be resisted as it fails to capture what is truly unique about our nature and functioning.

Second, human agents are characterized by plasticity of cognitive functioning and have an enormous capacity to acquire knowledge via social imitation and modeling. Their nature is not fixed, and, indeed, it relies heavily on social and cultural scaffolding for development of the abilities necessary to function independently and in a normatively acceptable way. To grasp why people act in socially destructive ways, it is imperative to examine innate dispositions, developmental history, current goals and psychological abilities, and the degree to which environments support continued offending, or indeed, contribute to its onset.

Third, human agents have cognitive systems that incorporate both internal and external components. We reject the *internalist* view that the mind resides entirely within the brain, or indeed, the body, and argue instead that cognitive systems extend into the external environment and integrate social, cultural, and technological resources when engaged in cognitive tasks such as problem-solving or inferring (Menary, 2007; Rowlands, 2010). We will discuss the distributed cognition or extended mind theory in greater depth in the following sections.

EMBODIMENT

The embodiment conception of personhood rests upon the idea that psychological properties emerge from the body and its interacting systems, in active engagement with the environment (or rather a range of external contexts; Baker, 1999; Gibbs, 2006). It is a holistic view and assumes that persons are the totality of their biological, social, and psychological properties. Moreover, according to the embodiment thesis, experience of being embodied colors and strongly determines the content of psychological concepts referring to actions and processes (Johnson, 2007). Theorists and researchers have argued that concepts such as justice, perception, language, and rationality arise from the phenomenological experience of bodies acting in the world rather than from a disembodied, Cartesian mind. For example, the conceptual metaphor that *understanding is seeing* is acquired by applying visual concepts (source) to the target domain of understanding. In this example, the object perceived equates to an idea, seeing an object is unpacked in terms of understanding, and visual focusing refers to mental attention. More abstract concepts can also be traced back to their embodied sources in a similar manner. For example, causation arguably is derived from the experience of pushing, and viewing life as a narrative process originates from the idea of a physical journey, whereas arriving at balanced ethical decision decisions may have its source in balancing physical objects.

Johnson has (2007, pp. 11–14) identified the core assumptions of the embodiment thesis: (1) mind and the body are not radically separated; (2) meaning is grounded in bodily experience; (3) reason is an embodied process—thus it cannot be identified with any specific parts (or modules) of the mind or brain; (4) the capacity to engage in imaginative thought depends on the use of body related metaphors and experiences; (5) human beings do not have radical freedom of the will in the sense that the capacity to make decisions depends crucially on a number of biological and physical factors; (6) emotional and rational processes are integrally linked, and have their basis in our physical nature. For example, gestures can be viewed as vehicles of meaning and also express emotional states; and (7) spirituality, or a sense of meaning and purpose, emerges from our relationship with the broader world rather than from a transcendent reality.

From a crime explanation viewpoint, the language agents use to talk abut their experiences and to make sense of their worlds depends in part on the physical environment. Understanding the particular nature of human beings' psychological and physical functioning and its historical (distal and proximal) development can assist us to appreciate why the world is constructed and conceptually parsed as it is. In so far as people share a common universal set of physical—embodied—properties then there will be universal conceptions of some aspects of human experience and shared sources of frustration and enjoyment. Additionally, the capacity for agency depends on body integrity and normal functioning. Physical stress created by such factors as poverty, crowding, intoxication, and physiological arousal will directly alter the salience of agents' goals and can compromise their ability to reflect critically on their actions. Finally, rehabilitation initiatives need to take the implications of embodiment into account and put as much emphasis on physical well-being as on social and physical functioning.

EMOTION

We argued in Chapter 8 that, from an agency perspective, emotions function as both normative markers and as initiators and regulators of action. Emotions are complex phenomena that are constituted from multiple, interacting psychological and biological systems, and involve physiological responses (e.g., heart rate, blood pressure), behavioral responses (facial displays and motor actions such as avoidance or escape), and subjective responses (e.g., feelings, verbally mediated thought; Mennin & Farach, 2007). Emotions signal to individuals how they are progressing with respect to important personal and interpersonal goals. In addition, they communicate to other people how the person experiencing a particular emotion is likely to act and, from a normative viewpoint, how they should respond. In other words, emotions have intrapersonal and interpersonal social meanings. According to Pennington, a major function of the emotional system is "...to allow goals and values to influence both perception and action selection rapidly and to adjust motivational state to fit changing environmental circumstances" (Pennington, 2002, p. 79). Emotional states and their associated values and motives orient the organism to its internal and external environment and enable it to deal with problems in a flexible and adaptive manner.

As stated earlier, an important function of emotions is normative; that is, they are inherently evaluative and centrally involved in human beings' experience of meaning. Expanding on the normative and meaning making purpose of emotions, Johnson (2007, p. 60) states that:

> ... every emotional response is part of a process in which there is some appraisal of how a given emotionally competent stimulus stands in relation to the potential well-being of the organism. Our emotional responses are based on both our nonconscious

and conscious assessments of the possible harm, nurturance, or enhancement that a given situation may bring to our lives.

Emotions often arise spontaneously and immediately orient us to actual or possible threats or benefits in our lives and press us to respond to the situations that evoke them. Emotions function as useful (and typically reliable) indicators of experiences of the "good," of what is perceived to be valuable. Thus the capacity to experience and respond to emotions is an adaptation that has increased human beings' ability to respond to well-being related cues in ways that promote survival, and even flourishing.

As a consequence of adverse developmental experiences and subsequent difficulties in identifying and regulating emotions, individuals may act in ways that are self-destructive and harmful to others. In these situations, offenders can benefit from learning how to reflect on their emotional experiences and their various components and ask themselves whether or not the values inherent in the situation are worthwhile. Cognitive skill programs for offenders such as Ross and Fabiano's (1985) Reasoning and Rehabilitation (R & R) program typically include a module on working with disruptive emotions. However, such programs tend not to be aligned with a comprehensive, evolutionary understanding of emotions, and therefore fail to address the positive ethical and prudential aspects of emotional functioning. Ward and Nee (2009; pp. 174–175) make this point in their recent article and comment:

> The limited focus that R & R puts on emotional competence addresses the disruptive aspects of emotion and also helps with the development of some of the emotional competence tasks. However, its does not appear to acknowledge the important role that emotions can play in orienting individuals to values and in the adaptive pursuit of goals. There is also a suspicion that R & R drives a wedge between emotion and cognition and fails to appreciate that emotions are partly cognitive in nature, and help to create a sense of meaning and purpose in people's lives. This occurs by virtue of the integral link between emotions and values identification.

Relatedly, once the importance of the agency level of explanation is appreciated, the role of what have been called *moral emotions* becomes significant from both crime preventive and management considerations. During the course of their evolution, human beings have acquired a number of emotions that promote group cohesion by motivating cooperation and conflict resolution (Kitcher, 2011; Sterelny, 2012). Emotions or affective states such as compassion, sympathy, empathy, anger, disgust, guilt, and shame are in part innate but require considerable cultural scaffolding if they are to become reliably linked to prosocial values and altruistic actions. The experience of social deprivation, injustice, and physical threats compromise the acquisition of norms that capitalize on these natural motivations, and should be taken into account when explaining and attempting to reduce the prevalence of crime. Communitarian responses to punishment, such as restorative justice, rely on moral emotions such as compassion, guilt, and empathy to a significant extent. Acceptance of accountability for harm inflicted and an associated experience of guilt is a desired response for offenders, although offering options for reconciliation is more likely to be effective if members of the community feel empathy and compassion.

DISTRIBUTED COGNITION

Recent theoretical and empirical research has suggested that human beings by virtue of their cognitive adaptations are able to functionally extend their minds out into the world by the construction of cognitive tools, much as a spider can extend its prey-hunting activities by spinning a web (Clark & Chalmers, 1998; Menary, 2007; Wilson, 2004). The research base for this proposal is diverse and ranges from developmental psychology, evolution of cognition, archeology, anthropology, and cognitive neuroscience (Clark, 2008; Sterelny, 2012).

There is evidence from cognitive neuroscience and developmental psychology that human beings' minds are not massively modular in the way sometimes depicted by evolutionary psychology (Clark, 2008; Gibbs, 2006). Rather, as stated previously, a critical human cognitive adaptation is the ability to use social learning by virtue of our considerable cognitive plasticity and cultural scaffolding in the acquisition of adaptive skills and knowledge of the world and ourselves. Although there does appear to be some degree of innate cognitive specialization such as face recognition, cheater detection, language acquisition, and selective attention, it is clear that human beings' capacity to adapt to moderately fast-changing environments is partly dependent on the existence of domain general learning mechanisms.

A related body of research has identified the marked ability of human beings to actively engineer their cultural and physical environments by using technology and social learning as unique characteristics of our species (Sterelny, 2012). Although many animals engage in niche construction activities, none do so to the same extend as human beings (Odling-Smee, Laland, & Feldman, 2003). Therefore, any explanation of human characteristics will necessarily involve cultural factors, including an understanding of the way technology assists and augments people's cognitive functioning. An adaptive advantage of cognitive plasticity and the facility to learn from others is that it enables individuals to distribute cognitive tasks among social groups. This allows for cognitive specialization among group members and arguably enhanced group performance and therefore increased chances of survival.

Thus the evidence indicates that human beings' ability to construct and in turn be shaped by their environments(s), in conjunction with their cognitive and behavioral plasticity and the role of culture and social learning in creating minds, means that it is a mistake to view human nature as biologically fixed and contained inside people's heads. Consistent with this view, Clark (2003) noted that human beings do not have a set nature with a "simple wrap-around of tools and culture; the tools and culture are as much determiners of our natures as products of it" (p. 86).

Ward summarizes the key ideas of the distributed cognition or external theory of mind approach (Ward, 2009, pp. 252–253):

> A notable characteristic of human beings is the fact that they are epistemic engineers who intentionally structure environments to facilitate problem-solving but who are also shaped by these very same environments. The creation of learning cocoons is arguably one of the features of human beings' knowledge-generating activities that enable them to achieve such control over themselves and the physical world...A considerable amount of the practical and theoretical knowledge required to engineer environments and to effectively achieve cognitive tasks resides in cultural and social institutions. The existence of such institutions directly enhances or ratchets-up individuals' cognitive abilities and capacity to continue to learn. In this respect, social networks and institutions can be regarded as potential components of a person's cognitive systems or extended mind.

The research and practice implications of the distributed cognition theory are striking and go well beyond the standard view that cognitive distortions exist solely within an offender's mind. It is necessary for practitioners to consider what type of environments offenders exist within and to what degree their attitudes, norms, and beliefs are actively supported, and in a sense created, by those around them (Ward, 2013). An example of environments that are effectively sources of offenders' distorted thinking and norms are pedophilic networks, subcultures endorsing hostile attitudes toward women, combat situations, and gang cultures. In such situations, it is hard to identify exactly where the distributed cognitions exist: Within the offender? The environment? Both? Perhaps the interaction between person and environment? And so on. When it comes to reducing reoffending rates, the construction of postrelease social environments that actively support normative thinking and behavior is especially important. In terms of crime prevention, the realization that human beings possess both natural predispositions and cognitive plasticity means that, although change is possible, any interventions should take into account the sensitivity of individuals to their social environments and the associated tendency to use external cues and prompts to partly regulate action. A nice example of an intervention for sex offenders that capitalizes on human beings' facility for distributed cognition, is the *Circles of Support* program (Wilson Pichec, Prinzo, & Cortoni, 2007). In brief, *Circles of Support* works with high-risk, socially isolated sex offenders who have been released into the community. Each offender has his own circle of support consisting of trained community volunteers who are supervised by qualified forensic practitioners. The support group assists the offender to become socially integrated, accompanies him to various events, and are available to give emotional support when necessary. The volunteers model socially appropriate attitudes and beliefs and function to strengthen prosocial norms. In a sense, they function as an external cognitive system as well as a source of support and means of social integration.

CONCLUSIONS

In our opinion, the four themes discussed here are conceptually associated with a dynamic, complex system view of human agency, embedded within a gene–culture coevolution framework. The physical embodiment of human agents means that emotion and cognition play an integral role in the adaptive functioning of the organism and can be compromised by physical as well as psychological threats. Emotions arise from individuals' fundamental commitments and needs and orient them to salient aspects of the environment that are likely to hinder or facilitate goal achievement. Moreover, emotions motivate people by providing feedback on the degree to which they are successful in implementing their plans and also contribute to the experience of meaning. The ability to create distributed cognitive systems enables individuals to take advantage of social and cultural institutions and personal social networks when formulating solutions to life problems.

We are aware that many criminologists will balk at the mention of evolution and crime in the same sentence and worry about reductionism and scientism, whereas biologically oriented researchers might dispute the claim that culture and social learning play an indispensable role in creating crime facilitative dispositions and contexts. Such a view, they could argue, is unscientific and hopelessly vague. In our opinion, both perspectives are partly correct and partly wrong. There is a strong, emerging body of research and theory that supports the conception of human beings as dynamic complex systems who are constituted by physical and psychological (and social) properties. The mix of dynamic and relational ideas in this conception of human beings means that any explanation of crime needs to be nuanced.

Thus, taking into account the systemic, dynamic nature of human beings and their sensitivity to the contexts in which they live, any explanation of offending will need to be multilevel, and ideally, conceptually linked. In other words, the appropriate epistemological stance to take is that of integrative pluralism. An adequate account of crime should be a deep one that explicitly builds into the explanatory picture the evolution of human beings and their adaptive capacity for agency and search for meaning. There is no necessary inconsistency between structural and functional, psychological and social, or social/cultural and biological theories of crime. However, to create consilience between the different types of theories currently evident in criminology, we propose that a gene–culture coevolution perspective is a promising way forward.

References

Abbott, J. H. (1981). *In the belly of the beast: Letters from prison*. New York: Random House.

Abel, G. G., Gore, D. K., Holland, C. L., Camp, N., Becker, J., & Rathner, J. (1989). The measurement of the cognitive distortions of child molesters. *Annals of Sex Research*, *2*, 135–153.

Adams, J., Stamp, E., Nettle, D., Milne, E. M. G., & Jagger, C. (2014). Socioeconomic position and the association between anticipated and actual survival in older English adults. *Journal of Epidemiology and Community Health*, 1–8. http://dx.doi.org/10.1136/jech-2014-203872.

Aebi, M. F., & Linde, A. (2012). Crime trends in Western Europe according to official statistics from 1990–2007. In J. Van Dijk, A. Tseloni, & G. Farrell (Eds.), *The international crime drop: New directions in research* (pp. 37–75). New York, NY: Palgrave Macmillan.

Afifi, A. O., & MacMillan, H. L. (2011). Resilience following child maltreatment: a review of protective factors. *Canadian Journal of Psychiatry*, *25*, 266–272.

Agnew, R. (2003). An integrated theory of the adolescent peak in offending. *Youth and Society*, *34*, 263–295.

Agnew, R. (2006). *Pressured into crime: An overview of general strain theory*. Los Angeles: Roxbury Publishing.

Agnew, R. (2009). *Juvenile delinquency: Causes and control* (3rd ed.). New York: Oxford University Press.

Agnew, R. (2011a). *Toward a unified criminology: Integrating assumptions about crime, people, and society*. New York, NY: New York University Press.

Agnew, R. (2011b). Crime and time: the temporal patterning of causal variables. *Theoretical Criminology*, *15*, 115–140. http://dx.doi.org/10.1177/1362480609356671.

Agnew, R. (2011c). Dire forecast: a theoretical model of the impact of climate change on crime. *Theoretical Criminology*, *16*, 21–42. http://dx.doi.org/10.1177/1362480611416843.

Agnew, R. (2013). Social concern and crime: moving beyond the assumption of self-interest. *Criminology*, *52*(1), 1–32. http://dx.doi.org/10.1111/1745-9125.12031.

Aharoni, E., & Fridlund, A. J. (2012). Punishment without reason: isolating retribution in lay punishment of criminal offenders. *Psychology, Public Policy, and Law*, *18*, 599–625. http://dx.doi.org/10.1037/a0025821.

Ainsworth, S. E., & Maner, J. K. (2012). Sex begets violence: mating motives, social dominance, and physical aggression in men. *Journal of Personality and Social Psychology*, *103*, 819–829. http://dx.doi.org/10.1037/a0029428.

Akers, R. L. (1977). *Deviant behavior: A social learning approach*. Belmont, CA: Wadsworth Publ. Co.

Akers, R. L., & Jensen, G. F. (2010). Social learning theory: process and structure in criminal and deviant behaviour. In E. McLaughlin, & T. Newburn (Eds.), *The Sage handbook of criminological theory* (pp. 56–71). London, UK: Sage Publications.

Akers, R. L., & Sellers, C. (2009). *Criminological theories: Introduction, evaluation and application*. New York, NY: Oxford University Press.

Albert, D., Chein, J., & Steinberg, L. (2013). The teenage brain: peer influences on adolescent decision making. *Current Directions in Adolescent Decision Making*, *22*, 114–120. http://dx.doi.org/10.1177/0963721412471347.

Alcock, J., & Sherman, P. (1994). The utility of the proximate-ultimate dichotomy in ethology. *Ethology*, *96*, 58–62.

Alter, A. L., Kernochan, J., & Darley, J. M. (2007). Transgression wrongfulness outweighs its harmfulness as a determinant of sentence severity. *Law and Human Behavior*, *31*, 319–335.

Alvard, M. (2013). Human sociality. In J. C. Mitani, J. Call, P. M. Kappeler, R. A. Palombit, & J. B. Silk (Eds.), *The evolution of primate societies* (pp. 585–604). Chicago: The University of Chicago Press.

Anderson, E. (1994). The code of the streets. *Atlantic Monthly, 273,* 81–94.

Anderson, E. (1999). *Code of the street: Decency, violence, and the moral life of the inner city.* New York: Norton.

Anderson, C. A., & Bushman, B. J. (2002). Human aggression. *Annual Review of Psychology, 53,* 27–51.

Andersson, M. (1982). Female choice selects for extreme tail length in a widowbird. *Nature, 299,* 818–820. http://dx.doi.org/10.1038/299818a0.

Andersson, M. (1994). *Sexual selection.* Princeton, NJ: Princeton University Press.

Andresen, M. A., & Felson, M. (2010). The impact of co-offending. *British Journal of Criminology, 50,* 66–81. http://dx.doi.org/10.1093/bjc/azp043.

Andrews, K. (2012). *Do apes read minds: Toward a new folk psychology.* Boston, MA: MIT Press.

Andrews, D. A., & Bonta, J. (2010). *The psychology of criminal conduct* (5th ed.). New Providence, NJ: Matthew Bender & Company Inc.

Andrews, P. W., Gangestad, S. W., & Matthews, D. (2002). Adaptationism – how to carry out an exaptationist program. *Behavioral and Brain Sciences, 25,* 489–553.

Antonaccio, O., & Tittle, C. R. (2008). Morality, self-control, and crime. *Criminology, 46,* 479–510.

Apostolou, M. (2014). Sexual selection in ancestral human societies: the importance of the anthropological and historical records. *Evolutionary Behavioral Sciences, 8,* 86–95. http://dx.doi.org/10.1037/h0099388.

Arcadi, A. C., & Wrangham, R. W. (1999). Infanticide in chimpanzees: review of cases and a new within-group observation from the Kanyawara study group in Kibale National Park. *Primates, 40,* 337–351.

Archer, J. (1998). *The behavioural biology of aggression.* Cambridge, UK: Cambridge University Press.

Archer, J. (2002). Sex differences in physically aggressive acts between heterosexual partners: a meta-analytic review. *Aggression and Violent Behavior, 7,* 313–351.

Archer, J. (2004). Sex differences in aggression in real-world settings: a meta-analytic review. *Review of General Psychology, 8,* 291–322. http://dx.doi.org/10.1037/1089-2680.8.4.291.

Archer, J. (2006a). Testosterone and human aggression: an evaluation of the challenge hypothesis. *Neuroscience and Biobehavioral Reviews, 30,* 319–345.

Archer, J. (2006b). Cross-cultural differences in physical aggression between partners: a social-role analysis. *Personality and Social Psychology Review, 10,* 133–153.

Archer, J. (2009a). Does sexual selection explain human sex differences in aggression? *Behavioral and Brain Sciences, 32,* 249–311. http://dx.doi.org/10.1017/S0140525X09990951.

Archer, J. (2009b). The nature of human aggression. *International Journal of Law and Psychiatry, 32,* 202–208. http://dx.doi.org/10.1016/j.ijlp.2009.04.001.

Archer, J. (2013). Can evolutionary principles explain patterns of family violence? *Psychological Bulletin, 139,* 403–440. http://dx.doi.org/10.1037/a0029114.

Archer, J., & Coyne, S. M. (2005). An integrated review of indirect, relational, and social aggression. *Personality and Social Psychology Review, 9,* 212–230. http://dx.doi.org/10.1207/s15327957pspr0903_2.

Ariew, A. (2003). Ernst Mayr's 'ultimate/proximate' distinction reconsidered and reconstructed. *Biology and Philosophy, 18,* 553–565. http://dx.doi.org/10.1023/A:1025565119032.

Armit, I. (2011). Violence and society in the deep human past. *British Journal of Criminology, 51,* 499–517. http://dx.doi.org/10.1093/bjc/azq076.

Arnett, J. J. (1999). Adolescent storm and stress, reconsidered. *American Psychologist, 54,* 317–326.

Arnett, J. J. (2000). Emerging adulthood: a theory of development from the late teens through the twenties. *American Psychologist, 55,* 469–480.

Arnhart, L. (1998). *Darwinian natural right: The biological ethics of human nature.* Albany, NY: State University of New York Press.

Arnqvist, G., & Rowe, L. (2005). *Sexual conflict*. Princeton: Princeton University Press.

Atkinson, I. A., & Greenwood, R. M. (1989). Relationships between moas and plants. *New Zealand Journal of Ecology, 12*, 67–96.

Baker, L. R. (1999). What is this thing called commonsense psychology? *Philosophical Explorations, 2*, 3–19. http://dx.doi.org/10.1080/13869799908520962.

Baker, L. A., Bezdjian, S., & Raine, A. (2006). Behavioral genetics: the science of antisocial behaviour. *Law and Contemporary Problems, 69*, 7–46.

Bakermans-Kranenburg, M. J., & van Ijzendoorn, M. H. (2011). Differential susceptibility to rearing environment depending on dopamine-related genes: new evidence and a meta-analysis. *Development and Psychopathology, 23*, 39–52. http://dx.doi.org/10.1017/S0954579410000635.

Bakermans-Kranenburg, M. J., & van Ijzendoorn, M. H. (2015). The hidden efficacy of interventions: gene × environment experiments from a differential susceptibility perspective. *Annual Review of Psychology, 66*. http://dx.doi.org/10.1146/annurev-psych-010814-015407.

Baldassarri, D., & Grossman, G. (2011). Centralized sanctioning and legitimate authority promote cooperation in humans. *Proceedings of the National Academy of Sciences, 108*, 11023–11027. http://dx.doi.org/10.1073/pnas.1105456108.

Baller, R. D., Zevenbergen, M. P., & Messner, S. F. (2009). The heritage of herding and Southern homicide: examining the ecological foundations of the code of honor thesis. *Journal of Research in Crime and Delinquency, 46*, 275–300.

Balliet, D., & van Lange, P. A. M. (2013). Trust, punishment, and cooperation across 18 societies: a meta-analysis. *Perspectives on Psychological Science, 8*, 363–379.

Bandura, A. (1999). Moral disengagement in the perpetration of inhumanities. *Personality and Social Psychology Review, 3*, 193–209.

Bandura, A. (2002). Selective moral disengagement in the exercise of moral agency. *Journal of Moral Education, 31*, 101–119.

Barak, G. (1998). *Integrating criminologies*. Boston, MA: Allyn and Bacon.

Barash, D. P., & Lipton, J. E. (2011). *Payback: Why we retaliate, redirect aggression, and take revenge*. Oxford, UK: Oxford University Press.

Barber, N. (2007). Evolutionary explanations for societal differences and historical change in violent crime and single parenthood. *Cross-Cultural Research, 37*, 123–148.

Barber, N. (2009). Countries with fewer males have more violent crime. Marriage markets and mating aggression. *Aggressive Behavior, 14*, 415–422.

Barber, N. (2011). Marriage markets and mating aggression help explain societal differences in violent crime. *Aggression and Violent Behavior, 16*, 420–427.

Barkow, J. H. (Ed.). (2005). *Missing the revolution: Darwinism for social scientists*. Oxford: Oxford University Press.

Barnett, G. D., & Mann, R. E. (2012). Empathy deficits and sexual offending: a model of obstacles to empathy. *Aggression and Violent Behavior, 18*, 228–239.

Baron, R. A. (1977). *Human aggression*. New York, NY: Plenum Press.

Baron, S. W., & Agnew, R. (2014). General strain theory and offending across the life-course. In M. Delisi, & K. M. Beaver (Eds.), *Criminological theory: A life course approach* (pp. 117–132). Burlington, MA: Jones and Bartlett.

Barr, K. N., & Quinsey, V. L. (2004). Is psychopathy pathology or a life strategy? Implications for social policy. In C. Crawford, & C. Salmon (Eds.), *Evolutionary psychology, public policy and personal decisions* (pp. 293–317). Mahwah, NJ: Erlbaum.

Barrett, H. C. (2012). A hierarchical model of the evolution of human brain specializations. *Proceedings of the National Academy of Sciences, 109*(Supplement 1), 10733–10740.

Barrett, L., Blumstein, D. T., Clutton-Brock, T. H., & Kappeler, P. M. (2013). Taking note of Tinbergen, or: the promise of a biology of behaviour. *Philosophical Transactions of the Royal Society B: Biological Sciences, 368*. http://dx.doi.org/10.1098/rstb.2012.0352.

Barrett, H. C., & Kurzban, R. (2006). Modularity in cognition: framing the debate. *Psychological Review, 113*, 628–647.

Batson, C. D. (2011). *Altruism in humans*. New York, NY: Oxford University Press.

Batson, C. D. (2014). Empathy-induced altruism and morality: no necessary connection. In H. L. Maibom (Ed.), *Empathy and morality* (pp. 41–58). New York, NY: Oxford University Press.

Baumard, N. (2011). Punishment is not a group adaptation: humans punish to restore fairness rather than to support group cooperation. *Mind and Society, 10*, 1–26. http://dx.doi.org/10.1007/s11299-010-0080-3.

Baumeister, R. F., Bratslavsky, E., Finkenauer, C., & Vohs, K. D. (2001). Bad is stronger than good. *Review of General Psychology, 5*, 323–370. http://dx.doi.org/10.1037//1089-2680.5.4.323.

Baumer, E. P., & Wolff, K. T. (2014). The breadth and causes of contemporary cross-national homicide trends. *Crime and Justice, 43*, http://dx.doi.org/10.1086/677663.

Beaver, K. M. (2013). The familial concentration and transmission of crime. *Criminal Justice and Behaviour, 40*, 139–155. http://dx.doi.org/10.1177/0093854812449405.

Beaver, K. M., & Connolly, E. J. (2013). Genetic and environmental influences on the development of childhood antisocial behavior: current evidence and directions for future research. In M. Delisi, & K. M. Beaver (Eds.), *Criminological theory: A life-course approach* (2nd ed.) (pp. 43–55). Burlington, MA: Jones and Bartlett Learning.

Beaver, K. M., Nedelec, J. L., Schwartz, J. A., & Connolly, E. J. (2014). Evolutionary behavioural genetics of violent crime. In T. K. Shackelford, & R. D. Hansen (Eds.), *The evolution of violence* (pp. 117–135). New York, NY: Springer.

Beech, A. R., & Craig, L. (2012). The current status of static and dynamic factors in sexual offender risk assessment. *Journal of Aggression, Conflict, and Peace Research, 4*, 169–185.

Beech, A., & Mitchell, I. (2005). A neurobiological perspective on attachment problems in sexual offenders and the role of selective serotonin re-uptake inhibitors in the treatment of such problems. *Clinical Psychology Review, 25*, 153–182. doi:apa.org/?uid=2005-01239-002.

Beech, A. R., & Ward, T. (2004). The integration of etiology and risk in sexual offenders: a theoretical framework. *Aggression and Violent Behavior, 10*, 31–63. http://dx.doi.org/10.1016/j.avb.2003.08.002.

Belsky, J. (2005). Differential susceptibility to rearing influence: en evolutionary hypothesis and some evidence. In B. J. Ellis, & D. F. Bjorklund (Eds.), *Origins of the social mind: Evolutionary psychology and child development* (pp. 139–163). New York, NY: The Guilford Press.

Belsky, J. (2012). The development of human reproductive strategies: Progress and prospects. *Current Directions in Psychological Science, 21*, 310–316.

Belsky, J., & Beaver, K. M. (2011). Cumulative-genetic plasticity, parenting and adolescent self-regulation. *Journal of Child Psychology and Psychiatry, 52*, 619–626. http://dx.doi.org/10.1111/j.1469-7610.2010.02327.x.

Belsky, J., & Pluess, M. (2009). Beyond diathesis stress: differential susceptibility to environmental influences. *Psychological Bulletin, 135*, 885–908. http://dx.doi.org/10.37/aa0017376.

Belsky, J., & Pluess, M. (2013). Beyond risk, resilience, and dysregulation: phenotypic plasticity and human development. *Development and Psychopathology, 25*, 1243–1261. http://dx.doi.org/10.1017/S095457941300059x.

Belsky, J., Schlomer, G. L., & Ellis, B. (2012). Beyond cumulative risk: distinguishing harshness and unpredictability as determinants of parenting and early life history strategy. *Developmental Psychology, 48*, 662–673. http://dx.doi.org/10.1037/a004454.

Belsky, J., Steinberg, L., & Draper, P. (1991). Childhood experience, interpersonal development, and reproductive strategy: an evolutionary theory of socialization. *Child Development, 62*, 647–670.

Betzig, L. (2012). Means, variances, and ranges in reproductive success: comparative evidence. *Evolution and Human Behavior, 33*(4), 309–317. http://dx.doi.org/10.1016/j.evolhumbehav.2011.10.008.

Betzig, L. (2014). Eusociality in history. *Human Nature, 25*, 80–99. http://dx.doi.org/10.1007/s12110-013-9186-8.

Biglan, A., & Cody, C. (2013). Integrating the human sciences to evolve effective policies. *Journal of Economic and Behavior Organization, 90s*, S152–S162. http://dx.doi.org/10.1016/j.jebo.2012.12.018.

Biglan, A., & Embry, D. D. (2013). A framework for intentional cultural change. *Journal of Contextual Behavioral Science*, 2, 95–104. http://dx.doi.org/10.1016/j.jcbs.2013.06.001.

Bjorklund, D. F., & Blasi, C. H. (2012). *Child and adolescent development: An integrated approach.* Belmont, CA: Wadsworth.

Bjorklund, D. F., & Ellis, B. J. (2014). Children, childhood, and development in evolutionary perspective. *Developmental Review*, *34*, 225–264. http://dx.doi.org/10.1016/j.dr.2014.05.005.

Bjorklund, D. F., & Hawley, P. H. (2014). Aggression grows up: looking through an evolutionary development lens to understand causes and consequences of human aggression. In T. K. Shackelford, & R. D. Hansen (Eds.), *The evolution of violence* (pp. 159–186). New York, NY: Springer Science+Business Media.

Blair, J., Mitchell, D., & Blair, K. (2005). *The psychopath: Emotion and the brain.* Malden, MA: Blackwell Publishing.

Blakemore, S., & Mills, K. L. (2014). Is adolescence a sensitive period for sociocultural processing? *Annual Review of Psychology*, *65*, 9.1–9.21. http://dx.doi.org/10.1146/annurev-psych-010213-115202.

Bloom, P. (2013). *Just babies: The origin of good and evil.* New York, NY: Random House.

Boehm, C. (2011). Retaliatory violence in human prehistory. *British Journal of Criminology*, *51*, 518–534. http://dx.doi.org/10.1093/bjc/azr020.

Boehm, C. (2012). *Moral origins: The evolution of virtue, altruism, and shame.* Philadelphia, PA: Basic Books.

Bond, W. J., Lee, W. G., & Craine, J. M. (2004). Plant structural defences against browsing birds: a legacy of New Zealand's extinct moas. *Oikos*, *104*, 500–508. http://dx.doi.org/10.1111/j.0030-1299.2004.12720.x.

Bonduriansky, R., & Day, T. (2009). Nongenetic inheritance and its evolutionary implications. *Annual Review of Ecology, Evolution, and Systematics*, *40*, 103–125. http://dx.doi.org/10.1146/annurev.ecolsys.39.110707.173441.

Bonta, J., Jesseman, R., Rugge, T., & Cormier, R. (2006). Restorative justice and recidivism: promises made, promises kept? In D. Sullivan, & L. Tifft (Eds.), *Handbook of restorative justice: A global perspective* (pp. 108–120). London: Routledge.

Boonin, D. (2008). *The problem of punishment.* New York, NY: Cambridge University Press.

Booth, A., & Dabbs, J. M. (1993). Testosterone and men's marriages. *Social Forces*, *72*, 463–477.

Borsboom, D. (2005). *Measuring the mind: Conceptual issues in contemporary psychometrics.* Cambridge, UK: Cambridge University Press.

Bourke, P., Ward, T., & Rose, C. (2012). Expertise and sexual offending: a preliminary empirical model. *Journal of Interpersonal Violence*, *27*, 2391–2414.

Boutwell, B. B. (2014). The intergenerational tranmission of antisocial behavior: Parenting, genes, and unsettling realities. In M. Delisi, & K. M. Beaver (Eds.), *Criminological theory: A life course approach* (2nd edition) (pp. 73–82). Burlington, MA: Jones and Bartlett.

Boutwell, B. B., Barnes, J. C., Deaton, R., & Beaver, K. M. (2013). On the evolutionary origins of life-course persistent offending: a theoretical scaffold for Moffitt's developmental taxonomy. *Journal of Theoretical Biology*, *322*, 72–80. http://dx.doi.org/10.1016/j.jtbi.2013.01.005.

Bowles, S., & Gintis, H. (2011). *A cooperative species: Human reciprocity and its evolution.* Princeton, NJ: Princeton University Press.

Boyce, W. T., & Ellis, B. J. (2005). Biological sensitivity to context: I. An evolutionary-developmental theory of the origins and functions of stress reactivity. *Development and Psychopathology*, *17*, 271–301.

Boyd, R., Gintis, H., Bowles, S., & Richerson, P. J. (2003). The evolution of altruistic punishment. *Proceedings of the National Academy of Science of the United States of America*, *100*, 3531–3535.

Boyd, R., Richerson, P. J., & Henrich, J. (2011). The cultural niche: why social learning is essential for human adaptation. *Proceedings of the National Academy of Science of the United States of America*, *108*, 10918–10925. http://dx.doi.org/10.1073/pnas.1100290108.

Braman, D., Kahan, D. M., & Hoffman, D. A. (2010). Some realism about punishment naturalism. *The University of Chicago Law Review*, *77*, 1531–1609.

Brannigan, A. (1997). Self control, social control and evolutionary psychology: towards an integrated perspective on crime. *Canadian Journal of Criminology, 39,* 403–431.

Brassett-Harknett, A., & Butler, N. (2007). Attention-deficit/hyperactivity disorder: an overview of the etiology and a review of the literature relating to the correlates and life course outcomes for men and women. *Clinical Psychology Review, 27,* 188–210.

Braveman, P., Egerter, S., & Williams, D. R. (2011). The social determinants of health: coming of age. *Annual Review of Public Health, 32,* 381–398. http://dx.doi.org/10.1146/annurev-publhealth-031210-101218.

Brenhouse, H. C., & Andersen, S. L. (2011). Developmental trajectories during adolescence in males and females: a cross-species understanding of underlying brain changes. *Neuroscience and Biobehavioral Reviews, 35,* 1687–1703. http://dx.doi.org/10.1016/j.neubiorev.2011.04.013.

Brennan, G., Eriksson, L., Goodin, R. E., & Southwood, N. (2013). *Explaining norms.* New York, NY: Oxford University Press.

Brisman, A. (2012). Toward a unified criminology: Integrating assumptions about crime, people and society: a commentary. *Journal of Theoretical and Philosophical Criminology, 4,* 54–64.

Brooks, R., Scott, I. M., Maklakov, A. A., Kasumovic, M. M., Clark, A. P., & Penton-Voak, I. S. (2011). National income inequality predicts women's preferences for masculinized faces better than health does. *Proceedings of the Royal Society B: Biological Sciences, 278,* 810–812. http://dx.doi.org/10.1098/rspb.2010.0964.

Brosnan, S. F., & de Waal, F. B. M. (2012). Fairness in animals: where to from here? *Social Justice Research, 25,* 336–351. http://dx.doi.org/10.1007/s11211-012-0165-8.

Brown, D. E. (1991). *Human universals.* New York, NY: McGraw Hill.

Brown, E., & Males, M. (2011). Does age or poverty level best predict criminal arrest and homicide rates? A preliminary investigation. *Justice Policy Journal, 8,* 1–30.

Brown, G. R., Dickins, T. E., Sear, R., & Laland, K. N. (2011). Evolutionary accounts of human behavioural diversity. *Philosophical Transactions of the Royal Society B: Biological Sciences, 366,* 313–324. http://dx.doi.org/10.1098/rstb.2010.0267.

Brown, G. R., & Richerson, P. J. (2014). Applying evolutionary theory to human behaviour: past differences and current debates. *Journal of Bioeconomics, 16,* 105–128. http://dx.doi.org/10.1007/s10818-013-9166-4.

Brown, P., Sutikna, T., Morwood, M. J., Soejono, R. P., Jatmiko, Saptomo, E. W., et al. (October 28, 2004). A new small-bodied hominin from the late Pleistocene of Flores, Indonesia. *Nature, 431,* 1055–1061. http://dx.doi.org/10.1038/nature02999.

Bruinsma, G. J., Pauwels, L. J., Weerman, F. M., & Bernasco, W. (2013). Social disorganization, social capital, collective efficacy and the spatial distribution of crime and offenders: an empirical test of six neighbourhood models for a Dutch city. *British Journal of Criminology, 53,* 942–963. http://dx.doi.org/10.1093/bjc/azt030.

Buckholtz, J. W., & Marois, R. (2012). The roots of modern justice: cognitive and neural foundations of social norms and their enforcement. *Nature Neuroscience Reviews, 15,* 655–661.

Buller, D. J. (2005). *Adapting minds: Evolutionary psychology and the persistent quest for human nature.* Cambridge, MA: MIT press.

Burkart, J. M., Hrdy, S. B., & Van Schaik, C. P. (2009). Cooperative breeding and human cognitive evolution. *Evolutionary Anthropology, 18,* 175–186. http://dx.doi.org/10.1002/evan.20222.

Buss, D. M. (1989). Sex differences in human mate preferences: evolutionary hypotheses tested in 37 cultures. *Behavioral and Brain Sciences, 12,* 1–14.

Buss, D. M. (1995). Evolutionary psychology: a new paradigm for psychological science. *Psychological Inquiry, 6,* 1–30. http://dx.doi.org/10.1207/s15327965pli0601_1.

Buss, D. M. (2005). *The murderer next door: Why the mind is designed to kill.* New York, NY: Penguin.

Buss, D. M. (2012). The evolutionary psychology of crime. *Journal of Theoretical and Philosophical Psychology, 1,* 90–98.

Buss, D. M., & Duntley, J. D. (2011). The evolution of intimate partner violence. *Aggression and Violent Behavior, 16,* 411–419. http://dx.doi.org/10.1016/j.avb.2011.04.015.

Buss, D. M., & Duntley, J. D. (2014). Intimate partner violence in evolutionary perspective. In D. M. Buss, & J. H. D. Duntley (Eds.), *The evolution of violence* (pp. 1–21). New York, NY: Springer.

Buss, D. M., & Greiling, H. (1999). Adaptive individual differences. *Journal of Personality, 67,* 209–243.

Buss, D. M., Haselton, M. G., Shackelford, T. K., Bleske, A. L., & Wakefield, J. C. (1998). Adaptation, exaptations, and spandrels. *American Psychologist, 53,* 533–548. http://dx.doi.org/10.1037/0003-066X.53.5.533.

Buss, D. M., & Shackelford, T. K. (1997). Human aggression in evolutionary psychological perspective. *Clinical Psychology Review, 17,* 605–619.

Byrd, A. L., & Manuck, S. B. (2014). MAOA, childhood maltreatment, and antisocial behavior: meta-analysis of a gene-environment interaction. *Biological Psychiatry, 75,* 9–17. http://dx.doi.org/10.1016/j.biopsych.2013.05.004.

Calcagno, J. M., & Fuentes, A. (Eds.), (2012). What makes us human? Answers from evolutionary anthropology. *Evolutionary Anthropology, 21,* 182–194. http://dx.doi.org/10.1002/evan.21328.

Campbell, A. (2005). Aggression. In D. M. Buss (Ed.), *Handbook of evolutionary psychology* (pp. 628–652). Hoboken, NJ: Wiley.

Campbell, A. (2007). Sex differences in aggression. In R. I. M. Dunbar, & L. Barrett (Eds.), *Oxford handbook of evolutionary psychology* (pp. 366–380). Oxford, UK: Oxford University Press.

Campbell, A. (2013a). The evolutionary psychology of women's aggression. *Philosophical Transactions of the Royal Society B: Biological Sciences 368.* http://dx.doi.org/10.1098/rstb.2013.0078.

Campbell, A. (2013b). *A mind of her own: The evolutionary psychology of women* (2nd ed.). Oxford, England: Oxford University Press.

Carlsmith, K. M. (2008). On justifying punishment: the discrepancy between words and actions. *Social Justice Research, 21,* 119–137. http://dx.doi.org/10.1007/s11211-008-0068-x.

Carlsmith, K. M., Darley, J. M., & Robinson, P. H. (2002). Why do we punish? Deterrence and just deserts as motives for punishment. *Journal of Personality and Social Psychology, 83,* 284–299. http://dx.doi.org/10.1037//0022-3514.83.2.284.

Carlson, N. R. (2014). *Foundations of behavioural neuroscience* (9th ed.). Boston, MA: Pearson.

Cartwright, J. (2000). *Evolution and human behaviour: Darwinian perspectives on human nature.* London, UK: Macmillan Press.

Casey, B. J., & Caudle, K. (2013). The teenage brain: self control. *Current Directions in Psychological Science, 22,* 82–87. http://dx.doi.org/10.1177/0963721413480170.

Casey, B. J., Getz, S., & Gavlán, A. (2008). The adolescent brain. *Developmental Review, 28,* 62–77. http://dx.doi.org/10.1016/j.dr.2007.08.003.

Caspi, A. (2000). The child is father of the man: personality continuities from childhood to adulthood. *Journal of Personality and Social Psychology, 78,* 158–172.

Caspi, A., McClay, L., Moffitt, T. E., Mill, J., Martin, J., Craig, I. W., et al. (2002). Role of genotype in the cycle of violence in maltreated children. *Science, 297,* 851–854. http://dx.doi.org/10.1126/science.1072290.

Cavadino, M., & Dignan, J. (2006). *Penal systems: A comparative approach.* London: Sage Publications.

Chapais, B. (2011). The deep social structure of humankind. *Science, 331,* 1276–1277. http://dx.doi.org/10.1126/science.1203281.

Chapais, B. (2013). Monogamy, strongly bonded groups, and the evolution of human social structure. *Evolutionary Anthropology, 22,* 52–65. http://dx.doi.org/10.1002/evan.21345.

Chein, J., Albert, D., O'Brien, L., Uckert, K., & Steinberg, L. (2011). Peers increase adolescent risk taking by enhancing activity in the brain's reward circuitry. *Developmental Science, 14,* F1–F10. http://dx.doi.org/10.1111/j.1467-7687.2010.01035.x.

Cheng, J. T., & Tracy, J. L. (2014). Toward a unified science of hierarchy: dominance and prestige are two fundamental pathways to human social rank. In J. T. Cheng, J. L. Tracy, & C. Anderson (Eds.), *The psychology of social status* (pp. 3–24). New York: Springer.

Collins, R. (2009). *Violence: A micro-sociological theory*. Princeton, NJ: Princeton University Press.

Cheng, J. T., Tracy, J. L., Foulsham, T., Kingstone, A., & Henrich, J. (2013). Two ways to the top: evidence that dominance and prestige are distinct yet viable avenues to social rank and influence. *Journal of Personality and Social Psychology, 104*, 103–125. http://dx.doi.org/10.1037/a0030398.

Cheng, J. T., Tracy, J. L., & Henrich, J. (2010). Pride, personality, and the evolutionary foundations of human social status. *Evolution and Human Behavior, 31*, 334–347. http://dx.doi.org/10.1016/j.evolhumbehav.2010.02.004.

Chiao, J. Y. (2011). Towards a cultural neuroscience of empathy and prosociality. *Emotion Review, 3*, 111–112.

Chiao, J. Y., & Blizinsky, K. D. (2010). Culture-gene coevolution of individualism-collectivism and serotonin transporter gene. *Proceedings of the Royal Society B: Biological Sciences, 277*, 529–537. http://dx.doi.org/10.1098/rspb.2009.1650.

Choudhury, S. (2010). Culturing the adolescent brain: what can neuroscience learn from anthropology? *Scan, 5*, 159–167. http://dx.doi.org/10.1093/scam/nsp030.

Christensen, W. (2012). Natural sources of normativity. *Studies in the History and Philosophy of Biological and Biomedical Sciences, 43*, 104–112. http://dx.doi.org/10.1016/j.shpsc.2011.05.009.

Christensen, W. D., & Hooker, C. A. (2000). An interactivist-constructivist approach to intelligence: self-directive anticipative learning. *Philosophical Psychology, 13*, 5–45. http://dx.doi.org/10.1080/09515080050002717.

Chudek, M., & Henrich, J. (2011). Culture-gene coevolution, norm psychology and the emergence of human prosociality. *Trends in Cognitive Sciences, 15*, 218–226.

Chudek, M., Zhao, W., & Henrich, J. (2013). Culture-gene coevolution, large-scale cooperation, and the shaping of human social psychology. In K. Sterelny, R. Joyce, B. Calcott, & B. Fraser (Eds.), *Cooperation and its evolution* (pp. 425–457). Cambridge, MA: MIT Press.

Chung, G. C., & Kuzawa, C. (2014). Intergenerational effects of early life nutrition: maternal leg length predicts offspring placental weight and birth weight among women in rural Luzon, Philippines. *American Journal of Human Biology, 26*, 652–659. http://dx.doi.org/10.1002/ajhb.22579.

Churchland, P. M. (1989). *A neurocomputational perspective: The nature of mind and the structure of science*. Cambridge, MA: MIT Press.

Chu, D. C., & Tusalem, R. F. (2013). The role of the state on cross-national homicide rates. *International Criminal Justice Review, 23*, 252–279. http://dx.doi.org/10.1177/1057567713500790.

Clark, A. (2003). *Natural Born Cyborgs: Minds, Technologies and the future of human Intelligence*. New York, NY: Oxford University Press.

Clark, A. (2008). *Supersizing the mind: Embodiment, action, and cognitive extension*. New York, NY: Oxford University Press.

Clark, A., & Chalmers, D. (1998). The extended mind. *Analysis, 58*, 7–19.

Clarke, R. V. (2004). Technology, criminology, and crime science. *European Journal on Criminal Policy and Research, 10*, 55–63. http://dx.doi.org/10.1023/B: CRIM.0000037557.42894.f7.

Clarke, R. V. (2008). Situational crime prevention. In R. Wortley, & L. Mazerolle (Eds.), *Environmental criminology and crime analysis* (pp. 178–192). Cullompton, UK: Willan Publishing.

Clutton-Brock, T. H. (2004). What is sexual selection? In P. M. Kappeler, & C. P. van Schaik (Eds.), *Sexual selection in primates: New and comparative perspectives* (pp. 24–54). Cambridge, UK: Cambridge University Press.

Clutton-Brock, T. (November 2009). Cooperation between non-kin in animal societies. *Nature, 462*, 51–57. http://dx.doi.org/10.1038/nature08366.

Clutton-Brock, T. H., & Parker, G. A. (1995). Punishment in animal societies. *Nature, 373*, 209–216. http://dx.doi.org/10.1038/373209a0.

Cohen, L. E., & Machalek, R. (1988). A general theory of expropriative crime: an evolutionary ecological approach. *American Journal of Sociology, 94*, 465–501.

Cohen, R. R., Panter, A. T., & Turan, N. (2012). Guilt proneness and moral character. *Current Directions in Psychological Science, 21*, 355–359. http://dx.doi.org/10.1177/0963721412454874.

Cohn, E. G., Farrington, D. P., & Iratzoqui, A. (2014). *Most-cited scholars in criminology and criminal justice, 1986–2010*. London: Springer.

Collins, R. (2009). *Violence: A micro-sociological theory*. Princeton, NJ: Princeton University Press.

Collins, S. A. (2000). Men's voice and women's choices. *Animal Behaviour, 60*, 773–780. http://dx.doi.org/10.1006/anbe.2000.1523.

Confer, J. C., Easton, J. A., Fleischman, D. S., Goetz, C. D., Lewis, D. M. G., Perilloux, C., et al. (2010). Evolutionary psychology: controversies, questions, prospects, and limitations. *American Psychologist, 65*, 110–126. http://dx.doi.org/10.1037/a0018413.

Cooke, D. J. (2008). Psychopathy as an important forensic construct: past, present, and future. In D. Canter, & R. Žukasukiene (Eds.), *Psychology and law: Bridging the gap* (pp. 167–191). Aldershot, Hampshire: Ashgate.

Cooke, D. J., & Michie, C. (2013). Violence risk assessment: from prediction to understanding- or from what? to why? In C. Logan, & L. Johnstone (Eds.), *Managing clinical risk: A guide to effective practice* (pp. 3–25). Abingdon, UK: Routledge.

Cooper, A., & Smith, E. L. (2011). *Homicide trends in the United States, 1980–2008*. NCJ 236018. Bureau of Justice Statistics.

Cooper, J. A., Walsh, A., & Ellis, L. (2010). Is criminology moving toward a paradigm shift? Evidence from a survey of the American Society of criminology. *Journal of Criminal Justice Education, 21*, 332–347. http://dx.doi.org/10.1080/10511253.2010.487830.

Cornwell, R. E., Palmer, C., Guinther, P. M., & Davis, H. P. (2005). Introductory psychology texts as a view of socio-biology/evolutionary psychology's role in psychology. *Evolutionary Psychology, 3*, 355–374.

Cosmides, L., & Tooby, J. (1987). From evolution to behavior: evolutionary psychology as the missing link. In J. Dupre (Ed.), *The latest on the best: Essays on evolution and optimality*. Cambridge, MA: MIT Press.

Cosmides, L., & Tooby, J. (2013). Evolutionary psychology: new perspectives on cognition and motivation. *Annual Review of Psychology, 64*, 201–229. http://dx.doi.org/10.1146/annurev.psych.121208.131628.

Coyne, J. A. (2009). *Why evolution is true*. New York, NY: Viking.

Crespi, B. (2014). The insectan apes. *Human Nature, 25*, 6–27. http://dx.doi.org/10.1007/s12110-013-9185-9.

Crone, E. A., & Dahl, R. E. (2012). Understanding adolescence as a period of social-affective engagement and goal flexibility. *Nature Reviews: Neuroscience, 13*, 636–650. http://dx.doi.org/10.1038/nrn3313.

Cross, C. P., & Campbell, A. (2011). Women's aggression. *Aggression and Violent Behavior, 16*, 390–398. http://dx.doi.org/10.1016/j.avb.2011.02.012.

Cross, C. P., Copping, L. T., & Campbell, A. (2011). Sex differences in impulsivity: a meta-analysis. *Psychological Bulletin, 137*, 97–130. http://dx.doi.org/10.1037/a0021591.

Crow, M. S., & Johnson, K. A. (2008). Race, ethnicity, and habitual-offender sentencing: a multilevel analysis of individual and contextual threat. *Criminal Justice Policy Review, 19*, 63–83.

Currie, T. E. (2013). Cultural evolution branches out: the phylogenetic approach in cross-cultural research. *Cross-Cultural Research, 47*, 102–130. doi:1069397112471803.

Dahl, R. E. (2004). Adolescent brain development: a period of vulnerabilities and opportunities. *Annals of the New York Academy of Sciences, 1021*, 1–22. http://dx.doi.org/10.1196/annals.1308.001.

Daly, M., & Wilson, M. (1988). *Homicide*. Hawthorne, NY: Aldine.

Daly, M., & Wilson, M. I. (1996). Violence against stepchildren. *Current Directions in Psychological Science 5*, 77–81.

Daly, M., & Wilson, M. (1997). Crime and conflict: homicide in evolutionary psychological perspective. *Crime and Justice, 22*, 51–100.

Daly, M., & Wilson, M. (2010). Cultural inertia, economic incentives, and the persistence of "Southern violence". In M. Schaller, A. Norenzayan, S. J. Heine, T. Yamagishi, & T. Kameda (Eds.), *Evolution, culture, and the human mind* (pp. 229–241). New York, NY: Psychology Press.

Daly, M., Wilson, M., & Vasdev, S. (2001). Income inequality and homicide rates in Canada and the United States. *Canadian Journal of Criminology, 43,* 219–236.

Daly, M., Wilson, M., & Weghorst, S. J. (1982). Male sexual jealousy. *Ethology and Sociobiology, 3,* 11–27.

Danchin, E., Charmantier, A., Champagne, F. A., Mesoudi, A., Pujol, B., & Blanchet, S. (2011). Beyond DNA: integrating inclusive inheritance into an extended theory of evolution. *Nature Reviews Genetics, 12,* 475–486. http://dx.doi.org/10.1038/nrg3028.

Dar-Nimrod, I., & Heine, S. J. (2011). Genetic essentialism: on the deceptive determinism of DNA. *Psychological Bulletin, 137,* 800–818. http://dx.doi.org/10.1037/a0021860.

Darley, J. M. (2009). Morality in the law: the psychological foundations of citizens' desires to punish transgressions. *Annual Review of Law and Social Science, 5,* 1–23. http://dx.doi.org/10.1146/annurev.lawsocsci.4.110707.172335.

Darley, J. M. (2010). Realism on change in moral intuitions. *University of Chicago Law Review, 77,* 1643–1653.

Darwin, C. (1859). *On the origin of species by natural selection.* London, UK: Murray.

Darwin, C. (1871). *The descent of man and selection in relation to sex.* London, UK: John Murray.

Dar-Nimrod, I., Heine, S. J., Cheung, B. Y., & Schaller, M. (2011). Do scientific theories affect men's evaluations of sex crimes? *Aggressive Behavior, 37,* 440–449. http://dx.doi.org/10.1002/ab.20401.

Davies, N. B., Krebs, J. R., & West, S. A. (2012). *An introduction to behavioural ecology* (4th ed.). Oxford, UK: Wiley-Blackwell.

Dawkins, R. (1976). *The selfish gene.* Oxford, UK: Oxford University Press.

Dawkins, R. (2004). *The ancestor's tale: A pilgrimage to the dawn of evolution.* Boston, MA: Houghton Mifflin.

Dawkins, R. (2009). *The greatest show on earth: The evidence for evolution.* London, UK: Bantam.

de Quervain, D. J., Fischbacher, U., Treyer, V., Schellhammer, M., Schnyder, U., Buck, A., et al. (August 27, 2004). The neural basis of altruistic punishment. *Science, 305,* 1254–1258. http://dx.doi.org/10.1126/science.1100735.

de Vries Robbé, M. (2014). *Protective factors: Validation of the structured assessment of protective factors for violence risk in forensic psychiatry.* Utrecht, NL: Van der Hoeven Kliniek.

de Waal, F. B. M. (1982). *Chimpanzee politics: Power and sex among apes.* Baltimore: Johns Hopkins University Press.

de Waal, F. B. M. (2006). *Primates and philosophers: How morality evolved.* Princeton, NJ: Princeton University Press.

de Waal, F. B. M. (May 18, 2012). The antiquity of empathy. *Science, 336,* 874–876. http://dx.doi.org/10.1126/science.1220999.

Dean, L. G., Kendal, R. L., Schapiro, S. J., Thierry, B., & Laland, K. N. (March 2, 2012). Identification of the social and cognitive processes underlying human cumulative culture. *Science, 335,* 1114–1118. http://dx.doi.org/10.1126/science.1213969.

Decety, J. (Ed.). (2012). *Empathy: From bench to bedside.* Cambridge, MA: The MIT Press.

Decety, J. (2014). The neuroevolution of empathy and caring for others: why if matters for morality. In J. Decety, & Y. Christen (Eds.), *New frontiers in social neuroscience* (pp. 127–151). Switzerland: Springer.

Decety, J., & Cowell, J. M. (2014). The complex relation between morality and empathy. *Trends in Cognitive Sciences, 18,* 337–339.

Degler, C. N. (1991). *In search of human nature: The decline and revival of Darwinism in American social thought.* Oxford, England: Oxford University Press.

DeKeseredy, W. S. (2012). The current condition of criminological theory in North America. In S. Hall, & S. Winlow (Eds.), *New directions in criminological theory* (pp. 66–80). London, UK: Routledge.

Del Frate, A. A., & Mugellini, G. (2012). The crime drop in 'non-Western' countries: a review of homicide data. In J. Van Dijk, A. Tseloni, & G. Farrell (Eds.), *The international crime drop: New directions in research* (pp. 134–158). New York, NY: Palgrave Macmillan.

Del Giudice, M. (2009). Sex, attachment, and the development of reproductive strategies. *Behavioral and Brain Sciences, 32,* 1–67. http://dx.doi.org/10.1017/S0140525X09000016.

Del Giudice, M., Angeleri, R., & Manera, V. (2009). The juvenile transition: a developmental switch point in human life history. *Developmental Review, 29,* 1–31. http://dx.doi.org/10.1016/j.dr.2008.09.001.

Del Giudice, M., & Belsky, J. (2011a). The development of life history strategies: toward a multistage theory. In D. M. Buss, & P. H. Hawley (Eds.), *Evolution of personality and individual differences* (pp. 154–176). New York, NY: Oxford University Press.

Del Giudice, M., & Belsky, J. (2011b). The development of life history strategies: toward a multi-stage theory. In D. M. Buss, & D. H. Hawley (Eds.), *The evolution of personality and individual differences* (pp. 154–176). Oxford, UK: Oxford University Press.

Del Giudice, M., Ellis, B. J., Hinnant, J. B., & El-Sheikh, M. (2012). Adaptive patterns of stress responsively: a preliminary investigation. *Developmental Psychology, 48,* 775–790. http://dx.doi.org/10.1037/a0026519.

Del Giudice, M., Ellis, B. J., & Shirtcliff, E. A. (2013). Making sense of stress: an evolutionary-developmental framework. In G. Laviola, & S. Macrí (Eds.), *Adaptive and Maladaptive Aspects of Developmental Stress* (pp. 23–43). New York, NY: Springer Science+Business.

Delisi, M. (2009). Introduction to the special issue on biosocial criminology. *Criminal Justice and Behaviour, 36,* 1111–1112. http://dx.doi.org/10.1007/s10612-013-9209-0.

Dennett, D. C. (1995). *Darwin's dangerous idea.* London, UK: Allen Lane.

Dennett, D. C. (2004). *Freedom evolves.* London, UK: Penguin.

d'Errico, F., & Stringer, C. B. (2011). Evolution, revolution or saltation scenarios for the emergence of modern cultures? *Philosophical Transactions of the Royal Society B: Biological Sciences, 366,* 1060–1069. http://dx.doi.org/10.1098/rstb.2010.0340.

Diamond, J. (1997). *Guns, germs and steel: A short history of everybody for the last 13,000 years.* London, UK: Vintage.

Diamond, J. (2005). *Collapse: How societies choose to fail or survive.* London, UK: Penguin.

Dickins, T. E., & Dickins, B. J. A. (2008). Mother nature's tolerant ways: why non-genetic inheritance has nothing to do with evolution. *New Ideas in Psychology, 26,* 41–54.

Dickins, T. E., & Rahman, Q. (2012). The extended evolutionary synthesis and the role of soft inheritance in evolution. *Proceedings of the Royal Society B: Biological Sciences, 279,* 2913–2921. http://dx.doi.org/10.1098/rspb.2012.0273.

Dishion, T. J., Ha, T., & Véronneau, M. (2012). An ecological analysis of the effects of deviant peer clustering on sexual promiscuity, problem behaviour, and childbearing from early adolescence to adulthood: an enhancement of the life history framework. *Developmental Psychology, 48,* 703–717. http://dx.doi.org/10.1037/a0027304.

Dixson, A. F. (2012). *Primate sexuality: Comparative studies of the Prosimians, monkeys, apes, and humans* (2nd ed.). Oxford, UK: Oxford University Press.

Dow, W. H., & Rehkopf, D. H. (2010). Socioeconomic gradients in health in international and historical contexts. *Annals of the New York Academy of Sciences, 1186,* 24–36. http://dx.doi.org/10.1111/j.1749-6632.2009.05384.x.

Duff, R. A. (2001). *Punishment, communication, and community.* New York, NY: Oxford University Press.

Dunbar, R. I. M. (2006). The social brain hypothesis and its implications for social evolution. *Annals of Human Biology, 36,* 562–572. http://dx.doi.org/10.1080/03014460902960289.

Duntley, J. D., & Buss, D. M. (2005). The plausibility of adaptations for homicide. In P. Carruthers, S. Laurence, & S. Stich (Eds.), *The structure of the innate mind.* New York, NY: Oxford University Press.

Duntley, J. D., & Buss, D. M. (2008). The origins of homicide. In J. Duntley, & T. Shackelford (Eds.), *Evolutionary forensic psychology.* New York, NY: Oxford University Press.

Duntley, J. D., & Buss, D. M. (2011). Homicide adaptations. *Aggression and Violent Behavior, 16*, 399–410. http://dx.doi.org/10.1016/j.avb.2011.04.016.

Duntley, J. D., & Shackelford, T. K. (2008a). Darwinian foundations of crime and law. *Aggression and Violent Behavior, 13*, 373–382. http://dx.doi.org/10.1093/acprof:oso/9780195325188.001.0001.

Duntley, J. D., & Shackelford, T. K. (Eds.). (2008b). *Evolutionary forensic psychology: Darwinian foundations of crime and law*. Oxford, UK: Oxford University Press.

Dupre, J. (2012). *Processes of life: Essays in the philosophy of biology*. Oxford, UK: Oxford University Press.

Durrant, R. (2009). Born to kill? A critical evaluation of homicide adaptation theory. *Aggression and Violent Behavior, 14*, 374–381. http://dx.doi.org/10.1016/j.avb.2009.06.005.

Durrant, R. (2011). Collective violence: an evolutionary perspective. *Aggression and Violent Behavior, 16*, 428–436. http://dx.doi.org/10.1016/j.avb.2011.04.014.

Durrant, R. (2013a). *An introduction to criminal psychology*. Oxford, UK: Routledge.

Durrant, R. (2013b). Alcohol and violence in evolutionary perspective. In M. McMurran (Ed.), *Alcohol-related violence: Prevention and treatment* (pp. 61–80). Chichester, UK: John Wiley & Sons.

Durrant, R., Adamson, S., Todd, F., & Sellman, D. (2009). Drug use and addiction: an evolutionary perspective. *Australian and New Zealand Journal of Psychiatry, 43*, 1049–1056. http://dx.doi.org/10.3109/00048670903270449.

Durrant, R., & Ellis, B. J. (2013). Evolutionary psychology. In R. J. Nelson, & S. J. Y. Mizumori (Eds.), *Handbook of psychology* (2nd ed.) *Behavioral neuroscience: Vol. 3* (pp. 26–51). Hoboken, NJ: John Wiley & Sons.

Durrant, R., & Haig, B. D. (2001). How to pursue the adaptationist program in psychology. *Philosophical Psychology, 14*, 357–380. http://dx.doi.org/10.1080/09515080120088067.

Durrant, R., & Thakker, J. (2003). *Substance use and abuse: Cultural and historical perspectives*. Thousand Oaks, CA: Sage Publications.

Durrant, R., & Ward, T. (2011). Evolutionary explanations in the social and behavioural sciences. *Aggression and Violent Behavior, 16*, 361–370. http://dx.doi.org/10.1016/j.avb.2011.02.010.

Durrant, R., & Ward, T. (2012). The role of evolutionary explanations in criminology. *Journal of Philosophical and Theoretical Criminology, 4*, 1–37.

Eagly, A. H., & Wood, W. (1999). The origins of sex differences in human behavior: evolved dispositions versus social roles. *American Psychologist, 54*, 408–423.

Eagly, A. H., & Wood, W. (2009). Sexual selection does not provide an adequate theory of sex differences in aggression. *Behavioral and Brain Sciences, 32*, 276–277. http://dx.doi.org/10.1017/S0140525X09990264.

Eck, J. E. (2002). Preventing crime at places. In L. W. Sherman, D. P. Farrington, B. C. Welsh, & D. L. MacKenzie (Eds.), *Evidence-based crime prevention* (rev. ed.) (pp. 241–295). New York, NY: Routledge.

Eisenberg, N., Eggum, N. D., & Di Giunta, L. (2010). Empathy-related responding: associations with prosocial behaviour, aggression, and intergroup relations. *Social Issues and Policy Review, 4*, 143–180.

Eisner, M. (2003). Long-term historical trends in violent crime. *Crime and Justice, 30*, 83–142.

Eisner, M. (2008). Modernity strikes back? A historical perspective on the latest increase in interpersonal violence (1960–1990). *International Journal of Conflict and Violence, 2*, 288–316.

Eisner, M. (2011). Killing kings: patterns of regicide in Europe, AD 600–1800. *British Journal of Criminology, 51*, 556–577. http://dx.doi.org/10.1093/bjc/azr004.

Eisner, M. (2012). What causes large-scale variation in homicide rates? In H. Hortüm, & J. Heinze (Eds.), *Aggression in humans and other primates: Biology, psychology, sociology* (pp. 137–162). Göttingen, Germany: De Gruyter.

Eisner, M. (2014). From swords to words: does macro-level change in self-control predict long-term variation in levels of homicide? *Crime and Justice, 43.*

Eisner, M., & Ghuneim, L. (2013). Honor killing attitudes amongst adolescents in Amman, Jordan. *Aggressive Behavior, 39*, 405–417. http://dx.doi.org/10.1002/ab.21485.

Elgar, F. J., & Aitken, N. (2010). Income inequality, trust and homicide in 33 countries. *European Journal of Public Health, 21*, 241–246. http://dx.doi.org/10.1093/eurpub/ckq068.

Elgar, F. J., Craig, W., Boyce, W., Morgan, A., & Vella-Zarb, R. (2009). Income inequality and school bullying: multilevel study of adolescents in 37 countries. *Journal of Adolescent Health, 45*, 351–359.

Ellis, B. J. (2004). Timing of pubertal maturation in girls: an integrated life history approach. *Psychological Bulletin, 130*, 920–958. http://dx.doi.org/10.1037/0033-2909.130.6.920.

Ellis, B. J., & Bjorklund, D. F. (2012). Beyond mental health: an evolutionary analysis of development under risky and supportive environmental conditions: an introduction to the special section. *Developmental Psychology, 48*, 591–597. http://dx.doi.org/10.1037/a0027651.

Ellis, B. J., & Boyce, W. T. (2005). Biological sensitivity to context 1: An evolutionary-developmental theory of the origins and functions of stress reactivity. *Development and Psychopathology, 17*, 271–301.

Ellis, B. J., & Boyce, W. T. (2011). Differential susceptibility to the environment: toward an understanding of sensitivity to developmental experiences and context. *Development and Psychopathology, 23*, 7–28. http://dx.doi.org/10.1037/s095457941000060x.

Ellis, B. J., Boyce, W. T., Belsky, J., Bakermans-Kranenburg, M. J., & van Ijzendoorn, M. H. (2011). Differential susceptibility to the environment: an evolutionary-neurodevelopmental theory. *Development and Psychopathology, 23*, 7–28. http://dx.doi.org/10.1017/s0954579410000611.

Ellis, B. J., & Del Giudice, M. (2014). Beyond allostatic load: rethinking the role of stress in regulating human development. *Development and Psychopathology, 26*, 1–20. http://dx.doi.org/10.1017/S0954579413000849.

Ellis, B. J., Dishion, T. J., Gray, P., Hawley, P. H., Volk, A. A., Del Giudice, M., et al., (2012). The evolutionary basis of risky adolescent behaviour: implications for science, polity and practice. *Developmental Psychology, 48*, 598–623. http://dx.doi.org/10.1037/a0026220.

Ellis, B. J., Figueredo, A. J., Brumbach, B. H., & Schlomer, G. L. (2009). Fundamental dimensions of environmental risk: the impact of harsh versus unpredictable environments of the evolution and development of life history strategies. *Human Nature, 20*, 204–268. http://dx.doi.org/10.1007/s12110-009-9063-7.

Ellis, L. (1989). *Theories of rape: Inquiries into the causes of sexual aggression.* New York, NY: Hemisphere Publishing Corp.

Ellis, L. (2005). A theory explaining biological correlates of criminology. *European Society of Criminology, 2*, 287–315. http://dx.doi.org/10.1177/1477370805054098.

Emlen, D. J. (2008). The evolution of animal weapons. *Annual Review of Ecology, Evolution and Systematics, 39*, 387–413. http://dx.doi.org/10.1146/annurev.ecolsys.39.110707.173502.

Eskridge, C. W. (2005). The state of the field of criminology: a brief essay. *Journal of Contemporary Criminal Justice, 21*, 296–308.

Fabio, A., Tu, L., Loeber, R., & Cohen, J. (2011). Neighbourhood socioeconomic disadvantage and the shape of the age-crime curve. *American Journal of Public Health, 101*, 325–332. http://dx.doi.org/10.2105/AJPH.2010.300034.

Fagan, A. A. (2014). Sociological explanations for the gender gap in offending. In K. M. Beaver, J. C. Barnes, & B. B. Boutwell (Eds.), *The nurture versus biosocial debate in criminology* (pp. 10–24). Los Angeles, CA: Sage Publications.

Fagan, B. M. (2012). *Ancient lives: An introduction to archaeology and prehistory* (5th ed.). Upper Saddle River, NJ: Pearson.

Fan, J., Dai, W., Liu, F., & Wu, J. (2005). Visual perception of male body attractiveness. *Proceedings of the Royal Society B: Biological Sciences, 272*, 219–226.

Farrell, G. (2013). Five tests for a theory of the crime drop. *Crime Science, 2*, 5.

Farrell, G., Tilley, N., & Tseloni, A. (2014). Why the crime drop? *Crime and Justice, 43*. http://dx.doi.org/10.1086/678081.

Farrell, G., Tilley, N., Tseloni, A., & Mailley, J. (2010). Explaining and sustaining the crime drop: clarifying the role of opportunity-related theories. *Crime Prevention and Community Safety, 12*, 24–41. http://dx.doi.org/10.1057/cpcs.2009.20.

Farrell, G., Tseloni, A., Mailley, & Tilley, N. (2011). The crime drop and the security hypothesis. *Journal of Research in Crime and Delinquency, 48*, 147–175. http://dx.doi.org/10.1177/0022427810391539.

Farrington, D. P. (2003). Developmental and life-course criminology: key theoretical and empirical issues – the 2002 Sutherland award address. *Criminology, 41*, 221–255.

Farrington, D. P. (2006). Key longitudinal-experimental studies in criminology. *Journal of Experimental Criminology, 2*, 121–141. http://dx.doi.org/10.1007/s11292-006-9000-2.

Farrington, D. P. (2010). Life-course and developmental theories in criminology. In E. McLaughlin, & T. Newburn (Eds.), *The Sage handbook of criminological theory* (pp. 249–270). London, UK: Sage Publications.

Farrington, D. P. (2014). Developmental and life course criminology: Theories and policy implications. In M. Delisi, & K. M. Beaver (Eds.), *Criminological theory: A life-course approach* (2nd Edition) (pp. 233–248). Burlington, MA: Jones and Bartlett.

Farrington, D. P., Jolliffe, D., Loeber, R., Stouthamer-Loeber, M., & Kalb, L. M. (2001). The concentration of offenders in families, and family criminality in the prediction of boys' delinquency. *Journal of Adolescence, 24*, 579–596. http://dx.doi.org/10.1006/jado.2001.0424.

Farrington, D. P., & Welsh, B. C. (2007). *Saving children from a life of crime: Early risk factors and effective interventions*. Oxford, UK: Oxford University Press.

Fedorenko, E., Duncan, J., & Kanwisher, N. (2013). Broad domain generality in focal regions of frontal and parietal cortex. *Proceedings of the National Academy of Sciences, 110*, 16616–16621. http://dx.doi.org/10.1073/pnas.1315235110.

Fehr, E., & Fischbacher, U. (2004). Social norms and human cooperation. *Trends in Cognitive Sciences, 8*, 185–190. http://dx.doi.org/10.1016/j.tics.2004.02.007.

Fehr, E., & Gächter, S. (2002). Altruistic punishment in humans. *Nature, 415*, 137–140.

Feixa, C. (2011). Past and present of adolescence in society: the 'teen brain' debate in perspective. *Neuroscience and Biobehavioral Reviews, 35*, 1634–1643. http://dx.doi.org/10.1016/j.neubiorev.2011.02.013.

Felson, M. (2008). Routine activity approach. In R. Wortley & L. Mazzerolle (Eds.), *Environmental criminology and crime analysis* (pp. 70–76). Cullompton, Devon: Willan Publishing.

Fergusson, D., Swain-Campbell, N., & Horwood, J. (2004). How does childhood economic disadvantage lead to crime? *Journal of Child Psychology and Psychiatry, 45*, 956–966.

Fergusson, D. M., Horwood, L. J., & Ridder, E. M. (2005). Show me the child at seven II: childhood intelligence and later outcomes in adolescence and young adulthood. *Journal of Child Psychology and Psychiatry, 46*, 850–858.

Fessler, D. M. T. (2007). From appeasement to conformity: evolutionary and cultural perspectives on shame, competition, and cooperation. In J. L. Tracy, R. W. Robins, & J. P. Tangney (Eds.), *The self-conscious emotions: Theory and research* (pp. 174–193). New York, NY: Guilford Press.

Fessler, D. M. T., Holbrook, C., & Gervais, M. M. (2014). Men's physical strength moderates conceptualizations of prospective foes in two disparate societies. *Human Nature, 25*, 393–409. http://dx.doi.org/10.1007/s12110-014-9205-4.

Fessler, D. M. T., Holbrook, C., & Snyder, J. K. (2012). Weapons make the man (larger): formidability is represented as size and strength in humans. *PLoS ONE, 7*, e32751. http://dx.doi.org/10.1371/journal.pone.0032751.

Feyerabend, P. (1975). How to defend science against society. *Radical Philosophy, 11*, 3–8.

Figueredo, A. J., Gladden, P. R., & Hohman, Z. (2011). The evolutionary psychology of criminal behavior. In S. C. Roberts (Ed.), *Applied evolutionary psychology* (pp. 201–221). New York, NY: Oxford University Press.

Fletcher, G. J. O., Simpson, J. A., Campbell, L., & Overall, N. C. (2013). *The science of intimate relationships*. Malden, MA: Wiley-Blackwell.

Flatley, J., Kershaw, C., Smith, K., Chaplin, R., & Moon, D. (2010). *Crime in England and Wales 2009/10. Findings from the British Crime Survey and police recorded crime*. London: Home Office.

Fletcher, G. J. O., Simpson, J. A., Campbell, L., & Overall, N. C. (2015). Pair-bonding, romantic love, and evolution: The curious case of *Homo sapiens*. Perspectives on Psychological Science, 10, 20–36. doi:10.1177/1745691614561683.

Flinn, M. V. (1988). Mate guarding in a Caribbean village. *Ethology and Sociobiology*, *9*, 1–28.

Flinn, M. V. (2011). Evolutionary anthropology of the human family. In C. A. Salmon, & T. K. Shackelford (Eds.), *The Oxford handbook of evolutionary family psychology* (pp. 12–32). New York, NY: Oxford University Press.

Foley, R., & Gamble, C. (2009). The ecology of social transitions in human evolution. *Philosophical Transactions of the Royal Society B: Biological Sciences*, *364*, 3267–3279. http://dx.doi.org/10.1098/rstb.2009.0136.

Foley, R. A., & Lahr, M. M. (2011). The evolution of the diversity of cultures. *Philosophical Transactions of the Royal Society B: Biological Sciences*, *366*, 1080–1089. http://dx.doi.org/10.1098/rstb.2010.0370.

Forsyth, A. J. M. (2013). Barroom approaches to prevention. In M. McMurran (Ed.), *Alcohol related violence: Prevention and treatment* (pp. 125–150). Chichester, England: John Wiley & Sons.

Foster, K. R., & Ratnieks, F. L. (2005). A new eusocial vertebrate? *Trends in Ecology and Evolution*, *20*, 363–364. http://dx.doi.org/10.1016/j.tree.2005.05.005.

Fox, J. A., & Piquero, A. R. (2003). Deadly demographics: population characteristics and forecasting homicide trends. *Crime and Delinquency*, *49*, 339–359. http://dx.doi.org/10.1177/0011128703253760.

Frankenhuis, W. E., & Del Giudice, M. (2012). When do adaptive developmental mechanisms yield maladaptive outcomes? *Developmental Psychology*, *48*, 628–642. http://dx.doi.org/10.1037/a0025629.

Frederick, D. A., & Haselton, M. G. (2007). Why is muscularity sexy? Tests of the fitness indicator hypothesis. *Personality and Social Psychology Bulletin*, *33*, 1167–1183. http://dx.doi.org/10.1177/0146167207303022.

Frick, P. J., Stickle, T. R., Dandreaux, D. M., Farrell, J. M., & Kimonis, E. R. (2005). Callous-unemotional traits in predicting the severity and stability of conduct problems and delinquency. *Journal of Abnormal Child Psychology*, *33*, 471–487.

Fry, D. P., & Souillac, G. (2013). The relevance of nomadic forager studies to moral foundations theory: moral education and global ethics in the twenty-first century. *Journal of Moral Education*, *42*, 346–359. http://dx.doi.org/10.1080/03057240.2013.817328.

Fukuyama, F. (2011). *The origins of political order: From prehuman times to the French Revolution*. London: Profile Books.

Furuichi, T. (2011). Female contributions to the peaceful nature of bonobo society. *Evolutionary Anthropology*, *20*, 131–142. http://dx.doi.org/10.1002/evan.2038.

Futuyma, D. J. (2009). *Evolution*. Sunderland, MA: Sinauer Associates.

Galluo, A. C., O'Brien, D. T., & Wilson, D. S. (2011). Intrasexual peer aggression and dating behavior during adolescence: an evolutionary perspective. *Aggressive Behavior*, *37*, 258–267. http://dx.doi.org/10.1002/ab.20384.

Gallup, A. C., O'Brien, D. T., & Wilson, D. S. (2011). Intrasexual peer aggression and dating behaviour during adolescence: an evolutionary perspective. *Aggressive Behavior*, *37*, 258–267.

Galván, A. (2010). Adolescent development of the reward system. *Frontiers in Neuroscience*, *4*, 1–9. http://dx.doi.org/10.3389/neuro.09.006.2010.

Galván, A. (2013). The teenage brain: sensitivity to rewards. *Current Directions in Psychological Science*, *22*, 88–93. http://dx.doi.org/10.1177/0963721413480859.

Gangestad, S. W. (2010). Evolutionary processes explaining the genetic variance in personality: an exploration of scenarios. In D. M. Buss, & P. Hawley (Eds.), *The evolution of personality and individual differences* (pp. 338–375). Oxford, UK: Oxford University Press.

Gangestad, S. W., Haselton, M. G., & Buss, D. M. (2006). Evolutionary foundations of cultural variation: evoked culture and mate preferences. *Psychological Inquiry, 17*, 75–95.

Gangestad, S. W., & Simpson, J. A. (2007). Whither science of the evolution of mind. In S. W. Gangestad, & J. A. Simpson (Eds.), *The evolution of mind: Fundamental questions and controversies* (pp. 397–437). New York, NY: The Guilford Press.

Gangestad, S. W., Thornhill, R., & Garver, C. E. (2002). Changes in women's sexual interests and their partner's mate-retention tactics across the menstrual cycle: evidence for shifting conflicts of interest. *Proceedings of the Royal Society of London. Series B: Biological Sciences, 269*, 975–982.

Gannon, T. A., & Polaschek, D. L. L. (2006). Cognitive distortions in child molesters: a re-examination of key theories and research. *Clinical Psychology Review, 26*, 1000–1019.

Gannon, T. A., Rose, M. R., & Ward, T. (2010). Pathways to female sexual offending: a preliminary study. *Psychology Crime and Law, 16*, 359–380.

Gannon, T., & Ward, T. (2014). Where has all the psychology gone? A critical review of evidence-based psychological practice in correctional settings. *Aggression and Violent Behavior, 19*, 435–436.

Gao, Y., Raine, A., Chan, F., Venables, P. H., & Mednick, S. A. (2010). Early maternal and paternal bonding, childhood physical abuse and adult psychopathic personality. *Psychological Medicine, 40*, 1007–1016.

Gardner, M., & Steinberg, L. (2005). Peer influence on risk taking, risk preference, and risky decision making in adolescence and adulthood: an experimental study. *Developmental Psychology, 41*, 625–635. http://dx.doi.org/10.1037/0012-1649.41.4.625.

Garland, D. (2001). *The culture of control*. Chicago, IL: University of Chicago Press.

Garland, D. (2011). Criminology's place in the academic field. In M. Bosworth, & C. Hoyle (Eds.), *What is criminology?* (pp. 298–317). Oxford, UK: Oxford University Press.

Garland, D. (2013). Penality and the penal state. *Criminology, 51*, 475–517. http://dx.doi.org/10.1111/1745-9125.12015.

Gartner, R. (2011). Sex, gender, and crime. In M. Tonry (Ed.), *The Oxford handbook of crime and criminal justice* (pp. 348–384). Oxford, UK: Oxford University Press.

Gat, A. (2009). So why do people fight? Evolutionary theory and the causes of war. *European Journal of International Relations, 15*, 571–599. http://dx.doi.org/10.1177/1354066109344661.

Geary, D. C. (2000). Evolution and proximate expression of human paternal investment. *Psychological Bulletin, 126*, 55–77. http://dx.doi.org/10.1037/0033-2909.126.1.55.

Geier, C. F., Terwilliger, R., Teslovich, T., Velanova, K., & Luna, B. (2009). Immaturities in reward processing and its influence on inhibitory control in adolescence. *Cerebral Cortex, 20*, 1613–1629. http://dx.doi.org/10.1093/cercor/bhp225.

Gelles, R. J. (2007). Family violence. In D. J. Flannery, A. T. Vazsonyi, & I. D. Walman (Eds.), *Cambridge handbook of violent behaviour* (pp. 403–417). Leiden: Cambridge University Press.

Gerbault, P., Liebert, A., Itan, Y., Powell, A., Currat, M., Burger, J., et al. (2011). Evolution of lacatase persistence: an example of human niche construction. *Philosophical Transactions of the Royal Society B: Biological Sciences, 366*, 863–877. http://dx.doi.org/10.1098/rstb.2010.0268.

Gettler, L. T., McDade, T. W., Feranil, A. B., & Kuzawa, C. W. (2011). Longitudinal evidence that fatherhood decreases testosterone in human males. *Proceedings of the National Academy of Sciences, 108*, 16194–16199. http://dx.doi.org/10.1073/pnas.1105403108.

Giancola, P. R. (2013). Alcohol and aggression: theories and mechanisms. In M. McMurran (Ed.), *Alcohol-related violence: Prevention and treatment* (pp. 37–60). Chichester, UK: John Wiley & Sons.

Giancola, P. R. (2013). Alcohol and aggression: theories and mechanisms. In M. McMurran (Ed.), *Alcohol related violence: Prevention and treatment* (pp. 37–60). Chichester, UK: John Wiley & Sons.

Gibbons, F. X., Roberts, M. E., Gerrard, M., Li, Z., Beach, S. R. H., Simons, R. L., et al. (2012). The impact of stress on the life history strategies of African American adolescents: cognitions, genetic moderation, and the role of discrimination. *Developmental Psychology, 48*, 722–739. http://dx.doi.org/10.1037/a0026599.

Gibbs, R. W. (2006). *Embodiment and cognitive science*. New York, NY: Cambridge University Press.

Gilbert, R., Widom, C. P., Browne, K., Fergusson, D., Webb, E., & Janson, S. (2009). Burden and consequences of child maltreatment in high-income countries. *Lancet, 373*, 68–81.

Gintis, H. (2011). Gene-culture coevolution and the nature of human sociality. *Philosophical Transactions of the Royal Society B: Biological Sciences, 366*, 878–888. http://dx.doi.org/10.1098/rstb.2010.0310.

Gintis, H., Henrich, J., Bowles, S., Boyd, R., & Fehr, E. (2008). Strong reciprocity and the roots of human morality. *Social Justice Research, 21*, 241–253.

Giordano, P. C., Longmore, M. A., Schroeder, R. D., & Seffrin, P. M. (2008). A life-course perspective on spirituality and desistance from crime. *Criminology, 46*, 99–132.

Glass, D. J., Wilson, D. S., & Geher, G. (2012). Evolutionary training in relation to human affairs is sorely lack in higher education. *EvoS Journal: The Journal of the Evolutionary Studies Consortium, 4*, 16–22.

Glenn, A. L., Kurzban, R., & Raine, A. (2011). Evolutionary theory and psychopathy. *Aggression and Violent Behavior, 16*, 371–380. http://dx.doi.org/10.1016/j.avb.2011.03.009.

Gluckman, P., Beedle, A., & Hanson, M. (2009). *Principles of evolutionary medicine*. Oxford: Oxford University Press.

Godfrey, B. S., Lawrence, P., & Williams, C. A. (2008). *History and crime*. Los Angeles, CA: Sage Publications.

Goetz, A. T. (2010). The evolutionary psychology of violence. *Psicothema, 22*, 15–21.

Goetz, J. L., Keltner, D., & Simon-Thomas, E. (2010). Compassion: an evolutionary analysis and empirical review. *Psychological Bulletin, 136*, 351–374. http://dx.doi.org/10.1037/a0018807.

Goetz, A. T., Shackelford, T. K., Romero, G. A., Kaighobadi, F., & Miner, E. J. (2008). Punishment, proprietrariness, and paternity: men's violence against women from an evolutionary perspective. *Aggression and Violent Behavior, 13*, 481–489. http://dx.doi.org/10.1016/j.avb.2008.07.004.

Goodwin, G. P., & Gromet, D. M. (2014). Punishment. *WIREs Cognitive Science, 5*, 561–572. http://dx.doi.org/10.1002/wcs.1301.

Gottfredson, M. R. (2011). Some advantages of a crime-free criminology. In M. Bosworth, & C. Hoyle (Eds.), *What is criminology?* Oxford: Oxford University Press.

Gottfredson, M. R., & Hirschi, T. (1990). *A general theory of crime*. Stanford, CA: Stanford University Press.

Gottschalk, M. (2006). *The prison and the gallows: The politics of mass incarceration in America*. Cambridge, UK: Cambridge University Press.

Gould, S. J. (1978). Sociobiology: the art of storytelling. *New Scientist, 16*, 530–533.

Gould, S. J. (1989). Sociobiology and the theory of natural selection. In M. Ruse (Ed.), *Philosophy of biology*. New York, NY: MacMillan.

Gould, W. A., & Heine, S. J. (2012). Implicit essentialism: genetic concepts are implicitly associated with fate concepts. *PloS ONE, 7*, e38176. http://dx.doi.org/10.1371/journal.pone.0038176.

Gould, S. J., & Lewontin, R. C. (1979). The spandrels of San Marco and the Panglossian paradigm: a critique of the adaptationist programme. *Proceedings of the Royal Society of London. Series B. Biological Sciences, 205*, 581–598.

Graham, J., Haidt, J., Koleva, S., Motyl, M., Iyer, R., Wojcik, S. P., et al. (2013). Moral foundations theory: the pragmatic validity of moral pluralism. *Advances in Experimental Psychology, 47*, 55–130. http://dx.doi.org/10.1016/B978-0-12-407236-7.00002-4.

Graham, J., Haidt, J., & Nosek, B. A. (2009). Liberals and conservatives rely on different sets of moral foundations. *Journal of Personality and Social Psychology, 96*, 1029–1046. http://dx.doi.org/10.1037/a0015141.

Graham, J., Nosek, B. A., Haidt, J., Iyer, R., Koleva, S., & Ditto, P. H. (2011). Mapping the moral domain. *Journal of Personality and Social Psychology, 101*, 366–385. http://dx.doi.org/10.1037/a0021847.

Graham, K., & Homel, R. (2008). *Raising the bar: Preventing aggression in and around bars, pubs, and clubs*. Devon, UK: Willan.

Graham-Kevan, N., & Archer, J. (2009). Control tactics and partner violence in heterosexual relationships. *Evolution and Human Behavior, 30*, 445–452.

Gray, P. B. (2013). Evolution and human sexuality. *American Journal of Physical Anthropology, 57*, 94–118.

Gray, P. B., Ellison, P. T., & Campbell, B. C. (2007). Testosterone and marriage among Ariaal men of Northern Kenya. *Current Anthropology, 48*, 750–755. http://dx.doi.org/10.1086/522061.

Gray, P. B., Kahlenberg, S. M., Barrett, E. S., Lipson, S. F., & Ellison, P. T. (2002). Marriage and fatherhood are associated with lower testosterone in males. *Evolution and Human Behaviour, 23*, 193–201.

Green, R. E., Krause, J., Briggs, A. W., Maricic, T., Stenzel, U., Kircher, M., et al. (2010). A draft sequence of the Neandertal genome. *Science, 328*, 710–722. http://dx.doi.org/10.1126/science.1188021.

Greenberg, D. F. (2008). Age, sex, and racial distributions of crime. In E. Goode (Ed.), *Out of control: Assessing the general theory of crime* (pp. 38–48). Stanford, CA: Stanford University Press.

Greene, J. (2013). *Moral tribes: Emotion, reason, and the gap between us and them*. New York, NY: The Penguin Press.

Greenwood, R. M., & Atkinson, I. A. E. (1977). Evolution of divaricating plants in New Zealand in relation to moa browsing. *Proceedings of the New Zealand Ecological. Society, 24*, 21–33.

Griffiths, P. E. (1996). The historical turn in the study of adaptation. *British Journal for the Philosophy of Science, 47*, 511–532.

Griskevicius, V., Tybur, J. M., Delton, A. W., & Robertson, T. E. (2011). The influence of mortality and socioeconomic status on risk and delayed rewards: a life history theory approach. *Journal of Personality and Social Psychology, 100*, 1–12. http://dx.doi.org/10.1037/a0022403.

Griskevicius, V., Tybur, J. M., Gangestad, S. W., Perea, E. F., Shapiro, J. R., & Kenrick, D. T. (2009). Aggress to impress: hostility as an evolved context-dependent strategy. *Journal of Personality and Social Psychology, 96*, 980–994. http://dx.doi.org/10.1037/a0013907.

Grueter, C. C., Chapais, B., & Zinner, D. (2012). Evolution of multilevel social systems in non-human primates and humans. *International Journal of Primatology, 33*, 1002–1037. http://dx.doi.org/10.1007/s10764-012-9618-z.

Gürerk, Ö., Irlenbusch, B., & Rockenbach, B. (2006). The competitive advantage of sanctioning institutions. *Science, 312*, 108–111. http://dx.doi.org/10.1126/science.1123633.

Gurr, T. R. (1981). Historical trends in violent crime: a critical review of the evidence. *Crime and Justice, 3*, 295–353.

Gurven, M. (2012). Human survival and life history in evolutionary perspective. In J. C. Mitani, J. Call, P. M. Kappeler, R. A. Palombit, & J. B. Silk (Eds.), *The evolution of primate societies* (pp. 293–314). Chicago, IL: Chicago University Press.

Haberl, H., Erb, K. H., Krausmann, F., Gaube, V., Bondeau, A., Plutzar, C., et al. (2007). Quantifying and mapping the human appropriation of net primary production in earth's terrestrial ecoystems. *Proceedings of the National Academy of Sciences, 104*, 12942–12947. http://dx.doi.org/10.1073/pnas.0704243104.

Haidt, J. (2007). The new synthesis in moral psychology. *Science, 316*, 998–1001. http://dx.doi.org/10.1126/science.1137651.

Haidt, J. (2012). *The righteous mind: Why good people are divided by politics and religion*. New York, NY: The Penguin Press.

Haig, B. D. (2014). *Investigating the psychological world: Scientific method in the behavioral sciences*. Cambridge, MA: MIT Press.

Hamilton, W. D. (1964). The genetical evolution of social behavior: I. *Journal of Theoretical Biology, 7,* 1–16. http://dx.doi.org/10.1016/0022-5193(64)90038-4.

Hamlin, J. K. (2013). Moral judgement and action in preverbal infants and toddlers: evidence for an innate moral core. *Current Directions in Psychological Science, 22,* 186–193. http://dx.doi.org/10.1177/0963721412470687.

Haney, C. (2003). Mental health issues in long-term solitary and "supermax" confinement. *Crime and Delinquency, 49,* 124–156.

Hare, B., Wobber, V., & Wrangham, R. (2012). The self-domestication hypothesis: evolution of bonobo psychology is due to selection against aggression. *Animal Behaviour, 83,* 573–585. http://dx.doi.org/10.1016/j.anbehav.2011.12.007.

Hare, R. D. (2001). Psychopaths and their nature: some implications for understanding human predatory violence. In A. Raine & J. Sanmartin (Eds.), *Violence and psychopathy* (pp. 5–34). New York, NY: Kluwer Academic.

Hare, R. D., & Neumann, C. S. (2008). Psychopathy as a clinical and empirical construct. *Annual Review of Clinical Psychology, 4,* 217–246. http://dx.doi.org/10.1146/annurev.clinpsy.3.022806.091452.

Harris, G. T., Hilton, N. Z., Rice, M. E., & Eke, A. W. (2007). Children killed by genetic parents versus stepparents. *Evolution and Human Behavior, 28,* 85–95. http://dx.doi.org/10.1016/j.evolhumbehav.2006.08.001.

Harvey, P. H., & Pagel, M. D. (1991). *The comparative method in evolutionary biology.* Oxford, UK: Oxford University Press.

Hauser, M. D. (2006). *Moral minds: How nature designed our universal sense of right and wrong.* New York, NY: Harper Collins.

Hawks, J., Wang, E. T., Cochran, G. M., Harpending, H. C., & Moyzis, R. K. (2007). Recent acceleration of human adaptive evolution. *Proceedings of the National Academy of Sciences of the United States of America, 52,* 20753–20758. http://dx.doi.org/10.1073/pnas.0707650104.

Hawkes, K. (2014). Primate sociality to human cooperation. *Human Nature, 25,* 28–48. http://dx.doi.org/10.1007/s12110-013-9184-x.

Henrich, J., Boyd, R., Bowles, S., Camerer, C., Fehr, E., & Gintis, H. (2004). *Foundations of human sociality: Economic experiments and ethnographic evidence from fifteen small-scale societies.* New York, NY: Oxford University Press.

Henrich, J., Boyd, R., Bowles, S., Camerer, C., Fehr, E., Gintis, H., et al. (2001). In search of homo economicus: behavioral experiments in 15 small-scale societies. *American Economic Review, 91,* 73–78.

Henrich, J., Boyd, R., & Richerson, P. J. (2012). The puzzle of monogamous marriage. *Philosophical Transactions of the Royal Society B: Biological Sciences, 367,* 657–669. http://dx.doi.org/10.1098/rstb.2011.0290.

Henrich, J., Ensminger, J., McElreath, R., Barr, A., Barrett, C., Bolyanatz, A., et al. (2010). Markets, religion, community size, and the evolution of fairness and punishment. *Science, 327,* 1480–1484. http://dx.doi.org/10.1126/science.1182238.

Henrich, J., & Gil-White, F. J. (2001). The evolution of prestige: freely conferred deference as a mechanism for enhancing the benefits of cultural transmission. *Evolution and Human Behavior, 22,* 165–196.

Henrich, J., & McElreath, R. (2007). Dual-inheritance theory: the evolution of human cultural capacities and cultural evolution. In R. I. M. Dunbar, & L. Barrett (Eds.), *The Oxford handbook of evolutionary psychology* (pp. 555–568). Oxford, UK: Oxford University Press.

Henrich, J., McElreath, R., Barr, A., Ensminger, J., Barrett, C., Bolyanatz, A., et al. (2006). Costly punishment across human societies. *Science, 312,* 1767–1770.

Henry, S. (2012). The challenges of integrating criminology: a commentary on Agnew's Toward a Unified Criminology. *Journal of Theoretical and Philosophical Criminology, 4,* 10–26.

Henry, S., & Einstadter, W. J. (2006). *Criminological theory: An analysis of its underlying assumptions.* Lanham, MD: Rowman & Littlefield Publishers.

Herrmann, E., & Tomasello, M. (2012). Human cultural cognition. In J. C. Mitani, J. Call, P. M. Kappeler, R. A. Palombit, & J. B. Silk (Eds.), *The evolution of primate societies* (pp. 701–714). Chicago, IL: University of Chicago Press.

Hess, N., Helfrecht, C., Hagen, E., Sell, A., & Hewlett, B. (2010). Interpersonal aggression among Aka hunter-gatherers of the Central African Republic. *Human Nature, 21,* 330–354. http://dx.doi.org/10.1007/s12110-010-9094-0.

Hicks, K., & Leonard, W. R. (2014). Developmental systems and inequality: linking evolutionary and political-economic theory in biological anthropology. *Current Anthropology, 55,* 523–550. http://dx.doi.org/10.1086/678055.

Hill, K., Barton, M., & Hurtado, M. (2009). The emergence of human uniqueness: characters underlying behavioural modernity. *Evolutionary Anthropology, 18,* 187–200.

Hill, K., & Hurtado, A. M. (1996). *Ache life history: The ecology and demography of a foraging people.* NJ: Transaction Publishers.

Hill, K. R., Walker, R. S., Božičević, M., Eder, J., Headland, T., Hewlett, B., et al. (2011). Co-residence patterns in hunter-gatherer societies show unique human social structure. *Science, 331*(6022), 1286–1289. http://dx.doi.org/10.1126/science.1199071.

Hirschi, T. (1969). *Causes of delinquency.* Berkeley, CA: University of California.

Hirschi, T., & Gottfredson, M. (1983). Age and the explanation of crime. *American Journal of Sociology, 89,* 552–584.

Hirschinger, N. B., Grisso, J. A., Wallace, D. B., McCollum, K. F., Schwarz, D. F., Sammel, M. D., et al. (2003). A case-control study of female-to-female nonintimate violence in an urban area. *American Journal of Public Health, 93,* 1098–1103.

Hitchcock, T., & Shoemaker, R. (2006). *Tales from the hanging court.* London, UK: Hodder and Arnold.

Hochberg, Z., & Belsky, J. (2013). Evo-devo of human adolescence: beyond disease models of early puberty. *BMC Medicine, 11,* 1–11. http://dx.doi.org/10.1186/1741-7015-11-113.

Hoffman, M. B. (2014). *The punisher's brain: The evolution of judge and jury.* New York, NY: Cambridge University Press.

Hollan, D. (2012). Emerging issues in the cross-cultural study of empathy. *Emotion Review, 4,* 70–78. http://dx.doi.org/10.1177/1754073911421376.

Hollan, D. (2014). Empathy and morality in ethnographic perspective. In H. Maibom (Ed.), *Empathy and morality* (pp. 230–250). Oxford, UK: Oxford University Press.

Hölldobler, B., & Wilson, E. O. (1990). *The ants.* Cambridge, MA: Harvard University Press.

Hölldobler, B., & Wilson, E. O. (1994). *Journey to the ants.* Cambridge, MA: Harvard University Press.

Hooker, C. A. (1987). *A realistic theory of science.* New York, NY: State University of New York Press.

Hooker, C. A. (2009). Interaction and bio-cognitive order. *Synthese, 166,* 513–546. http://dx.doi.org/10.1007/s11229-008-9374-y.

Horne, C. (2009). *The rewards of punishment: A relational theory of norm enforcement.* Stanford, CA: Stanford University Press.

Horney, J., Tolan, P., & Weisburd, D. (2012). Contextual influences. In R. Loeber, & D. P. Farrington (Eds.), *From juvenile delinquency to adult Crime: Criminal careers, Justice policy, and prevention* (pp. 86–117). Oxford, UK: Oxford University Press.

House, B. R., Henrich, J., Brosnan, S. F., & Silk, J. B. (2012). The ontogeny of human prosociality: behavioral experiments with children aged 3 to 8. *Evolution and Human Behaviour, 33,* 291–308. http://dx.doi.org/10.1016/j.evolhumbehav.2011.10.007.

Howell, C. J., Kelly, D., & Turnbull, M. H. (2002). Moa ghosts exorcised? New Zealand's divaricate shrubs avoid photoinhibition. *Functional Ecology, 16,* 232–240.

Hrdy, S. (2009). *Mothers and others: The evolutionary origins of mutual understanding.* Cambridge, MA: Harvard University Press.

Huang, J. Y., & Bargh, J. (2014). The selfish goal: autonomously operating motivational structures as the proximate cause of human judgment and behavior. *Behavioral and Brain Sciences*, *37*, 121–134. http://dx.doi.org/10.1017/S0140525X13000290.

Ingram, J. R., Patchin, J. W., Huebner, B. H., McCluskey, J. D., & Bynum, T. S. (2007). Parents, friends, and serious delinquency: an examination of direct and indirect effects among at-risk early adolescents. *Criminal Justice Review*, *32*, 380–400. http://dx.doi.org/10.1177/0734016807311463.

Irwin, J., & Owen, B. (2005). Harm and the contemporary prison. In A. Liebling, & S. Maruna (Eds.), *The effects of imprisonment* (pp. 94–117). Cullompton, Devon: Willan Publishing.

Jablonka, E., & Lamb, M. J. (2005). *Evolution in four dimensions: Genetic, epigenetic, behavioural, and symbolic variation in the history of life.* Cambridge, MA: MIT Press.

Jablonka, E., & Lamb, M. J. (2008). Soft inheritance: challenging the modern synthesis. *Genetics and Molecular Biology*, *31*, 389–395. http://dx.doi.org/10.1590/S1415-47572008000300001.

Jablonka, E., & Lamb, M. J. (2010). Transgenerational epigenetic inheritance. In M. Pigliucci & G. B. Muller (Eds.), *Evolution: The extended synthesis* (pp. 137–174). Cambridge, MA: MIT press.

Jacard, J., Blanton, H., & Dodge, T. (2005). Peer influences on risk behaviour: an analysis of the effects of a close friend. *Developmental Psychology*, *41*, 135–147. http://dx.doi.org/10.1037/0012-1649.41.1.135.

Jacob, F. (1977). Evolution and tinkering. *Science*, *196*, 1161–1166.

Jacobs, D., & Richardson, A. M. (2008). Economic inequality and homicide in developed nations from 1975–1995. *Homicide Studies*, *12*, 28–45. http://dx.doi.org/10.1177/1088767907311849.

James, J., Ellis, B. J., Schlomer, G. L., & Garber, J. (2012). Sex-specific pathways to early puberty, sexual debut, and sexual risk taking: tests of an integrated evolutionary-developmental model. *Developmental Psychology*, *48*, 687–702. http://dx.doi.org/10.1037/a0026427.

Jennings, W. G., & Reingle, J. M. (2012). On the number and shape of developmental/life-course violence, aggression, and delinquency trajectories: a state-of-the-art review. *Journal of Criminal Justice*, *40*, 472–489. http://dx.doi.org/10.1016/j.crimjus.2012.07.001.

Jensen, K. (2010). Punishment and spite: the dark side of cooperation. *Philosophical Transactions of the Royal Society B: Biological Sciences*, *365*, 2635–2650. http://dx.doi.org/10.1098/rstb.2010.0146.

Jensen, K. (2012). Social regard: evolving a psychology of cooperation. In J. C. Mitani, J. Call, P. M. Kappeler, R. A. Palombit, & J. B. Silk (Eds.), *The evolution of primate societies* (pp. 565–584). Chicago, IL: University of Chicago Press.

Jepperson, R., & Meyer, J. W. (2011). Multiple levels of analysis and the limitations of methodological individualisms. *Sociological Theory*, *29*, 54–73. http://dx.doi.org/10.1111/j.1467-9558.2010.01387.x.

Jessor, R. (1987). Problem-behavior theory, psychosocial development, and adolescent problem drinking. *British Journal of Addiction*, *82*, 331–342.

Jobling, M., Hollox, E., Hurles, M., Kivisild, T., & Tyler-Smith, C. (2013). *Human evolutionary genetics.* New York, NY: Garland Science.

Johnson, D. T. (2008). The homicide drop in postwar Japan. *Homicide Studies*, *12*, 146–160. http://dx.doi.org/10.1177/1088767907310854.

Johnson, M. (2007) *The meaning of the body: Aesthetics of human understanding.* Chicago, IL: University of Chicago Press.

Johnson, R. T., Burk, J. A., & Kirkpatrick, L. A. (2007). Dominance and prestige as differential predictors of aggression and testosterone levels in men. *Evolution and Human Behavior*, *28*, 345–351. http://dx.doi.org/10.1016/j.evolhumbehav.2007.04.003.

Johnstone, G., & Van Ness, D. W. (2007). The meaning of restorative justice. In G. Johnstone, & D. W. Van Ness (Eds.), *Handbook of restorative justice* (pp. 5–23). Cullompton, UK: Willan Publishing.

Jolliffe, D., & Farrington, D. P. (2004). Empathy and offending: a systematic review and meta-analysis. *Aggression and Violent Behavior*, *9*, 441–476.

Jolliffe, D., & Farrington, D. P. (2006). Examining the relationship between low empathy and bullying. *Aggressive Behavior*, *32*, 540–550.

Jolliffe, D., & Farrington, D. P. (2007). Examining the relationship between low empathy and self-reported offending. *Legal and Criminological Psychology, 12,* 265–286.

Jonason, P. K., & Tost, J. (2010). I just cannot control myself: the dark triad and self-control. *Personality and Individual Differences, 49,* 611–615. http://dx.doi.org/10.1016/j.paid.2010.05.031.

Jonason, P. K., LI, N. P., Webster, G. D., & Schmitt, D. P. (2009). The dark triad: facilitating a short-term mating strategy in men. *European Journal of Personality, 23,* 5–18. http://dx.doi.org/10.1002/per.698.

Jones, O. D., & Kurzban, R. (2010). Intuitions of punishment. *The University of Chicago Law Review, 77,* 1643–1653.

Joyce, R. (2006). *The evolution of morality.* Cambridge, MA: MIT Press.

Kaighobadi, F., Shackelford, T. K., & Goetz, A. T. (2009). From mate retention to murder: evolutionary psychological perspectives on men's partner-directed violence. *Review of General Psychology, 13,* 327–334.

Kanazawa, S. (2008). Theft. In J. D. Duntley, & T. K. Shackelford (Eds.), *Evolutionary forensic psychology: Darwinian foundations of crime and law* (pp. 160–175). Oxford, UK: Oxford University Press.

Kanazawa, S., & Still, M. C. (2000). Why men commit crime (and why they desist). *Sociological Theory, 18,* 434–447. http://dx.doi.org/10.1111/0735-2751.00110.

Kaplan, H. S., & Gangestad, S. W. (2005). Life history theory and evolutionary psychology. In D. M. Buss (Ed.), *The handbook of evolutionary psychology* (pp. 68–95). Hoboken, NJ: John Wiley.

Kaplan, H. S., Hooper, P. L., & Gurven, M. (2009). The evolutionary and ecological roots of human social organization. *Philosophical Transactions of the Royal Society B: Biological Sciences 364,* 3289–3299. http://dx.doi.org/10.1098/rstb.2009.0115.

Kazemian, L. (2007). Desistance from crime: theoretical, empirical, methodological, and policy considerations. *Journal of Contemporary Criminal Justice, 23,* 5–27.

Keeley, L. H. (1996). *War before civilization: The myth of the peaceful savage.* New York, NY: Oxford University Press.

Kekes, J. (1989). *Moral tradition and individuality.* Princeton, NJ: Princeton University Press.

Kelly, R. L. (2013). *The lifeways of hunter-gatherers: The foraging spectrum.* Cambridge, UK: Cambridge University Press.

Kesebir, S. (2012). The superorganism account of human sociality: how and when human groups are like beehives. *Personality and Social Psychology Review, 4,* 738–744. http://dx.doi.org/10.1177/1088868311430834.

Ketelaar, T., & Ellis, B. J. (2000). Are evolutionary explanations unfalsifiable? Evolutionary psychology and the Lakatosian philosophy of science. *Psychological Inquiry, 11,* 1–22. http://dx.doi.org/10.1207/S15327965PLI1101_01.

King, P. (2014). Exploring and explaining the geography of homicide: patterns of lethal violence in Britain and Europe 1805–1900. *European Review of History, 20,* 967–987. http://dx.doi.org/10.1080/13507486.2013.852516.

Kitcher, P. (1985a). *Vaulting ambition: Sociobiology and the quest for human nature.* Cambridge, MA: MIT Press.

Kitcher, P. (1985b). Two approaches to explanation. *The Journal of Philosophy, 82,* 632–639.

Kitcher, P. (2010). Varieties of altruism. *Economics and Philosophy, 26,* 121–148. http://dx.doi.org/10.1017/S0266267110000167.

Kitcher, P. (2011). *The ethical project.* Cambridge, MA: MIT press.

Kivivuori, J. (2014). Understanding trends in personal violence: does cultural sensitivity matter? *Crime and Justice, 43.* http://dx.doi.org/10.1086/677664.

Klein, R. G. (2008). Out of Africa and the evolution of human behaviour. *Evolutionary Anthropology, 17,* 267–281. http://dx.doi.org/10.1002/evan.20181.

Knott, C. D. (2009). Orangutans: sexual coercion without sexual violence. In M. N. Muller, & R. W. Wrangham (Eds.), *Sexual coercion in primates and humans: An evolutionary perspective on male aggression against females* (pp. 81–111). Cambridge, MA: Harvard University Press.

Koster, F., Foudriaan, H., & van der Schans, C. (2009). Shame and punishment: an international comparative study on the effects of religious affiliation and religiosity on attitudes to offending. *European Journal of Criminology, 6*, 481–495. http://dx.doi.org/10.1177/1477370809341129.

Krasnow, M. M., Cosmides, L., Pedersen, E. J., & Tooby, J. (2012). What are punishment and reputation for? *Plos ONE, 7*. http://dx.doi.org/10.1371/journal.pone.0045662.

Krebs, D. L. (2008). Morality: an evolutionary account. *Perspectives on Psychological Science, 3*, 149–172. http://dx.doi.org/10.1111/j.1745-6924.2008.00072.x.

Kruger, D. J., Fisher, M. L., & Wright, P. (2014). Patriarchy, male competition, and excess male mortality. *Evolutionary Behavioral Sciences, 8*, 3–11. http://dx.doi.org/10.1037/h0097244.

Kruger, D. J., & Nesse, R. M. (2006). An evolutionary life-history framework for understanding sex differences in human mortality rates. *Human Nature, 17*, 74–97.

Kugler, M. B., Funk, F., Braun, J., Gollwitzer, M., Kay, A. C., & Darley, J. M. (2013). Differences in punitiveness across three cultures: a test of American exceptionalism in justice attitudes. *Journal of Criminal Law and Criminology, 103*, 1071–1114.

Kuhn, T. S. (1970). *The structure of scientific revolutions* (2nd ed.). Chicago. IL: The University of Chicago Press.

Kurzban, R., Burton-Chellew, M. N., & West, S. A. (2014). The evolution of altruism in humans. *Annual Review of Psychology, 66*, 10.1–10.25. http://dx.doi.org/10.1146/annurev-psych-010814-015355.

Kurzban, R., & Haselton, M. (2006). Making hay out of straw? Real and imagined controversies in evolutionary psychology. In J. Barkow (Ed.), *Missing the revolution: Darwinism for social scientists* (pp. 149–162). Oxford, UK: Oxford University Press.

Kuzawa, C. W., & Bragg, J. M. (2012). Plasticity in human life strategy: implications for contemporary human variation and the evolution of the genus *Homo. Current Anthropology, 53*, S369–S382.

Kuzawa, C. W., & Sweet, E. (2009). Epigenetics and the embodiment of race: developmental origins of US racial disparities in cardiovascular health. *American Journal of Human Biology, 21*, 2–15. http://dx.doi.org/10.1002/ajhb.20822.

Kuzawa, C. W., & Thayer, Z. M. (2011). Timescales of human adaptation: the role of epigenetic processes. *Epigenomics, 3*, 221–234. http://dx.doi.org/10.2217/EPI.11.11.

Laland, K. N., & Brown, G. (2011). *Sense and nonsense: Evolutionary perspectives on human behaviour.* Oxford, UK: Oxford University Press.

Laland, K. N., & Galef, B. G. (Eds.). (2009). *The question of animal culture.* Cambridge, MA: Harvard University Press.

Laland, K. N., Odling-Smee, F. J., & Myles, S. (2010). How culture shaped the human genome: bringing genetics and the human sciences together. *Nature Reviews Genetics, 11*, 137–148. http://dx.doi.org/10.1038/nrg2734.

Laland, K. N., Sterelny, K., Odling-Smee, J., Hoppitt, W., & Uller, T. (2011). Cause and effect in biology revisited: is Mayr's proximate-ultimate dichotomy still useful? *Science, 334*, 1512–1516. http://dx.doi.org/10.1126/science.1210879.

Laland, K. N., Sterelny, K., Odling-Smee, J., Hoppitt, W., & Uller, T. (2013). More on how and why: cause and effect in biology. *Biology and Philosophy, 28*, 719–745. http://dx.doi.org/10.1007/s10539-012-9335-1.

Lalumière, M. L., Mishra, S., & Harris, G. T. (2008). In cold blood: the evolution of psychopathy. In J. D. Duntley, & T. K. Shackelford (Eds.), *Evolutionary forensic psychology: Darwinian foundations of crime and law* (pp. 176–193). Oxford, UK: Oxford University Press.

Land, K. C., McCall, P. L., & Cohen, L. E. (1990). Structural covariates of homicide rates: are there any invariances across time and social space? *American Journal of Sociology, 95*, 922–963.

Langergraber, K. E. (2012). Cooperation among kin. In J. C. Mitani, J. Call, P. M. Kappeler, R. A. Palombit, & J. B. Silk (Eds.), *The evolution of primate societies* (pp. 491–513). Chicago, IL: University of Chicago Press.

Lassek, W. D., & Gaulin, S. J. C. (2009). Costs and benefits of fat-free muscle mass in men: relationship to mating success, dietary requirements, and native immunity. *Evolution and Human Behavior, 30*, 322–328. http://dx.doi.org/10.1016/j.evolhumbehav.2009.04.002.

Laub, J. H. (2006). Edwin H. Sutherland and the Michael-Adler report: searching for the soul of criminology seventy years later. *Criminology, 44*, 235–257.

Laub, J. H., & Sampson, R. J. (2003). *Shared beginnings, divergent lives: Delinquent boys to age 70.* Cambridge, MA: Harvard University Press.

Laub, J. H., Sampson, R. J., & Sweeten, G. A. (2006). Assessing Sampson and Laub's life course theory of crime. In F. T. Cullen, J. P. Wright, & K. R. Blevins (Eds.), *Taking stock: The status of criminological theory* (pp. 313–334). New Brunswick, NJ: Transaction Publishers.

Lauritsen, J. L., Rezey, M. L., & Heimer, K. (2014). Violence and economic conditions in the United States, 1973–2011: gender, race, and ethnicity patterns in the National Crime Victimization Survey. *Journal of Contemporary Criminal Justice, 30*, 7–28. http://dx.doi.org/10.1177/1043986213509024.

Laws, D. R., & Ward, T. (2011). *Desistance and sexual offending: Alternatives to throwing away the keys.* New York, NY: Guilford Press.

Lee, M. R., & Shihadeh, E. S. (2009). The spatial concentration of Southern whites and argument-based lethal violence. *Social Forces, 87*, 1671–1694.

Leigh, E. G. (2010). The group selection controversy. *Journal of Evolutionary Biology, 23*, 6–19. http://dx.doi.org/10.1111/j.1420-9101.2009.01876.

Levin, H. (2013). *The earth through time* (10th ed.). Hoboken, NY: John Wiley & Sons.

Lewin, R. (1974). Accidental career. *New Scientist, August, 8*, 322–325.

Lewontin, R. C. (1979). Sociobiology as an adaptationist program. *Behavioral Science, 24*, 5–14.

Lewontin, R. C. (1990). The evolution of cognition. In D. N. Osheron, & E. E. Smith (Eds.), *Thinking: An introduction to cognitive science.* Cambridge, MA: MIT Press.

Liddle, J. R., Shackelford, T. K., & Weekes–Shackelford, V. A. (2012). Why can't we all just get along? Evolutionary perspectives on violence, homicide, and war. *Review of General Psychology, 16*, 24–36. http://dx.doi.org/10.1037/a0026610.

Liebling, A. (2007). Prison suicide and its prevention. In Y. Jewkes (Ed.), *Handbook of prisons* (pp. 423–446). Cullompton, UK: Willan Publishing.

Lloyd, E. (1999). Evolutionary psychology: the burdens of proof. *Biology and Philosophy, 14*, 211–233.

Loeber, R. (2012). Does the study of the age-crime curve have a future? In R. Loeber, & B. C. Welsh (Eds.), *The future of criminology* (pp. 11–19). Oxford, UK: Oxford University Press.

Loeber, R., & Farrington, D. P. (2012). Introduction. In R. Loeber, & D. P. Farrington (Eds.), *From juvenile delinquency to adult Crime: Criminal careers, Justice policy, and prevention* (pp. 3–13). Oxford, UK: Oxford University Press.

Lombroso, C. (1884/2006). *Criminal man.* Durham, NC: Duke University Press.

Luckenbill, D. F. (1977). Criminal homicide as a situated transaction. *Social Problems, 25*, 176–186.

MacDougall-Shackleton, S. A. (2011). The levels of analysis revisited. *Philosophical Transactions of the Royal Society B: Biological Sciences, 366*, 2076–2085. http://dx.doi.org/10.1098/rstb.2010.0363.

Mace, R., & Jordan, F. M. (2011). Macro-evolutionary studies of cultural diversity: a review of empirical studies of cultural transmission and cultural adaptation. *Philosophical Transactions of the Royal Society B: Biological Sciences, 366*, 402–411. http://dx.doi.org/10.1098/rstb.2010.0238.

Maibom, H. L. (2012). The many faces of empathy and their relation to prosocial action and aggression inhibition. *WIREs Cognitive Science, 3*, 253–263. http://dx.doi.org/10.1002/wcs.1165.

Maibom, H. L. (2014). Introduction: (almost) everything you wanted to know about empathy. In H. L. Maibom (Ed.), *Empathy and morality* (pp. 1–40). New York, NY: Oxford University Press.

Maise, M. (2011). *Embodiment, emotion, and cognition*. Basingstoke, UK: Palgrave Macmillan.

Malone, N., Fuentes, A., & White, F. J. (2012). Variation in the social systems of extant hominoids: comparative insight into the social behaviour of early hominins. *International Journal of Primatology, 33*, 1251–1277. http://dx.doi.org/10.1007/s10764-012-9617-0.

Maner, J. K., DeWall, C. N., & Gailliot, M. T. (2008). Selective attention to signs of success: social dominance and early stage interpersonal perception. *Personality and Social Psychology Bulletin, 34*, 488–501. http://dx.doi.org/10.1177/0146167207311910.

Manicas, P. T. (2006). *A realist philosophy of social science: Explanation and understanding*. Cambridge, UK: Cambridge University Press.

Mann, R. E., & Barnett, G. D. (2013). Victim empathy intervention with sexual offenders: rehabilitation, punishment, or correctional quackery? *Sexual Abuse: A Journal of Research and Treatment, 25*, 282–301.

Mann, R. E., Hanson, R. K., & Thornton, D. (2010). Assessing risk for sexual recidivism: some proposals on the nature of psychologically meaningful risk factors. *Sexual Abuse: A Journal of Research and Treatment, 22*, 191–217. http://dx.doi.org/10.1177/1079063210366039.

Manuck, S. B., & McCaffery, J. M. (2014). Gene environment interaction. *Annual Review of Psychology, 65*, 41–70. http://dx.doi.org/10.1146/annurev-psych-010213-115100.

Mare, R. D. (2011). A multigenerational view of inequality. *Demography, 48*, 1–23. http://dx.doi.org/10.1007/s13524-011-0014-7.

Mares, D. M. (2009). Civilization, economic change, and trends in interpersonal violence in western societies. *Theoretical Criminology, 13*, 419–449. http://dx.doi.org/10.1177/1362480609340401.

Marlowe, F. W. (2012). The socioecology of human reproduction. In J. C. Mitani, J. Call, P. M. Kappeler, R. A. Palombit, & J. B. Silk (Eds.), *The evolution of primate societies* (pp. 469–486). Chicago, IL: Chicago University Press.

Marsh, I. (2011). *Crime and criminal justice*. New York, NY: Routledge.

Marshall, W. L. (1989). Intimacy, loneliness, and sexual offenders. *Behavior Research and Therapy, 27*, 491–503.

Marshall, W. L., Hudson, S. M., Jones, R., & Fernandez, Y. M. (1995). Empathy in sex offenders. *Clinical Psychology Review, 15*, 99–113.

Marshall, W. L., Marshall, L. E., Serran, G. A., & Fernandez, Y. M. (2006). *Treating sexual offenders: An integrated approach*. New York, NY: Routledge.

Maruna, S. (2001). *Making good: How ex-convicts reform and rebuild their lives*. Washington, DC: American Psychological Association.

Matthew, S., & Boyd, R. (2014). The cost of cowardice: punitive sentiments towards free riders in Turkana raids. *Evolution and Human Behaviour, 35*, 58–64. http://dx.doi.org/10.1016/j.evolhumbehav.2013.10.001.

Matthew, S., Boyd, R., & van Veelen, N. (2012). Human cooperation among kin and close associates may require enforcement of norms by third parties. In P. J. Richerson, & M. H. Strüngmann (Eds.), *Cultural evolution: Society, technology, language, and religion* (pp. 45–60). Cambridge, MA: MIT Press.

Matza, D., & Sykes, G. M. (1961). Juvenile delinquency and subterranean values. *American Sociological Review, 26*, 712–719.

Mayhew, P. (2012). The case of Australia and New Zealand. In J. Van Dijk, A. Tseloni, & G. Farrell (Eds.), *The international crime drop: New directions in research* (pp. 76–102). New York, NY: Palgrave Macmillan.

Mayhew, P., & Reilly, J. (2007). *The New Zealand crime & Safety Survey 2006: Key findings*. Wellington , NZ: Ministry of Justice.

Mayr, E. (1961). Cause and effect in biology: kinds of causes, predictability, and teleology are viewed by a practicing biologist. *Science, 134*, 1501–1506. http://dx.doi.org/10.1126/science.134.3489.1501.

Mayr, E. (1993). Proximate and ultimate causations. *Biology and Philosophy, 8*, 93–94. http://dx.doi.org/10.1007/BF00868508.

Mazerolle, L., Wickes, R., & McBroom, J. (2010). Community variations in violence: the role of social ties and collective efficacy in comparative context. *Journal of Research in Crime and Delinquency, 47*, 3–30.

Mazur, A. (2009). Testosterone and violence among young men. In A. Walsh, & K. M. Beaver (Eds.), *Biosocial criminology: New direction in theory and research* (pp. 191–204). New York, NY: Routledge.

Mazur, A., & Michalek, J. (1998). Marriage, divorce, male testosterone. *Social Forces, 77*, 315–330.

McBrearty, S., & Brooks, A. S. (2000). The revolution that wasn't: a new interpretation of the origin of modern human behavior. *Journal of Human Evolution, 39*, 453–563.

McCall, P. L., Land, K. C., & Parker, K. F. (2010). An empirical assessment of what we know about structural covariates of homicide rates: a return to a classic 20 years later. *Homicide Studies, 14*, 219–243. http://dx.doi.org/10.1177/1088767910371166.

McCall, P. L., & Nieuwbeerta, P. (2007). Structural covariates of homicide rates: a European city cross-national comparative analysis. *Homicide Studies, 11*, 167–188. http://dx.doi.org/10.1177/1088767907304072.

McCall, G. S., & Shields, N. (2008). Examining the evidence from small-scale societies and early prehistory and implications for modern theories of aggression and violence. *Aggression and Violent Behavior, 13*, 1–9.

McCauley, R. N. (1996). Explanatory pluralism and the coevolution of theories in science. In R. N. McCauley (Ed.), *The Churchlands and their critics* (pp. 17–47). Oxford, UK: Blackwell.

McCord, J., & Conway, K. P. (2005). *Co-offending and patterns of juvenile crime.* Washington, DC: US Department of Justice, Office of Justice Programs, National Institute of Justice.

McCullough, M. E., Kurzban, R., & Tabak, B. A. (2012). Cognitive systems for revenge and forgiveness. *Behavioral and Brain Sciences, 36*, 1–58. http://dx.doi.org/10.1017/S0140525X11002160.

McCullough, M. E., Kurzban, R., & Tabak, B. A. (2013). Cognitive systems for revenge and forgiveness. *Behavioral and Brain Sciences, 36*, 1–58.

McCullough, M. E., Pedersen, E. J., Schroder, J. M., Tabak, B. A., & Carver, C. S. (2013). Harsh childhood environmental characteristics predict exploitation and retaliation in humans. *Proceedings of the Royal Society B: Biological Sciences, 280*, 2012–2104. http://dx.doi.org/10.1098/rspb.2012.2104.

McDonald, M. N., Donnellan, M. B., & Navarrete, C. D. (2012). A life history approach to understanding the dark triad. *Personality and Individual Differences, 52*, 601–605. http://dx.doi.org/10.1016/j.paid.2011.12.003.

McGlone, M. S., & Webb, C. J. (1981). Selective forces influencing the evolution of divaricating plants. *New Zealand Journal of Ecology, 4*, 20–28.

McGuire, J. (2004). *Understanding psychology and crime: Perspectives on theory and action.* New York, NY: Open University Press.

McHenry, H. M. (2009). Human evolution. In M. Ruse, & J. Travis (Eds.), *Evolution: The first four billion years* (pp. 256–280). Cambridge, MA: Belknap Press.

McKee, I. R., & Feather, N. T. (2008). Revenge, retribution, and values: social attitudes and punitive sentencing. *Social Justice Research, 21*, 138–163.

McKibbin, W. F., Shackelford, T. K., Goetz, A. T., & Starratt, V. G. (2008). Why do men rape? An evolutionary psychological perspective. *Review of General Psychology, 12*, 86–97. http://dx.doi.org/10.1037/1089-2680.12.1.86.

McLaughlin, E., & Newburn, T. (2010a). Introduction. In E. McLaughlin, & T. Newburn (Eds.), *The Sage handbook of criminological theory* (pp. 1–18). London, UK: Sage Publications.

McLaughlin, E., & Newburn, T. (Eds.). (2010b). *The Sage handbook of criminological theory.* London, UK: Sage Publications.

McNeill, F. (2006). A desistance paradigm for offender management. *Criminology & Criminal Justice, 6*, 39–62.

McNeill, F. (2009). What works and what's just? *European Journal of Probation, 1*, 21–40.

McNeill, F., Batchelor, S., Burnett, R., & Knox, J. (2005). *21st century social work. Reducing re-offending: Key practice skills.* Edinburgh, UK: Scottish Executive.

Mealey, L. (1995). The socio-biology of sociopathy: an integrated evolutionary model. *Behavioral and Brain Sciences, 18,* 523–599.

Menary, R. (2007). *Cognitive integration: Mind and cognition unbounded.* Basingstoke, UK: Palgrave MacMillan.

Mennin, D., & Farach, F. (2007). Emotion and evolving treatments for adult psychopathology. *Clinical Psychology: Science and Practice, 14,* 329–352.

Merton, R. K. (1938). Social structure and anomie. *American Sociological Review, 3,* 672–682.

Mesoudi, A. (2011a). *Cultural evolution: How Darwinian theory can explain human culture and synthesize the social sciences.* Chicago, IL: University of Chicago Press.

Mesoudi, A. (2011b). Culture and the Darwinian renaissance in the social sciences and humanities. *Journal of Evolutionary Psychology, 9,* 109–124. http://dx.doi.org/10.1556/JEP.9.2011.29.1.

Mesoudi, A., Blanchet, S., Charmantier, A., & Pujol, B. (2013). Is non-genetic inheritance just a proximate mechanism? A corroboration of the extended evolutionary synthesis. *Biological Theory, 7,* 189–195. http://dx.doi.org/10.1007/s13752-013-0091-5.

Mesoudi, A., Whiten, A., & Laland, K. N. (2006). Towards a unified science of cultural evolution. *Behavioral and Brain Sciences, 29,* 329–347. http://dx.doi.org/10.1017/S0140525X06009083.

Messner, S. F. (2012). Morality, markets, and the ASC: 2011 presidential address to the American Society of Criminology. *Criminology, 50,* 5–25. http://dx.doi.org/10.1111/j.1745-9125.2011.00264.x.

Messner, S. F., & Rosenfeld, R. (2013). *Crime and the American dream.* Belmont, CA: Wadsworth.

Messner, S. F., Rosenfeld, R., & Karstedt, S. (2013). Social institutions and crime. In F. T. Cullen, & P. Wilcox (Eds.), *The Oxford handbook of criminological theory* (pp. 405–424). New York, NY: Oxford University Press.

Miller, G. F. (2010). Are pleiotropic mutations and Holocene selective sweeps the only evolutionary-genetic processes left for explaining heritable variation in human psychological traits? In D. M. Buss, & P. Hawley (Eds.), *The evolution of personality and individual differences* (pp. 376–399). Oxford, UK: Oxford University Press.

Miller, D. T., & Vidmar, N. (1981). The social psychology of punishment reactions. In *The justice motive in social behavior* (pp. 145–172). US: Springer.

Mitani, J. C., Call, J., Kappeler, P. M., Palombit, R. A., & Silk, J. B. (Ed.), (2012). *The evolution of primate societies.* Chicago, IL: Chicago University Press.

Mitchell, O. (2005). A meta-analysis of race and sentencing research: explaining the inconsistencies. *Journal of Quantitative Criminology, 21,* 439–466.

Mitchell, S. D. (2004). *Why integrative pluralism?* E:CO, Vol. 6, 81–91.

Mitchell, S. D. (2009). *Unsimple truths: Science, complexity, and policy.* Chicago, IL: University of Chicago Press.

Moffett, M. W. (2013). Human identity and the evolution of societies. *Human Nature, 24,* 219–267. http://dx.doi.org/10.1007/s12110-013-9170-3.

Moffitt, T. E. (1993). Adolescence-limited and life-course-persistent antisocial behaviour: a developmental taxonomy. *Psychological Review, 100,* 674–701.

Moffitt, T. E. (2000). Life-course-persistent versus adolescence-limited antisocial behavior. In D. Cicchetti, & D. J. Cohen (Eds.), *Developmental psychopathology* (2nd ed.) (pp. 570–598). Hoboken, NJ: Wiley.

Moffitt, T. E. (2006). A review of research on the taxonomy of life-course persistent versus adolescence-limited antisocial behaviour. In F. T. Cullen, J. P. Wright, & K. R. Blevins (Eds.), *Taking stock: The status of criminological theory. Advances in criminological theory: volume 15.* (pp. 277–311). New Brunswick, NJ: Transaction Publishers.

Moffitt, T. E., Caspi, A., Harrington, H., & Milne, B. J. (2002). Males on the life-course-persistent and adolescence-limited antisocial pathways: follow-up at age 26 years. *Development and Psychopathology, 14,* 179–207.

Monahan, K. C., Cauffman, E., & Steinberg, L. (2009). Affiliation with antisocial peers, susceptibility to peer influence, and antisocial behaviour during the transition to adulthood. *Developmental Psycholog, 45*, 1520–1530. http://dx.doi.org/10.1037/a0017417.

Monahan, K. C., Steinberg, L., Cauffman, E., & Mulvey, E. P. (2013). Psychosocial (im)maturity from adolescence to early adulthood: distinguishing between adolescence-limited and persisting antisocial behavior. *Development and Psychopathology, 25*, 1093–1105. http://dx.doi.org/10.1017/S0954579413000394.

Morris, A. (2002). Critiquing the critics: a brief response to critics of restorative justice. *British Journal of Criminology, 42*, 596–615.

Morris, I. (2011). *Why the West rules – For now: The patterns of history, and what they reveal about the future.* New York, NY: Farrar, Straus & Giroux.

Morris, I. (2012). The evolution of war. *Cliodynamics, 3*, 9–37.

Morris, I. (2013). *The measure of civilization: How social development decides the fate of nations.* Princeton, NJ: Princeton University Press.

Morris, I. (2014). *War, what is it good for? The role of conflict in civilization from primates to robots.* London, UK: Profile Books.

Morwood, M. J., & Jungers, W. L. (2009). Conclusions: implications of the Liang Bua excavations for hominin evolution and biogeography. *Journal of Human Evolution, 57*, 640–648.

Muftic, L. R. (2009). Macro-micro theoretical integration: an unexplored theoretical frontier. *Journal of Theoretical and Philosophical Criminology, 1*, 33–71.

Mulder, M. B. (2007). On the utility, not the necessity, of tracking current fitness. In S. Gangestad, & J. Simpson (Eds.), *The evolution of mind: Fundamental questions and controversies* (pp. 78–85). New York, NY: Guilford Press.

Muller, M. N., Kahlenberg, S. M., & Wrangham, R. W. (2009). Male aggression and sexual coercion in primates. In M. N. Muller, & R. W. Wrangham (Eds.), *Sexual coercion in primates and humans: An evolutionary perspective on male aggression against females* (pp. 3–22). Cambridge, MA: Harvard University Press.

Muller, M. N., & Wrangham, R. W. (Eds.). (2009). *Sexual coercion in primates and humans: An evolutionary perspective on male aggression against females.* Cambridge, MA: Harvard University Press.

Mullins, D. A., Whitehouse, H., & Atkinson, Q. D. (2013). The role of writing and record-keeping in the cultural evolution of human cooperation. *Journal of Economic Behaviour and Organization, 90*, 141–151. http://dx.doi.org/10.1016/j.jebo.2012.12.017.

Murray, J. (2005). The effects of imprisonment on families and children of prisoners. In A. Liebling, & S. Maruna (Eds.), *The effects of imprisonment* (pp. 442–462). Cullompton, Devon: Willan Publishing.

Murray, J., & Farrington, D. P. (2005). Parental imprisonment: effects on boys' antisocial behaviour and delinquency through the life-course. *Journal of Child Psychology and Psychiatry, 46*, 1269–1278.

Navathe, S., Ward, T., & Rose, C. (2013). The development of the sexual offender relationship frames model. *Psychiatry Psychology & Law, 20*, 60–72.

Nedelec, J. L., & Beaver, K. M. (2012). The association between sexual behaviour and antisocial behaviour: insights from an evolutionary informed analysis. *Journal of Contemporary Criminal Justice, 28*, 329–345. http://dx.doi.org/10.1177/1043986212450230.

Nelissen, R. M. A., Breugelmans, S. M., & Zeelenberg, M. (2013). Reappraising the moral nature of emotions in decision making: the case of shame and guilt. *Social and Personality Psychology Compass, 7*, 355–365. http://dx.doi.org/10.1111/spc3.12030.

Nelkin, D. (2000). Less selfish than sacred? Genes and the religious impulse in evolutionary psychology. In H. Rose, & S. P. R. Rose (Eds.), *Alas, poor Darwin: Arguments against evolutionary psychology* (pp. 17–32). New York, NY: Harmony.

Nesse, R. M. (1994). An evolutionary perspective on substance abuse. *Ethology and Sociobiology, 15*, 339–348.

Nesse, R. M., & Stearns, S. C. (2008). The great opportunity: evolutionary applications to medicine and public health. *Evolutionary Applications, 1*, 28–48.

Nettle, D. (2006). The evolution of personality variation in humans and other animals. *American Psychologist, 61*, 622–631. http://dx.doi.org/10.1037/0003-066X.61.6.622.

Nettle, D. (2009). Social class through the evolutionary lens. *Journal of the Royal Anthropological Institute, 15*, 223–240.

Nettle, D. (2010). Dying young and living fast: variation in life history across English neighborhoods. *Behavioral Ecology, 21*, 387–395. http://dx.doi.org/10.1093/beheco/arp202.

Nettle, D., Gibson, M. A., Lawson, D. W., & Sear, R. (2013a). Human behavioral ecology: current research and future prospects. *Behavioral Ecology, 24*, 1031–1040. http://dx.doi.org/10.1093/beheco/ars222.

Nettle, D., Harper, Z., Kidson, A., Stone, R., Penton-Voak, I. S., & Bateson, M. (2013b). The watching eyes effect on the dictator game: it's not how much you give, it's being seen to give something. *Evolution and Human Behavior, 34*, 35–40. http://dx.doi.org/10.1016/j.evolhumbehav.2012.08.004.

Neumann, C. S., & Hare, R. D. (2008). Psychopathic traits in a large community sample: links to violence, alcohol use, and intelligence. *Journal of Consulting and Clinical Psychology, 76*, 893–899.

Nieuwbeerta, P., McCall, P. L., Elffers, H., & Wittebrood, K. (2008). Neighborhood characteristics and individual homicide risks effects of social cohesion, confidence in the police, and socioeconomic disadvantage. *Homicide Studies, 12*, 90–116. http://dx.doi.org/10.1177/1088767907310913.

Nisbett, R. E. (1993). Violence and US regional culture. *American Psychologist, 48*, 441–449. http://dx.doi.org/10.1037/0003-066X.48.4.441.

Nivette, A. E. (2011a). Violence in non-state societies: a review. *British Journal of Criminology, 51*, 578–598. http://dx.doi.org/10.1093/bjc/azr008.

Nivette, A. E. (2011b). Cross-national predictors of crime: a meta-analysis. *Homicide Studies, 15*, 103–131. http://dx.doi.org/10.1177/1088767911406397.

Nivette, A. E., & Eisner, M. (2013). Do legitimate polities have fewer homicides? A cross-national analysis. *Homicide Studies, 17*, 3–26. http://dx.doi.org/10.1177/1088767912452131.

Nivette, A. E., Eisner, M., Malti, T., & Ribeaud, D. (2014). Sex differences in aggression among children of low and high gender inequality backgrounds: a comparison of gender role and sexual selection theories. *Aggressive Behavior, 5*, 451–464. http://dx.doi.org/10.1002/ab.21530.

Noe, A. (2009). *Out of our heads: Why you are not your brain and other lessons from the biology of consciousness.* New York, NY: Hill & Wang.

Norenzayan, A. (2013). *Big gods: How religion transformed cooperation and conflict.* Princeton, NJ: Princeton University Press.

Norenzayan, A. (2014). Does religion make people moral? *Behaviour, 151*, 365–384. http://dx.doi.org/10.1163/1568539X-00003139.

Nowak, M. A., & Highfield, R. (2011). *Supercooperators. Altruism, evolution, and why we need each other to succeed.* New York, NY: Simon & Schuster.

Nowak, M. A., Tarnita, C. E., & Wilson, E. O. (2010). The evolution of eusociality. *Nature, 466*, 1057–1062. http://dx.doi.org/10.1038/nature09205.

O'Brien, M. J., & Laland, K. N. (2012). Genes, culture and agriculture: an example of human niche construction. *Current Anthropology, 53*, 434–470. http://dx.doi.org/10.1086/666585.

Odling-Smee, J. (2010). Niche inheritance. In M. Pigliucci, & G. B. Müller (Eds.), *Evolution: The extended synthesis* (pp. 175–207). Cambridge, MA: MIT Press.

Odling-Smee, F. J., Laland, K. N., & Feldman, M. W. (2003). *Niche construction: The neglected process in evolution.* Princeton, NJ: Princeton University Press.

O'Gorman, R., Wilson, D. S., & Miller, R. R. (2008). An evolved cognitive bias for social norms. *Evolution and Human Behavior, 29*, 71–78. http://dx.doi.org/10.1016/j.evolhumbehav.2007.07.002.

Öhman, A., & Mineka, S. (2003). The malicious serpent snakes as a prototypical stimulus for an evolved module of fear. *Current Directions in Psychological Science, 12*(1), 5–9. http://dx.doi.org/10.1111/1467-8721.01211.

Olds, D. L., Sadler, L., & Kitzman, H. (2007). Programs for parents of infants and toddlers: recent evidence from randomized trials. *Journal of Child Psychology and Psychiatry, 35,* 1171–1190.

Oswald, M. E., & Stucki, I. (2009). A two-process model of punishment. In M. E. Oswald, S. Bieneck, & J. Hupfeld-Heinemann (Eds.), *Social psychology of punishment and crime* (pp. 173–190). New York, NY: John Wiley & Sons.

Ouimet, M. (2012). A world of homicides: the effect of economic development, income inequality, and excess infant mortality on the homicide rate for 165 countries in 2010. *Homicide Studies, 16,* 238–258. http://dx.doi.org/10.1177/1088767912442500.

Ousey, G. C., & Lee, M. R. (2010). The Southern culture of violence and homicide-type differentiations: an analysis across cities and time points. *Homicide Studies, 14,* 268–295.

Oxley, J. C. (2011). *The moral dimensions of empathy: Limits and applications in ethical theory and practice.* London, UK: Palgrave Macmillan.

Parker, G. A. (2006). Sexual conflict over mating and fertilization: an overview. *Philosophical Transactions of the Royal Society B: Biological Sciences, 361,* 235–259.

Payne, B. K., Gainey, R. R., Triplett, R. A., & Danner, M. J. E. (2004). What drives punitive beliefs? Demographic characteristics and justifications for sentencing. *Journal of Criminal Justice, 32,* 195–206. http://dx.doi.org/10.1016/j.jcrimjus.2004.02.007.

Pedersen, E. J., Kurzban, R., & McCullough, M. E. (2013). Do humans *really* punish altruistically? A closer look. *Proceedings of the Royal Society of London B: Biological Sciences, 280,* 2012–2723. http://dx.doi.org/10.1098/rspb.2012.2723.

Pennington, B. F. (2002). *The development of psychopathology: Nature and nurture.* New York, NY: Guilford Press.

Peper, J. S., & Dahl, R. E. (2013). The teenage brain: surging hormones – brain-behavior interactions during puberty. *Current Directions in Psychological Science, 22,* 134–139. http://dx.doi.org/10.1177/0963721412473755.

Perry, G., & Mace, R. (2010). The lack of acceptance of evolutionary approaches to human behaviour. *Journal of Evolutionary Psychology, 8,* 105–125. http://dx.doi.org/10.1556/JEP.8.2010.2.2.

Peters, B. M. (2013). Evolutionary psychology: neglecting neurobiology in defining the mind. *Theory & Psychology, 23,* 305–322. http://dx.doi.org/10.1177/0959354313480269.

Peterson, M. B., Sell, A., Tooby, J., & Cosmides, L. (2010). Evolutionary psychology and criminal justice: a recalibrational theory of punishment and reconciliation. In H. Hogh-Oleson (Ed.), *Human morality and sociality* (pp. 72–131). New York, NY: Palgrave MacMillan.

Peterson, M. B., Sznycer, D., Sell, A., Cosmides, L., & Tooby, J. (2013). The ancestral logic of politics: upper-body strength regulates men's assertion of self-interest over economic redistribution. *Psychological Science, 24,* 1098–1103.

Pfeifer, J. H., & Allen, N. B. (2012). Arrested development? Reconsidering dual-systems models of brain function in adolescence and disorders. *Trends in Cognitive Sciences, 16,* 322–329. http://dx.doi.org/10.1016/j.tics.2012.04.011.

Pierce, J., & Bekoff, M. (2012). Wild justice redux: what we know about social justice in animals and why it matters. *Social Justice Research, 25,* 122–139. http://dx.doi.org/10.1007/s11211-012-0154-y.

Pigliucci, M. (2009). An extended synthesis for evolutionary biology. *Annals of the New York Academy of Science, 1168,* 218–228. http://dx.doi.org/10.1111/j.1749-6632.2009.04578.x.

Pigliucci, M., & Kaplan, J. (2006). *Making sense of evolution: The conceptual foundations of evolutionary biology.* Chicago, IL: Chicago University Press.

Pigliucci, M., & Müller, G. B. (Eds.). (2010). *Evolution, the extended synthesis.* Cambridge, MA: MIT press.

Pinker, S. (1997). *How the mind works.* London, UK: Penguin.

Pinker, S. (2002). *The blank slate.* London, UK: Penguin Books.

Pinker, S. (2011). *The better angels of our nature: The decline of violence in history and its causes.* London, UK: Penguin Books.

Piquero, A. R., Hawkins, J. D., & Kazemian, L. (2012). Criminal career patterns. In R. Loeber, & D. Farrington (Eds.), *From juvenile delinquency to adult crime: Criminal careers, justice policy, and prevention* (pp. 14–46). Oxford, UK: Oxford University Press.

Piquero, A. R., Jennings, W. G., & Barnes, J. C. (2012). Violence in criminal careers: a review of the literature from a developmental life-course perspective. *Aggression and Violent Behavior, 17*, 171–179. http://dx.doi.org/10.1016/j.avb.2012.02.008.

Piquero, N. L., Piquero, A. R., & Stewart, E. S. (2014). Soicological viewpoint on the race-crime relationships. In K. M. Beaver, J. C. Barnes, & B. B. Boutwell (Eds.), *The nurture versus biosocial debate in criminology: On the origins of criminal behavior and criminality* (pp. 43–54). Los Angeles, CA: Sage Publications.

Plotkin, H. (2004). *Evolutionary thought in psychology: A brief history.* Oxford, UK: Blackwell Publishing.

Pluess, M., & Belsky, J. (2013). Vantage sensitivity: individual differences in response to positive experiences. *Psychological Bulletin, 139*, 901–916. http://dx.doi.org/10.1037/a0030196.

Polaschek, D. L. L. (2003). Empathy and victim empathy. In T. Ward, D. R. Laws, & S. M. Hudson (Eds.), *Sexual deviance: Issues and controversies.* Thousand Oaks, CA: Sage Publications.

Polk, K. (1995). Lethal violence as a form of masculine conflict resolution. *Australian and New Zealand Journal of Criminology, 28*, 93–115.

Polk, K. (1999). Males and honor contest violence. *Homicide Studies, 3*, 6–29.

Popper, K. R. (1959). *The logic of scientific discovery.* London, UK: Hutchinson.

Porporino, F. R. (2008). *Bringing sense and sensitivity to corrections: From programs to 'fix' offenders to services to support desistance.* USA: A research brief submitted to the National Institute of Corrections.

Porter, S., & Woodworth, M. (2006). Psychopathy and aggression. In C. J. Patrick (Ed.), *Handbook of psychopathy* (pp. 481–493). New York, NY: The Guilford Press.

Potochnik, A., & McGill, B. (2012). The limitations of hierarchical organization. *Philosophy of Science, 79*, 120–140. http://dx.doi.org/10.1086/663237.

Potts, R. (2012a). Environmental and behavioural evidence pertaining to the evolution of early *Homo. Current Anthropology, 53*(Suppl. 6), S299–S317. http://dx.doi.org/10.1086/667704.

Potts, R. (2012b). Evolution and environmental change in early human prehistory. *Annual Review of Anthropology, 41*, 151–167. http://dx.doi.org/10.1146/annurev-anthro-092611-145754.

Powell, R. (2012). The future of human evolution. *British Journal for the Philosophy of Science, 63*, 145–175.

Powell, A., Shennan, S., & Thomas, M. G. (2009). Late Pleistocene demography and the appearance of modern human behaviour. *Science, 324*, 1298–1301. http://dx.doi.org/10.1126/science.1170165.

Pratt, J. (2000). Emotive and ostentatious punishment: its decline and resurgence in modern society. *Punishment and Society, 2*, 417–439.

Pratt, J. (2008). Scandinavian exceptionalism in an era of penal excess part I: the nature and roots of Scandinavian exceptionalism. *British Journal of Criminology, 48*, 119–137. http://dx.doi.org/10.1093/bjc/azm072.

Pratt, T. C., & Cullen, F. T. (2000). The empirical status of Gottfredson and Hirschi's general theory of crime: a meta-analysis. *Criminology, 38*, 931–964.

Pratt, T. C., & Cullen, F. T. (2005). Assessing macro-level predictors and theories of crime: a meta-analysis. *Crime and Justice, 32*, 373–450.

Pratt, T. C., Cullen, F. T., Sellers, C. S., & Gau, J. M. (2010). The empirical status of social learning theory: a meta-analysis. *Justice Quarterly, 27*, 765–802. http://dx.doi.org/10.1080/07418820903379610.

Pratt, J., & Eriksson, A. (2012). *Contrasts in punishment: An explanation of Anglophone excess and Nordic exceptionalism.* (272 pp) Routledge.

Pridemore, W. A., & Trent, C. L. S. (2010). Do the invariant findings of Land, McCall, and Cohen generalize to cross-national studies of social structure and homicide? *Homicide Studies*, 14, 296–335. http://dx.doi.org/10.1177/1088767910371184.

Pusey, A., Murray, C., Wallauer, W., Wilson, M., Wroblewski, E., & Goodall, J. (2008). Severe aggression among female Pan troglodytes schweinfurthii at Gombe National Park, Tanzania. *International Journal of Primatology*, 29, 949–973.

Puts, D. A. (2010). Beauty and the beast: mechanisms of sexual selection in humans. *Evolution and Human Behavior*, 31, 157–175. http://dx.doi.org/10.1016/j.evolhumbehav.2010.02.005.

Puts, D. A., Apicella, C. L., & Cárdenas, R. A. (2011). Masculine voices signal men's threat potential in forager and industrial societies. *Proceedings of the Royal Society B: Biological Sciences*, 279, 601–609. http://dx.doi.org/10.1098/rspb.200.0829.

Rafter, N. (2008). *The criminal brain: Understanding biological theories of crime*. New York, NY: New York University Press.

Raihani, N. J., Thornton, A., & Bshary, R. (2012). Punishment and cooperation in nature. *Trends in Ecology and Evolution*, 27, 288–295. http://dx.doi.org/10.1016/j.tree.2011.12.004.

Raine, A. (2008). From genes to brain to antisocial behavior. *Current Directions in Psychological Science*, 17, 323–328. http://dx.doi.org/10.1111/j.1467-8721.2008.00599.x.

Raine, A. (2013). *The anatomy of violence: The biological roots of crime*. New York, NY: Pantheon Books.

Raine, A., Moffitt, T. E., Caspi, A., Loeber, R., Stouthamer-Loeber, M., & Lynam, D. (2005). Neurocognitive impairments in boys on the life-course persistent antisocial path. *Journal of Abnormal Psychology*, 114, 38–49. http://dx.doi.org/10.1037/0021-843X.114.1.38.

Rendell, L., Fogart, L., Hoppitt, W. J. E., Morgan, T. J. H., Webster, M. M., & Laland, K. N. (2011). Cognitive culture: theoretical and empirical insights into social learning strategies. *Trends in Cognitive Sciences*, 15, 68–76. http://dx.doi.org/10.1016/j.tics.2010.12.002.

Reyna, V. F., & Farley, F. (2006). Risk and rationality in adolescent decision making: implications for theory, practice, and public policy. *Association for Psychological Science*, 7, 1–44. http://dx.doi.org/10.1111/j.1529-1006.2006.00026.x.

Reyna, V. F., & Farley, F. (January 2007). Is the teen brain too rational? *Scientific American Mind*, 17, 68–75.

Rhee, S. H., & Waldman, I. D. (2002). Genetic and environmental influences on antisocial behavior: a meta-analysis of twin and adoption studies. *Psychological Bulletin*, 128, 490–529. http://dx.doi.org/10.1037//0033-2909.128.3.490.

Richards, R. J. (1987). *Darwin and the emergence of evolutionary theories of mind and behaviour*. Chicago, IL: University of Chicago Press.

Richardson, R. C. (2007). *Evolutionary psychology as maladapted psychology*. Cambridge, MA: MIT press.

Richerson, P. J., & Boyd, R. (2005). *Not by genes alone: How culture transformed human evolution*. Chicago, IL: Chicago University Press.

Richerson, P. J., Boyd, R., & Henrich, J. (2010). Gene-culture coevolution in the age of genomics. *Proceedings of the National Academy of Sciences of the United States of America*, 107(Suppl. 2), 8985–8992. http://dx.doi.org/10.1073/pnas.0914631107.

Richerson, P. J., & Henrich, J. (2012). Tribal social instincts and the cultural evolution of institutions to solve collective action problems. *Cliodynamics: The Journal of Theoretical and Mathematical History*, 3, 38–80.

Riedl, K., Jensen, K., Call, J., & Tomasello, M. (2012). No third-party punishment in chimpanzees. *Proceedings of the National Academy of Science of the United States of America*, 109, 14824–14829. http://dx.doi.org/10.1073/pnas.1203179109.

Rigdon, M., Ishii, K., Watabe, M., & Kitayama, S. (2009). Minimal social cues in the dictator game. *Journal of Economic Psychology*, 30, 358–367. http://dx.doi.org/10.1016/j.joep.2009.02.002.

Roach, J., & Pease, K. (2013). *Evolution and crime*. London, UK: Routledge.

Roberts, J. V. (2008). *Punishing persistent offenders: Exploring community and offender perspectives*. Oxford, UK: Oxford University Press.

Roberts, J. V., & Hough, M. (2005). *Understanding public attitudes to criminal justice*. New York, NY: Open University Press.

Robinson, A. (2010). Domestic violence. In F. Brookman, M. Maguire, H. Pierpoint, & T. Bennett (Eds.), *Handbook on crime* (pp. 245–270). Cullompton, Devon: Willan Publishing.

Robinson, P. H. (2013). Natural law & lawlessness: modern lessons from pirates, lepers, eskimos, and survivors. *University of Illinois Law Review, 2013*, 433.

Robinson, P. H., Jackowitz, S. E., & Bartels, D. M. (2012). Extralegal punishment factors: a study of forgiveness, hardship, good deeds, apology, remorse, and other such discretionary factors in assessing criminal punishment. *Vanderbilt Law Review, 65*, 737–826.

Robinson, P. H., Jones, O. D., & Kurzban, R. (2010). Realism, punishment, and reform. *University of Chicago Law Review, 77*, 1611–1641.

Robinson, P. H., & Kurzban, R. (2007). Concordance and conflict in intuitions of justice. *Minnesota Law Review, 91*, 1829–1907.

Rose, S., Kamin, L. J., & Lewontin, R. C. (1984). *Not in our genes: Biology, ideology, and human nature*. New York, NY: Pelican Books.

Rosenfeld, R. (2011). The big picture: 2010 presidential address to the American Society of criminology. *Criminology, 49*, 1–26. http://dx.doi.org/10.1111/j.1745-9125.2010.00216.x.

Rosenfeld, R. G., & Nicodemus, B. C. (2003). The transition from adolescence to adult life: physiology of the 'transition' phase and its evolutionary basis. *Hormone Research, 60*, 74–77.

Ross, R. R., & Fabiano, E. A. (1985). *Time to think: A cognitive model of delinquency prevention and offender rehabilitation*. Johnson City, TN: Institute of Social Sciences and Arts.

Rossi, P. H., & Berk, R. A. (1997). *Just punishments: Federal guidelines and public views compared*. New York, NY: Aldine de Gruyter.

Roth, R. (2001). Child murder in New England. *Social Science History, 25*, 101–147.

Roth, R. (2009). *American homicide*. Cambridge, MA: Harvard University Press.

Roth, R. (2011). Biology and the deep history of homicide. *British Journal of Criminology, 51*, 535–555. http://dx.doi.org/10.1093/bjc/azr029.

Roth, R. (2012). Measuring feelings and beliefs that may facilitate (or deter) homicide: a reach note on the causes of historic fluctuations in homicide rates in the United States. *Homicide Studies, 16*, 197–216. http://dx.doi.org/10.1177/1088767912442501.

Rowlands, M. (2010). *The new science of the mind: From extended mind to embodied phenomenology*. Cambridge, MA: MIT Press.

Ruddell, R., & Urbina, M. G. (2004). Minority threat and punishment: a cross-national analysis. *Justice Quarterly, 21*, 903–931.

Ruse, M. (2009). The history of evolutionary thought. In M. Ruse, & J. Travis (Eds.), *Evolution: The first four billion years* (pp. 1–48). Cambridge, MA: Belknap Press.

Russell, K., & Darjee, R. (2013). Managing the risk posed by personality-disordered sexual offenders in the community. In C. Logan, & L. Johnstone (Eds.), *Managing clinical risk: A guide to effective practice* (pp. 88–114). Abingdon, UK: Routledge.

Rutter, M. (2003). Crucial paths from risk indicator to causal mechanism. In B. B. Lahey, T. E. Moffitt, & A. Caspi (Eds.), *Causes of conduct disorder and juvenile delinquency* (pp. 5–24). New York: The Guilford Press.

Rutter, M. (2007). Gene-environment interdependence. *Developmental Science, 10*, 12–18. http://dx.doi.org/10.111/j.1467-7687.2007.00557.x.

Sagarin, B. J., Martin, A. L., Coutinho, S. A., Edlund, J. E., Patel, L., Skowronski, J. J., et al. (2012). Sex differences in jealousy: a meta-analytic examination. *Evolution and Human Behavior, 33*, 595–614. http://dx.doi.org/10.1016/j.evolhumbehav.2012.02.006.

Salekin, R. T. (2008). Psychopathy and recidivism from mid-adolescence to young adulthood: cumulating legal problems and limiting life opportunities. *Journal of Abnormal Psychology, 117*, 386–395.

Salmon, W. (1989). Four decades of scientific explanation. In P. Kitcher, & W. Salmon (Eds.), *Scientific explanation*. Minneapolis, MN: Minneapolis Press.

Salmon, C. A., & Hehman, J. A. (2014). The evolutionary psychology of sibling conflict and siblicide. In T. K. Shackelford, & R. D. Hansen (Eds.), *The evolution of violence* (pp. 137–157). New York, NY: Springer.

Salmon, C. A., & Malcolm, J. (2011). Parent–offspring conflict. In C. Salmon, & T. K. Shackelford (Eds.), *The Oxford handbook of evolutionary family psychology* (pp. 83–96). Oxford, UK: Oxford University Press.

Sampson, R. J. (2012). *Great American city: Chicago and the enduring neighbourhood effect*. Chicago, IL: Chicago University Press.

Sampson, R. J. (2013). The place of context: a theory and strategy for criminology's hard problems. *Criminology, 51*, 1–31. http://dx.doi.org/10.1111/1745-9125.12002.

Sampson, R. J., & Laub, J. H. (2005). A life-course view of the development of crime. *The ANNALS of the American Academy of Political and Social Science, 602*, 12–45. http://dx.doi.org/10.1177/0002716205280075.

Sampson, R. J., Raudenbush, S. W., & Earls, F. (1997). Neighborhoods and violent crime: a multilevel study of collective efficacy. *Science, 277*, 918–924.

Sanday, P. R. (2003). Rape-free versus rape-prone: how culture makes a difference. In C. B. Travis (Ed.), *Evolution, Gender and Rape* (pp. 337–361). Cambridge, MA: MIT Press.

Santrock, J. W. (2012). *A topical approach to lifespan development*. New York, NY: McGraw Hill.

Savage, J., & Kanazawa, S. (2002). Social capital, crime, and human nature. *Journal of Contemporary Criminal Justice, 18*, 188–211. http://dx.doi.org/10.1177/1043986202018002005.

Savage, J., & Vila, B. (2003). Human ecology, crime, and crime control: linking individual behaviour and aggregate crime. *Social Biology, 50*, 77–101. http://dx.doi.org/10.1080/19485565.2003.9989066.

Schacht, R., Rauch, K. L., & Borgerhoff Mulder, M. (2014). Too many men: the violence problem? *Trends in Ecology & Evolution, 29*, 214–222. http://dx.doi.org/10.1016/j.tree.2014.02.001.

Schlegel, A. (1995). A cross-cultural approach to adolescence. *Ethos, 23*, 15–32.

Schlegel, A., & Hewlett, B. (2011). Contributions of anthropology to the study of adolescence. *Journal of Research on Adolescence, 21*, 281–289. http://dx.doi.org/10.1111/j.1532-7795.2010.0079.x.

Schlomer, G. L., Del Giudice, M., & Ellis, B. J. (2011). Parent-offspring conflict theory: an evolutionary framework for understanding conflict within human families. *Psychological Review, 118*, 496–521. http://dx.doi.org/10.1037/a0024043.

Schmidt, M. F. H., & Tomasello, M. (2012). Young children enforce social norms. *Current Directions in Psychological Science, 21*, 232–236. http://dx.doi.org/10.1177/0963721412448659.

Schmitt, D. P., Jonason, P. K., Byerley, G. J., Flores, S. D., Illbeck, B. E., O'Leary, N., et al. (2012). A reexamination of sex differences in sexuality: new studies reveal old truths. *Current Directions in Psychological Science, 21*, 135–139.

Schützwohl, A. (2005). Sex differences in jealousy: the processing of cues to infidelity. *Evolution and Human Behavior, 26*, 288–299. http://dx.doi.org/10.1016/j.evolhumbehav.2004.09.003.

Scott-Phillips, T. C., Dickins, T. E., & West, S. A. (2011). Evolutionary theory and the ultimate-proximate distinction in the human behavioural sciences. *Perspectives on Psychological Science, 6*, 38–47. http://dx.doi.org/10.1177/1745691610393528.

Sear, R., & Mace, R. (2008). Who keeps children alive? A review of the effects of kin on child survival. *Evolution and Human Behavior, 29*, 1–18.

Seeley, T. D. (1995). *The wisdom of the hive*. Cambridge, MA: Harvard University Press.

Segerstråle, U. (2000). *Defenders of the truth: The battle for science in the sociobiology debate and beyond*. Oxford, UK: Oxford University Press.

Seligman, M. E., & Hager, J. L. (1972). *Biological boundaries of learning.*

Sell, A., Bryant, G. A., Cosmides, L., Tooby, J., Sznycer, D., von Reuden, C., et al. (2010). Adaptations in humans for assessing physical strength from the voice. *Proceedings of the Royal Society B*, 3509–3518. http://dx.doi.org/10.1098/rspb.2010.0769.

Sell, A., Hone, L. S. E., & Pound, N. (2012). The importance of physical strength to human males. *Human Nature, 23*, 30–44. http://dx.doi.org/10.1007/s12110-012-9131-2.

Seymour, B., Singer, T., & Dolan, R. (2007). The neurobiology of punishment. *Nature Reviews Neuroscience, 8*, 300–311. http://dx.doi.org/10.1038/nrn2119.

Shackelford, T. K., Buss, D. M., & Peters, J. (2000). Wife killing: risk to women as a function of age. *Violence and Victims, 15*, 273–281.

Shackelford, T. K., Buss, D. M., & Weekes-Shackelford, V. A. (2003). Wifekillings committed in the context of a "lovers triangle". *Basic and Applied Social Psychology, 25*, 127–133.

Shackelford, T., & Duntley, J. (2008). Evolutionary forensic psychology. In J. Duntley, & T. Shackelford (Eds.), *Evolutionary forensic psychology.* New York, NY: Oxford University Press.

Sharkey, P. (2008). The intergenerational transmission of context. *American Journal of Sociology, 113*, 931–969. http://dx.doi.org/10.1086/522804.

Shaw, C. R., & McKay, H. D. (1942). *Juvenile delinquency and urban areas.* Chicago, IL: Chicago University Press.

Shaw, A., & Olson, K. (2014). Fairness as partiality aversion: the development of procedural justice. *Journal of Experimental Child Psychology, 119*, 40–53. http://dx.doi.org/10.1016/j.jecp.2013.10.007.

Shenhav, A., & Greene, J. D. (2014). Integrative moral judgment: dissociating the roles of the amygdala and ventromedial prefrontal cortex. *The Journal of Neuroscience, 34*, 4741–4749.

Sheppard, P., Garcia, J. R., & Sear, R. (2014). A not-so-grim tale: how childhood family structure influences reproductive and risk-taking outcomes in a historical U.S. population. *PLOS ONE, 9*, e89539. http://dx.doi.org/10.1371/journal.pone.0089539.

Sherman, P. W. (1988). The levels of analysis. *Animal Behavior, 36*, 616–619.

Sherry, D. F., & Verhulst, S. (2009). Forword: four decades on from the "four questions". In J. J. Bolhuis, & S. Verhulst (Eds.), *Tinbergen's legacy: Function and mechanism in behavioural biology* (pp. ix–xx). Cambridge, UK: Cambridge University Press.

Sheskin, M., Bloom, P., & Wynn, K. (2014). Anti-equality: social comparison in young children. *Cognition, 130*, 152–156. http://dx.doi.org/10.1016/j.cognition.2013.10.008.

Shryock, A., & Smail, D. L. (Eds.). (2011). *Deep history: The architecture of past and present.* Berekley, CA: University of California Press.

Shulman, E. P., Harden, K. P., Chein, J. M., & Steinberg, L. (2014). Sex differences in the developmental trajectories of impulse control and sensation-seeking from early adolescence to early adulthood. *Journal of Youth and Adolescence, 44*, 1–17. http://dx.doi.org/10.1007/s10964-014-0116-9.

Shulman, E. P., Steinberg, L. D., & Piquero, A. R. (2013). The age-crime curve in adolescence and early adulthood is not due to age differences in economic status. *Journal of Youth and Adolescence, 42*, 848–860. http://dx.doi.org/10.1007/s10964-013-9950-4.

Shultz, S., Nelson, F., & Dunbar, R. I. M. (2012). Hominin cognitive evolution: identifying patterns and processes in the fossil and archaeological record. *Philosophical Transactions of the Royal Society B: Biological Sciences, 367*, 2130–2140. http://dx.doi.org/10.1098/rstb.2012.0115.

Silk, J. B., & Boyd, R. (2010). From grooming to giving blood: the origins of human altruism. In P. M. Kappeler, & J. B. Silk (Eds.), *Mind the gap: Tracing the origins of human universals* (pp. 223–244). London, UK: Springer.

Simon, H. A. (1962). The architecture of complexity. *Proceedings of the American Philosophical Society, 106*, 467–482.

Simons, R. L., & Lei, M. K. (2013). Enhanced susceptibility to context: a promising perspective on the interplay of genes and the social environment. In C. L. Gibson, & M. D. Krohn (Eds.), *Handbook of life-course criminology: Emerging trends and directions for future research* (pp. 57–66). New York, NY: Springer Science+Business Media.

Simons, R. L., Simons, L. G., Chen, Y.-F., Brody, G. H., & Lin, K.-H. (2007). Identifying the psychological factors that mediate the association between parenting practices and delinquency. *Criminology, 45*, 481–517.

Simpson, J. A., & Campbell, L. (2005). Methods of evolutionary science. In D. Buss (Ed.), *Handbook of evolutionary psychology* (pp. 119–144). Hoboken, NJ: John Wiley & Sons.

Simpson, J. A., Griskevicius, V., Kuo, S. -I., Sung, S., & Collins, W. A. (2012). Evolution, stress, and sensitive periods: the influence of unpredictability in early versus late childhood on sex and risky behaviour. *Developmental Psychology, 3*, 674–686. http://dx.doi.org/10.1037/a0027293.

Singer, P. (1999). *A Darwinian left: Politics, evolution and cooperation.* New Haven, CT: Yale University Press.

Skeem, J. L., & Cooke, D. J. (2010). Is criminal behaviour a central component of psychopathy? Conceptual directions for resolving the debate. *Psychological Assessment, 22*, 433–445. http://dx.doi.org/10.1037/a0008512.

Skeem, J. L., Polaschek, D. L. L., Patrick, C. J., & Lilienfeld, S. O. (2011). Psychopathic personality: bridging the gap between scientific evidence and public policy. *Psychological Science in the Public Interest, 12*, 95–162. http://dx.doi.org/10.1177/1529100611426706.

Skoglund, P., & Jakobsson, M. (2011). Archaic human ancestry in East Asia. *Proceedings of the National Academy of Sciences of the United States of America, 45*, 18301–18306. http://dx.doi.org/10.1073/pnas.1108181108.

Slingerland, E., Henrich, J., & Norenzayan, A. (2013). The evolution of prosocial religions. In P. J. Richerson, & M. H. Christiansen (Eds.), *Cultural evolution: Society, technology, language, and religion* (pp. 335–348). Cambridge, MA: MIT press.

Smallbone, S., & Cale, J. Situational theories. In T. Ward & A.R. Beech. (Eds.), *Theories of sexual offending.* Oxford, UK: Wiley-Blackwell, in press.

Smil, V. (2011). Harvesting the biosphere: the human impact. *Population and Development Review, 37*, 613–636. http://dx.doi.org/10.1111/j.1728-4457.2011.00450.x.

Smith, M. E. (2010). The archaeological study of neighborhoods and districts in ancient cities. *Journal of Anthropological Archaeology, 29*, 137–154. http://dx.doi.org/10.1016/j.jaa.2010.01.001.

Smith, E. L., & Cooper, A. (2013). Homicide in the U.S. known to law enforcement, 2011. U.S. Department of Justice. Retrieved from http://www.bjs.gov/content/pub/pdf/hus11.pdf .

Smith, E. A., Mulder, M., & Hill, K. (2001). Controversies in the evolutionary social sciences: a guide for the perplexed. *Trends in Ecology and Evolution, 16*, 128–135. http://dx.doi.org/10.1016/S0169-5347(00)02077-2.

Sober, E. (2000). *Philosophy of biology* (2nd ed.). Boulder, CO: Westview Press.

Sober, E., & Wilson, D. S. (1998). *Unto others: The evolution and psychology of unselfish behaviour.* Cambridge, MA: Harvard University Press.

Somerville, L. H. (2013). The teenage brain: sensitivity to social evaluation. *Current Directions in Psychological Science, 22*, 121–127. http://dx.doi.org/10.1177/0963721413476512.

Somerville, L. H., & Casey, B. J. (2010). Developmental neurobiology of cognitive control and motivational systems. *Current Opinion in Neurobiology, 20*, 236–241. http://dx.doi.org/10.1016/j.conb.2010.01.006.

Somerville, L. H., Jones, R. M., & Casey, B. J. (2010). A time of change: behavioural and neural correlates of adolescent sensitivity to appetitive and aversive environmental cues. *Brain and Cognition, 72*, 124–133. http://dx.doi.org/10.1016/j.bandc.2009.07.003.

Spear, L. P. (2013). Adolescent neurodevelopment. *Journal of Adolescent Health, 52*, S7–S13. http://dx.doi.org/10.1016/j.jadohealth.2012.05.006.

Spierenburg, P. (2008). *Violence and punishment: Civilizing the body through time.* Cambridge, UK: Polity.

Spiranovic, C. A., Roberts, L. D., & Indermaur, D. (2012). What predicts punitiveness? An examination of predictors of punitive attitudes towards offenders in Australia. *Psychiatry, Psychology & Law, 19*, 249–261. http://dx.doi.org/10.1080/13218719.2011.561766.

Sporer, S. L., & Goodman-Delahunty, J. (2009). Disparities in sentencing decisions. In M. E. Oswald, S. Bieneck, & J. Hupfeld-Heinemann (Eds.), *Social psychology of punishment and crime* (pp. 379–401). Hoboken, NJ: John Wiley & Sons.

Stearns, S. C., Allal, N., & Mace, R. (2008). Life history theory and human development. In C. Crawford, & D. Krebs (Eds.), *Foundations of evolutionary psychology* (pp. 47–69). New York, NY: Taylor & Francis Group.

Steinberg, L. (2007). Risk taking in adolescence: new perspectives from brain and behavioural science. *Current Directions in Psychological Science, 16*, 55–59. http://dx.doi.org/10.1111/j.1467-8721.2007.00475.x.

Steinberg, L. (2009). Adolescent development and juvenile justice. *Annual Review of Clinical Psychology, 5*, 47–73. http://dx.doi.org/10.1146/annurev.clinpsy.032408.153603.

Steinberg, L. (2010). A dual systems model of adolescent risk-taking. *Developmental Psychobiology, 52*, 216–224. http://dx.doi.org/10.1002/dev.20445.

Sterelny, K. (1990). *The representational theory of mind: An introduction.* Cambridge, MA: Blackwell.

Sterelny, K. (2003). *Thought in a hostile world: The evolution of human cognition.* Oxford, UK: Blackwell Publishing.

Sterelny, K. (2011). From hominins to humans: how sapiens became behaviourally modern. *Philosophical Transactions of the Royal Society B: Biological Sciences, 366*, 809–822. http://dx.doi.org/10.1098/rstb.2010.0301.

Sterelny, K. (2012). *The evolved apprentice: How evolution made humans unique.* Cambridge, MA: MIT Press.

Stewart-Williams, S., & Thomas, A. G. (2013). The age that thought it was a peacock: does evolutionary psychology exaggerate human sex differences? *Psychological Inquiry: An International Journal for the Advancement of Psychological Theory, 24*, 137–168. http://dx.doi.org/10.1080/1047840x.2013.80489.

Stewart, E. A., & Simons, R. L. (2010). Race, code of the street, and violent delinquency: a multilevel investigation of neighbourhood street culture and individuals norms of violence. *Criminology, 48*, 569–605.

Stolzenberg, L., & D'Alessio, S. J. (2008). Co-offending and the age-crime curve. *Journal of Research in Crime and Delinquency, 45*, 65–86. http://dx.doi.org/10.1177/0022427807309441.

Strang, N. M., Chein, J. M., & Steinberg, L. (2013). The value of the dual systems model of adolescent risk-taking. *Frontiers in Human Neuroscience, 7*, 1–4. http://dx.doi.org/10.3389/fnhum.2013.00223.

Straus, M. A. (2008). Bucking the tide in family violence research. *Trauma Violence Abuse, 9*, 191–213.

Straus, M. A. (2011). Gender symmetry and mutuality in perpetration of clinical-level partner violence: empirical evidence and implications for prevention and treatment. *Aggression and Violent Behavior, 16*, 279–288.

Stringer, C. (2011). *The origin of our species.* London, UK: Allen Lane.

Stuewig, J., Tangney, J. P., Kendall, S., Folk, J. B., Meyer, C. R., & Dearing, R. L. (2014). Children's proneness to shame and guilt predict risky and illegal behaviors in young adulthood. *Child Psychiatry and Human Development.* http://dx.doi.org/10.1007/s10578-014-0467-1.

Stylianou, S. (2003). Measuring crime seriousness perceptions: what have we learned and what else do we want to know? *Journal of Criminal Justice, 31*, 37–56.

Suhler, C. L., & Churchland, P. (2011). Can innate, modular "foundations" explain morality? Challenges for Haidt's moral foundations theory. *Journal of Cognitive Neuroscience, 23*, 2103–2116.

Sutherland, E. H. (1947). *Principles of criminology.* Philadelphia, PA: J. P. Lippincott.

Sutherland, A., Brunton-Smith, I., & Jackson, J. (2013). Collective efficacy, deprivation and violence in London. *British Journal of Criminology, 53*, 1050–1074. http://dx.doi.org/10.1093/bjc/azt050.

Sutton, A., Cherney, A., & White, R. (2008). *Crime prevention: Principles, perspectives, and practices*. Cambridge, UK: Cambridge University Press.

Sweeten, G., Piquero, A. R., & Steinberg, L. (2013). Age and the explanation of crime, revisited. *Journal of Youth and Adolescence, 42*, 921–938. http://dx.doi.org/10.1007/s10964-013-9926-4.

Sykes, G. M., & Matza, D. (1957). Techniques of neutralization: a theory of delinquency. *American Sociological Review, 22*, 664–670.

Tangney, J. P., Stuewig, J., Malouf, E. E., & Youman, K. (2013). Communicative functions of shame and guilt. In K. Sterelny, R. Joyce, B. Calcott, & B. Fraser (Eds.), *Cooperation and its evolution* (pp. 485–502). Cambridge, MA: MIT Press.

Tangney, J. P., Stuewig, J., & Martinez, A. G. (2014). Two faces of shame: the role of shame and guilt in predicting recidivism. *Psychological Science, 25*, 799–805. http://dx.doi.org/10.1177/0956797613508790.

Tangney, J. P., Stuewig, J., & Mashek, D. J. (2007). Moral emotions and moral behaviour. *Annual Review of Psychology, 58*, 345–372. http://dx.doi.org/10.1146/annurev.psych.56.091103.070145.

Temrin, H., Nordlund, J., Rying, M., & Tullberg, B. S. (2011). Is the higher rate of parental child homicide in stepfamilies an effect of non-genetic relatedness? *Current Zoology, 57*, 253–259.

Tennie, C., Call, J., & Tomasello, M. (2009). Ratcheting up the ratchet: on the evolution of cumulative culture. *Philosophical Transactions of the Royal Society B: Biological Sciences, 364*, 2405–2415. http://dx.doi.org/10.1098/rstb.2009.0052.

Thagard, P. (1992). *Conceptual revolutions*. Princeton, NJ: Princeton University Press.

Thagard, P. (2012). The self as a system of multilevel interacting mechanisms. *Philosophical Psychology, 2012*, 1–19. http://dx.doi.org/10.1080/09515089.2012.725715.

The Chimpanzee Sequencing and Analysis Consortium (2005). Initial sequence of the chimpanzee genome and comparison with the human genome. *Nature, 437*, 69–87. http://dx.doi.org/10.1038/nature04072.

Theobald, D., & Farrington, D. P. (2009). Effects of getting married on offending: results from a prospective longitudinal survey of males. *European Journal of Criminology, 6*, 496–516. http://dx.doi.org/10.1177/1477370809341226.

Theobald, D., & Farrington, D. P. (2010). Why do the crime-reducing effects of marriage vary with age? *British Journal of Criminology, 51*, 136–158. http://dx.doi.org/10.1093/bjc/azq060.

Thierry, B. (2005). Integrating proximate and ultimate causation: just one more go! *Current Science, 89*, 1180–1183.

Thompson, M. E. (2013). Comparative reproductive energetics of humans and non-human primates. *Annual Review of Anthropology, 42*, 287–304.

Thomsen, L., Frankenhis, W. E., Ingold-Smith, M., & Carey, S. (2011). Big and mighty: preverbal infants mentally represent social dominance. *Science, 331*, 477–480.

Thornberry, T. P., Giordano, P. C., Uggen, C., Matsuda, M., Masten, A. S., Bulten, E., et al. (2012). Explanations for offending. In R. Loeber, & D. P. Farrington (Eds.), *From Juvenile delinquency to adult crime: Criminal careers, justice policy and prevention* (pp. 47–85). Oxford, UK: Oxford University Press.

Thornhill, R., & Fincher, C. L. (2014). *The parasite stress theory of values and sociality: Infectious disease, history, and human values world wide*. London, UK: Springer.

Thornhill, R., & Palmer, C. P. (2000). *A natural history of rape*. Cambridge, MA: MIT Press.

Thornton, D. (2013). Implications of our developing understanding of risk and protective factors in the treatment of adult male sexual offenders. *International Journal of Behavioral Consultation and Therapy, 8*, 62–65.

Thornton, A., & Clutton-Brock, T. (2011). Social learning and the development of individual and group behaviour in mammal societies. *Philosophical Transactions of the Royal Society B: Biological Sciences, 366*, 978–987. http://dx.doi.org/10.1098/rstb.2010.0312.

Tinbergen, N. (1963). On aims and methods in ethology. *Zeitschrift Für Tierpsychologie, 20*, 410–433. http://dx.doi.org/10.1111/j.1439-0310.1963.tb01161.x.

Tither, J. M., & Ellis, B. J. (2008). Impact of fathers on daughters' age at menarche: a genetically and environmentally controlled sibling study. *Developmental Psychology, 44*, 14091420. http://dx.doi.org/10.1037/a0013065.

Tolan, P., Gorman-Smith, D., & Henry, D. (2006). Family violence. *Annual Review of Psychology, 57*, 557–583.

Tomasello, M., & Vaish, A. (2013). Origins of human cooperation and morality. *Annual Review of Psychology, 64*, 231–255. http://dx.doi.org/10.1146/annurev-psych-113001-143812.

Tonry, M. (2009). Explanations of American punishment policies: a national history. *Punishment and Society, 11*, 377–394. http://dx.doi.org/10.1177/1462474509334609.

Tooby, J., & Cosmides, L. (1990). The past explains the present: emotional adaptations and the structure of ancestral environments. *Ethology and Sociobiology, 11*, 375–424.

Tooby, J., & Cosmides, L. (1992). The psychological foundations of culture. In J. Barkow, L. Cosmides, & J. Tooby (Eds.), *The adapted mind: Evolutionary psychology and the generation of culture*. New York, NY: Oxford University Press.

Tooby, J., & Cosmides, L. (2005). Conceptual foundations of evolutionary psychology. In D. M. Buss (Ed.), *The handbook of evolutionary psychology* (pp. 5–67). Hoboken, NJ: John Wiley & Sons.

Travis, J., & Reznick, D. N. (2009). Adaptation. In M. Ruse, & J. Travis (Eds.), *Evolution: The first four billion years* (pp. 105–131). Cambridge, MA: Belknap Press.

Trivers, R. L. (1971). The evolution of reciprocal altruism. *Quarterly Review of Biology, 46*, 35–57.

Trivers, R. L. (1972). Parental investment and sexual selection. In B. Campbell (Ed.), *Sexual selection and the descent of man: 1871–1971* (pp. 136–179). Chicago, IL: Aldine.

Trivers, R. L. (1974). Parent-offspring conflict. *American Zoologist, 14*, 249–264.

Truman, J. L., & Rand, M. R. (2010). *Criminal victimization, 2009*. Washington, DC: Bureau of Justice Statistics. U.S. Department of Justice.

Tseloni, A., Mailley, J., Farrell, G., & Tilley, N. (2010). Exploring the international decline in crime rates. *European Journal of Criminology, 7*, 375–394. http://dx.doi.org/10.1177/1477370810367014.

Turchin, P. (2006). *War and peace and war: The life cycles of imperial nations*. New York, NY: Pi Press.

Turchin, P. (2009). A theory for formation of large empires. *Journal of Global History, 4*, 191–217. http://dx.doi.org/10.1017/S174002280900312X.

Turchin, P. (2012). Dynamics of political instability in the United States, 1780–2010. *Journal of Peace Research*, 1–15. http://dx.doi.org/10.1177/0022343312442078.

Turchin, P. (2013). The puzzle of human ultrasociality: how did large-scale complex societies evolve? In P. J. Richerson, & M. H. Christiansen (Eds.), *Cultural evolution: Society, technology, language, and religion* (pp. 61–73). Cambridge, MA: MIT press.

Turchin, P., & Gavrilets, S. (2009). Evolution of complex hierarchical societies. *Social Evolution and History, 8*, 167–198.

Tybur, J. M., & Griskevicius, V. (2013). Evolutionary psychology: a fresh perspective for understanding and changing problem behaviour. *Public Administration Review, 73*, 12–22. http://dx.doi.org/10.1111/puar.12003.

Ulmer, J. T., & Steffensmeier, D. (2015). The age and crime relationship: social variation, social explanations. In K. M. Beaver, J. C. Barnes, & B. B. Boutwell (Eds.), *The nurture versus biosocial debate in criminology: On the origins of criminal behaviour and criminality* (pp. 377–396). Los Angeles, CA: Sage.

Uniform Crime Reports. (2010). *Crime in the United States, 2009*. U.S. Department of Justice. Retrieved from: http://www.fbi.gov/about-us/cjis/ucr/ucr. 05.11.11.

United Nations Office on Drugs and Crime. (2014). *Global study on homicide 2013*. Vienna: United Nations Office of Drugs and Crime.

Unnever, J. D. (2012). The power of one? Reflections on Agnew's unified theory of crime. *Journal of Theoretical and Philosophical Criminology, 2*, 40–53.

van Fraassen, B. C. (1977). The pragmatics of explanation. *American Philosophical Quarterly, 14*, 143–150.

Van Goozen, S. H. M., Fairchild, G., & Harold, G. T. (2008). The role of neurobiological deficits in childhood antisocial behavior. *Current Directions in Psychological Science, 17,* 224–228. http://dx.doi.org/10.1111/j.1467-8721.2008.00579.xvv.

van Langen, M. A. M., Wissink, I. B., van Vugt, E. S., van der Stouwe, T., & Stams, G. J. J. (2014). The relationship between empathy and offending: a meta-analysis. *Aggression and Violent Behavior, 19,* 179–189. http://dx.doi.org/10.1016/j.avb.2014.02.003.

Van Mastrigt, S. B., & Farrington, D. P. (2009). Co-offending, age, gender and crime type: implications for criminal justice policy. *British Journal of Criminology, 49,* 552–573. http://dx.doi.org/10.1093/bjc/azp021.

Van Ness, D. W. (2005). An overview of restorative justice around the world. In *Eleventh United Nations Congress on Crime Prevention and Criminal Justice.* Retrieved 21.08.07, from: http://www.icclr.law.ubc.ca/Publications/Reports/11_un/Dan%20van%20Ness%20fin al%20paper.pdf.

Van Vugt, M. (2009). Sex differences in intergroup competition, aggression, and warfare: the male warrior hypothesis. *Annals of the New York Academy of Science, 1167,* 124–134. http://dx.doi.org/10.1111/j.1749-6632.2009.04539.x.

Vila, B. (1994). A general paradigm for understanding criminal behaviour: extending evolutionary ecological theory. *Criminology, 32,* 311–359. http://dx.doi.org/10.1111/j.1745-9125.1994.tb01157.x.

Vila, B. (1997). Human nature and crime control: improving the feasibility of nurturant strategies. *Politics and the Life Sciences, 16,* 3–21.

von Rueden, C., Gurven, M., & Kaplan, H. (2008). The multiple dimensions of male social status in an Amazonian society. *Evolution and Human Behaviour, 29,* 402–415.

von Rueden, C., Gurven, M., & Kaplan, H. (2010). Why do men seek status? Fitness payoffs to dominance and prestige. *Proceedings of the Royal Society B: Biological Sciences, 278,* 2223–2232. http://dx.doi.org/10.1098/rspb.2010.2145.

Wade, N. (2014). *A troublesome inheritance: Genes, race and human history.* Penguin Press.

Walgrave, L. (1993). Beyond rehabilitation: in search of a constructive alternative in the judicial response to juvenile crime. *European Journal on Criminal Policy and Research, 2,* 57–75.

Walgrave, L. (2008). *Restorative justice, self-interest, and responsible citizenship.* Devon, UK: Willan Publishing.

Walker, M. U. (2006). *Moral repair: Reconstructing moral relations after wrongdoings.* New York, NY: Cambridge University Press.

Walker, R. S., Flinn, M. V., & Hill, K. R. (2010). Evolutionary history of partible paternity in lowland South America. *Proceedings of the National Academy of Sciences of the United States of America, 107,* 19195–19200. http://dx.doi.org/10.1073/pnas.1002598107/-/DCsupplemental.

Walker, R. S., Hill, K. R., Flinn, M. V., & Ellsworth, R. M. (2011). Evolutionary history of hunter-gatherer marriage practises. *PILO ONE, 6,* 1–6. http://dx.doi.org/10.1371/journal.pone.0019066.

Walsh, A. (2000). Evolutionary psychology and the origins of justice. *Justice Quarterly, 17,* 841–864.

Walsh, A. (2006). Evolutionary psychology and criminal behavior. In J. Barkow (Ed.), *Missing the revolution: Darwinism for social scientists* (pp. 225–268). Oxford, UK: Oxford University Press.

Walsh, A. (2009). *Biology and criminology: The biosocial synthesis.* New York, NY: Routledge.

Walsh, A. (2011). *Social class and crime: A biosocial approach.* London, UK: Routledge.

Walsh, A. (2012). Editor's introduction: Tinbergen's four questions and the holism of biosocial criminology. *Journal of Contemporary Criminal Justice, 28,* 232–236. http://dx.doi.org/10.1177/1043986212450215.

Walsh, A., & Beaver, K. M. (Eds.). (2009). *Biosocial Criminology: New directions in theory and research.* New York, NY: Routledge.

Walsh, A., & Bolen, D. (2012). *The neurobiology of criminal behaviour: Gene-brain-culture interaction.* Burlington, VT: Ashgate.

Walsh, A., & Ellis, L. (2004). Ideology: criminology's Achilles' heel? *Quarterly Journal of Ideology*, *27*, 1–25.

Walsh, A., & Ellis, L. (2006). *Criminology: An interdisciplinary approach*. Thousand Oaks, CA: Sage Publications.

Walsh, A., & Yun, I. (2011). Race and criminology in the age of genomic science. *Social Science Quarterly*, *5*, 1279–1296.

Walsh, A., & Yun, I. (2014). Epigenetics and allostasis: implications for criminology. *Criminal Justice Review*, 1–21. http://dx.doi.org/10.1177/0734016814530148.

Wang, X. T., Kruger, D. J., & Wilke, A. (2009). Life history variables and risk-taking behaviour. *Evolution and Human Nature*, *30*, 77–84. http://dx.doi.org/10.1016/j.evolhumbehav.2008.09.006.

Ward, T. (2009). The extended mind theory of cognitive distortions in sex offenders. *Journal of Sexual Aggression*, *15*, 247–259.

Ward, T. (2013). The explanation of sexual offending: from single factor theories to integrative pluralism. *Journal of Sexual Aggression*, *20*, 130–141. http://dx.doi.org/10.1080/13552600.2013.870242.

Ward, T. (2014). The explanation of sexual offending: from single factor theories to integrative pluralism. *Journal of Sexual Aggression*, *20*, 130–141.

Ward, T., & Beech, T. (2006). An integrated theory of sexual offending. *Aggression and Violent Behavior*, *11*, 44–63.

Ward, T., & Beech, A. (2014). Dynamic risk factors: a theoretical dead-end? *Psychology, Crime & Law*, *21*, 100–113.

Ward, T., & Casey, A. (2010). Extending the mind into the world: a new theory of cognitive distortions in sexual offenders. *Aggression and Violent Behavior*, *15*, 49–58.

Ward, T., & Durrant, R. (2011a). Evolutionary psychology and the rehabilitation of offenders: constraints and consequences. *Aggression and Violent Behavior*, *16*, 444–452. http://dx.doi.org/10.1016/j.avb.2011.02.011.

Ward, T., & Durrant, R. (2011b). Evolutionary behavioural science: etiological and intervention implications. *Legal and Criminological Psychology*, *16*, 193–210.

Ward, T., & Durrant, R. (2013). Altruism, empathy, and sex offender treatment. *International Journal of Behavioral Consultation and Therapy*, *8*, 66–71.

Ward, T., & Durrant, R. (2014). Psychological altruism, empathy, and offender rehabilitation. In H. L. Maibom (Ed.), *Empathy and morality* (pp. 210–229). Oxford, UK: Oxford University Press.

Ward, T., Fox, A., & Garber, M. (2014). Restorative justice, offender rehabilitation, and desistance. *Restorative Justice: An International Journal*, *2*, 24–42.

Ward, T., Mann, R., & Gannon, T. (2007). The good lives model of offender rehabilitation: clinical implications. *Aggression and Violent Behavior*, *12*, 87–107.

Ward, T., Hudson, S., & Marshall, W. L. (1996). Attachment style in sex offenders: a preliminary study. *Journal of Sex Research*, *33*, 17–26.

Ward, T., & Langlands, R. (2009). Repairing the rupture: restorative justice and offender rehabilitation. *Aggression and Violent Behavior*, *14*, 205–214.

Ward, T., & Laws, D. R. (2010). Desistance from sex offending: motivating change, enriching practice. *The International Journal of Forensic Mental Health*, *9*, 11–23.

Ward, T., & Maruna, S. (2007). *Rehabilitation: Beyond the risk assessment paradigm*. London, UK: Routledge.

Ward, T., & Nee, C. (2009). Surfaces and depths: evaluating the theoretical assumptions of the cognitive skills programmes. *Psychology, Crime & Law*, *15*, 165–182.

Ward, T., Polaschek, D., & Beech, A. R. (2006). *Theories of sexual offending*. Chichester, UK: John Wiley.

Ward, T., & Salmon, K. (2009). The ethics of punishment: implications for correctional practice. *Aggression and Violent Behavior*, *14*, 239–247.

Ward, T., & Siegert, R. J. (2002). Toward a comprehensive theory of child sexual abuse: a theory knitting perspective. *Psychology, Crime and Law*, *8*, 319–351.

Ward, T., & Stewart, C. A. (2003). The treatment of sex offenders: risk management and good lives. *Professional Psychology: Research and Practice, 34*(4), 353–360. http://dx.doi.org/10.1037/0735-7028.34.4.353.

Warr, M. (1989). What is the perceived seriousness of crimes? *Criminology, 27,* 795–821.

Warr, M. (2002). *Companions in crime: The social aspects of criminal conduct.* Cambridge, UK: Cambridge University Press.

Watts, D. P. (2012). The apes: taxonomy, biogeography, life histories, and behavioral ecology. In J. C. Mitani, J. Call, P. M. Kappeler, R. A. Palombit, & J. B. Silk (Eds.), *The evolution of primate societies.* Chicago: Chicago University Press (pp. 113–142). Chicago, IL: Chicago University Press.

Webber, C. (2010). *Psychology and crime.* Los Angeles, CA: Sage Publications.

Webster, G. D. (2007). Evolutionary theory's increasing role in personality and social psychology. *Evolutionary Psychology, 5,* 84–91.

Weekes-Shackelford, V. A., & Shackelford, T. K. (2004). Methods of filicide: stepparents and genetic parents kill differently. *Violence and Victims, 19,* 75–81.

Weigard, A., Chein, J., Albert, D., Smith, A., & Steinberg, L. (2014a). Effects of anonymous peer observation on adolescents' preference for immediate rewards. *Developmental Science, 17,* 71–78. http://dx.doi.org/10.1111/desc.12099.

Weigard, A., Chein, J., Albert, D., Smith, A., & Steinberg, L. (2014b). Effects of anonymous peer observation of adolescents' preference for immediate rewards. *Developmental Science, 17,* 71–78. http://dx.doi.org/10.1111/desc.12099.

Weisburd, D., & Piquero, A. R. (2008). How well do criminologists explain crime? Statistical modelling in published studies. *Crime and Justice: A Review of Research, 37,* 453–502.

Weisfeld, G. E., & Janisse, H. E. (2005). Some functional aspects of human adolescence. In B. J. Ellis, & D. F. Bjorklund (Eds.), *Origins of the social mind: Evolutionary psychology and child development* (pp. 189–218). New York, NY: Guildford Press.

Wells, J. C. (2012). Ecological volatility and human evolution: a novel perspective of life history and reproductive strategy. *Evolutionary Anthropology, 21,* 277–288. http://dx.doi.org/10.1002/evan.21334.

Welsh, B. C., & Farrington, D. P. (2006). Closed-circuit television surveillance. In B. C. Welsh, & D. P. Farrington (Eds.), *Preventing crime: What works for children, offenders, victims, and places* (pp. 193–209). Dordrecht, NL: Springer.

Welsh, B. C., & Farrington, D. P. (2007). Scientific support for early prevention of delinquency and later offending. *Victims and Offenders, 2,* 125–140.

West-Eberhard, M. J. (2003). *Developmental Plasticity and evolution.* Oxford, London, UK: Oxford University Press.

West, S. A., El Mouden, C., & Gardner, A. (2011). Sixteen common misconceptions about the evolution of cooperation in humans. *Evolution and Human Behaviour, 32,* 231–262. http://dx.doi.org/10.1016/j.evolhumbehav.2010.08.001.

Wheeldon, J., Heidt, J., & Dooley, B. (2014). The trouble(s) with unification: debating assumptions, methods, and expertise in criminology. *Journal of Theoretical and Philosophical Criminology, 6,* 111–128.

White, M. (2011). *Atrocitology: Humanity's 100 Deadliest Achievements.* Edinburgh, UK: Canongate Books.

White, J. L., Moffitt, T. E., Caspi, A., Bartusch, D. J., Needles, D. J., & Stouthamer-Loeber, M. (1994). Measuring impulsivity and examining its relationship to delinquency. *Journal of Abnormal Psychology, 103,* 192–205.

Whiten, A., & Erdal, D. (2012). The human socio-cognitive niche and its evolutionary origins. *Philosophical Transactions of the Royal Society B: Biological Sciences, 367,* 2119–2129. http://dx.doi.org/10.1098/rstb.2012.0114.

Whiten, A., & van Schaik, C. P. (2007). The evolution of animal 'cultures' and social intelligence. *Philosophical Transactions of the Royal Society B: Biological Sciences, 362,* 603–620. http://dx.doi.org/10.1098/rstb.2006.1998.

Whitman, J. Q. (2005). The comparative study of criminal punishment. *Annual Review of Law and Society, 1,* 17–34. http://dx.doi.org/10.1146/annurev.lawsocsci.1.041604.115833.

Wiebe, R. P. (2012). Integrating criminology through adaptive strategy and life history theory. *Journal of Contemporary Criminal Justice, 28,* 346–365. http://dx.doi.org/10.1177/1043986212450231.

Wiessner, P. (2005). Norm enforcement among the Ju/'hoansi Bushmen: a case of strong reciprocity? *Human Nature, 16,* 115–145.

Wikström, P. H. (2006). Individuals, settings and acts of crime: situational mechanisms and the explanation of crime. In P. H. Wikström, & R. J. Sampson (Eds.), *The explanation for crime: Context, mechanisms and development* (pp. 61–107). Cambridge, UK: Cambridge University Press.

Wikström, P. H., Oberwittler, D., Treiber, K., & Hardie, B. (2012). *Breaking rules: The social and situational dynamics of young people's urban crime.* Oxford, UK: Oxford University Press.

Wilkinson, R., & Pickett, K. (2009). *The spirit level: Why equality is better for everyone.* London, UK: Penguin Books.

Williams, G. C. (1966). *Adaptation and natural selection.* Princeton, NJ: Princeton University Press.

Willoughby, T., Good, M., Adachi, P. J. C., Hamza, C., & Tavernier, R. (2013). Examining the link between adolescent brain development and risk taking from a social-developmental perspective. *Brain and Cognition, 83,* 315–323. http://dx.doi.org/10.1016/j.bandc.2013.09.008.

Wilson, E. O. (1975). *Sociobiology: The new synthesis.* Cambridge, MA: Harvard University Press.

Wilson, E. O. (1978). *On human nature.* Cambridge, MA: Harvard University Press.

Wilson, R. (2004). *Boundaries of the mind: The individual in the fragile sciences.* New York, NY: Oxford University Press.

Wilson, R. J. (2007). Circles of support and accountability: empowering communities. In D. Prescott (Ed.), *Knowledge and practice: Practical applications in the treatment and supervision of sexual abusers* (pp. 280–309). Oklahoma City, OK: Wood and Barnes.

Wilson, E. O. (2012). *The social conquest of earth.* New York, NY: W.W. Norton.

Wilson, M., & Daly, M. (1985). Competitiveness, risk taking, and violence: the young male syndrome. *Ethology and Sociobiology, 6,* 59–73.

Wilson, M. I., & Daly, M. (1996). Male sexual proprietariness and violence against wives. *Current Directions in Psychological Science, 5,* 77–81.

Wilson, M. I., & Daly, M. (2009). Coercive violence by human males against their female partners. In M. M. Muller, & R. W. Wrangham (Eds.), *Sexual coercion in primates and humans* (pp. 271–291). Cambridge, MA: Harvard University Press.

Wilson, D. S., Dietrich, E., & Clark, A. B. (2003). On the inappropriate use of the naturalistic fallacy in evolutionary psychology. *Biology and Philosophy, 18,* 669–681. http://dx.doi.org/10.1023/A:1026380825208.

Wilson, D. S., & Gowdy, J. M. (2013). Evolution as a general theoretical framework for economics and public policy. *Journal of Economic Behaviour and Organization, 90,* S3–S10. http://dx.doi.org/10.1016/j.jebo.2012.12.008.

Wilson, D. S., Hayes, S. C., Biglan, A., & Embry, D. D. (2014). Evolving the future: toward a science of intentional change. *Behavioral and Brain Sciences, 37,* 395–460. http://dx.doi.org/10.1017/S0140525X13001593.

Wilson, M., Johnson, H., & Daly, M. (1995). Lethal and nonlethal violence against wives. *Canadian Journal of Criminology, 37,* 331–361.

Wilson, R., Picheca, J., Prinzo, M., & Cortoni, F. (2007). Circles of support and accountability: engaging community volunteers in the management of high-risk sexual offenders. *The Howard Journal, 46,* 1–15.

Wilson, D. S., & Wilson, E. O. (2007). Rethinking the theoretical foundations of sociobiology. *Quarterly Review of Biology, 82,* 327–348. http://dx.doi.org/10.1086/522809.

Winking, J., Gurven, M., & Kaplan, H. (2011). The impact of parents and self-selection on child survival among the Tsimane of Bolivia. *Current Anthropology, 52,* 277–284.

Winterhalder, B., & Smith, E. A. (2000). Analyzing adaptive strategies: human behavioural ecology at twenty-five. *Evolutionary Anthropology, 9,* 51–72.

Wolfgang, M. E., & Ferracuti, F. (1967). *The subculture of violence: Toward an integrated theory in criminology.* Devon, UK: Tavistock Publications.

Wood, J. C. (2011). A change of perspective: integrating evolution psychology into the historiography of violence. *British Journal of Criminology, 51,* 479–498. http://dx.doi.org/10.1093/bjc/azq077.

Wood, B., & Baker, J. (2011). Evolution in the genus *Homo. Annual Review of Ecology, Evolution, and Systematics, 42,* 47–69. http://dx.doi.org/10.1146/annurev-ecolsys-102209-144653.

World Health Organization. (2002). *World report on violence and health.* Geneva: World Health Organization.

Wrangham, R. (1999). Evolution of coalitionary killing. *Yearbook of Physical Anthropology, 42,* 1–30.

Wrangham, R., & Carmody, R. (2010). Human adaptation to the control of fire. *Evolutionary Anthropology, 19,* 187–199. http://dx.doi.org/10.1002/evan.20275.

Wrangham, R. W., & Glowacki, L. (2012). Intergroup aggression in chimpanzees and war in nomadic hunter-gatherers: evaluating the chimpanzee model. *Human Nature, 23,* 5–29. http://dx.doi.org/10.1007/s12110-012-9132-1.

Wrangham, R. W., Wilson, M. L., & Muller, M. N. (2006). Comparative rates of violence in chimpanzees and humans. *Primates, 47,* 14–26. http://dx.doi.org/10.1007/s10329-005-0140-1.

Wright, J. P., & Cullen, F. T. (2012). The future of biosocial criminology: beyond scholars' professional ideology. *Journal of Contemporary Criminal Justice, 28,* 237–253. http://dx.doi.org/10.1177/1043986212450216.

Wright, J. P., & Morgan, M. A. (2014). Human biodiversity and the egalitarian fiction. In K. M. Beaver, J. C. Barnes, & B. B. Boutwell (Eds.), *The nurture versus biosocial debate in criminology: On the origins of criminal behavior and criminality* (pp. 55–74). Los Angeles, CA: Sage Publications.

Yang, Y., Gao, Y., Glenn, A., Peskin, M., Schug, R. A., & Raine, A. (2014). Biosocial bases of antisocial behaviour. In M. Delisi, & K. M. Beaver (Eds.), *Criminological theory: A life course approach* (2nd ed.) (pp. 3–25). Burlington, MA: Jones and Bartlett Learning.

Yao, S., Långström, N., Temrin, H., & Walum, H. (2014). Criminal offending as part of an alternative reproductive strategy: investigating evolutionary hypotheses using Swedish total population data. *Evolution and Human Behavior, 35,* 481–488. http://dx.doi.org/10.1016/j.evolhumbehav.2014.06.007.

Young, J. (2011). *The criminological imagination.* Cambridge, UK: Polity Press.

Young, J. T. N., Rebellon, C. J., Barnes, J. C., & Weerman, F. M. (2014). Unpacking the black box of peer similarity in deviance: understanding the mechanisms linking personal behaviour, peer behaviour, and perceptions. *Criminology, 52,* 60–86. http://dx.doi.org/10.1111/1745-9125.12029.

Zehr, H., & Mika, H. (1998). Fundamental concepts of restorative justice. *Contemporary Justice Review, 1,* 47–55.

Zehr, H., & Toews, B. (2004). *Critical issues in restorative justice.* Cullompton, Devon, UK: Willan Publishing.

Zhong, C. B., Bohns, V. K., & Gino, F. (2010). A good lamp is the best police: darkness increases dishonesty and self-interested behaviour. *Psychological Science, 21,* 311–314. http://dx.doi.org/10.1177/0956797609360754.

Zimring, F. E. (2013). American youth violence: a cautionary tale. *Crime and Justice, 42,* 265–298. http://dx.doi.org/10.1086/670399.

Zuk, M. (2014). *Paleofantasy: What evolution really tells us about sex, diet, and how we live.* New York, NY: W.W. Norton.

Index

Edwards Brothers Malloy
Thorofare, NJ USA
November 6, 2015